The new jersey income-maintenance experiment

volume II

Labor-supply responses

Institute for Research on Poverty
Monograph Series

Vernon L. Allen, Editor, *Psychological Factors in Poverty*

Frederick Williams, Editor, *Language and Poverty: Perspectives on a Theme*

Murray Edelman, *Politics as Symbolic Action: Mass Arousal and Quiescence*

Joel F. Handler and Ellen Jane Hollingsworth, *"The Deserving Poor": A Study of Welfare Administration*

Robert J. Lampman, *Ends and Means of Reducing Income Poverty*

Larry L. Orr, Robinson G. Hollister, and Myron J. Lefcowitz, Editors, with the assistance of Karen Hester, *Income Maintenance: Interdisciplinary Approaches to Research*

Charles E. Metcalf, *An Econometric Model of the Income Distribution*

Glen G. Cain and Harold W. Watts, Editors, *Income Maintenance and Labor Supply: Econometric Studies*

Joel F. Handler, *The Coercive Social Worker: British Lessons for American Social Services*

Larry L. Orr, *Income, Employment, and Urban Residential Location*

Stanley H. Masters, *Black–White Income Differentials: Empirical Studies and Policy Implications*

Irene Lurie, Editor, *Integrating Income Maintenance Programs*

Peter K. Eisinger, *Patterns of Interracial Politics: Conflict and Cooperation in the City*

David Kershaw and Jerilyn Fair, *The New Jersey Income-Maintenance Experiment, Volume I: Operations, Surveys, and Administration*

Fredrick L. Golladay and Robert H. Haveman, *The Economic Impacts of Tax–Transfer Policy: Regional and Distributional Effects*

Morgan Reynolds and Eugene Smolensky, *Public Expenditures, Taxes, and the Distribution of Income: The United States, 1950, 1961, 1970*

Marilyn Moon, *The Measurement of Economic Welfare: Its Application to the Aged Poor*

In Preparation

Harold W. Watts and Albert Rees, Editors, *The New Jersey Income–Maintenance Experiment, Volume II: Labor-Supply Responses*

Marilyn Moon and Eugene Smolensky, Editors, *Improving Measures of Economic Well-Being*

Murray Edelman, *Political Language: Words That Succeed and Policies That Fail*

The new jersey income-maintenance experiment

volume II

Labor-supply responses

Edited by

Harold W. Watts and Albert Rees

Institute for Research on Poverty
The University of Wisconsin
Madison, Wisconsin

ACADEMIC PRESS   New York   San Francisco   London

A Subsidiary of Harcourt Brace Jovanovich, Publishers

This book is one of a series sponsored by the Institute for Research on Poverty of the University of Wisconsin pursuant to the provisions of the Economic Opportunity Act of 1964.

Copyright © 1977 by the Regents of the University of Wisconsin System on behalf of the Institute for Research on Poverty
All Rights Reserved
No portion of this book may be reproduced in any form by print, microfilm, or any other means without permission from Academic Press

ACADEMIC PRESS, INC.
111 Fifth Avenue, New York, New York 10003

United Kingdom Edition published by
ACADEMIC PRESS, INC. (LONDON) LTD.
24/28 Oval Road, London NW1

Library of Congress Cataloging in Publication Data

Main entry under title

The New Jersey income-maintenance experiment.

    Vol. 2 edited by H. W. Watts and A. Rees.
    Includes bibliographical references and Index.
    CONTENTS: v. 1.   Operations, surveys, and administration.—v. 2.   Labor-supply responses.
    1.   Negative income tax—New Jersey   2.   Income maintenance programs—New Jersey.   I.   K_____, David
II.   Fair, Jerilyn.   III.   Watts, Harold W.   IV.   Title.
V.   Series: Wisconsin. University—Madison. Institute for Research on Poverty. Monograph series.
HC107.N53I514   1976   326.5   75-16882
ISBN 0-12-738502-9 (v. 2)

PRINTED IN THE UNITED STATES OF AMERICA

 The Institute for Research on Poverty is a national center for research established at the University of Wisconsin in 1966 by a grant from the Office of Economic Opportunity. Its primary objective is to foster basic, multidisciplinary research into the nature and causes of poverty and means to combat it.

In addition to increasing the basic knowledge from which policies aimed at the elimination of poverty can be shaped, the Institute strives to carry analysis beyond the formulation and testing of fundamental generalizations to the development and assessment of relevant policy alternatives.

The Institute endeavors to bring together scholars of the highest caliber whose primary research efforts are focused on the problem of poverty, the distribution of income, and the analysis and evaluation of social policy, offering staff members wide opportunity for interchange of ideas, maximum freedom for research into basic questions about poverty and social policy, and dissemination of their findings.

Contents

List of Figures	xi
List of Tables	xiii
List of Contributors	xix
Foreword	xxi
Preface	xxiii

part I Labor-supply responses to the experiment

Introduction   3

1 The labor-supply results of the experiment: a summary   5
Albert Rees

1.	What We Expected to Find	5
2.	How We Analyze the Data	15
3.	What We Found	22
4.	Conclusions	31
References		32

2 Sample, variables, and concepts used in the analysis   33
Harold W. Watts, Dale J. Poirier,
and Charles Mallar

1.	Dimensions of the Sample	33
2.	Labor-Force Variables	41
3.	Measurement of Nonearned Income	45
4.	Variables Measuring Treatment and Time	47
5.	Wage and Income Variables for Labor-Supply Models	51
References		56

3 Labor-supply response of husbands   57
Harold W. Watts and David Horner

1.	Summary of the Findings for Husbands	58
2.	Analysis Using a Simplified Labor-Supply Model	64
3.	Labor-Supply Response Disaggregated by Time and Ethnic Group	77

4.	Labor-Supply Responses as Mediated by Earning Capacity	85
5.	Conclusions and Interpretations	110
	References	113

4 Labor-supply response of wives   115
Glen G. Cain, Walter Nicholson, Charles Mallar, and Judith Wooldridge

1.	Summary of Results	115
2.	The Special Importance of the Work Behavior of Married Women	117
3.	The Statistical Model: General Considerations	121
4.	The Application of the Basic Model: Statistical Results	126
5.	Additional Results Using Various Other Samples and Models	154
6.	An Interpretation of the Findings	158
	References	162

5 The educational and labor-supply responses of young adults in experimental families   163
Charles D. Mallar

1.	Methodological Considerations	165
2.	The Educational Response	169
3.	The Labor-Supply Response	178
4.	Activity Rates and Simultaneous Models	181
5.	Conclusions	183
	References	184

6 Family labor-supply response in the new jersey experiment   185
Robinson G. Hollister and Charles E. Metcalf

1.	Basic Experimental Response	187
2.	Looking for Response Differences among Experimental Plans	197
3.	Control Variables for Normal Earnings When Interacted with Experimental Effects	202
4.	Differential Response among Individuals, Using Interactions between $\hat{Y}$ and Experimental Variables	212
5.	Conclusions	215
	Appendix: The Development of Control-based Estimates of Normal Earnings and Normal Hours	216
	References	220

7 The effect of negative income tax payments on job turnover and unemployment duration   221
Seymour Spilerman and Richard E. Miller

1.	Preliminary Considerations	224
2.	The Effect of the Payments on Job Turnover	230
3.	The Effects of the Payments on Duration of Unemployment	239

Appendix A: Construction of the Job Satisfaction Measures   247
Appendix B: Supplementary Tables   249
References   250

8 The impact of the experiment on job selection   253
Seymour Spilerman and Richard E. Miller

1. Earnings and Status   255
2. Satisfaction   279
3. Conclusions   281
References   283

part II Factors modifying the labor-supply response

Introduction   287

9 The effects of health on the supply of and returns to labor   289
David Elesh and M. J. Lefcowitz

1. Hypotheses   290
2. Methodological Issues   294
3. Labor Supply of Husbands   303
4. Labor Supply of Wife   309
5. Conclusion   311
Appendix A: Operational Definitions of Variables   312
Appendix B: Supplementary Detailed Tabulations   315
References   319

10 Social psychological characteristics and labor-force response of male heads   321
Sonia Wright

1. The Culture of Poverty   322
2. Sample and Model   323
3. Results   329
4. Summary and Discussion   335
Appendix A: The Items Making Up the Eight Dimensions Expected to Influence Work Behavior   342
References   345

11 Information levels and labor response   347
Jon Helge Knudsen, John Mamer, Robert A. Scott, and Arnold R. Shore

1. Models of Subjects' Understanding   350
2. Measurement of Information Levels   352

3. Numeric Measurement of Tax Rate and Guarantee Level	354
4. The Choice of Equations and Variables	355
5. Labor-Supply Equations and Information Level	358
6. Equations for Husbands	360
7. Equations for Wives	361
8. Regression of Perceived Parameters on Assigned Parameters and Other Variables	363
9. The Nature of the Reduced Sample	365
10. Conclusion	367
References	368

12 Spline functions and their applications in regression analysis   369
Dale J. Poirier

1. Linear Splines	370
2. Cubic Splines	372
3. Periodic Cubic Splines	374
4. Bilinear Splines	376
References	381

13 The application of an error components model to experimental panel data   383
Robert Avery and Harold W. Watts

1. Three-Component Error Components Model	384
2. Parametric Estimates	387
3. Two-Component Model	387
4. Two-Component Model with Missing Data	389
5. Summary	390
References	391

14 The estimation of normal wage rates and normal income   393
Harold W. Watts and Dale Poirier

1. Specification of Models	395
2. Estimates of the Systematic Components of Wage Rates and Family Income	401
3. Calculation of Individual Deviations	410
References	414

Subject Index   415

List of figures

1.1	Response to a Negative Income Tax	6
3.1	Relationship of Net Benefits to Income in the Range of Sample Observations	77
7.1	Interaction between Guarantee Level (Spline 2) and Job Characteristic, "Percentage with Earnings Greater than $6000," Whites' Job Departures	238
7.2	Interaction between $BENEFIT$ 1 and Job Characteristic, "Percentage with Earnings Greater than $8000," Whites' Job Departures	239
7.3	Interaction between $BENEFIT$ 2 and Head's Earnings ($H.E.$), Blacks' Unemployment Duration	245
7.4	Interaction between the Tax Rate (Spline 3) and Wife's Earnings ($W.E.$), Whites' Unemployment Duration	245
7.5	Interaction between the Guarantee Level (Spline 2) and Head's Education, Whites' Unemployment Duration	246
8.1	Interaction between Guarantee Level (Spline 2) and Head's Education, in Equation for "Duncan Status Score (V_8)," Total Sample	267
8.2	Interaction between Presence in Experimental Group (Spline 1) and Job Characteristic, "Percentage with Earnings Greater than $6000 ($V_0$)," in Equation for "Percentage with Earnings Greater than $6000 ($V_8$)," White Subsample	275
8.3	Interaction between Tax Rate (Spline 3) and Job Characteristic "Duncan Status Score (V_0)," in Equation for "Duncan Status Score (V_8)," White Subsample	276
8.4	Interaction between Tax Rate (Spline 3) and Head's Age, In Equation for "Average Earnings (V_8)," Black Subsample	277
8.5	Interaction between Guarantee Level (Spline 2) and Head's Education, in Equation for "Duncan Status Score (V_8)," Black Subsample	278
8.6	Interaction between Guarantee Level (Spline 2) and Head's Education, in Equation for "Duncan Status Score (V_8)," Spanish-speaking Subsample	279
12.1	Linear Spline with Three Segments	370
12.2	Limiting Case in Which One Knot Approaches Another Knot	371
12.3	Rectangular Grid	378
14.1	Male Age Profiles for Full-Time Wage Rates in Trenton, at Preenrollment, for an Operative in Durable Manufacturing Whose Wife Is Not Employed	402
14.2	Female Age Profiles for Full-Time Wage Rates in Trenton, at Preenrollment, for a Service Worker Whose Husband Is Employed	403

14.3	Family Age–Income Profiles for Like-Aged Couple, Both with Eight Years of Education, Living in Trenton at Preenrollment, Husband Healthy	404
14.4	Family Age–Income Profiles for Like-Aged Couple, Both with Twelve Years of Education, Living in Trenton at Preenrollment, Husband Healthy	404
14.5	Wage-Rate Index for Male Sample during Experimental Period, Estimated Natural Cubic Calendar Time Splines	406
14.6	Wage-Rate Index for Female Sample during Experimental Period, Estimated Natural Cubic Calendar Time Spline	407
14.7	Index of Total Family Income during Experimental Period for Control Families, Including Seasonal Pattern	408
14.8	Structure of Experimental Component by Plan, Tax-Guarantee Splines for Male Wage Rates, by Ethnic Group	409
14.9	Structure of Experimental Component by Plan, Tax-Guarantee Spline for Female Wage Rates	410
14.10	Relative Experimental–Control Differential for Male Wage Rates	411
14.11	Relative Experimental–Control Differential for Female Wage Rates	412

List of tables

1.1	Number of Families, by Payment Plan	18
1.2	Average Payments in Dollars per Four-Week Period, Continuous Husband–Wife Families, by Site	19
1.3	Average Payments in Dollars per Four-Week Period, Continuous Husband–Wife Families, by Ethnic Group	20
1.4	Average Payments in Dollars per Four-Week Period, Continuous Husband–Wife Families, by Plan, Second Experimental Year	21
1.5	Percentage Change in Average Payments between First and Third Year, Continuous Husband–Wife Families, by Plan	21
1.6	Unadjusted Mean Values of Key Variables, Male Heads of Husband–Wife Families, Quarters 3–10	22
1.7	Labor-Force-Participation Rates of Wives, Selected Time Periods	26
1.8	Labor-Supply Response of Wives in Husband–Wife Families, Quarters 3–10	27
1.9	Estimates of Family Labor-Supply Response Differentials, Quarters 3–10	29
2.1	The New Jersey Sample Characteristics, Total Sample	34
2.2	The New Jersey Sample Characteristics, Continuous Husband–Wife Sample	35
2.3	Average Weekly Family Income in Dollars, by Ethnic Group and by Site	36
2.4	Average Weekly Family Earnings in Dollars, by Ethnic Group and by Site	37
2.5	Average Weekly Family Hours Worked, by Ethnic Group and by Site	37
2.6	Average Family Size, by Ethnic Group and by Site	38
2.7	Number of Employed Persons per Family, by Ethnic Group and by Site	38
2.8	Average Number of Employed Male Heads per Family, by Ethnic Group and by Site	39
2.9	Average Weekly Hours Worked by Male Head, by Ethnic Group and by Site	39
2.10	Nonearned Income Statistics by Income Category, Full Sample	40
2.11	Nonearned Income Statistics by Income Category, Continuous Husband–Wife Sample	41
3.1	Unadjusted Mean Values for Key Variables, by Ethnic Group and Experimental Status, Husbands	59
3.2	Basic Experimental Differentials for Husbands	61
3.3	Labor-Supply Response of Husbands' Coefficients, Three Primary Models	68

LIST OF TABLES

3.4	Estimated Hours Response for Illustrative Values of the Treatment (Q), by Plan	70
3.5	Predicted Hours Response, for Selected Treatment (Q) Levels, by Age and Education	72
3.6	Statistics Associated with Entering Alternative Experimental Combinations	74
3.7	The Pattern of Adjustment of Response as Measured by Coefficients of Q	76
3.8	Distribution of Sample Families, by Plan Generosity and Ethnicity	78
3.9	Experimental Response according to Plan Generosity for Four Indicators of Labor Supply, by Ethnicity and Time Period	80
3.10	Distribution of Sample by Welfare Ratio at Preenrollment	83
3.11	Selected Differentials from Family Income Classification at Preenrollment, by Ethnicity and Time Period	84
3.12	Means and Standard Deviations of θ (Income Relative to Breakeven)	87
3.13	Specimen Regression Estimates for White Husbands' Labor Force Participation, Averaged over Quarters 3–10	89
3.14	Experimental Response in Husbands' Labor Force Participation as Conditioned by θ, Central Two Years, by Ethnicity	90
3.15	Distribution of θ for Different Breakeven Levels	91
3.16	Experimental Response in Husbands' Labor Force Participation as Conditioned by θ, Spanish-speaking, All Three Years	92
3.17	Experimental Response in Husbands' Employment as Conditioned by θ, Central Two Years, by Ethnicity	94
3.18	Experimental Response in Husbands' Employment as Conditioned by θ, Spanish-speaking, All Three Years	95
3.19	Experimental Response in Husbands' Unemployment as Related to θ and Plan, by Ethnicity, Various Time Periods	96
3.20	Derivatives of Experimental Response in Husbands' Employment for Two Levels of θ, from Regressions for Central Two Years	99
3.21	Experimental Response in Husbands' Hours Worked per Week as Conditioned by θ, Whites, Central Two Years and Last Two Years	100
3.22	Experimental Response in Husbands' Hours Worked per Week as Conditioned by θ, Blacks, Central Two Years and Last Two Years	101
3.23	Experimental Response in Husbands' Hours Worked per Week as Conditioned by θ, Spanish-speaking, Central Two Years and Last Two Years	102
3.24	Estimated Response in Hours Worked per Week Derived from Smoothed Response Surface, by Plan Generosity, All Three Years	103
3.25	Coefficients of Specimen Regression for Husbands' Hours Worked per Week Conditional on Employment, Whites, Quarters 1–12 (Pooled Data, Variance Components Estimation Procedure)	106
3.26	Experimental Response in Husbands' Hours Worked per Week Conditional on Employment, by Ethnicity, Quarters 4, 8, and 12 (Pooled Data, Variance Components Estimation Procedure)	108
3.27	Derivatives of Experimental Response in Husbands' Hours Worked per Week for Two Levels of θ, by Ethnicity, Central Two Years	110
3.28	Derivatives of Experimental Response in Husbands' Hours Worked per Week for Two Levels of θ, Conditional on Employment, Quarters 4, 8, and 12	111

LIST OF TABLES

4.1	Labor-Force-Participation Rates at Preenrollment and for Each Year	116
4.2	Labor-Force-Participation Rates for the Whole Period and by Quarter	122
4.3	Statistics of the Independent Variables, Quarters 1–12 Averaged	128
4.4	Representative Regression Results for the Independent Variables, Quarters 3–10 Averaged	130
4.5	Labor-Supply Response of Wives, Regression Results, Quarters 3–10	135
4.6	Labor-Supply Response of Wives, Regression Results, Quarters 1–12	136
4.7	Labor-Supply Response for Each Experimental Plan, Including Ethnicity Interactions, Quarters 3–10	138
4.8	Labor-Supply Response for Each Experimental Plan, Including Ethnicity Interactions, Quarters 1–4	139
4.9	Labor-Supply Response for Each Experimental Plan, Including Ethnicity Interactions, Quarters 5–8	140
4.10	Labor-Supply Response for Each Experimental Plan, Including Ethnicity Interactions, Quarters 9–12	141
4.11	Labor-Supply Regression Coefficients and Predicted Effects by Plan, All Wives, Quarters 3–10	144
4.12	Labor-Supply Regression Coefficients and Predicted Effects by Plan, White Wives, Quarters 3–10	145
4.13	Labor-Supply Regression Coefficients and Predicted Effects by Plan, Black Wives, Quarters 3–10	146
4.14	Labor-Supply Regression Coefficients and Predicted Effects by Plan, Spanish-speaking Wives, Quarters 3–10	147
4.15	Coefficients of Treatment Variables and Predicted Effects, by Experimental Status and Payment Level and Tax Rate below Breakeven, Various Time Periods	148
4.16	Coefficients of Treatment Variables and Predicted Effects, by Experimental Status and Payment Level and Tax Rate below Breakeven, with Ethnicity Interactions, Quarters 3–10	149
4.17	Coefficients of Treatment Variables and Predicted Effects, by Experimental Status and Payment Level and Tax Rate below Breakeven, with Ethnicity Interactions, Quarters 1–12	150
4.18	Earnings and Hours Worked Regressions, Coefficients of Treatment Variables for Two Measures of Preexperimental Labor Supply, Two Treatment Specifications, Quarters 3–10	153
4.19	Effects on Hours Worked for Two Preenrollment Employment Statuses, Pooled Regressions, Quarters 1–12	157
5.1	Differentials in Probability of High School Completion for Youths, by Plan	173
5.2	Differentials in Years of Schooling Attained for Youths, by Plan	174
5.3	Treatment Response in Educational Activity of Youths, Predicted Marginal Effects Evaluated at Appropriate Probabilities	176
5.4	Treatment Response in Labor-Supply Activity of Youths, Predicted Marginal Effects in Middle Two Years	179
5.5	Treatment Response in Labor Force Participation of Youths, Predicted Marginal Effects Evaluated at Appropriate Probabilities	180
5.6	Treatment Response in Education and/or Labor-Force Activity of Youths, Predicted Marginal Effects Evaluated at Appropriate Probabilities	182

6.1	Unadjusted Mean Earnings and Labor Supply, Continuous Husband–Wife Sample, Preenrollment Through Twelfth Quarter	188
6.2	Unadjusted Mean Earnings and Labor Supply, White Families, Preenrollment through Twelfth Quarter	189
6.3	Unadjusted Mean Earnings and Labor Supply, Black Families, Preenrollment through Twelfth Quarter	190
6.4	Unadjusted Mean Earnings and Labor Supply, Spanish-speaking Families, Preenrollment through Twelfth Quarter	191
6.5	Labor-Supply Differentials for Three Proxy Control Variable Specifications, White Families, Quarters 3–10 Pooled	195
6.6	Labor-Supply Differentials for Three Proxy Control Variable Specifications, Black Families, Quarters 3–10 Pooled	196
6.7	Labor-Supply Differentials for Three Proxy Control Variable Specifications, Spanish-speaking Families, Quarters 3–10 Pooled	196
6.8	Labor-Supply Differentials for Three Proxy Control Variable Specifications, White Families, Quarters 3–10 Averaged	197
6.9	Labor-Supply Differentials for Three Proxy Control Variable Specifications, Black Families, Quarters 3–10 Averaged	198
6.10	Labor-Supply Differentials for Three Proxy Control Variable Specifications, Spanish-speaking Families, Quarters 3–10 Averaged	198
6.11	Labor-Supply Differentials by Tax Rate and Guarantee Differences, Control-based Proxy Control Variable, Quarters 3–10 Pooled	200
6.12	Experimental Interaction with Proxy Income Control Variable ($\hat{Y}$) for Three Proxy Specifications, White Families, Quarters 3–10 Pooled	205
6.13	Experimental Interaction with Proxy Income Control Variable ($\hat{Y}$) for Three Proxy Specifications, Black Families, Quarters 3–10 Pooled	206
6.14	Experimental Interaction with Proxy Income Control Variable ($\hat{Y}$) for Three Proxy Specifications, Spanish-speaking Families, Quarters 3–10 Pooled	207
6.15	Estimated Biases for Experimental Interactions with Control-based Proxy Income Control Variable ($\hat{Y}$), Quarters 3–10 Pooled	211
6.16	Differential Responses among Experimentals by Plan Generosity Relative to Income, White Families, Quarters 3–10 Pooled	214
6.17	Differential Responses among Experimentals by Plan Generosity Relative to Income, Black Families, Quarters 3–10 Pooled	214
6.18	Differential Responses among Experimentals by Plan Generosity Relative to Income, Spanish-speaking Families, Quarters 3–10 Pooled	215
6A.1	Variables for Control-based Proxies: Total Family Earnings and Hours	218
7.1	Characteristics of the Male Family Heads Employed at Preenrollment	226
7.2	Regressions of Job Characteristics on Individual Attributes for Male Family Heads at Preenrollment	229
7.3	Regressions of Job Departure Decision on Subject Characteristics, Additive Effects Model, Two Formulations	234
7.4	Regression Coefficients for Significant Interactions with Experimental Variables, for Job Departures	237
7.5	Regressions of Unemployment Duration on Subject Characteristics, Additive Effects Model, Two Formulations	242
7.6	Regression Coefficients for Significant Interactions with Experimental Variables, for Unemployment Duration	244
7B.1	Characteristics of the Census and Parnes Samples	249

LIST OF TABLES

7B.2	Coefficients of Job Characteristics, from Additive Regression Models (Spline Formulation), for Job Departures	250
8.1	Changes in Job Characteristic Means under Employment Transition, by Total Sample and by Ethnic Group	256
8.2	Characteristic Average Earnings (V_8), Additive Effects Model	260
8.3	Regression Equations for Job Characteristic, Percentage with Earnings > \$6000 (V_8), Additive Effects Model	262
8.4	Regression Equations for Job Characteristic, Percentage with Earnings > \$8000 (V_8), Additive Effects Model	263
8.5	Regression Equations for Job Characteristic, Average Education (V_8), Additive Effects Model	264
8.6	Regression Equations for Job Characteristic, Occupational Status (Duncan) Score (V_8), Additive Effects Model	265
8.7	Regression Coefficients for Significant Interactions with Experimental Variables (Splines), for Employment Transition, Total Sample	268
8.8	Regression Coefficients for Significant Interactions with Experimental Variables (Splines), for Employment Transition, Whites	270
8.9	Regression Coefficients for Significant Interactions with Experimental Variables (Splines), for Employment Transition, Blacks	272
8.10	Regression Coefficients for Significant Interactions with Experimental Variables (Splines), for Employment Transition, Spanish-speaking	274
9.1	Estimated Effects on Head's Average Labor Supply for the Entire Experiment, Health Status and Experimental Parameters	304
9.2	Regression Coefficients for Health Status (Defined for Each Year of the Experiment) and Experimental Parameter, from Equations Estimating Head's Labor Supply in Each Year of the Experiment	306
9.3	Estimated Effects of Health Status on Head's Labor Supply for Specified Time Periods (Unhealthy Defined as Those Who Were Unhealthy for All Three Years)	307
9.4	Estimated Average Hours Worked per Week by Husband for Each Year of the Experiment, by Benefits and Health Status	308
9.5	Estimates of Three-Year Labor Supply of Wives, by Benefits and Health Status	310
9.6	Estimated Hours Worked per Week by Wives, for Each Experimental Year, by Benefits and Health Status	311
9B.1	Effects of Health Status and Experiment on Husband's Average Labor Supply over Entire Experiment: Regression Coefficients in Full Equation for Models I and II	315
9B.2	Estimated Effects on Head's Average Labor Supply for the Middle Two Years of the Experiment, by Health Status and Experimental Parameters	316
9B.3	Regression Coefficients for Health Status and Experimental Benefits Received, from Equations Estimating Husband's Labor Supply for Years in the Experiment	317
9B.4	Effect of Health Status and Experiment on Wife's Average Labor Supply over Entire Experiment: Regression Coefficients in Full Equation	318
10.1	Social Psychological and Experimental Effects on Labor-Force Activity	330
10.2	Social Psychological and Experimental Effects on Work Activity, High Culture of Poverty Integration	336

10.3	Social Psychological and Experimental Effects on Work Activity, Negative Personality Traits and Work Ethic	338
11.1	Levels of Information: Guarantee and Tax Rate	356
11.2	Basic Labor-Supply Equations for the Total Family	360
11.3	Husband Labor-Supply Equation, Interaction of Under–Correct–Over Information Dummy Variables with Guarantee Level Dummy Variables	362
11.4	Predicted Percentage Differences in Earnings, (Eighth-Pre)/Pre, for a Hypothetical Husband	363
11.5	Perceived Guarantee Level as the Dependent Variable	364
11.6	Predicted Guarantee Level for a Hypothetical Family	365
11.7	Probability of Being Excluded from the Sample	366
11.8	Probability of Exclusion for a Hypothetical Case, by Plan	366
11.9	Included and Excluded Members of the Sample, by Selected Variables	367
12.1	Transformed Variables for a Natural Cubic Spline Over $\Delta = [0, 2, 6, 12]$	374
12.2	Transformed Variables for a Periodic Cube Spline Over $\Delta = [0, 3, 6, 9, 12]$	377
14.1	Binary Variable Specification for f_2 (Z_3, Z_4)	397
14.2	Sample Statistics for Normal Wage and Income Variables and Their Components, Husband–Wife Continuous Sample	413

List of contributors

Numbers in parentheses indicate the pages on which the authors' contributions begin.

Robert Avery (383), Department of Economics, Carnegie Mellon University, Pittsburgh, Pennsylvania

Glen G. Cain (115), Department of Economics and Institute for Research on Poverty, University of Wisconsin, Madison, Wisconsin

David Elesh (289), Department of Sociology, Temple University, Philadelphia, Pennsylvania

Robinson G. Hollister (185), Department of Economics, Swarthmore College, Swarthmore, Pennsylvania

David Horner (57), Mathematica Policy Research, P.O. Box 2393, Princeton, New Jersey

Jon Helge Knudsen (347), vei 815 nr 318, 5033 Fyllingsdalen, Fyllingsdalen, Norway

Myron J. Lefcowitz (289), School of Social Work, University of Wisconsin, Madison, Wisconsin

Charles Mallar (33, 115, 163), Mathematica Policy Research, P.O. Box 2393, Princeton, New Jersey (on leave from Department of Political Economy, Johns Hopkins University, Baltimore, Maryland 21218)

John Mamer (347), Mathematica Policy Research, P.O. Box 2393, Princeton, New Jersey

Charles E. Metcalf (185), Mathematica Policy Research, P.O. Box 2393, Princeton, New Jersey

Richard E. Miller (221, 253), Department of Sociology, University of Wisconsin, Madison, Wisconsin

Walter Nicholson (115), Department of Economics, Amherst College, Amherst, Massachusetts

Dale J. Poirier (33, 369, 393), Department of Economics, University of Toronto, Toronto, W5S 1A1, Ontario, Canada

Albert Rees (5), Department of Economics, Princeton University, Princeton, New Jersey

Robert A. Scott (347), Department of Sociology, Princeton University, Princeton, New Jersey

Arnold R. Shore (347), Russell Sage Foundation, 230 Park Avenue, New York, New York

Seymour Spilerman (221, 253), Department of Sociology and Institute for Research on Poverty, University of Wisconsin, Madison, Wisconsin

Harold W. Watts (33, 57, 383, 393), Department of Economics and Center for the Social Sciences, Columbia University, New York, New York

Judith Wooldrige (115), Mathematica Policy Research, P.O. Box 2393, Princeton, New Jersey

Sonia Wright (321), Department of Sociology, University of Massachusetts, Amherst, Massachusetts

Foreword

The New Jersey Income-Maintenance Experiment is important for two reasons. It is the first social science experiment conducted on a large scale, and it addresses a critical current public policy issue.

The New Jersey Income-Maintenance Experiment cost $8 million, involved 1350 families, and lasted for a period of five years. No social science experiment of this magnitude had even been carried out before. Compared with nonexperimental, individual, social science research projects, the New Jersey experiment and the other large social science experiments that have followed it—three more Income-Maintenance Experiments, an Educational Performance Contracting Experiment, a Health Insurance Experiment, a Housing Allowance Experiment, and a Supported Work Experiment, to name the most important ones—are expensive. Compared with either the expenditures on experimental research in the physical sciences, or the total expenditures of nonexperimental individual social science research projects, or expenditures on demonstration programs, or, finally, expenditures on actual social programs, however, expenditures on large-scale social science research are small.

The experiment has weaknesses and flaws. Many of these have already been recognized and analyzed by the researchers who conducted the experiment. Some are discussed in this book. Still others are discussed in the forthcoming third volume of *The New Jersey Income-Maintenance Experiment.* In retrospect, weaknesses and flaws had to be expected. The first experiments in physical science were very crude indeed compared to current physical science experiments. The social sciences are much younger than the physical sciences. Social science experimentation is younger yet. If, as I assume, social science experimentation grows in importance, the historical importance of the first experiment will also grow.

The New Jersey Income-Maintenance Experiment is also important because it was designed to assess what effect a negative income tax program would have on the work effort of its beneficiaries. This question is of interest to nonbeneficiaries both because an income-maintenance program will be more costly to them the greater are the labor-supply reductions induced by that program, and because many people would object to an income-maintenance program that flagrantly violated the work ethic by inducing a large number of the able-bodied to quit work. (Of course, an appropriately defined work test may prevent some abuse. But, for a variety of reasons that no longer seem persuasive to me, advocates of negative income tax programs were opposed to work tests.)

Support for a universal negative income tax had been growing during the 1960s. By 1966, numerous officials in the Office of Economic Opportunity were committed to the idea. Because of the Vietnam War, however, President Johnson was unwilling to consider such a new domestic program. Moreover, many people still opposed a universal negative income tax because they feared that such a program would lead to massive labor-force withdrawals. In order to keep the idea of a negative income tax on the national agenda, and to test the effects of such a program on work effort, officials within the OEO Office of Planning and Evaluation initiated the Graduated Work Incentive Experiment, popularly known as the New Jersey Income-Maintenance Experiment.

This is the second of a three-volume set that contains revisions of the research that constituted the Official Report to the Office of Economic Opportunity on the New Jersey Graduated Work Incentive Experiment. The first volume deals with the administration and data-collection facets of the experiment. This volume contains papers on the experimental labor-supply response. The third volume will contain papers on other behavioral responses—in terms of expenditures, health, and social behavior—of experimental subjects.

Writing the foreword to this book is a special pleasure for me. When I was still a graduate student, I heard about the New Jersey Income-Maintenance Experiment and the Poverty Institute, was excited by both, and decided that, if possible, I would like to be a part of both. I did come to the Institute in 1970 and one year later was asked by Harold Watts, then the director of the Institute and a principal investigator in the experiment, to examine how the existence of a relatively generous welfare program in New Jersey affected the experimental results. The work I did on this problem during the ensuing three years was some of the most exciting that I have ever done. The question itself was intellectually intriguing. But, participating in the New Jersey Income-Maintenance Experiment was exciting per se, precisely because it was the first large social science experiment and it addressed a critical current public policy issue.

IRWIN GARFINKEL

Director, Institute for Research on Poverty

Preface

This project grew from a great many roots, and historians will draw different conclusions about the course of events that led to the funding and fielding of the first negative income tax experiment. However, the path that was most apparent to the experimental staff itself led from a clear imperative in the era of the early War on Poverty to do something about the welfare "mess." The concept of a negative income tax was outlined by Milton Friedman and elaborated and expanded by James Tobin. In the mid-1960s, this was developed into a welfare reform proposal but was rejected for various reasons—one of the major ones being concern about the effect of unconditional income supplements upon the labor supply of able-bodied men among the recipient group.

This issue of the labor-supply response to variations in income supplements and net wage rates was perceived as potentially amenable to scientific inquiry. But it was also one in which existing theory and sources of empirical evidence seemed unable to provide either intellectually or politically convincing answers. It was clear that experimental implementation of such a scheme offered the possibility of providing more convincing evidence.

Thoughts in this direction were crystallized in a specific proposal drawn up by Heather Ross for the United Planning Organization in Washington, D.C. Although it was rejected as initially proposed, this proposal was widely reviewed, and served to move the discussion to a point where OEO solicited a proposal for experimental research. This in turn elicited a proposal from Mathematica, Inc., of New Jersey, which enlisted William Baumol and Albert Rees, as well as Heather Ross, in its drafting.

The basic concept was approved by OEO. They were, however, reluctant to authorize a direct operation on the part of a profit-making private firm and requested the Institute for Research on Poverty to take primary responsibility for the experiment and to participate in its implementation in any way necessary to discharge that responsibility. The Institute and the University of Wisconsin agreed. In the summer of 1967, a grant was awarded to the Institute for Research on Poverty, and a subcontract agreement simultaneously reached with Mathematica to undertake the field operations and contribute to the research output.

The operation of the experiment, which finally took more than six years to complete, has involved some 1357 experimental and control families, four cities (Trenton, Paterson–Passaic, and Jersey City, in New Jersey; and Scranton, Pennsylvania), and a total cost of $7.9 million, of which one-third represented direct cash payments to sample families.

Any undertaking as large and long as this one inevitably involves a great many people. When the undertaking is also important and exciting, those people exert their best efforts—and this experiment is certainly no exception. It is an immense and finally impossible task to acknowledge fully all their contributions, but it is no less necessary to provide here an enumeration of the contributors who have in their various ways been crucial to bringing the experiment to a successful conclusion.

Many, many thanks are due to the Office of Economic Opportunity and its research, funding, and monitoring personnel. That the necessary financial support was forthcoming is obvious. But gratitude for that does not begin to do justice to the equally important forms of support that established, protected, and enhanced the undertaking as a scientifically significant and policy-relevant venture into the largely unexplored area of social experimentation. A succession of OEO assistant directors, their research chiefs, and related staff have been indispensable at various points and sympathetically supportive at all times. Mention must be made, in particular, of Robert A. Levine, Walter Williams, James Lyday, John Wilson, Tom Glennan, and Larry Orr.

Second, thanks go to the University of Wisconsin administration and the Research Committee of the Institute for Research on Poverty, particularly Martin Loeb.

Third, Professor James Tobin of Yale contributed his patience and wisdom in hearing out a major econometric dispute between Mathematica and the Poverty Institute over the design allocation model. The experiment is most grateful for his willingness to render a judgment, on which the actual allocation was based.

The first fourteen months of the contract, prior to initial pilot operations in Trenton, were spent by the staff both at Mathematica and at the Institute for Research on Poverty in specifying the experimental design. This entailed both technical and statistical specification of treatments and sample allocation, and also creation of detailed operational rules and procedures for administering payments and for collecting data.

INSTITUTE PERSONNEL

In Madison, work on drafting the model "statute"—the unit subject to the negative income tax, the kinds of income included in the tax base, the period of time over which income is measured, as well as the plethora of minor regulations regarding when reports had to be made, contingencies for failure to report, provision for appeals and so on—was undertaken by a group that included Joel

Handler, Joe Heffernan, Robinson Hollister, William Klein, Jack Lefcowitz, Jan and Theodore Marmor, and Robert Lampman (chairman). Particular thanks are due to William Klein, who did all the basic drafting.

The Madison work on the statistical design to specify the numbers and classes of families to be assigned to the experimental and control cells was done by a committee that included Dennis Aigner, John Conlisk, Robinson Hollister, Seymour Spilerman, Karl Taeuber, and Harold Watts (chairman). Special thanks are due to John Conlisk, who co-authored, with Watts, the technical design paper on the sample allocation method chosen, and also wrote and operated the computer programs required to render the conceptual design operational.

Another design task was the development of the questionnaires administered periodically to the families. Specification of essential baseline data required an intensive initial effort on the part of all the sociologists on the experiment staff. In addition, as the experiment progressed, there were new questions to be drafted and other important decisions to be made. In this connection, Sonia Wright carried responsibility on the Madison side for formulating and coordinating suggested questions and modifications of existing questions.

Although the primary responsibility for data coding and processing resided with Mathematica, a substantial and indispensable technical capability for dealing with data—particularly for early tabulations from incomplete and only partially processed files—was needed. Nancy Williamson provided this expertise. In the last year of the project, when the demands for analytic data processing became acute, Dennis Bindley coordinated and processed data requests, and always succeeded in producing what was required. He and Nancy, along with the many research assistants whose names appear in the separate papers, performed difficult feats under stringent deadlines.

An enormous and indispensable contribution was made by Felicity Sikdmore, the assistant director of the project in Madison, who kept the major research tasks on track and moving forward. Her sense and judgment with regard to the complex interaction of personalities and imperfect communication on the tripartite (OEO, Wisconsin, Mathematica) management of the project was a critical contribution. During the final, analytic phase of the experiment she had responsibility, with the help of Jill Isaacson, Angela Kenyon, and (during the summer of 1973) Renee Barnow, for organizing the production of the final report and the subsequent monographs—coaxing out manuscripts, editing them, getting them reviewed, revised, and ultimately typed and reproduced. Suzette Swoboda was most valuable in helping to organize the effort of turning the final report into three monographs.

MATHEMATICA PERSONNEL

At the Mathematica end, there was no clear assignment of research staff to the various design and planning issues or separation between research and planning for the field operations. The following research staff worked on a wide variety of tasks, including site selection, planning of the payments system, questionnaire design, and negotiation with state and federal agencies. Heather Ross, whose original idea for an experiment was the stimulus to the whole effort, spent her full time on the project, participating in a critical way in every facet of the early planning and operation of the study. William J. Baumol, William H. Branson, Robert A. Scott, and Michael Taussig participated part time; and (starting slightly later) Arnold Shore devoted full time, particularly to questionnaire development.

The critical field decisions necessary to implement the experiment were the responsibility of Mathematica (with Institute staff acting, when asked, as consultants and advisers). These decisions were made by the small group of senior operational people in Princeton, whose jobs during the course of the experiment varied with the needs of the study. Jeri Fair coordinated operational activities during most of the experiment as the project administrator; Cheri Marshall, as director of interview development, was responsible for coordinating the development of virtually all the survey instruments; Frank Mason originated and developed the QUEST data processing system used to enter, clean, store, and extract all the survey data.

Another group of dedicated people at Mathematica originated and developed the procedures used in the payments and interviewing aspects of the experiment. In payments, Wendy Cavanaugh, Anne Freeman, Mickey Olsen, and Marsha Shore all served at various times as Payments Department supervisors and Council for Grants to Families field coordinators. On the interviewing (Urban Opinion Surveys) side of the study, training and field coordination activities were the responsibilities of Sandra Carter, Diane Lewis, and Andrea Schutz.

Supporting the payments activities as either payments analysts or field representatives were Ann Amalfitano, Mary Capouya, Sylvia Figueroa, Catalina Fleming, Sheila Jones, Linda Roggenburg, Mary Scowcroft, Lilian Setta, Arne Shore, Peggy Torres, and Patti Uvegas. Interviewing activities were supported by Madeline Bellow, Nancy Feldman, Jimmye Abrams, Leon Redding, Audrey MacDonald, Marianne Stevenson, and Carl Weary.

The massive amounts of data were cleaned, entered, stored, and extracted by a group whose key members included Jules Balogh, Elaine Chanley, Betty Cohen, Barbara Genovese, Ellen Harralson, Rosemary Lechner, Regina Pasche, Eric Richardson, George Sabo, and Michael Watts.

Our last and perhaps greatest debt of gratitude is to David N. Kershaw, who joined the Mathematica staff as project director of the experiment in the spring of 1968. It is quite impossible to enumerate the many ways in which his talents, efforts, and dedication have contributed to the accomplishment of this unprecedented social experiment. While it is clear with hindsight that a person with his combination of abilities is absolutely necessary to the success of an experimental operation of this magnitude, we were extremely fortunate to have found him, because we would not have had the wit to invent him.

part I
Labor-supply responses to the experiment

Introduction

This volume is organized into three major parts. The first part deals, as its title suggests, with the labor-supply behavior of the families enrolled in the eight negative income tax plans tested in the New Jersey experiment. Chapter 1 describes the basic hypotheses of the designers of the experiment, provides a short survey of the nonexperimental literature of labor supply, and summarizes the four components of the central labor-supply analysis—husbands, wives, young adults, and the family. Chapter 2 describes the characteristics of the sample, the data base, and the major concepts used in the analysis. The labor-supply response of husbands is examined in Chapter 3. Chapter 4 deals with the response of wives. Chapter 5 looks at young adults. Chapter 6 deals with the labor supply of the family as a unit. The last two chapters of Part I analyze the effect of the experiment on job turnover and job selection.

Part II deals with factors—such as health, social psychological characteristics, and the information level of the participants about the program—which might be expected to modify, or mediate, the response. Part III contains technical expositions of the three major methodological innovations that run through the labor-supply analysis—spline functions, the adaptation of a variance components model to intermittent panel data, and the construction of "normal" income and wage variables. Part III is intended for the reader interested in the statistical underpinnings of the labor-supply analyses. The rest of the book can be read quite adequately without it.

1 The labor-supply results of the experiment: a summary

Albert Rees

The purpose of this chapter is to provide a summary of the findings of the graduated work incentives experiment on labor supply, and to do so in a way that makes them accessible to readers not concerned with the finer points of methodology and technique.[1] A full account of the methods of analysis and the design of the experiment will be found in the chapters that follow. As a necessary preface to the summary of findings, we begin with a discussion of what we expected to find, and why.

1. WHAT WE EXPECTED TO FIND

The sponsors of the experiment and the researchers all expected from the outset that the payment of substantial amounts of unearned income to poor families would reduce the amount of labor they supplied, though not by very large amounts. These expectations were based in part on theory and in part on the results of nonexperimental empirical research. We

---

[1] Large parts of this chapter have appeared in Rees (1974:158–180) and Rees and Watts (1975:60–87).

begin by reviewing what will be called here the static theory of the labor–leisure choice.

Static Theory

Figure 1.1 shows the labor–leisure choices of a hypothetical worker capable of earning $2 an hour. We assume that he is able to vary his weekly hours by such devices as voluntary overtime, part-time work, and multiple job holding; we also assume, for simplicity, that all hours worked are paid at the straight-time rate. In the initial situation, the worker is in equilibrium at point X on indifference curve I_0, where he works forty hours a week and receives a weekly income of $80. He is then offered a negative income tax plan that guarantees him $60 a week if he has no earned income and "taxes" earned income at 50 percent by reducing the guaranteed payment as earned income rises. This plan has a "breakeven" at point C with an earned income of $120; to the left of this point, the worker

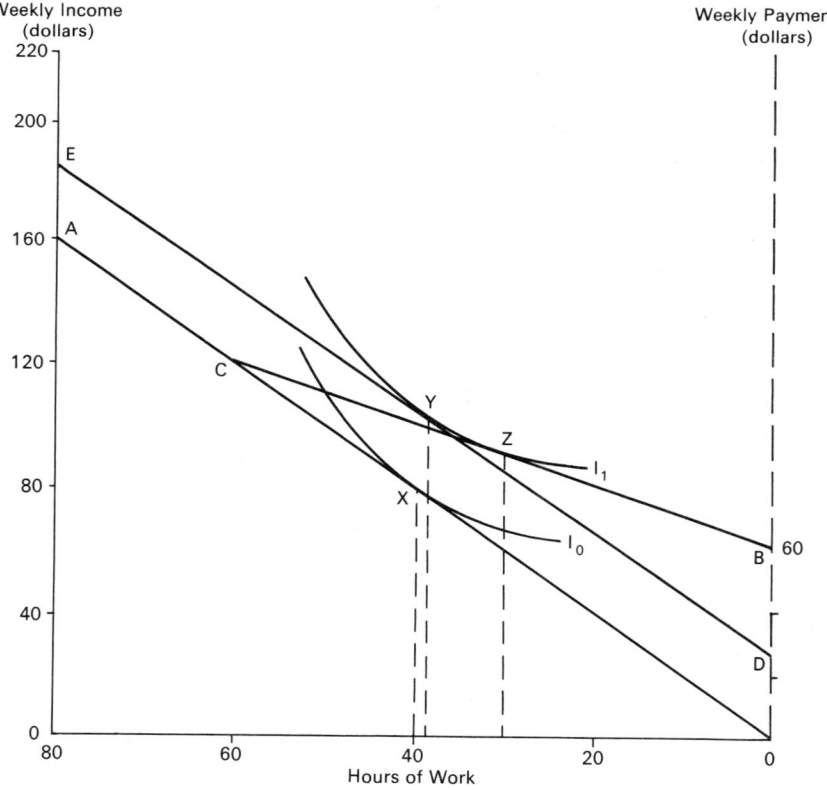

Figure 1.1 Response to a negative income tax.

receives no payments. The opportunity set facing him is now BCA rather than OA, and he chooses point Z on indifference curve I_1. His hours and earned income have decreased and his total income has increased.

The reduction in hours from X to Z can be divided into an income effect and a substitution effect by drawing line DE parallel to AO, which is tangent to I_1 at Y. The distance DO shows the payment amount that would yield as much satisfaction as the original negative income tax plan if the tax rate were zero. The horizontal distance from X to Y is the pure income effect on hours since the wage rate, or the price of "leisure" (the term used, for convenience, to include all nonwork activity), is the same at both points. The horizontal distance from Y to Z is the pure substitution effect of the tax rate, since the level of satisfaction is the same at both points. It should be noted that the income effect refers to the combined effect on welfare or satisfaction of the guarantee and the tax—not that of the guarantee alone. A guarantee of $60 a week with no tax would enable the worker to reach an indifference curve lying above I_1.

As Figure 1.1 is drawn, both the income effect and the substitution effect of the negative income tax reduce hours of work. The negative substitution effect follows from the usual constraints of neoclassical utility theory on the shapes of indifference curves. If the curves are convex from the origin (lower left) and BC is flatter than OA, then Z must lie to the right of Y. There is no such necessary relation between X and Y. The expectation that Y will lie to the right of X rests on empirical evidence. This is the evidence that, as real income has risen through time, hours of work have tended to fall and that, in cross section, hours of work tend to be shorter in high-paid than in low-paid jobs. In other words, the empirical evidence all indicates that leisure is a normal good. That leisure is not an inferior good might be expected from the fact that most inferior goods have preferred close substitutes, and there is no close substitute for leisure.

In the case of wage increases, not only is the income effect negative, but it is sufficiently large to outweigh the positive substitution effect of a wage increase, which of course makes leisure more expensive. In the case of a negative income tax, both the income effect and the substitution effect will tend to reduce the amount of work supplied. The experiment enables us to observe points X and Z as the behavior of the control and experimental subjects, respectively. (It should be noted that point Y is not observable.)

The preceding discussion has been cast in terms of the choice of hours of work by a single worker. If we think of the family as a single decision-making unit having a collective indifference map, the same analysis would apply to a family. Moreover, it would apply to decisions about labor force participation as well as decisions about hours. Thus a negative income tax might be expected to induce some members of the household to withdraw from the work force, particularly those whose wage rate was low and who had good nonmarket uses for their time. Teenagers might withdraw to devote their full time to schooling, or wives to devote full time to keeping house.

Our expectations about labor force participation rest more heavily on substitution effects than do those about hours of work. As real wages have risen through time, male labor-force-participation rates have fallen, suggesting (as in the case of hours) that negative income effects outweigh the positive substitution effects of real wage increases. For married women, however, the evidence is mixed. In cross section, holding education constant, the participation rate of wives falls as husbands' incomes rise. However, the participation rate of wives has risen through time as real wages have risen. Either the income effects are smaller than substitution effects in this context, or they are offset by other changes in the opportunity set confronting wives—such as the availability of work-saving home appliances and prepared foods.

In the presentation above, we have assumed only one specification of the negative income tax plan. In the actual experiment, there are eight, with four different guarantee levels and three different tax rates. The general expectation from the theory is that the plans with higher tax rates will have larger substitution effects and hence will produce greater reductions in labor supply though, strictly speaking, this is true only among plans that permit the family to achieve the same level of satisfaction. Similarly, one would expect from the empirical evidence on hours of work that, at the same tax rate, the plans with the most generous payments would cause the largest reduction in labor supply, whether generosity is measured in guarantee levels or in the average payments that would be made at the family's normal (preenrollment) income.

Dynamic Considerations

The theory sketched above is too simple in at least three respects. (1) It assumes that the wage rate confronting each worker is exogenously given, and that he can do nothing to affect it. (2) It implicitly assumes that the negative income tax is a permanent change in the opportunity set facing the worker. (3) It assumes that the negative income tax plan is introduced into a world without existing welfare plans. Relaxation of these assumptions gives rise to what can loosely be called dynamic modifications of the standard theory. Each will be discussed in turn.

ENDOGENOUS WAGE CHANGE

The worker could change his market wage in at least three different ways. First, he might withdraw from the labor force or reduce his hours in order to undertake training that would raise his wage at some future time. A permanent negative income tax would make it easier to do this by providing some income during the period of training. A temporary experiment provides an even stronger incentive in the short run, since in this case the training would have to be completed before the end of the experiment. These considerations suggest that there might be a greater reduction in labor supply early in the experiment than the static theory suggests, but that toward the end of the experiment this might no longer be true. If labor supply is measured in earnings rather than in man-hours, the effect toward the end of the experiment could even be to have a larger labor supply from the experimental group than from the control group. However, few of us gave sufficient weight to this line of argument at the beginning of the experiment to expect this result.

A second set of arguments suggests that earnings might fall more than hours throughout the experiment. The jobs open to a person of given skill and experience usually differ in the extent to which they are pleasant or unpleasant. Some involve heavy physical labor, disagreeable working conditions, inconvenient working hours, or inaccessible places of work. Others are lighter, more pleasant, and more convenient. Under conditions of sustained full employment, the less desirable jobs can be filled only at higher wages; the wage differentials thus called forth are known as compensating differentials.

The payment of a negative income tax could lead workers to shift toward pleasant jobs, sacrificing compensating differentials previously earned. Instead of substituting leisure for labor, they would substitute more agreeable work for disagreeable work. Such behavior would cause earnings to fall more than hours.

To the extent that average hours are reduced, there is another source of reduction in hourly earnings. By choosing not to work voluntary overtime, workers would reduce the hours paid at premium rates. In shifting from full-time jobs to part-time jobs, workers might have to accept lower straight-time rates. It is not uncommon for part-time workers to receive less for similar work than full-time workers; for example, such differentials are often found in collective bargaining agreements for clerks in retail food stores.

Another possible influence of experimental payments on wages is through their effects on job search. One of the standard arguments in favor of unemployment insurance is that it permits the unemployed worker to search for a suitable job rather than being forced by lack of income to accept one of the first job offers he receives, even if the wage offered is very low. More generally, any payments that are increased when a worker is not working will lower the cost of search, increase the optimum length of search, and increase the expected wage of the job offer finally accepted. Negative income tax payments fall into this category, serving as income supplements for workers entitled to unemployment insurance and even more strongly for those workers not eligible for unemployment insurance payments. Low-income workers are less likely to receive unemployment insurance. Some are in uncovered industries such as local government, domestic service, and agriculture. Some are new entrants to the labor force or new residents in the state. Finally, some will have quit their last jobs or have been discharged for cause. Any difference between experimental and control families in the incidence and duration of unemployment should be considered as a change in labor supply rather than a result of deficient demand. This is because experimentals and controls were selected from the same population and face the same demand conditions.

LIMITED DURATION OF THE EXPERIMENT

We turn next to consideration of the effects on labor supply of the limited duration of the experiment. These, too, do not all work in the same direction. Consider first the male household head with a steady job involving hard work and long hours. If he knew that negative tax payments were permanent, he might instead take a job with lighter work and more normal hours. Yet for a period of three years, such a shift might seem too risky. At the end of the experiment, he would need the higher earned income but might be unable to get his old job back. For the steadily employed male head, the probability is that an experiment of limited duration will have smaller effects on labor supply than will a permanent program.

For other members of the household, whose attachment to the labor force is less secure, the effects of limited duration may be quite the opposite. Wives, teenagers, and other adults in the household are likely to be in and out of the labor force as family circumstances change. To the extent that periods of withdrawal from the labor force are planned in advance, a temporary experiment encourages the concentration of such periods during the experimental years, when the costs of not working are lower than normal. This may be particularly true toward the end of the experiment.

THE LABOR-SUPPLY RESULTS OF THE EXPERIMENT: A SUMMARY

PRESENCE OF WELFARE

The final consideration is the presence of preexisting welfare plans. At the beginning of the experiment, New Jersey did not give welfare to households with a male head—that is, it did not have the program known as Aid to Families with Dependent Children and Unemployed Parents (AFDC-UP). This, indeed, was one of the important reasons for choosing New Jersey as the experimental site. Moreover, we did not plan at the outset to include a site in Pennsylvania, a move which became necessary to enroll enough non-Spanish-speaking whites. In January 1969 (three months after the Trenton enrollment but before enrollment in the other sites), New Jersey introduced a welfare program for intact families. Until they were cut back in July 1971, benefits under this plan were more generous than those of most welfare programs in the country, and more generous, over certain income ranges, than some of the experimental plans.

The presence of welfare complicates the comparison between control and experimental families. In the ninth experimental quarter, 25 percent of control families and 13 percent of experimental families were on welfare (these figures are the highest percentages for any quarter). Among experimental families, the percentage varied by plan, decreasing with plan generosity; ninth-quarter figures show 23 percent of those on the 50–50 and 75–70 plans choosing welfare, compared with only 7 percent of those on the 125–50 plan. It also varied by site, from 6 percent in Jersey City to 21 percent in Paterson–Passaic in the ninth quarter.

The general effect of welfare, again according to theoretical principles, is to make the observed differences between experimental and control groups smaller than they would be in the absence of welfare. The underestimate occurs essentially because welfare may induce some withdrawal of work effort in the control group. On the other hand, the estimates derived from an experiment in the presence of welfare are perhaps more appropriate estimates of the net effect of a new national income-maintenance program that would be superimposed on existing programs.

Taken as a group, these three arguments led us to look for certain patterns in the experimental results. However, they did not modify substantially the overall expectations generated by the static theory because, for the household as a whole, they tend to be offsetting.

The Nonexperimental Literature

Since World War II, there has been substantial empirical research on labor supply. The resulting literature was important in forming our initial expectations. The studies fall into three general groups—studies of hours of work, studies of labor force participation, and studies concentrating on the effects of nonlabor income on labor supply.

HOURS OF WORK

The findings from studies on hours of work led us to expect some reduction in labor supply for the experimental group, because they suggested that the income effect as well as the substitution effect of a negative income tax would be to diminish the amount of work supplied.

It should be noted, however, that these studies were not confined to low-income workers. They suggest that, at or near the mean wage, increases in wage rates are associated with decreases in hours worked; but this need not be true at wages well below the mean, when the desire for added consumer goods may be stronger and the desire for additional leisure weaker. Low-income workers may have a desire to reach the average level of living of their communities stronger than the desire of middle-income workers to rise above it. Indeed, this is exactly what is indicated by the usual textbook diagrams of the backward-bending supply curve of labor, which show a forward-rising curve at very low wages, becoming vertical and finally bending back as some higher level of wages is reached. Unfortunately, there is no empirical basis for the forward-sloping portion of the curve. Moreover, even if substitution effects are stronger than income effects at low wages, the total effect of a negative income tax will still be to reduce hours, since the tax-induced reduction in net wage rates will not produce an income loss, as would a wage cut with no income transfer. The unique feature of a negative income tax plan is that income is increased at the same time the net wage rate is reduced.

LABOR FORCE PARTICIPATION

The relevant portion of the labor-force-participation literature deals with the differences in strength of attachment to the labor force by age, sex, and marital status. The studies of such attachment show very high rates of participation by married men with wives present, only weakly affected by differences in education or the strength of demand. For teenagers, the elderly, and married women, average rates of participation are much lower, and such forces as differences in education or in the strength of demand induce much larger differences in participation rates.

Because of the previous studies of participation rates, we never expected any substantial fraction of the male heads of households to withdraw from the labor force when they received payments. It seemed much more likely that the response of male heads would be shorter hours or longer periods of search between jobs. For wives, teenagers, and the elderly, however, reductions in labor-force-participation rates seemed a much more likely outcome.

We were aware, of course, of the popular view that large transfer payments can cause widespread idleness. There are experiences that support such a view, the experience with unemployment benefits for returning veterans after World War II, for instance—payments that were sometimes called "rocking chair money." However, many of the veterans involved were single rather than household heads, and they lacked recent civilian work experience. Popular current views about the effect of welfare on work behavior are similarly based largely on experience other than that of male household heads—in this case mothers without husbands—and, even here, tend to be based on anecdotal information rather than systematic evidence. If any scholars expected our experimental treatment to cause large declines in the participation rates of male heads, they were not in our research group.

NONLABOR INCOME

The last relevant category of research consists of studies emphasizing the effects of nonlabor income on labor supply. Several of these studies were designed explicitly to simulate, from nonexperimental data, the effects of a negative income tax program. Nevertheless, they were not influential in forming our expectations—in part, of course, because most of them have appeared since we began the experiment. The most striking thing about them is the very wide range of values in their results—a lack of agreement that weakens confidence in any of their findings.

First of all, these studies face a problem that may be insurmountable. Much of the nonlabor income reported in income surveys consists of transfer payments such as unemployment compensation; workmen's compensation; old age, survivors', and disability insurance; and temporary disability insurance. All these payments except survivors' insurance are totally or partially work conditioned—that is, they cannot legally be received by those who work, or by those who work and earn more than a stated amount. Work behavior determines whether nonlabor income is received, and in what amount. If any of these types of work-conditioned transfers are included in the measure of nonlabor income used to simulate a negative income tax, the size of the negative effects on work effort will be overestimated, perhaps very greatly. There are, of course, types of nonlabor income that are not work conditioned, particularly dividends, interest, and certain types of pensions. However, the dividend and interest income of the nonaged poor is negligible, and pensions tend to be received by those past prime working age. Nonlabor income of the working poor that is not work conditioned is hard to find in such existing data bases as the Census or the Survey of Economic Opportunity. Some investigators, searching for this needle in the haystack, seem to have seized in desperation at the handiest pitchfork instead. Even those clearly aware of the problem of work-conditioned transfers sometimes report amounts of nonlabor income (supposedly *not* work conditioned) so large as to call their definitions or procedures into question.

A second general difficulty with the simulation studies of negative income taxes is that they sometimes truncate their samples by current income. This will tend to include a disproportionate number of households that supply, perhaps temporarily, less than average amounts of labor—a selection which could bias the estimated coefficients toward large supply effects. Truncation on a measure such as hourly wages, which is uncorrelated or less highly correlated with the amount of labor currently supplied, would be far preferable. To be sure, the New Jersey experiment sample was also truncated on family income, which may not have been the best variable to choose for this purpose. However, the problem is far less serious in a study that estimates labor-supply effects in a period subsequent to that used to select the sample, that also derives these estimates from a comparison of experimental and control groups, where the experimental group receives an exogenous treatment.

It should also be pointed out that the nonexperimental studies estimate substitution effects from cross-sectional differences in average hourly earnings that may not be entirely independent of the effects of the amount of labor supplied. Those who work over forty hours per week will receive premium pay for overtime; those who only want to work part time may have to accept lower hourly earnings. In an experiment, differential tax rates create a truly exogenous source of differences in net wages.

Despite these deficiencies, the studies that focus on the effects of nonlabor income reinforce the more general labor-supply studies in one important respect—they consistently find larger supply effects for women than for men. The estimated effects for men, indeed, are sometimes very close to zero.

A Summary of Expectations

The researchers involved in the experiment never agreed on, or set down in advance, a summary of what they felt was the most likely outcome for labor supply. In retrospect, this is unfortunate. Any attempt to do so now is bound to reflect, to some extent, our present knowledge of the results and thus understate the degree to which we have been surprised. Despite this caveat, it still seems useful to attempt a summary in retrospect.

We never expected able-bodied male heads of households to withdraw from the labor force in response to temporary payments too small to support large families. We did expect some of them to reduce their hours of work or to spend more time searching for new jobs when they lost or quit their jobs. We expected some teenagers to return to school or to stay in school longer as a result of the payments. We expected some working wives to leave the labor force in order to spend all their time in household work.

On the whole, the reduction in labor supply we expected to find in the experimental group was on the order of 10 to 15 percent. We did not expect to find any differential effects by ethnic group. However, we did expect to find that higher tax rates and higher guarantees would produce greater reductions in labor supply.

2. HOW WE ANALYZE THE DATA

The results presented in the following chapters are more complex and somewhat more ambiguous than we anticipated, and they are not easy to summarize. In attempting to do so, we must explain why we regard some of the results as more salient than others. This in turn requires some brief discussion of our methods of analysis, which will deal with dependent variables, the control variables, the treatment variables, and the time period.

The Dependent Variables

There are at least four possible measures of the amount of labor supplied by the household: labor-force-participation rates, employment rates, total hours of work, and total earnings. Total hours of work includes those not at work as supplying zero hours, and therefore the average level of this variable will be below the average weekly hours of those at work. With hours defined this way, the measures listed above are in order of increasing comprehensiveness. Employment includes changes in labor force participation and in unemployment, which (as pointed out earlier) must be considered as a supply phenomenon in the context of differences between experimentals and controls. Hours includes variations in the two preceding variables and, in addition, variations in hours per week of those at work. Earnings reflects variations in all three preceding variables and, in addition, variation in earnings per hour worked.

It therefore seems that earnings furnishes the best summary measure of the effects on labor supply. Unfortunately, however, there is a possible bias in the use of the earnings variable not present in the other measures. Experimental families filled out an income reporting form every four weeks; control families did not. The experimental families may therefore have learned more quickly than control families that what was to be furnished was gross rather than net earnings (that is, earnings before taxes and other deductions, *not* take-home pay). This differential learning process may have caused a spurious differential in earnings in favor of the experimental group, especially during the early part of the experiment.

Because of this possible bias in the earnings measure, the hours measure is emphasized in summarizing the results. An exception is made in discussing the labor supply of the household *as a whole,* where the earnings measure, despite its defects, serves as an appropriate way of weighting the hours of different members of the household by the value of the labor they supply. It should also be recalled that family earnings provided the basis on which payments were determined.

Control Variables

In measuring supply effects, a large set of control variables was typically entered on the right-hand side of the regression equations. In part, these were necessary to control for differences between the experimental and control groups resulting from the fact that families were not assigned to these groups by simple random assignment, but by a more complex stratified design. In part, however, their inclusion was in response to the fact that even in a simple random design it is important to control for systematic differences that may survive the randomization process.

The control variables are used in two different ways. First, they are entered into the labor-supply equations as variables in their own right. Second, they are often interacted with the variables representing experimental treatments to see whether the treatment has differential effects in different subgroups of the treated population. A control variable that is highly significant in the first of these contexts may not be significant in the second.

One of the most important control variables is the preenrollment value of the dependent variable. Thus, if the dependent variable is hours, hours at preenrollment is usually entered on the right-hand side. This procedure captures the effect of many taste variables that cannot be specified individually, but will also reduce the significance of the control variables that are separately specified. It is worth noting that this kind of control vari-

THE LABOR-SUPPLY RESULTS OF THE EXPERIMENT: A SUMMARY 17

able cannot be used in a nonexperimental study based on a single body of cross-sectional data.

Some of these control variables, although they could be expected to be very significant, in fact were not. Thus, after control for ethnicity, there was little systematic difference among experimental sites. In most cases, separate results by site will therefore not be summarized here. On the other hand, health status turned out to be a very important variable, and all the results summarized below control for it. In effect, they can be thought of as results for people in good health. Ethnicity turns out to be tremendously important, even when many other control variables are present. For this reason, most of the chapters that follow run separate regressions for the three ethnic groups (white, black, and Spanish-speaking), and we shall summarize these results separately.

It is also important to control for potential earned income, since average income levels are not the same in experimental and control groups as a result of the complexities of the design model, and since there may be differential responses at different income levels. The income variable used for this purpose should be free of any influence from the experimental treatment. For this purpose, we have used estimates of normal hourly earnings, either based entirely on observations from the control group or derived by methods that isolate and abstract from treatment effects.

The foregoing brief account is by no means a complete listing of control variables. It would be tedious and unnecessary to discuss each of them in this summary. Two important additional variables should be mentioned here, however. (1) In studying the labor supply of wives, rather elaborate control variables are used for the number and ages of children. (2) Education frequently appears as a control variable, though it is less powerful than in most labor-supply studies because of the truncation of the sample by income.

Treatment Variables

In one sense, the experimental treatment is very simple—it consists of giving families cash payments. These can be specified much more precisely than the relatively amorphous treatments involved in experimental evaluation of counseling, training, or psychotherapy programs. In another sense, however, the treatment is complex. There were eight different payment plans, and within each of these, there was variation in payments by family size. Table 1.1 shows the number of experimental families by payment plan.

Table 1.1 **Number of Families, by Payment Plan**

Guarantee Level[a] (Percentage)	Tax Rate (Percentage)		
	30	50	70
125	no plan	138	no plan
100	no plan	77	86
75	100	117	85
50	46	76	no plan

Total treatment families:	725
Total control families:	632
Grand total	1357

[a] Guarantee as percent of the following basic support levels, referred to throughout as the "poverty levels":

2 persons	2000	6 persons	4050
3 persons	2750	7 persons	4350
4 persons	3300	8+ persons	4600
5 persons	3700		

These differ slightly from the official poverty levels as of 1968. They were increased annually by the change in the Consumer Price Index (CPI).

In the design stages of the experiment, we all confidently expected significant overall effects of the treatment on labor supply, and attention was focused on measuring differential effects of the treatment plans. In retrospect, this emphasis may have been somewhat misplaced, since the overall treatment effect is not always unambiguous.

In general, two different methods of introducing treatment effects are used. The first is to include a dummy variable for any experimental treatment and two additional sets of variables that specify tax rates and guarantee levels. The second method uses the experimental dummy and a variable measuring average payments levels. The payments reflect guarantee level, tax rate, family size, and earned income. To avoid introducing experimental response into the treatment variable, the preenrollment level of income is used in calculating payments. The payments calculation is useful in identifying families who are initially above the breakeven point of their plans, since although they are in the experimental group, they all appear at preenrollment with zero payments.

In practice, two of our plans were dominated by New Jersey welfare during most of the period of the experiment, and attrition from these plans was very high. These were, of course, the two least generous plans—the 50 percent of poverty guarantee with a 50 percent tax rate (50–50 plan) and the 75 percent guarantee with a 70 percent tax rate (75–70 plan). In much of the analysis, these plans are omitted from the treatment group.

Before we discuss effects, it will be useful for the reader to have some idea of the size of the payments and their variation by plan. Table 1.2 gives, by experimental site, the average size of payments to continuous husband–wife families who received payments in a given four-week period for each of the three years of the experiment. The average payments per period can, of course, be converted to annual averages by multiplying by thirteen. Thus the first-year annual average for all such families is $1183. The average payments are slightly lower for all families than for continuous husband–wife families. We show the data for the latter here, since most of the labor-supply analysis is based on these families.

The data in Table 1.2 show a mildly rising trend through time, except in Trenton. This trend comes from two sources. First, guarantee levels were escalated annually during the course of the experiment, according to the Consumer Price Index (CPI). The increase was based on July-to-July changes in the CPI and was implemented in all sites where payments were then being made in September 1969 (5.5 percent), October 1970 (5.9 percent), and September or October 1971 (4.4 percent). Because of differences in the timing of the experimental period in different sites, Trenton received the first two cost-of-living adjustments, cumulating to 11.7 percent; Paterson–Passaic and Jersey City received all three, cumulating to 16.6 percent; and Scranton received the last two, cumulating to 10.5 percent. In Paterson–Passaic and Jersey City, the third increase in guarantees was in effect for less than a full year before the end of payments, in Scranton for less than two months, and in Jersey City for about seven months. The average increase in guarantee levels over the experimental period in the two sites that received all three increments thus lies between 11.7 and 16.6 percent, closer to the former figure in Paterson–Passaic and slightly closer to the latter in Jersey City. Comparing these

Table 1.2 **Average Payments in Dollars per Four-Week Period, Continuous Husband–Wife Families, by Site**

	All Sites	Trenton	Paterson–Passaic	Jersey City	Scranton
First year	91.03	69.93	79.43	107.80	91.46
Second year	93.25	71.91	80.67	109.86	94.72
Third year	96.84	58.67	84.92	120.35	98.26
Percentage change, first to third year	6.4	−16.1	6.9	11.6	5.2

increases with the increases in average payments shown in Table 1.2, it can be seen that in every case the increase in payments is less than the increase in guarantees—and by substantial amounts in all sites but Jersey City.

The second factor tending to produce increasing average payments over time is rising unemployment rates. A weighted average unemployment rate for the four sites rose from 4.4 percent in 1969 to 7.1 percent in 1971, a factor that would also tend to produce rising payments as members of the experimental families who lost jobs experienced greater difficulty finding new ones.

In light of the increases in guarantees and the rise in unemployment, the smallness of the rise in average payments over the life of the experiment suggests that there was neither an increasing withdrawal of labor supply nor any growing falsification of income reports as experimental subjects learned to "beat the system." Either of these kinds of behavior would have produced more rapidly rising payments.

Table 1.3 gives, by ethnic group, the same kind of data as Table 1.2. The average payments rise most rapidly for Spanish-speaking families. Since their payments rise more than those for all ethnic groups in any one site, something more than the distribution of ethnic groups by site must be at work.

Table 1.4 shows the average payments to continuous husband–wife families by experimental plan for the second experimental year. These vary from $187 per four-week period in the most generous plan to $22 in the least generous. In addition, of course, there is substantial variation within plans because of differences in family size and earned income.

Changes in payments from the first to the third year also vary by plan as shown in Table 1.5. In the three plans with guarantees equal to or above the poverty line, payment increases lie between 9 and 14 percent. The low guarantee plans vary more, but three of the five show decreases in pay-

Table 1.3 Average Payments in Dollars per Four-Week Period, Continuous Husband–Wife Families, by Ethnic Group

	All	White	Black	Spanish-speaking
First year	91.03	87.65	97.65	86.96
Second year	93.25	91.03	96.59	92.23
Third year	96.84	90.11	102.83	100.32
Percentage increase, first to third year	6.4	2.8	5.3	15.4

THE LABOR-SUPPLY RESULTS OF THE EXPERIMENT: A SUMMARY

Table 1.4 Average Payments in Dollars per Four-Week Period, Continuous Husband–Wife Families, by Plan, Second Experimental Year

Guarantee Level (Percentage)	Tax Rate (Percentage)		
	30	50	70
125	no plan	187.28	no plan
100	no plan	123.72	66.07
75	103.54	44.17	34.91
50	46.23	21.66	no plan

ments. The decreases include both the plans with the lowest (30 percent) tax rate.

Experimental Time

We expected before the experiment began that the best results would be obtained during the middle part of the experimental period. At the outset, we expected participants to be still learning how to report income and how their payments would vary with changes in income. We expected that toward the end of the experiment, anticipation of the termination of payments might also affect labor supply, producing unknown kinds of "end game" effects. Where results are presented separately by years, then, results for the middle year should generally be the most reliable. Often we use the central two years—that is, quarters 3 through 10. For some purposes, we average observations over the entire period.

It should also be recalled that experimental time does not have the same meaning in each site in terms of calendar time, because each site entered and left the experiment at different dates. To control for trends in the economy, calendar time is sometimes entered into the analysis in addition to experimental time.

Table 1.5 Percentage Change in Average Payments between First and Third Year, Continuous Husband–Wife Families, by Plan

Guarantee Level (Percentage)	Tax Rate (Percentage)		
	30	50	70
125	no plan	8.9	no plan
100	no plan	9.1	13.9
75	−4.5	−10.3	15.1
50	−2.6	3.2	no plan

3. WHAT WE FOUND

This section will summarize findings for three groups of participants —married men, married women, and the family as a whole. Within each grouping, attention will be given to differences by ethnic group. The analyses of the three groups were done simultaneously by different members of the research team. Although the methods used for each group have important features in common, there are also important differences, and results are not always directly comparable from one group to another.

Husbands

The first step in the analysis of husbands' work behavior was to calculate the differences in work behavior between experimentals and controls for male heads of continuous husband–wife families.[2] They were, as we expected, very small. Contrary to our expectations, however, these differences did not all show a clear and significant pattern; indeed, they showed a discernible pattern only after a great deal of refined analysis. The results, in the crude form of unadjusted means, are reproduced in Table 1.6 for quarters 3 to 10, the central two years of the experiment. Experimentals show a slightly higher participation rate than controls, a lower employment rate, and a correspondingly higher unemployment rate. The unemployment rate difference carries over into hours worked per week. However, on the two measures of earnings, experimentals do better than controls—a result that may reflect greater misreporting of earnings by controls.

The higher unemployment rate of male experimentals did not result from higher job turnover. Indeed, the experimental treatment was found

Table 1.6 **Unadjusted Mean Values of Key Variables, Male Heads of Husband–Wife Families, Quarters 3–10**

	All Controls	All Experimentals	Experimentals on High and Medium Plans
Participation rate	93.7	94.7	95.5
Employment rate	87.0	86.4	86.8
Unemployment rate	6.7	8.3	8.7
Hours	33.6	33.1	32.9
Earnings	$84.1	$89.9	$89.4
Earnings per hour	$ 2.50	$ 2.72	$ 2.72

[2] This section summarizes the research reported in detail in Chapters 3, 7, and 8.

unambiguously to reduce job turnover—although there was also evidence of an increase in the duration of unemployment for heads in the experimental group who did become unemployed. For younger, better educated heads, there was also evidence of an improvement in occupational status and job satisfaction after changing jobs. Thus at least some members of the experimental group may have looked for work longer and been more choosy about the jobs they accepted.

The next step in the analysis of male heads was to calculate a set of simple multiple regressions with the labor-supply measures as dependent variables. These were done separately for each time period and ethnic group, with fourteen or fifteen control variables for age, education, preenrollment hours, weeks worked in the year before the experiment, site, and family size. The coefficients of interest are those giving the size of the differential between experimental and control groups for several dependent variables. Except for the suspect earnings measure, where the differential is positive, none of these coefficients are statistically significant, even at the 10 percent level, for the critical central two years. There are significant (at the 5 percent level) negative coefficients for the treatment variables in the regressions for white hours in the last year, and for Spanish-speaking hours and employment in the first year. The coefficients for blacks are never significant and are usually positive.

These regressions have several limitations. They include, in the experimental group, families who received the very low payments provided by the two least generous plans; these plans were dominated by welfare and had high attrition. Nor do the regressions allow for differential response at different income levels. The third step in the analysis was therefore to run a set of regressions that controlled for normal wages and normal income as a fraction of the poverty level, permitted nonlinear wage effects, and analyzed the experimental plans separately in three groups of high, medium, and low generosity.

These regressions do little better than the first set in revealing significant effects of the treatment. There are some significant negative coefficients for experimental treatment for white employment and hours, but they occur most often for the low-payment plans where one would least expect them. The coefficients for blacks remain insignificant except for earnings, and almost entirely positive. Coefficients for the Spanish-speaking are preponderantly negative, but never both negative and significant.

The remaining step in the analysis of husbands discarded the suspect earnings variable as a measure of labor supply, using a variable scaled in hours. It also eliminated the two least generous experimental plans on the grounds that they were dominated by welfare and therefore contained few families actually facing their experimental parameters. This was done, however, at the cost of dropping most of the 70 percent tax rate, reducing our ability to measure the effects of tax rate variation. It also attempted to deal with a potential problem of underestimation of the size of the response to payments caused by the presence of families in the experimental group but above their breakeven point.

In the regressions discussed so far, there is no explicit way of allowing for the fact that some of the experimental families were above the breakeven point of their plans and therefore received no payments and did not, in fact, face high marginal tax rates. Nevertheless, these families were counted as being in the experimental group. The normal income variable, when introduced as an interaction, allows for differential responses at different normal incomes but does not specifically identify families above their breakeven points. In the remaining analysis of male heads, therefore, a variable called θ is introduced, which measures the distance between a family's normal income and its breakeven point. This variable is scaled in hours of work at the male head's normal wage. It is equal to 0 if the family is a control family or if it is an experimental family whose head could forego twenty hours or more of work per week without the family's normal income falling below the breakeven. It is equal to 2 when normal income is at the breakeven level, and to 4 when it would take twenty hours more work at the normal wage to reach breakeven. The mean value of θ for all experimentals is approximately 5.

The experimental response function takes each of the plan parameters (guarantee and tax rate) and interacts it multiplicatively with θ and with θ^2, thus estimating a nonlinear response function that typically changes sign over different values of θ. The significance of the response functions is then evaluated by an F-test where the null hypothesis is that there is no experimental response.

In the central two years, the null hypothesis for labor force participation and employment cannot be rejected for whites or blacks, but is rejected at the 1 percent level for the Spanish-speaking, for whom the treatment decreased labor-force-participation rates. For hours, the null hypothesis is rejected at the 5 percent level for white heads and at the 1 percent level for Spanish-speaking heads, but it cannot be rejected for blacks. For white and Spanish-speaking heads, whose estimated response is significant, let us examine the size and pattern of the response. For this purpose, we look at a relatively generous plan (guarantee of 100 and tax rate of 50, that is the 100–50 plan) and at a typical value of θ, namely 5. (Recall that a family for whom $\theta = 5$ needs 30 more hours of work per week at the male head's estimated normal wage to reach its breakeven point.) The estimated reduction in hours per week at this point in the response surface is 2.4 hours for white heads and a substantial 7.3 hours for Spanish-speaking heads. The reductions are larger for higher values of θ (that is, for poorer families).

These two hours effects seem to arise in different ways. For the Spanish-speaking heads, a 9 percentage-point decrease in the employment rate is estimated for the central two years at $\theta = 5$ for the 100–50 plan. This accounts for much of the decrease in hours. It suggests that Spanish-speaking heads were unemployed more when in the experimental group, and this is verified by analyzing unemployment rates directly. For whites, however, the employment response at these values is positive and very small. The entire hours effect is a reduction in hours per week for those at work. This is confirmed in separate estimates of the hours response for those who are employed; the response for white heads is significant at the 1 percent level, but is not significant for the other two ethnic groups.

The hours response for white heads is strongest in the last year, when it is significant at the 1 percent level and is estimated at -7.3 hours per week at $\theta = 5$ for the 100–50 plan. For Spanish-speaking heads, the time pattern is opposite. The negative hours responses in the first year and the central two years become predominantly positive and significant at the 5 percent level in the last year.

Some information is also gained by looking at the results for the central two years in terms of the plans. For Spanish-speaking heads, the estimates are ordered by tax rates, as we would expect, with higher tax rates producing substantially stronger disincentives. For whites, the reverse is true—the largest disincentives are estimated for the plans with the lowest tax rates. In neither case is there a strong or consistent ordering by guarantee levels—indeed, the most generous plan (125–50) shows the smallest effects.

By far the most surprising result of the analysis for male heads is the complete failure to find any significant effect for black male heads in any of the analyses, despite the fact that black husband–wife families received larger average payments than similar families in the other two ethnic groups. Indeed, the estimated supply response for blacks is not only insignificant, but preponderantly positive. This kind of finding for blacks is not limited to male heads; it recurs in the analysis of other components of the household.

We certainly did not anticipate this outcome; moreover, we have no plausible explanation for it after the fact. There is some indication in the earnings data that something peculiar happened to the black control group, but we don't know why. While there is always some possibility that the result arises from sampling variability, we should note that black continuous husband–wife families are more than a third of the total, and are a larger group than the Spanish-speaking, for whom negative supply effects were found.

Wives

The supply response of married women with husbands present can be seen fairly clearly from some simple descriptive statistics, reproduced in Table 1.7.[3] These give, separately for experimentals and controls, the labor-force-participation rates of wives at the preenrollment interview and averages for the four interviews in each of the next three years.

One of the first things to note is that the participation rates are very low—less than half the 1971 rates of all married women in the U.S. population as a whole. This is in part because the average family size in the experiment is very large, and we overrepresent families with small children. In part, it is an unfortunate consequence of the decision to truncate the sample by family income, a decision that led to an underrepresentation of working wives, even among large families. In retrospect, it might have been preferable to truncate on the basis of husband's income or, still better, husband's wage rate. The same decision probably accounts in part for the rather sharp rise in participation rates of control wives over time, since at the outset we overrepresent families where the wife is temporarily out of the labor force. The difference in the average rates at preenrollment is a result of the experimental design model, which assigned more of the higher-income families to the experimental group. The effect of the treatment is shown by the drop in the participation rate of experimental wives during the first two years of the experiment. By the third year, the rate for experimental wives is above the preenrollment rate, but still slightly below the rate for wives in the control group.

The regression analysis for wives controls for the presence of children

Table 1.7 **Labor-Force-Participation Rates of Wives, Selected Time Periods**

	Preenrollment	First Year	Second Year	Third Year
Experimental wives	16.0	14.0	15.2	18.0
Control wives	13.4	16.3	16.5	18.5

NOTE: These numbers show the percentage of wives in the labor force during the survey week. For the last three columns, the numbers are averages of the four quarterly interviews for the appropriate year.

[3] This section summarizes the research reported in detail in Chapter 4.

by detailed age, for the health of both husband and wife, and for education, age, and previous work experience. Two methods of entering the treatment parameters are used. We shall summarize here the results for the method that defines treatment by a dummy variable (with the value of 1 when the family is in the experimental group, and 0 for controls), a variable for average payments based on preenrollment income, and a variable that gives the tax rate of the experimental plan if the payments are positive (that is, the family was below breakeven at preenrollment). The results of this analysis are summarized in Table 1.8. The effects shown are from regressions in which the treatment effect applies to wives in families below their breakeven level and is evaluated at the mean level of payments and a tax rate of 50 percent. The coefficient for all wives is the weighted average of three ethnic effects in a regression in which treatment and ethnicity interact.

The analysis shows significant negative effects on labor-force-participation rates for all experimental wives. These rates are defined as the proportion of quarterly surveys in which the wife was in the labor force in the survey week. When the results are disaggregated by ethnic group, they are seen to arise almost entirely from the behavior of white wives—the effects of the treatment on the participation rates of black and Spanish-speaking wives being close to 0 and sometimes positive. When the dependent variable is hours, the results are generally similar, but somewhat weaker. The estimated effect for black wives is positive and significantly different from that for white wives. Once again, we have no plausible explanation for the strong differences in results by ethnic group.

Table 1.8 Labor-Supply Response of Wives in Husband–Wife Families, Quarters 3–10

	Percentage of Survey Weeks in Labor Force	Hours of Work in Survey Week
White	-8***	-1.8
Black	-0.2**	$+0.6$***
Spanish-speaking	$+5$**	$+.05$
All	-3***	-0.6**
Control group mean	17	4

NOTE: Significance levels of treatment variables on the F-test: *** = 1 percent; ** = 5 percent; * = 10 percent. The F-test for the white subgroup applies to the three treatment variables and tests for an overall effect that is significantly different from 0. The F-tests for the two minority ethnic groups apply to their respective interactions with these same three treatment variables, and the significance levels are with respect to differences from the *white* subgroup.

Where the regressions include treatment variables that distinguish among experimental plans, the pattern of results by the parameters of the plans is consistent with expectations. The estimated negative response is quite consistently larger the higher the level of payments, and the differences are usually significant. Moreover, with payments levels held constant, it is generally larger the higher the tax rate, though this effect is usually small and never significant.

The size of the estimated effects on labor supply are subject to two rather different interpretations. In the central two years (quarters 3 through 10) the average estimated reduction in labor force participation for all wives as shown in Table 1.8 is 3 percentage points; for white wives, it is 8 percentage points. These are not large absolute changes, but given the low rates from which they start, they are very large relative changes. The mean participation rate for all control wives in quarters 3 through 10 is only 17 percent. The estimated percentage reduction in labor supply for all experimental wives is 20 percent and for white wives a startling 50 percent.

The results thus indicate that a temporary negative income tax program would cause a substantial percentage reduction in the proportion of working wives in large, low-income families, at least among white wives. How such a result is evaluated in terms of social priorities will depend on one's views about the value of having mothers care for their own children. It should also be remembered that these estimated effects are probably larger than those to be expected in an otherwise similar permanent income-maintenance program. For the control families, no more than 19 percent of wives were in the labor force in any one quarter, but 41 percent were in the labor force in at least one of the thirteen quarters (counting preenrollment). In other words, this is a group that enters and leaves the labor force frequently. The experimental treatment creates a strong incentive to concentrate periods out of the labor force during the life of the experiment. A permanent program could therefore be expected to have a somewhat smaller impact.

The Family

The analysis summarized in this subsection covers the labor supply of the family as a whole, including male heads, wives, and all other members of the household sixteen years of age and over.[4] The sample is still restricted to continuous husband–wife families and results will again be presented for the central two years of the experiment, quarters 3 through

---

[4] This section summarizes the research reported in Chapter 6.

10. As mentioned earlier, earnings as a dependent variable has more relevance for the whole family than for its components, since it provides a natural way of weighting hours by value. Results for earnings as well as for hours will, therefore, be reported in this summary, despite the possible reporting bias for earnings.

The regression model used for the basic family labor-supply analysis incorporates three separate measures of "normal" earnings as a control variable. All three are reported here, because the results are somewhat different. The first is simply the preenrollment value of the labor-supply variable. The usefulness of this variable is limited because it does not incorporate information about trends in earnings after enrollment. Two additional measures are, therefore, used: (a) a variable derived from an equation relating earnings over the course of the experiment to demographic characteristics, time, and seasonality, using control-group data only; and (b) a variable derived from a similar estimating procedure but using information on both controls and experimentals. The endogenous experimental effects are separated out by estimating an additive function of experimental parameters and then subtracting the value of this function from the predicted values. Table 1.9 shows what was found for the middle two years of the experiment. The results for all three specifications of the normal earnings control variable are generally consistent with estimates for the separate family members. For white families, there is a highly significant disincentive effect in both earnings and hours—on the order of 10 percent for earnings and 15 percent for hours. For the black subsample,

Table 1.9 Estimates of Family Labor-Supply Response Differentials, Quarters 3–10

	"Normal" Earnings Control Variable		
	Preenrollment Earnings	Estimated from Control Group	Estimated from Controls & Experimentals
Whites			
Dollar earnings per week	−14.5***	−14.1***	−10.4***
(% of control group mean)	(−11.7)	(−11.4)	(−8.4)
Hours per week	−7.5***	−7.5***	−6.3***
Blacks			
Dollar earnings per week	9.6	12.1*	10.3
Hours per week	−0.81	0.16	−0.40
Spanish-speaking			
Dollar earnings per week	−1.36	4.4	4.7
Hours per week	−3.33	−1.65	−1.26

* Significant at the 10 percent level.
*** Significant at the 1 percent level.

the earnings differentials are positive, although only one is significant (at the 10 percent level) and the hours differentials are, practically speaking, zero. For the Spanish-speaking, none of the results are significant, although they tend to suggest some disincentive.

The regressions reported in Table 1.9 control in a general way for the effects of normal earnings as a determinant of labor supply. However, there are two reasons to suppose that the strength of the experimental response varies systematically according to the level of normal earnings. The first reason is that some families had incomes that placed them consistently above their breakeven points, and thus above the range where they faced any experimental tax rate on additional earnings. For these families, therefore, there may be little, if any, experimental labor-supply response—which could affect not only the means but also the differential response by experimental parameter. The second reason is that response may vary in a nonlinear way according to earnings capacity (as measured by normal earnings), and economic theory gives us no guidance as to whether and how the underlying income and substitution effects might vary across income levels.

To test this hypothesis requires the use of interactions between the normal earnings measures and treatment variables. These proved to be extremely sensitive to the method used to generate the earnings proxy. It was not, therefore, possible to develop quantitative estimates in which a great deal of confidence could be placed. Certain statements can, however, be made. For whites, there does appear to be an increase in the disincentive response with increases in normal earnings, mainly manifested as a difference between below- and above-breakeven experimentals, but probably also associated with tax rate differences. For the Spanish-speaking, there was again evidence of a differential response among experimentals. For blacks, there was no such apparent difference.

The results for the family as a whole for whites are thus consistent with those from the separate analyses of male heads and wives in showing appreciable and significant negative effects on labor supply. For blacks, the results again show anomalous but not significant positive responses for family earnings (though not for hours). For Spanish-speaking families, the effects are generally negative, though not significant.

If we regard the hours estimates as somewhat more reliable than the earnings estimates because of the possible bias in reporting earnings, then a rough summary estimate of the effects of labor supply at the 50 percent tax rate is a reduction in family labor supply of something like three hours. This suggests an overall reduction of family labor supply of about 7 percent.

4. CONCLUSIONS

In general, the estimated effects of the experimental treatment on labor supply are in accord with our expectations. The major surprise is the absence of any negative effect on the labor supply of black households. For white and Spanish-speaking families, and for the group as a whole, the effects are negative, always significant for whites, but not very large. They consist of a reduction in hours of white male heads, an increase in the unemployment rate of Spanish-speaking male heads, and a large relative reduction in the labor-force-participation rate of white wives.

If one calculates the cost of a negative income tax program on the assumption of no supply response, then these results strongly suggest that the estimated cost will be too low. However, the added cost produced by the supply response is a rather small portion of the total cost—not over 10 percent and probably closer to 5 percent. The estimates suggest that a substantial part of this will, in effect, represent added benefits for mothers whose withdrawal from paid employment is likely to be offset by increased "employment" at home. There is a further suggestion that tax rates higher than 50 percent may lead to a more pronounced supply response and consequently a larger increment to total cost. Whatever the percentage change in income, a higher tax rate requires that more of that change will be made up in benefits.

If the results we found by ethnic group were applied to the national low-income urban population using national ethnic weights, then the importance of our results for whites would rise and the importance of the results for the Spanish-speaking would fall. It is not at all clear that results for Puerto Ricans in New Jersey say anything at all about Mexican Americans in the Southwest.

We place less weight on our results for blacks for a different reason. They are strange results that appear to arise from the unusual behavior of the black control group, whose labor supply and, especially, earnings fell relative to other control groups for reasons we do not understand. That the experimental treatment effects for blacks are often statistically significant is no assurance that they are not biased.

The patterns of labor-supply response that we found are not as clear as we expected. Yet in many ways, they are clearer and more sensible than the results of much of the nonexperimental literature. Certainly they call into serious question the very large effects estimated in some of the nonexperimental studies. The burden of proof now appears to be on those who assert that income-maintenance programs for intact families will have very large effects on labor supply. Considering how little had been done in the experimental testing of economic policies when we began, we do not find our results disappointing.

REFERENCES

Rees, A. 1974. An overview of the labor-supply results. *Journal of Human Resources* 9(2):158–180.

Rees, A., and Watts, H. W. 1975. An overview of the labor-supply results. In *Work incentives and income guarantees: The New Jersey negative income tax experiment*, ed. J. A. Pechman and P. M. Timpane, pp. 60–87. Washington D.C.: Brookings Institution.

2 Sample, variables, and concepts used in the analysis

Harold W. Watts
Dale J. Poirier
Charles Mallar

The chapters that follow differ in the analytical and statistical models used to explore the phenomenon of labor-supply response. Nevertheless, the problem and the data are fundamentally the same. Although each chapter pursues a specific aspect of the problem, certain standard concepts and measurement conventions emerged which together form a major part of the "overhead" explanations of the data base and of the variables used in the separate analytic studies. This chapter, therefore, presents a description of the samples, the basic variables utilized in the labor-supply analysis, and the general approach taken to the analytic problems of measurement in the experiment.

1. DIMENSIONS OF THE SAMPLE

A total of 1357 families were enrolled in the experiment—725 experimental families and 632 control families. Only 491 control families were originally assigned; 141 "new controls" were enrolled in Trenton and Paterson–Passaic after the beginning of the experiment. There were four experimental sites: Trenton, Paterson–Passaic, Jersey City, and Scranton. Eight different experimental negative income tax plans were used, and sample families were divided, according to a rough measure of their "normal" income, into three income strata for assignment to the various plans. The lowest stratum (I) included those families whose income was below the official poverty line, the next (II) included families with incomes at the poverty line and up to 124 percent of the poverty line. Stratum III included those with incomes higher than 124 percent but not higher than 150 percent of poverty. Families were assigned to the various plans according to a deliberately nonsymmetrical design whose objective was to maximize the desired information within the constraint of experimental cost (Metcalf, forthcoming). The initial distribution of families among plans is shown in Table 1.1.

Table 2.1 displays a breakdown of the total sample at the time of the preenrollment (or baseline) interview by ethnicity, by site, and by income stratum. Virtually all the Scranton sample was white, and Paterson–Passaic contained a heavy concentration of Spanish-speaking persons. Less than one-third of the sample was initially below the poverty level of income.

Table 2.1 **The New Jersey Sample Characteristics, Total Sample**

	All	White	Black	Spanish-speaking
Total sample	1357 (100)	440 (100)	502 (100)	415 (100)
Negative income tax plan				
50–30	48 (3.5)	19 (4.3)	19 (3.8)	10 (2.4)
50–50	73 (5.4)	15 (3.4)	28 (5.6)	30 (7.2)
75–30	101 (7.4)	26 (5.9)	41 (8.1)	34 (8.2)
75–50	117 (8.6)	33 (7.5)	43 (8.6)	41 (9.9)
75–70	85 (6.3)	31 (7.0)	38 (7.6)	16 (3.9)
100–50	77 (5.7)	22 (5.0)	32 (6.4)	23 (5.5)
100–70	86 (6.3)	25 (5.7)	34 (6.8)	27 (6.5)
125–50	138 (10.2)	61 (13.9)	47 (9.4)	30 (7.2)
Original controls	491 (36.2)	196 (44.5)	151 (30.1)	144 (34.7)
New controls	141 (10.4)	12 (2.7)	69 (13.7)	60 (14.5)
Site				
Trenton	159 (11.7)	25 (5.7)	105 (20.9)	29 (7.0)
Paterson–Passaic	490 (36.1)	49 (11.1)	194 (38.6)	247 (59.5)
Jersey City	390 (28.7)	52 (11.8)	199 (39.6)	139 (33.5)
Scranton	318 (23.4)	314 (71.4)	4 (0.8)	0 (0.0)
Income stratum				
I (0–99 percent of poverty)	414 (30.5)	119 (27.0)	139 (27.7)	156 (37.6)
II (100–124 percent of poverty)	454 (33.5)	153 (34.8)	173 (34.5)	128 (30.8)
III (125–150 percent of poverty)	489 (36.0)	168 (38.2)	190 (37.8)	131 (31.6)

NOTE: Numbers in parentheses are percentages of appropriate totals.

SAMPLE, VARIABLES, AND CONCEPTS USED IN THE ANALYSIS

Most of the analysis has been done on a subsample of these 1357 families—the relatively homogeneous group of 693 families that continued throughout the experiment to consist of married couples (and usually some additional persons) who remained active as questionnaire respondents throughout the three years.[1] These 693 families comprise the so-called "continuous husband–wife sample." A similar breakdown of their characteristics is shown in Table 2.2.

Several major components of the difference between the total sample and the continuous husband–wife sample should be noted. (1) A few families did not include a "primary" husband–wife couple at enrollment, and many were separated or divorced during the experiment. (2) New controls were excluded from the analysis (and therefore from the continuous husband–wife subsample) because they were enrolled late and did not have records for the full experimental period. (3) Certain families dropped out

Table 2.2 **The New Jersey Sample Characteristics, Continuous Husband–Wife Sample**

	All	White	Black	Spanish-speaking
Total	693 (100)	310 (100)	234 (100)	149 (100)
Negative income tax plan				
50–30	27 (3.9)	13 (4.2)	8 (3.4)	6 (4.0)
50–50	32 (4.6)	11 (3.5)	12 (5.1)	9 (6.0)
75–30	60 (8.7)	22 (7.1)	23 (9.8)	15 (10.1)
75–50	65 (9.4)	24 (7.7)	25 (10.7)	16 (10.7)
75–70	48 (6.9)	24 (7.7)	21 (9.0)	3 (2.0)
100–50	44 (6.3)	20 (6.5)	14 (6.0)	10 (6.7)
100–70	53 (7.6)	21 (6.8)	17 (7.3)	15 (10.1)
125–50	96 (13.9)	46 (14.8)	31 (13.2)	19 (12.8)
Controls	268 (38.7)	129 (41.6)	83 (35.5)	56 (37.6)
Site				
Trenton				
Paterson–Passaic	60 (8.7)	12 (3.9)	38 (16.2)	10 (6.7)
Jersey City	158 (22.8)	30 (9.7)	59 (25.2)	69 (46.3)
Scranton	236 (34.0)	32 (10.3)	134 (57.3)	70 (47.0)
Income stratum	239 (34.5)	236 (76.1)	3 (1.3)	0 (0.0)
I (0–99 percent of poverty)	179 (25.8)	71 (22.9)	53 (22.6)	55 (36.9)
II (100–124 percent of poverty)	237 (34.2)	105 (33.9)	85 (36.3)	47 (31.5)
III (125–150 percent of poverty)	277 (40.0)	134 (43.2)	96 (41.0)	47 (31.5)

NOTE: Numbers in parentheses are percentages of appropriate totals.

[1] The specific definition was that the husband–wife families had to have answered both the preenrollment questionnaire and the twelfth quarterly interview, and they also had to have missed no more than five of the regular quarterly interviews, of which not more than two lapses could be consecutive.

during the experiment, either because they were unwilling to continue or because they moved and could not be located. Note that a more than proportionate number of Spanish-speaking families were lost from the continuous husband–wife sample. The control group and the low-benefit plans also suffered more than proportionately.

Tables 2.3 through 2.9 provide descriptive statistics on the basic income and labor-supply characteristics of the full sample (except for the 141 new controls and 3 families with no preenrollment record) at the preenrollment interview, and the continuous sample at preenrollment and at the end of each twelve-month period in the experiment. Average values are tabulated for all controls and experimental families and also for the respective ethnic groups. The averages for the four sites are also shown. The differences between the two samples are not great. The continuous sample is shown to have somewhat larger families, have somewhat higher initial income and earnings, and to work somewhat more throughout the period. Crude indications of the nature of the response to the experiment can be drawn from these tables. It should be noted that divergence between control and experimental averages often comes as a result of movement of both groups in the same direction but at different rates. Clearly there is no gross evidence of widespread or major abandonment of

Table 2.3 **Average Weekly Family Income in Dollars, by Ethnic Group and by Site**

	Total Sample (N = 1213)	Continuous Husband–Wife Sample (N = 693)			
	Pre[a]	Pre[a]	First Year	Second Year	Third Year
Total sample	98.27	103.09	117.31	130.71	143.63
All					
Experimentals	98.20	102.30	117.32	129.45	140.28
Controls	98.38	104.34	117.30	132.71	148.93
Whites					
Experimentals	109.59	111.09	118.93	133.18	145.84
Controls	104.45	111.51	123.92	144.64	165.12
Blacks					
Experimentals	93.50	99.21	121.41	133.39	144.07
Controls	93.59	97.00	113.13	121.82	133.54
Spanish-speaking					
Experimentals	91.89	90.18	107.56	115.78	123.31
Controls	95.14	98.74	108.25	121.35	134.44
By site					
Trenton	87.90	91.45	107.46	123.32	142.62
Paterson–Passaic	91.78	96.16	118.74	130.57	139.55
Jersey City	99.52	102.44	119.15	126.37	137.86
Scranton	108.60	111.22	117.03	136.94	152.26

[a] Pre = at preenrollment.

Table 2.4 **Average Weekly Family Earnings in Dollars, by Ethnic Group and by Site**

	Total Sample (N = 1213)	Continuous Husband–Wife Sample (N = 693)			
	Pre[a]	Pre[a]	First Year	Second Year	Third Year
Total sample	89.00	94.93	107.06	113.55	125.43
All					
Experimentals	88.86	95.18	108.16	113.63	123.93
Controls	89.20	94.54	105.31	113.41	127.80
Whites					
Experimentals	96.18	100.24	106.67	114.49	126.26
Controls	92.11	98.02	107.37	122.17	143.38
Blacks					
Experimentals	86.71	94.40	115.30	120.24	128.38
Controls	86.11	89.73	104.87	104.26	109.83
Spanish-speaking					
Experimentals	83.65	86.60	99.47	101.23	112.19
Controls	88.49	93.64	101.23	106.80	118.54
By site					
Trenton	87.90	91.45	102.46	107.55	116.30
Paterson–Passaic	81.37	86.90	107.64	109.68	123.01
Jersey City	93.23	98.45	113.35	115.92	123.55
Scranton	93.37	97.64	101.62	115.27	131.17

[a] Pre = at preenrollment.

Table 2.5 **Average Weekly Family Hours Worked, by Ethnic Group and by Site**

	Total Sample (N = 1213)	Continuous Husband–Wife Sample (N = 693)			
	Pre[a]	Pre[a]	First Year	Second Year	Third Year
Total sample	39.5	40.6	40.9	40.4	42.4
All					
Experimentals	39.3	40.6	39.9	39.2	40.8
Controls	39.9	40.7	42.6	42.4	44.9
Whites					
Experimentals	41.5	42.3	39.6	39.8	42.2
Controls	40.7	42.2	44.0	45.5	50.9
Blacks					
Experimentals	37.9	40.3	41.8	39.9	40.5
Controls	37.1	36.2	40.6	38.7	37.3
Spanish-speaking					
Experimentals	38.6	37.8	37.2	36.8	38.4
Controls	41.9	43.9	42.2	40.7	42.3
By site					
Trenton	41.8	44.3	42.8	39.8	39.8
Paterson–Passaic	36.4	36.5	38.4	38.8	40.9
Jersey City	40.0	40.1	41.6	39.5	39.7
Scranton	41.8	43.0	41.4	42.6	46.6

[a] Pre = at preenrollment.

Table 2.6 Average Family Size, by Ethnic Group and by Site

	Total Sample (N = 1213)	Continuous Husband–Wife Sample (N = 693)			
	Pre[a]	Pre[a]	First Year	Second Year	Third Year
Total sample	5.9	6.1	6.2	6.2	6.3
All					
Experimentals	6.0	6.3	6.3	6.4	6.4
Controls	5.7	5.9	6.0	6.1	6.1
Whites					
Experimentals	5.7	5.9	5.9	5.9	5.9
Controls	5.4	5.7	5.8	5.8	5.8
Blacks					
Experimentals	6.5	7.0	7.1	7.2	7.3
Controls	6.0	6.3	6.4	6.5	6.5
Spanish-speaking					
Experimentals	5.7	5.8	5.9	6.0	6.0
Controls	5.7	5.9	5.9	6.0	6.3
By site					
Trenton	6.1	6.4	6.5	6.6	6.8
Paterson–Passaic	5.7	6.1	6.2	6.2	6.2
Jersey City	6.3	6.6	6.6	6.7	6.8
Scranton	5.5	5.6	5.7	5.7	5.7

[a] Pre = at preenrollment.

Table 2.7 Number of Employed Persons per Family, by Ethnic Group and by Site

	Total Sample (N = 1213)	Continuous Husband–Wife Sample (N = 693)			
	Pre[a]	Pre[a]	First Year	Second Year	Third Year
Total sample	1.08	1.06	1.10	1.08	1.12
All					
Experimentals	1.08	1.07	1.07	1.04	1.07
Controls	1.06	1.04	1.16	1.15	1.19
Whites					
Experimentals	1.14	1.11	1.07	1.08	1.14
Controls	1.07	1.05	1.17	1.26	1.37
Blacks					
Experimentals	1.06	1.05	1.10	1.05	1.04
Controls	1.04	0.98	1.16	1.07	0.98
Spanish-speaking					
Experimentals	1.05	1.03	0.98	0.94	0.97
Controls	1.08	1.13	1.13	1.04	1.08
By site					
Trenton	1.13	1.12	1.11	1.05	1.08
Paterson–Passaic	1.02	0.98	1.07	1.02	1.06
Jersey City	1.05	1.06	1.12	1.04	1.02
Scranton	1.15	1.10	1.11	1.12	1.25

[a] Pre = at preenrollment.

Table 2.8 Average Number of Employed Male Heads per Family, by Ethnic Group and by Site

	Male Head Sample (N = 1160)	Continuous Husband–Wife Sample (N = 693)			
	Pre[a]	Pre[a]	First Year	Second Year	Third Year
Total sample	.873	.885	.890	.868	.841
All					
Experimentals	.866	.887	.895	.863	.836
Controls	.885	.881	.882	.876	.849
Whites					
Experimentals	.881	.906	.884	.856	.826
Controls	.895	.907	.884	.886	.876
Blacks					
Experimentals	.870	.861	.911	.881	.829
Controls	.825	.783	.828	.840	.786
Spanish-speaking					
Experimentals	.880	.892	.890	.847	.866
Controls	.929	.964	.955	.906	.906
By site					
Trenton	.831	.817	.883	.825	.771
Paterson–Passaic	.836	.816	.883	.831	.834
Jersey City	.908	.919	.905	.909	.858
Scranton	.890	.912	.881	.863	.846

NOTE: The maximum = 1.
[a] Pre = at preenrollment.

Table 2.9 Average Weekly Hours Worked by Male Head, by Ethnic Group and by Site

	Male Head Sample (N = 1160)	Continuous Husband–Wife Sample (N = 693)			
	Pre[a]	Pre[a]	First Year	Second Year	Third Year
Total sample	33.5	34.7	34.2	33.0	33.0
All					
Experimentals	32.9	34.6	34.2	32.8	32.6
Controls	34.4	34.8	34.1	33.4	33.7
Whites					
Experimentals	34.1	35.3	33.9	32.4	32.1
Controls	35.5	36.9	35.3	34.7	36.2
Blacks					
Experimentals	31.8	34.1	35.3	33.2	32.1
Controls	30.6	29.6	30.7	30.2	28.9
Spanish-speaking					
Experimentals	33.0	33.8	33.0	32.9	34.4
Controls	36.7	37.8	36.6	35.4	35.2
By site					
Trenton	33.0	34.5	34.6	31.8	28.9
Paterson–Passaic	30.6	30.7	31.7	31.2	32.5
Jersey City	35.6	35.7	35.2	34.2	33.3
Scranton	34.5	36.3	34.7	33.5	34.2

[a] Pre = at preenrollment.

work on the part of any of the experimental groups. There is, however, a pattern of slightly reduced labor supply.

To complete the income picture, Tables 2.10 and 2.11 display the nonearned income statistics for the whole sample and for the husband–wife continuous sample. They are generally in accord with economists' expectations. Relatively few of our sample, as is true in general for low-income families, received any nonearned income. The percentage on welfare (income category 1 in Tables 2.10 and 2.11) can be expected to be slightly higher for controls, because at least some experimental families would undoubtedly have been on welfare in the absence of their experimental plan, but chose not to during the duration of the experiment since, for them, the experimental budget constraint dominated the welfare budget constraint. The percentage on welfare and the mean welfare payment both grew initially (reflecting the newness of some of these programs, which were initiated at approximately the same time as the experiment) and then tapered off toward the end of the experiment with the cut in New Jersey welfare guarantees. The slightly larger mean welfare payment received by experimentals is probably a consequence of the experimental plans' tendency to dominate welfare payments at higher levels of earned income, resulting in the experimental families who chose welfare being

Table 2.10 **Nonearned Income Statistics by Income Category, Full Sample**

	Nonearned Income Category					
	(1)	(2)	(3)	(4)	(5)	Total
Controls (N = 388)						
Number ever receiving	173	146	1	60	86	293
Percentage ever receiving	44.6	37.6	0.3	15.5	22.2	75.5
Mean for those receiving ($ per week)	54.83	46.61	6.15	22.51	23.77	47.27
Sample mean ($ per week)	13.72	5.35	0.00	0.87	0.86	20.80
Experimentals (N = 625)						
Number ever receiving	269	247	6	87	153	479
Percentage ever receiving	43.0	39.5	1.0	13.9	24.5	76.6
Mean for those receiving ($ per week)	57.25	47.70	14.17	21.38	24.11	47.03
Sample mean ($ per week)	12.59	5.20	0.03	1.11	0.97	19.90
Total (N = 1013)						
Number ever receiving	442	393	7	147	239	772
Percentage ever receiving	43.6	38.8	0.7	14.5	23.6	76.2
Mean for those receiving ($ per week)	56.25	47.27	13.70	21.73	23.99	47.12
Sample mean ($ per week)	13.02	5.26	0.02	1.02	0.93	20.25

NOTE: (1) = public assistance payments; (2) = nonwelfare work-conditioned payments; (3) = unearned income from family business; (4) = rent, interest, dividends; (5) = other.

Table 2.11 Nonearned Income Statistics by Income Category, Continuous Husband–Wife Sample

	Nonearned Income Category					
	(1)	(2)	(3)	(4)	(5)	Total
Controls (N = 268)						
Number ever receiving	102	99	1	42	54	195
Percentage ever receiving	38.1	36.9	0.4	15.7	20.1	72.8
Mean for those receiving ($ per week)	53.50	46.21	6.15	25.36	17.77	45.78
Sample mean ($ per week)	10.66	4.66	0.00	0.95	0.51	16.78
Experimentals (N = 425)						
Number ever receiving	135	166	4	66	100	303
Percentage ever receiving	31.8	39.1	0.9	15.5	23.5	71.3
Mean for those receiving ($ per week)	48.54	48.29	11.88	19.31	19.18	39.86
Sample mean ($ per week)	6.76	4.87	0.03	1.11	0.71	13.24
Total (N = 693)						
Number ever receiving	237	265	5	108	154	498
Percentage ever receiving	34.2	38.2	0.7	15.6	22.2	71.9
Mean for those receiving ($ per week)	50.94	47.49	11.50	21.07	18.71	42.29
Sample mean ($ per week)	8.12	4.79	0.02	1.05	0.63	14.61

NOTE: (1) = public assistance payments; (2) = nonwelfare work-conditioned payments; (3) = unearned income from family business; (4) = rent, interest, dividends; (5) = other.

those with relatively lower incomes and therefore receiving larger welfare payments than control families on welfare. For husband–wife continuous families, the same pattern does not appear, probably because of the greater reluctance of this category of family to try to get on welfare if there is any other option.

2. LABOR-FORCE VARIABLES

The central analysis of the experimental data is concerned with the labor-force responses, if any, to the experimental treatments. For this purpose, labor-force behavior has been divided into responses of the married male heads of household; the female spouse; young adults, meaning people between the ages of sixteen and twenty-two; and the families as a whole.

The initial survey instrument was closely patterned after the Bureau of Labor Statistics Monthly Survey, which uses the week preceding the interview as the base period for inquiry. Although such a limited snapshot was found to be unsatisfactorily incomplete for the data purposes of the experiment and a major revision[2] was made in the labor-force core of the quarterly questionnaires partway through the experiment (Kershaw and Fair, 1976: Chapter 9), the analysis in this volume has been limited to the weekly data because they can be readily obtained on a comparable basis for the entire experimental period.

Four basic indicators of labor supply will be analyzed in subsequent chapters: labor force participation, employment status, hours worked, and earnings. These will be discussed in turn below, but before such a discussion, a word should be said about why we used both labor force participation *and* employment measures. The usual interpretation of the difference between the two (that is, unemployment) cannot, in the context of simultaneous comparisons between experimentals and controls, be regarded simply as a demand phenomenon. This is not to say that all unemployment is voluntary, but it is to say that if differential levels of unemployment appear between the control and experimental groups, such differences should be regarded as a component of response—whether or *not* that component is the result of consciously voluntary choices.

Labor Force Participation

Labor force participation was defined in the traditional way to include people who are employed as well as those who are actively seeking work. The questions answered on the questionnaire were as follows:[3]

a. What were you doing most of last week?
b. Did you do any work for pay last week?
c. Did you have a job (or business) from which you were temporarily absent last week?
d. Why were you absent from work last week?
e. Were you looking for work in the past four weeks?

---

[2] The revision (the "New Core") augmented the weekly data by asking additional questions about the three weeks preceding the week immediately prior to the interview (or a month, if pay was on a monthly basis). The revision was instituted in the summer of 1970, so the monthly data are not available for any site for the entire experimental period, and the period for which they are available differs for each site.

[3] For the New Core, the questionnaire items regarding labor force participation are:

(a) What were you doing most of last month?
(b) Did you do any work for pay last month?
(c) Did you have a job (or business) from which you were temporarily absent last month?
(d) Why were you absent from work during those weeks?
(e) Were you looking for work during the weeks that you weren't working?

SAMPLE, VARIABLES, AND CONCEPTS USED IN THE ANALYSIS

The answers to these questions were used as the basis for assigning six labor-force-participation codes as follows:

- −1. Could not ascertain
- 1. Not in labor force
- 2. In labor force, no further classification possible
- 3. Unemployed, without a job
- 4. Unemployed, with a job
- 5. Employed, but not at work last week
- 6. Employed and at work last week

All individuals were classified as being in the labor force if they were coded 2 through 6. Those coded −1 and 1 were classified as not in the labor force.

Employment

Employment status was assigned on the basis of the same questions and the same codes. Individuals were classified as employed if they were coded 5 or 6, unemployed if coded 2 through 4.

Hours

The questionnaire questions from which this variable was constructed were as follows:[4]

a. How many hours did you work last week at all jobs?
b. Did you lose any time or take any time off from work last week for any reason such as illness, holiday, or slack work? If so, how many?
c. Did you work any overtime or extra hours last week? If so, how many?
d. Did you work at more than one job or for more than one employer last week? If so, how many hours did you work on this extra job or jobs last week?

[4] For the New Core, the questionnaire items regarding hours are:

(a) I would like to find out about the work you have done on your *main* job in the *past month*. Could you tell me about how many hours you spent working for each week in the *past month?* I want the total number of hours, including overtime if you had any.
(b) Does that include any overtime? If so, how many hours of overtime did you work that week?
(c) Did you ever have more than one job at the *same time* during the *past month?* If so, about how many hours per *week* over the *past month* did you work on the extra job(s) . . . ?

Any individual for whom the labor-force-participation code was not 6 was assigned zero hours. For those with a labor force participation of 6, three hours variables were constructed as follows: (a) total hours worked last week at all jobs, including overtime; (b) regular hours worked last week on main job only; (c) total hours worked last week at main job. The labor-supply analyses in this volume use the first of the three definitions —namely, total hours actually worked during the period preceding the interviews—on the ground that it is the simplest and most comprehensive measure.

Earnings

The questionnaire items on which the earnings variables are based were as follows:[5]

a. How much were your total earnings from all jobs, before taxes and any other deductions?
b. Are you getting wages or salary from any of the time off last week? If yes, how much?

For the analyses reported in subsequent chapters the earnings definition chosen (like the one for hours) is the simplest and most comprehensive, and therefore encompasses total cash compensation for labor services received the week prior to the interview. This includes all overtime pay, sick pay, and paid vacation receipts.

Data Cleaning

As with any set of microdata, procedures had to be set up for detecting inconsistencies and gaps in the data. Tests were designed to confirm that the data were coded according to the skip logic of the questionnaires.

---

[5] For the New Core, the questionnaire items regarding earnings are:

(a) Could you tell me how you were paid—is it by week, every two weeks, twice a month, monthly, irregularly, or what? Could you tell me the amount of *each* paycheck you received during the past month before taxes and other deductions?
(b) Did you receive pay for any of the time you were not working, was it an unpaid layoff, or were you self-employed? If yes, how much did you receive for the time you were not working? (This pertains only to the *most recent part-time* week and thus may or may not be used in the construction of last week's earnings.)

. . . and how much did you make *per week* from it (them)? (This pertains to extra job(s) pay and is the ending to question [c] under hours.)

(c) Did you receive pay for any of the time you were not working, was it an unpaid layoff, or were you self-employed? If yes, how much did you receive? (This pertains to any of the weeks in the past month when this adult worked zero hours.)

More basic checking was done on key questions to ensure that no illegal codes were used. Consistency checks were also performed on constructed variables, that is, those variables inserted into the data file after they had been built up from questionnaire questions during coding or initial processing.

When problems were highlighted by these checks, the following steps were taken. (1) The original questionnaire was checked for coding errors or errors in skip logic. (2) If the inconsistency or gap remained, there was a longitudinal check. Adjacent quarterlies were consulted, plus the Annual Income Schedule, plus the three-year work history on the eleventh quarterly. (3) In stubborn cases with apparently inconsistent wage rates, further longitudinal checking was done into possible changes in employer or job. All proposed solutions to data gaps or inconsistencies were then submitted to an independent team who checked them again with the raw questionnaires. On close decisions or in the most difficult cases, the principal investigators, Harold Watts and Albert Rees, made the final decisions as to whether to impute or not.

A record was maintained of all the alterations made to the basic data. The construction of an imputation flag (added to the data file itself) indicated what type of change was made. A change list was also developed containing, for each observation point for the family in question, the list of permanent answer numbers altered by imputation, along with the original response given.

3. MEASUREMENT OF NONEARNED INCOME

Quarterly series for various categories of nonearned income were constructed for all families enrolled in the experiment. The breakdown of income sources was designed to fulfill two basic requirements: (1) to ascertain the quantity and magnitude of work-conditioned transfers the families were receiving over the duration of the experiment, in order to be able to generalize the results obtained from our sample to groups eligible for various actual transfer programs; and (2) to have data available on the amount of non-work-conditioned, nonearned income in order to be able to obtain estimates that are, at least asymptotically, unbiased of the effects of changes in income on the labor supply of persons in low-income households.

Family nonearned income from all possible sources was broken down into the following five categories:

  a. Work conditioned, consisting of welfare or public assistance from the government.

b. Work conditioned, consisting of Social Security, pensions, or retirement income; Unemployment Insurance; workmen's compensation; and veterans' disability payments.
c. Income from business run by someone in the family, not reported as earned income.
d. Non-work-conditioned, consisting of rent (which includes room and/or board payments); and interest or dividend payments.
e. Other (mostly non-work-conditioned), consisting of lottery and other prizes; monetary gifts; alimony payments; and separation pay, bonuses, and so on, not reported as earned income.

It is clear from the above classifications that our nonearned-income series includes only income received as cash or vouchers (for example, food stamps) and does not include such items as the rental value of owner-occupied housing or the rental value of durable goods.

Welfare or public assistance payments from the government were assigned to a unique category of work-conditioned, nonearned income because of their potential use in attacking the substantive problems involved in drawing generalized conclusions from experimental sites with atypical welfare programs. Over most of the duration of the experiment, the welfare programs in the experimental locations were found to be considerably more generous than the United States norm, but there was at least one major shift in generosity—consisting of the massive reduction in New Jersey welfare guarantee levels beginning in July 1971 (toward the end of the experiment).

A section on nonearned income was added to the labor-force section of the quarterly questionnaires at the fourth quarter in every city except Scranton, where it was administered to half the families at the third quarter. When possible, the data were taken directly from this source. For previous quarters, however, the data had to be constructed by allocating by quarter the data from a special questionnaire, administered at the end of every calendar year, called the Annual Income Supplement (AIS). (The AIS was used merely as a consistency check for the quarters which had data directly usable from the labor-force core.) All questions relating to nonearned income sources were used to allocate the data from the Annual Income Supplement to the appropriate quarters. For welfare payments, county welfare audit lists were also utilized for all quarters and cities except Paterson–Passaic, where the welfare authorities did not permit a welfare audit until too late to be incorporated into the data base. Most of the imputational problems were related to the welfare category, and especially to the sporadic reporting of food stamps.

All sources were converted to a weekly dollar amount and, for the families who reported food stamps, the weekly difference between their cash

SAMPLE, VARIABLES, AND CONCEPTS USED IN THE ANALYSIS

value and the amount paid was recorded. An attempt was made to minimize the additional source of error for early quarters by using all information available for both control and experimental families. Data from the payments file was intentionally not used, since it was obviously not available for control families, and we did not wish to make imputations for control and experimental families differentially.

4. VARIABLES MEASURING TREATMENT AND TIME

Treatment Variables

The experiment was designed to estimate a response surface that varied by tax rate and guarantee. Three tax rates and four guarantees were chosen, combined in such a way that eight experimental plans were tested, as specified in the previous chapter. A variety of treatments was thus administered, and the "mix" was not identical across sites, ethnic groups, or income strata—with the result that an "average" experimental effect can refer to different mixtures of treatments. A procedure was worked out, therefore, to provide a straightforward way of exploring the variation in response, by progressively complicating the permissible shape of the response surface in four stages.

Consider a general formulation of an additive model for control–experimental comparisons:

$$y = f(\mathbf{Z}) + R(\mathbf{X}, \mathbf{XZ}) + u,$$

where $\mathbf{X}$ denotes the variables which characterize particular variants of the treatment—guarantee and tax rate in our case; $\mathbf{Z}$ is a vector of whatever other variables are relevant; and the $\mathbf{XZ}$ argument indicates the possibility of interactions of some or all of the $\mathbf{Z}$ variables with treatment variation. The expression $f(\mathbf{Z})$ is the function that "explains" y in the absence of any experimental treatment; and $R(\mathbf{X}, \mathbf{XZ})$ is the response to the treatment (that is, the amount by which experimentals differ from controls with the same $\mathbf{Z}$ vector). The variable, u, is of course the "unexplained" part of y, which is assumed to be generated randomly. The following paragraphs specify possible functional forms for $R(\mathbf{X}, \mathbf{XZ})$ in the context of the experiment, first dealing with the simple case of no interaction between $\mathbf{X}$ and $\mathbf{Z}$, and then showing how these may be added.

A convenient sequence of variables can be defined that form a family of response surfaces which progressively exploit and finally exhaust the variation of G and t provided by the eight experimental treatment combinations in four stages of progressively increasing complexity. Call this the "spline series" and denote by $S(k)$ the spline-series response surface with k terms.[6] The general response surface can thus be written as

$$S(k) = \sum_{i=1}^{k} a_i s_i(x, G, t).$$

The a_i are unknown coefficients to be estimated and the $s_i(x, G, t)$ constitute a set of eight variables (spline components) defined on the experimental space.

The first stage of complexity is the familiar dummy variable device for measuring an average or constant experimental differential. For the dummy variable case, s_1 equals x, which equals 1 for all experimental observations and 0 for all controls. Thus

$$S(1) = a_1 x.$$

The second stage of complexity is to fit a simple linear surface, call it $S(3)$, to denote three degrees of freedom, and evaluate it at some "central" coordinate. To do this, two more spline components are added:

$$s_2 = s_1(G - .75) \text{ and}$$
$$s_3 = s_1(t - .50),$$

where G is the guarantee level expressed as a fraction of the basic poverty schedule, and t is the (fractional) tax rate. Thus,

$$S(3) = a_1 s_1 + a_2[s_1(G - .75)] + a_3[s_1(t - .50)].$$

Here the coordinate (.75,.50) in (G, t) space has been arbitrarily chosen as an origin from which interplan variation is measured. It is a real plan that is close to the mean coordinate—approximately (.85,.50)—among experimentals. The coefficients have the following interpretation:

a_1 measures the (planar) experimental differential evaluated at $G = .75, t = .50$;
a_2 is the "slope" with respect to changes in G;
a_3 is the "slope" with respect to changes in t.

Hence, the estimated response for the (1.00,.70) plan would be

$$a_1 + .25 a_2 + .20 a_3.$$

The third stage is to allow nonlinear, but still additive, effects of G and t by adding s_4, s_5, and s_6, as follows.

Let $s_4 = \max(s_2, 0)$
$s_5 = \max(s_3, 0)$
$s_6 = \max(G - 1.00, 0)$.

---

[6] For a detailed definition and exposition of splines, see Chapter 13.

SAMPLE, VARIABLES, AND CONCEPTS USED IN THE ANALYSIS

These terms are linear spline variables and do not have to be added in any particular sequence; s_4 is equal to zero for all observations with negative values of s_2 and equal to s_2 for all nonnegative s_2 and so on. Introduction of s_4 allows for a change in the G slope at $G = .75$. The interpretation of a_1 and a_3 is the same as above. A "student t" test of a_4 tests the null hypothesis of equal slopes above and below $G = .75$ (given a linear tax effect). A similar change in the t slope at $t = .50$ is added with s_5. Here a_3 estimates the t slope where $t < .50$ and $a_3 + a_5$ estimates the slope above $t = .50$. This time a test of a_5 is a test of the hypothesis of a constant t slope given a (possible) differential slope in the G dimension. A further degree of nonlinearity for the guarantee is added by s_6. Note that s_6 differs from zero only for $G > 1.00$; a_6, consequently, estimates the change in slope which occurs at $G = 1.00$. The slope beyond $G = 1.00$ is thus $a_2 + a_4 + a_6$. Between .75 and 1.00 the slope is $a_2 + a_4$; and below .75, it is a_2.

At this point, the possible additive or "main-effect" terms have been exhausted. The three values of t in the experimental design have been used to estimate two parameters, and the four G values have been used to obtain three slopes for G.

The fourth (and last) stage provides for interactions, that is, nonadditive effects.

Define $s_7 = s_2 * s_3 - s_4 * s_5$
$s_8 = s_4 * s_5.$

The expression s_7 is nonzero for the region $G < .75$ *and* $t < .50$. The only experimental plan in that region is at (.50,.30), where $s_7 = .05$. Thus, nonadditivity is allowed in the sense that a_7 estimates the amount (times 20) by which the (.50,.30) plan deviates from the extrapolation of a plane passing through the responses at (.75,.30), (.75,.50), and (.50,.50).

The expression s_8 adds a term allowing for similar interaction among the four plans (.75,.50), (1.00,.50), (.75,.70) and (1.00,.70), with a_8 estimating the deviation of the last from a plan determined by the other three. Separate tests of a_7 and a_8 amount to tests of the only two interaction components that the design affords.

The formulation using all eight s_i is equivalent to inserting eight "dummy" variables, one for each distinct treatment, in that the estimated values at each plan–coordinate will be the same as the dummy coefficients. (The R^2 and other statistics will be the same also.) The advantage of the suggested sequence is that it provides more interpretable intermediate coefficients (using less than eight degrees of freedom) than the dummy representation and yields directly the more relevant tests of the presence of interactions and nonlinearities.

Further variations on this sequence can be specified. First, it may be argued that the absolute or dollar value of the guarantee is more appropriate than its ratio to a family-size-related index of need, that is, the poverty schedule. This can be accomplished by multiplying s_2 and s_6 by the dollar poverty level evaluated at the family size appropriate for the given observation. Secondly, a similar argument may be made that it is not the tax rate which is relevant, but rather the (dollar) amount by which hourly earnings are reduced. In this case, s_3 can be multiplied by the hourly earning rate for the particular observation.

Time Variables

The sample was drawn from four different sites, which were phased into operation sequentially. Trenton was enrolled in August 1968, Paterson and Passaic in January 1969, Jersey City in June 1969, and Scranton, Pennsylvania, in September 1969. The experimental period lasted for three years at each site. Questionnaires were administered prior to enrollment and at quarterly intervals thereafter for a total of thirteen regularly spaced interviews.

The sequencing in time of the experimental treatments and the interviews thus provided a set of common problems for all analysts. Each experimental family was "on" the experiment for three years following enrollment, but the entire time period during which payments were being made extended from August 1968 through September 1972—a four-year period. Because the interviews were scheduled to be (roughly) synchronous in terms of elapsed time after enrollment, "experimental time" has been used as the primary dimension for organizing the data. An additional cogent reason for using experimental time is that any response to the experimental treatment could be expected to develop with some lag, because acquiring information and adjusting to the changed situation both take time. Similarly, as the end of the payments period moved closer, some anticipatory adjustment could be expected to take place—both events, of course, associated with experimental time rather than calendar time.

In taking account of the time dimension, it is useful to separate response variables measured once or infrequently from those (primarily labor-force variables) collected every quarter. For the former, the difference in calendar time at the various sites only adds another reason for expecting possible intersite differences; and if such differences are controlled, say, by a dummy variable, the calendar time differences will be adequately allowed for (even though thoroughly confounded with other sources of site differences).

For variables collected on a panel basis, there is an additional question

SAMPLE, VARIABLES, AND CONCEPTS USED IN THE ANALYSIS

as to how, or whether, the repeated measurements should be aggregated or averaged. A rough overall measurement can be obtained by aggregating or averaging over the entire three-year period. This provides a good first test. It may average some weak initial or end responses with stronger middle ones, but the averaging process eliminates some random variation or "noise" and affords better precision. At the other extreme, each interview wave could be treated as a separate cross section; but this fragments the results so much that major secondary summarization is necessary. An intermediate procedure is to average over segments of the time period, such as the middle two years (quarters 3–10); or compute each of the three years as separate averages (quarters 1–4, 5–8, 9–12), which isolates the central part of the experimental period where the strongest responses may be expected, and provides a basis for comparison with the initial and end responses.

Finally, it is possible to combine the measurements from all the quarterly surveys into a pooled analysis which allows for a simple form of non-independence of successive observations on the same unit. This formulation makes it possible to estimate response as an explicit function of experimental time, either by using a series of binary variables or by using a spline representation. In this framework, it is also possible to control separately for calendar time and seasonal variations.[7]

All these ways of tackling the time dimension are used in the chapters that follow.

5. WAGE AND INCOME VARIABLES FOR LABOR-SUPPLY MODELS

The critical importance of wage rates and the measurement of family income for econometric analysis of labor supply does not need extensive discussion here. These variables are the basis for the opportunity locus in the familiar diagram of labor–leisure choice and, econometrically, they provide the basis for estimating income and substitution parameters. The problems of their measurement also provide a large part of the uncertainty and imprecision of estimates based on cross-sectional studies (Cain and Watts, 1973: Chapter 9).

In the analysis of longitudinal labor-supply data from an experiment that deliberately manipulated net wage rates and unearned income, these variables are still crucial. Their role in the analysis is somewhat different,

---

[7] For technical discussions of the methodology involved in this approach, see Chapters 12 and 13. An application is detailed in Chapter 14.

however, and the opportunities and problems for their estimation are changed. This section will briefly discuss these differences and outline the strategy finally adopted. A more extensive discussion and further technical detail appear in Chapter 14.

In the case of nonexperimental data, the spontaneous variation of wage rates and incomes are the direct basis for estimation of income and price or substitution effects. In this experiment, however, the net wage rate is manipulated by variation of the tax rate, and the unearned part of total income is altered by the amount of the guarantee. And the net response to these exogenously administered changes is the objective of estimation. The "natural" variation of wage rates and income is still present, of course, but the main objective now is to control for such variation—to hold it constant so that appropriately net comparisons can be made. In addition, there is a strong possibility that nonlinearities and/or interactions will require models involving combinations of the natural and experimental variation in both wages and income.

Because the experiment yielded longitudinal or panel data on individual earners, there are in many cases multiple observations on family income and wage rates (more precisely, average hourly earnings). This feature provides an opportunity to develop estimates of wage rates or income that are less affected by simple measurement errors or actual but transitory fluctuations. Since we are concerned here with estimating average labor-supply behavior over substantial periods of time rather than the week-to-week variations, it seems appropriate to use variables which reflect average circumstances. This is not feasible, of course, in typical cross-sectional analyses, and more crude methods have to be used to eliminate transient and accidental variation (along with the danger of eliminating most of the actual variation).

But an additional problem exists, in that our panel data on wages and income reflect possible experimental response. Any response in earnings by any family member will be reflected by definition in family income (exclusive of any experimental payment) during the experiment. While the a priori case for similar response in terms of wage rates is less strong, a substantial differential did appear in the experiment. A major question concerns whether this is real or spurious, which is discussed elsewhere (Watts and Mamer, forthcoming). For our present purposes, we shall assume that the appropriate concept, both for income and wage rates, is the value those variables would have had for a family at a particular time and place if no experimental treatment had been administered (that is, their *ex ante* values). The existence of a control group, which received no treatment, is thus of direct usefulness as a basis for isolation and removal of the experimental component.

SAMPLE, VARIABLES, AND CONCEPTS USED IN THE ANALYSIS

The approach used for the development of W and Y—the estimates of the appropriate "normal" wage rate and income variables used in subsequent labor-supply models—follows. The general framework is the same for both wage rates and family income, although the exposition will use notation and language for individual wage rates.

The observed wage rate of an arbitrary individual, i, at an arbitrary point of time, T, during the experiment is assumed to be composed of four multiplicative components. Consequently we write

$$\ln W_{iT} = \ln W^*_{iT} + \ln \tilde{W}_{iT} + \ln \mu_i + \nu_{iT},$$

where

W^*_{iT} = the average wage rate at time T for persons with observed characteristics equivalent to those of the ith persons in the absence of experimental effects;

$\tilde{W}_{iT}$ = the average proportional displacement from W^*_{iT} which is associated with the experimental treatment at time T. This is zero for all persons in the control group and varies with experimental treatment;

μ_i = the proportion by which the wage of individual i typically departs from the average of persons like himself on measured characteristics;

ν_{iT} = a random variable with zero mean for individuals, groups, or time intervals representing measurement error and/or transient influences.

Given the decomposition of observed wage rates, the strategy is to obtain the best possible estimates of the three nonrandom components and to form $\ln \hat{W}_{iT}$ as the sum of the first and third components. In other words, the component that is associated with the existence or level of the treatment is excluded, along with the noise component. The W^* component is quite analogous to the "permanent" wage functions employed by many investigators of cross-sectional data to eliminate transitory bias. Since such equations explain a very small part of the variation of wage rates, however, they are suspected of eliminating much permanent variation as well. The μ_i component implicitly represents that part of permanent wage rates which is not accounted for by W^*. Estimates of persistent departures for individuals can be made with multiple observations and should be interpreted as due to unmeasured characteristics of the individual.

The estimation of the components used data from the preenrollment questionnaire and the twelve quarterly questionnaires administered during the experiment. Separate subfunctions for $\ln W^*$ and $\ln \tilde{W}$ were jointly estimated using regression techniques appropriate for a two-component model of error. The component $\ln \mu_i$ was specified to be constant over time for each individual. (See Chapter 14 for a more complete description of the two-component regression model and the estimator used.) Given estimates of $\ln W^*$ and $\ln \tilde{W}$, observed residuals were averaged for each individual to provide explicit estimates of the $\ln \mu_i$. Finally, the sum of $\ln W^*_{iT} + \ln \mu_i$ was exponentiated to provide a complete series, $\hat{W}_{iT}$, known as the normal wage rate.

So far, the explanation of the general approach parallels the procedures used for the normal income estimates. But several differences in the application must be pointed out. Normal wage estimates are needed for each adult member of sample families to indicate their market opportunities at each point in time. But many of these adults, particularly wives and older teenagers, are not working most of the time. Normal *income* estimates, in contrast, are needed for family units and, with minor exceptions, there is a usable observation for each family in the continuous husband–wife sample at every quarter.

A full panel of 9009 observations could, thus, be used (693 families × 13 questionnaires) for estimating normal income. Separate normal income estimates could be made for the three ethnic subgroups, with as many as 1937 observations available for even the smallest (Spanish-speaking) sample. To estimate normal wages, however, there were only 4340 observations on 618 different male individuals and 493 observations on 129 female individuals. This was because only those quarters in which persons worked thirty-five to forty hours were used—in order to estimate full-time wage rates uncontaminated by overtime, second jobs, or paid holidays. (Workers over fifty-five or with some college education were also eliminated as representing very atypical observations for our sample.) For males, the number of observations for the normal wage calculations was still large enough to permit separate estimates to be made by ethnic group; for females, only a single model could be estimated, adding ethnic adjustments for W^* and $\tilde{W}$ within the model.

In developing the estimates of time-persistent deviations, μ_i, all observations which provided a nonzero observation were used. This included all families in the normal income case, of course; but for wages, a larger subset of individual observations entered the calculation of μ_i than was used to estimate W^*. For all cases with no observed wages, μ_i was set equal to zero. In this manner, it was possible to obtain an estimate of the normal wage rate for each adult in the sample. Clearly, the estimate is more accurate for those who worked full time during most of the experiment and is most dubious for those, including many females, who did not work at all. For the latter, the nature of the estimated wage is most similar to the "permanent" wage function used for cross-sectional studies—mainly a log-linear function of age and education.

While the estimation of normal income, $\hat{Y}$, did not suffer from a fractional sample basis, there was an additional problem involved in its estimation. For estimating the experimental component of wage rates, $\tilde{W}$, it was regarded as sufficient to specify $\tilde{W}$ as a function of assigned experimental parameters and time elapsed after the start of the experiment. But for estimating the analogous component of family income, $\tilde{Y}$, it was necessary to include average normal income, Y^*, in the subfunction for capturing $\tilde{Y}$. Symbolically we have

$$\ln Y_{iT} = \ln Y^*(\mathbf{Z}_{iT}) + \ln \tilde{Y}(Y^*_{iT}\mathbf{X}_{iT}) + \ln \mu_i + \epsilon_{iT},$$

where $\mathbf{Z}_{iT}$ is a vector of family characteristics and the time variable and $\mathbf{X}_{iT}$ is a vector of experimental parameters and the time variable. This specification should be interpreted as saying that the effect of the experimental treatment on family income depends on the expected income level for that family; for example, families with incomes well above their breakeven may be less affected than families who are far below it.

Because it was impractical to substitute all the variables in the $\mathbf{Z}_{iT}$ vector into the $\tilde{Y}$ function (with appropriate constraints), an iterative process was used. Starting off with $Y^*_{iT} = Y_{i0}$ (or preenrollment income) in the $\tilde{Y}$ function, a first-round estimate of $\ln Y^*(\mathbf{Z}_{iT})$ was obtained. This estimate was used to revise the coefficients of the $\ln \tilde{Y}$ function, and then a second round estimate of $\ln Y^*$ could be obtained. This process was continued until $Y^*(\mathbf{Z}_{iT})$ stabilized. At every stage, the components-of-variance regression model was used to allow for nonindependence of residuals for the same family.

By these methods, normal wage estimates, $\hat{W}_{iT}$, were obtained for every adult member of the husband–wife sample, and normal income estimates, $\hat{Y}_{iT}$, were formed for every family in that sample. These somewhat novel procedures are described in more detail in Chapter 13, and some discussion of alternatives is provided. For present purposes, however, it should be noted that this technique uses most of the available information from a longitudinal data base to eliminate noise and transitory influences. The variables produced are used as control variables for isolating net response to experimental variation rather than as the primary variation from which income and substitution effects are estimated. Whether such estimates could be recommended for the latter purpose is an interesting question not addressed here. What is implied by their use in subsequent analysis is the more modest claim of providing a sound basis for defining comparability between control and experimental groups (or among experimental variations).

REFERENCES

Cain, G. G., and Watts, H. W., eds. 1973. *Income maintenance and labor supply: Econometric studies*. New York: Academic Press.

Kershaw, D. N., and Fair, J. 1976. *The New Jersey Income-Maintenance Experiment*. Vol. 1. *Operations, surveys, and administration*. New York: Academic Press.

Metcalf, C. Forthcoming. Implications of the sample design for the use of experimental data. In *The New Jersey Income-Maintenance Experiment*. Vol. 3. *Expenditures, health, and social behavior; and the quality of the evidence,* ed. H. W. Watts and A. Rees. New York: Academic Press.

Watts, H. W., and Mamer, J. Forthcoming. The problem of a spurious wage rate response. In *The New Jersey Income-Maintenance Experiment*. Vol. 3. *Expenditures, health, and social behavior; and the quality of the evidence,* ed. H. W. Watts and A. Rees. New York: Academic Press.

3 Labor-supply response of husbands

Harold W. Watts
David Horner

The labor-supply response of male heads of poor and near-poor families to an income subsidy program such as a negative income tax is crucial from two points of view. First, the earnings of the male are typically the major source of earnings for such families, and few have important amounts of income other than earnings. As the major earner, then, he has a large potential for labor-force withdrawal in response to a transfer payment—large enough, in fact, to negate the augmentation in money income from the transfer, which is less likely to be true for the subsidiary earners. Second, there is a popular view that any reduction in work for pay on the part of husbands with heavy family responsibilities is unrelieved either by offsetting gains in output from work at home, such as that expected of wives, or by investments toward future income, such as that expected from adult children (whose alternatives may be successful completion of high school or added training of some sort). Whether these views are accurate is less important here than their prevalence. They do, in any case, provide reasons for concern about any weakening of the traditional "breadwinner" effort that are different from those regarding the work effort of secondary earners.

1. SUMMARY OF THE FINDINGS FOR HUSBANDS

Nonexperimental studies have found married, nonaged males in general to have high rates of labor force participation and to be quite insensitive to price (wage) and income variation. Hence, *if* poor and near-poor male heads respond to such economic stimuli in about the same way as more general populations, and *if* the nonexperimental studies have not somehow misled us about that response, we should not expect to find large responses for this group. With some complicating qualifications, this is what is found in the analysis that follows. The overall responses to tax rates that (on average) cut net wages in half and to income guarantees that were equal to a substantial fraction of preexperimental income are barely detectable, and could be interpreted as being so minor that further analysis is unwarranted. Further analysis was, however, carried out and tended both to confirm prior hypotheses about the direction of response and to support previous nonexperimental findings of low elasticities of labor supply for prime-age male breadwinners.

The basic factual context for the analysis below is shown in Table 3.1 which gives mean values for the key labor-supply variables to be used. These are simple, unadjusted means for the first, second, and third years of the experiment, and for the two-year period obtained by dropping the first two and the last two quarterly observations. The sample consists of the 693 continuous husband–wife families described in Chapter 2 and used for most of the following analysis. The white, black, and Spanish-speaking control groups are shown separately to give a description of the performance base from which the experimental differentials are measured. The aggregated control sample is also shown and can be contrasted both with the aggregated experimental group and with the subgroup of experimentals in the medium and high plans, that is, those not dominated by AFDC-UP. The mean values are unadjusted averages of the relevant quarterly observations.

All three groups have participation rates above 90 percent, with the Spanish-speaking group the highest. Relatively little variation in participation occurs during the three years, and the experimental groups appear to maintain a small lead over the controls. These rates should be interpreted in light of the fact that the male family heads are all between nineteen and fifty-nine years old (in the middle year), are married, and started out in the sample without any disability or school obligation preventing their employment.

Employment, and hence the unemployment implied by the difference between employment and participation, shows more variation. There is a tendency for unemployment to increase during the three years of the

Table 3.1 Unadjusted Mean Values for Key Variables, by Ethnic Group and Experimental Status, Husbands

	Quarters	Labor Force Participation (Percentage)	Employment (Percentage)	Unemployment (Percentage)	Hours per Week	Earnings per Week (Dollars)	Earnings per Hour (Dollars)
Controls							
All	1–4	93.0	88.2	4.8	33.8	82.6	2.44
	5–8	94.1	87.6	6.5	33.4	83.8	2.51
	9–12	93.1	84.9	8.2	33.7	87.7	2.60
	3–10	93.7	87.0	6.7	33.6	84.1	2.50
White	1–4	92.1	88.4	3.7	35.3	84.2	2.39
	5–8	94.4	88.6	5.8	34.7	88.2	2.54
	9–12	93.0	87.6	5.4	36.2	94.3	2.60
	3–10	93.7	88.1	5.6	35.1	88.0	2.51
Black	1–4	91.6	82.8	8.8	30.7	79.4	2.59
	5–8	91.6	84.0	7.6	30.2	76.6	2.54
	9–12	90.4	76.8	13.6	28.9	77.5	2.68
	3–10	91.4	82.5	8.9	30.3	77.8	2.57
Spanish-speaking	1–4	97.3	95.5	1.8	36.6	83.5	2.28
	5–8	97.3	90.6	6.7	35.4	84.7	2.39
	9–12	97.8	90.6	7.2	35.2	87.6	2.49
	3–10	97.3	91.3	6.0	35.4	84.6	2.39
Experimentals							
All	1–4	94.6	89.5	5.1	34.2	90.1	2.63
	5–8	94.8	86.3	8.5	32.8	89.0	2.71
	9–12	94.2	83.6	10.6	32.6	90.8	2.78
	3–10	94.7	86.4	8.3	33.1	89.9	2.72
Medium and high plans[a]	1–4	95.1	89.9	5.2	34.1	89.8	2.63
	5–8	95.6	86.8	8.8	33.1	88.7	2.68
	9–12	95.5	84.4	11.1	32.5	89.8	2.76
	3–10	95.5	86.8	8.7	32.9	89.4	2.72

[a] These are the plans not dominated by welfare (AFDC-UP).

experiment for the control sample, and this tendency is stronger for the experimental sample. The black control sample shows the greatest unemployment which, along with the largest rate of nonparticipation, yields an employment rate some 9 points lower than the rate for the Spanish-speaking control sample over the middle two years, and 5½ points lower than the rate for whites over the same period. Average hours worked per week largely mirrors the employment variation. Average hours per employed person range from 37 hours for the black control sample to 39–40 hours for the white and Spanish-speaking groups—a much narrower range than that for the averages shown, which are not conditional on being employed.

Earnings and earnings per hour (which are computed as the ratio of mean earnings to mean hours) both show a tendency to increase and are centered around $2.50 per hour (in 1968 prices)—a little higher for blacks and a little lower for Spanish-speakers. The difference between control and experimental earnings rates, which (as noted in Chapter 1) is suspect in that it may reflect differential misreporting rather than a "real" difference, is clearly visible in these means.

Table 3.2 provides more controlled comparisons than the simple control–experimental differences that can be calculated from Table 3.1. The gross differences between control and experimental husbands shown in Table 3.2 are estimated from a multiple regression which adjusts for the following variables:

1. Hours worked per week at preenrollment
2. Weeks worked in year prior to enrollment
3. Age (nonlinear)
4. Education (nonlinear)
5. Experimental site
6. Number of adults in the family
7. Number of children in the family

Holding these variables constant, the differences shown in Table 3.2 emerged between the control group and the entire collection of families eligible for experimental benefits.[1] These forty-eight measurements are derived from forty-eight separate regressions controlling for the variables listed above. In only two cases are the differentials significant at the 5 percent level; two more are significant at 10 percent. That is slightly less than the expected number for forty-eight independent tests on entirely random

---

[1] These differentials do not agree exactly with those shown for quarters 3–10 in the official summary of the experimental results (U.S. Department of Health, Education, and Welfare: 1973) because simple linear adjustments for age and education were used for their estimation.

Table 3.2 Basic Experimental Differentials for Husbands

	Quarters	Labor Force Participation (Percentage)	Employment (Percentage)	Unemployment (Percentage)	Hours per Week	Earnings per Week (Dollars)
All	1–4	1.8	0.2	1.6	−0.91	2.51
	5–8	−1.2	−3.0	1.8	−1.97	−0.02
	9–12	−0.7	−4.4	3.7	−3.46**	−3.84
	3–10	−0.4	−2.5	2.1	−2.07	−0.08
Black	1–4	−0.9	2.5	−3.4	1.86	6.93
	5–8	0.1	−0.3	0.4	0.54	8.10
	9–12	−1.1	1.1	0.0	1.00	8.01
	3–10	0.1	1.1	−1.0	0.93	8.29*
Spanish-speaking	1–4	−0.5	−6.9**	6.4	−3.37*	2.64
	5–8	−1.0	−4.1	3.1	−1.20	2.23
	9–12	−0.1	−1.0	0.9	0.95	6.93
	3–10	−0.9	−4.0	3.1	−0.98	4.48

NOTE: Control variables include age, education, preenrollment hours, weeks worked in year before experiment, site, and family size. Regressions estimated 15 parameters (14 for Spanish-speakers) including experimental differential.
* Significant at the 10 percent level.
** Significant at the 5 percent level.

data. White husbands showed a significant negative response in the third year for hours. Notably, this significance is lacking for the midexperimental aggregates of both hours and earnings, which have the same negative sign but a smaller magnitude. Spanish-speaking husbands show a significantly different level of unemployment in the first year, which is partially reflected in the hours differential. The significance of this is also absent in the two middle time periods, and any hint of the effect has vanished by the third year. The blacks generally show positive differentials, and in the case of earnings the difference is significant at 10 percent for the two-year average.[2]

This survey of the simple differentials suggests that overall they are neither large nor reliable. The few significant results are quite consistent with the null hypothesis, and even *they* seem concentrated at the beginning and end of the experiment.

The following sections report on three approaches to the problem of searching for intelligible patterns of response within the small average differentials shown above. The results confirm a small but significant overall reduction in labor supply that is somewhat concentrated in the groups which have the lowest earning potential, and for which high guarantees and/or tax rates relative to the other experimental plans drastically reduce the incentive to work. But the patterns are not clearly evident in the data, nor are they always consistent across ethnic groups. And in no case does the analysis point to complete withdrawals from work or even drastic reductions for any subgroup of the sample.

Section 2 reports on the estimation of a simplified labor-supply model derived from utility assumptions which imply linear expenditure functions à la Becker.[3] This model enables the response to be captured in a single parameter and strictly constrains the pattern of response to variations in tax rates and guarantee levels. The estimated response in terms of hours worked during quarters 7–10 indicates a 4 percent reduction in hours for husbands earning $2.67 per hour who were assigned to a 50 percent tax rate and a guarantee equal to the poverty level. The response parameter is just significant at the .05 level for this sample, which includes all husbands who reported regularly during quarters 7–10.

The Section 2 analysis explores variations in response by age and education. While the patterns are not statistically significant, it is noteworthy that, for the median or modal age groups with less than a high school education, the response was much smaller than the overall average of 4 per-

---

[2] Earnings results reflect, in part, the persistence of the wage-rate differential discussed in Watts and Mamer (forthcoming).

[3] Section 2 is the work of David Horner.

cent. The overall estimate was raised by larger reductions among the distinctly older or younger than average husbands and among those who had graduated from high school. Here it should be noted that no allowance is made for ethnicity, which is somewhat confounded with education in this sample.

The time pattern of response and the effects of attrition are also explored briefly in terms of the one-parameter model. The response is shown to be more consistently negative in the middle two years, and to be somewhat more negative for the continuous sample during quarters 7–10 than for the more inclusive sample on which most of the analysis is based.

Section 3 provides an analysis of a wider range of measures of labor-supply—labor force participation, employment, hours, and earnings.[4] Here three ethnic groups are analyzed separately: non-Spanish whites, Spanish-speaking whites (primarily Puerto Ricans), and blacks. This section also explores the variations in response among the various guarantees and tax rates and the effects of preenrollment earnings levels on response.

The way is thus prepared for more intensive analysis in Section 4 in several ways. As mentioned above, crude and mainly descriptive models are used to explore variation in response by treatment levels and earning capacity. In addition, there is a discussion of measurement biases which suggests the elimination of earnings as a reliable indicator of relative labor supply, and a further elimination of those families on the two least generous plans because these plans yielded less generous benefits for those eligible to receive payments than the New Jersey welfare alternative. Very few of them, therefore, chose the experimental payments.

Section 4 proceeds on this more limited sample with a more elaborate model, incorporating a specification of a vanishing response as income rises substantially beyond the breakeven level. The ethnic subsamples of continuous husband–wife families are treated separately, and participation, employment, and hours are all analyzed for their contribution to the experimental response. There is some confirmation of the hypothesis that response is greater for husbands the farther they are below the breakeven level, and that the response is more than proportional to that distance. Only the Spanish-speaking subsample displays income and substitution effects which are significant and of the expected sign. The white subsample, while showing some significant response in hours for employed husbands, does not show a pattern of response which is consistent with theoretical predictions. The blacks persistently show a *positive* response to the experimental subsidies which is not statistically significant. This

---

[4] Sections 3 and 4 are the work of Harold W. Watts.

contrary finding calls for explanation, and a brief examination of trends for subgroups of the black sample is provided at the end of the section.

The final section draws together the evidence provided in the body of the chapter and provides tentative conclusions. The general finding of small labor-supply reductions is seen as relatively robust, though weak. It is to be hoped that the analysis of other experiments will clarify areas of uncertainty and resolve some newly uncovered puzzles.

2. ANALYSIS USING A SIMPLIFIED LABOR-SUPPLY MODEL

This section approaches the analysis of the experimental response by male family heads using a generous measure of theoretically derived prior specification. It achieves a much more parsimonious empirical model than the ones used in subsequent sections and, by limiting the analysis to response in terms of hours worked, secures a further simplification. Within this framework, the possible interaction of individual or family characteristics with the experimental treatment can be effectively explored and some interesting patterns by age and education displayed. Tests of the adequacy and validity of the theoretically derived measures give strong support to this strategy. Additional estimates examine the time pattern of response and the effect of attrition on the estimated response.

Theoretical Background

The theory underlying the model used here follows that of Becker and others in their work on the household allocation of time.[5] However, the reduced form of the constrained utility function is analogous to and, hence, has the same general properties as the log-linear function used in many expenditure models.[6]

Assume there is associated with each family a utility function

$$U = U[Z(Y, L_m, L_f, L_o)], \qquad (1)$$

where Z represents an aggregation of the outputs of the various activities

---

[5] The basic model of time allocation is contained in Becker (1967).

[6] For a detailed statement of the standard theory of work–leisure choice, see Horner (1972: Chapter 2). A survey of consumer expenditures models is contained in Goldberger (1967).

a family is engaged in, Y represents an aggregation of the goods which are input to those activities, and L_m, L_f, and L_o are the leisure or nonmarket time inputs of the male head, his spouse, and any other family members.[7]

Assume further that Z is produced by a simple Cobb–Douglas production function and that utility is proportional to the logarithm of Z (that is, marginal utility declines as the inverse of Z). The solution for the demand equations has the familiar property that fixed proportions of net "whole" income are devoted to purchases of goods and leisure time of the relevant family members. In particular:

$$(1 - t)W_m L_m = \beta_m[(1 - t)(W_m T_m + W_f T_f + W_o T_o) + G] \qquad (2)$$

where
  W = market wage rate for family members;
  T = total available time for family members;
  t = tax rate applied to earnings;
  G = income guarantee.

From (2) and the identity, $H_m = T_m - L_m$, it can be inferred that the change in labor supplied to the market, H_m, caused by introduction of a tax rate, t, and guarantee, G, will be

$$\Delta H_m = -\beta_m[G/(1 - t)W_m], \qquad (3)$$

assuming no change in wage rates or time availabilities for any family member. This suggests that the husbands' response to introduction of a nonzero tax and income guarantee for low income families should be proportional to the ratio of the guarantee to the husbands' wage rate net of tax. This variable, rescaled by 1/2000 to put the guarantee on an hourly basis, is denoted by Q in the following empirical work.

The response parameter, β_m, may be a function of the characteristics of a family or of its male breadwinner. By its derivation, β_m should be positive if the nonmarket time input has positive productivity for Z.

In the following applications, Q is employed to detect the experimental response, sometimes alone and sometimes with interactions allowing cross-sectional variation in β_m. Change in hours worked from preenrollment levels is used as the indicator of labor supply. The control variables introduced in the regressions—age, education, health status, prior work experience, and experimental site—are necessary both to reduce variation and to allow for possible nonrandom associations between these variables and experimental status. Preenrollment hours, H_0, is introduced as a

---

[7] In other specifications, Z and Y are generally disaggregated into multiple dimensions, but our simplification does not affect the conclusions.

control variable and, since the dependent variable is formed as $H_t - H_0$, the models can also be interpreted as explaining H_t if the appropriate adjustment is made in the coefficient of H_0. Finally, an estimate of $1/W_m$ is introduced to avoid contamination of the experimental coefficient, since Q also varies with $1/W_m$.

Basic Findings

The data used for this analysis were collected in the preenrollment interview and the twelve quarterly interviews of the experiment. In addition to hours worked and the experimental variables, a number of variables representing characteristics of the husband and his family are used. The usable sample consisted of all husbands for whom there were data at preenrollment, the fourth quarterly, and at least three other quarterlies.[8] In the actual regressions presented, observations were deleted if there was a missing value for one of the variables.[9]

The dependent variable, ΔH, which is used to measure work effort in the primary results, is the change in average work effort for the seventh through tenth quarters, where hours worked are measured for the week prior to the interview. Thus, $\Delta H = [(H_7 + H_8 + H_9 + H_{10})/4] - H_0$, where the subscripts indicate the quarter in which the hours are worked. This choice was made for two reasons. First, the average of four periods was used so that seasonal factors could be adjusted for. (Analysis of the adjustment path indicates that the quarter-to-quarter adjustment is not smooth.) Second, the analysis is predicated on the assumption that recipients view the experiment as permanent, at least until shortly before the end of the program. Given the three-year period of the experiment, this assumption is questionable and remains to be tested. However, it is reasonable to expect that as the experiment neared its end, the labor-supply response would become more conditioned than before by the prospect of the termination of experimental payments. The adjustment path revealed a decrease in work effort which continued through the tenth quarter but was then sharply reversed. Thus, the seventh through tenth quarters can legitimately be viewed as the longest time period in which to allow for a labor-supply adjustment.

The treatment variable is constructed by dividing the four-person sub-

[8] Note that this sample is more inclusive than the 693 families in the continuous husband–wife sample used for Tables 3.1 and 3.2 and for the subsequent analysis.

[9] In cases where a variable was used in dummy form, it was possible to include observations with missing values for that particular variable by including an additional dummy which indicates that the value of the variable was missing.

sidy, expressed as an hourly rate (for example, $1.65 for families assigned to a 100 percent guarantee plan) by an estimate of the husband's normal wage rate net of the tax rate assigned to the family.[10]

Table 3.3 presents the estimates of what will be called the three primary regressions. All the regressions from which these were chosen were of the general form

$$\Delta H = \mathbf{B}'_0 \overline{\mathbf{X}}_0 + \mathbf{B}'_1 \overline{X}_1 Q + e, \tag{4}$$

where

ΔH = the measure of work-effort change described above;
$\overline{\mathbf{X}}_0$ = a vector of variables characterizing the husband and his family;
$\overline{X}_1$ = a subgroup of characteristics which interact with Q;
Q = the experimental variable, described above;
$\mathbf{B}'_0$ = vector of parameters of the control function;
$\mathbf{B}'_1$ = vector of parameters of the response function;
e = an error term with assumed distribution $(0, \sigma^2)$.

Both the control and the interaction variables were chosen based on a

---

[10] For each individual the estimated wage, $\overline{W}$, was constructed as follows. A wage rate was determined for the preenrollment period and each of the first eight quarterly interviews by dividing the individual's earnings by his hours worked. If the wage rate for a particular quarter was below $1.40 per hour or above $4.50 per hour, or if the hours worked were 0, the observation for that quarter was thrown out. If the individual did not have at least two remaining wage rates, he was excluded from the construction. The quarterly wage rates for the remaining individuals were adjusted so that the adjusted mean wage rate of all remaining individuals in a particular quarter was equal to the mean wage rate in the fourth quarter. This was done to eliminate the bias caused by the general upward trend in wage rates which occurred during the two-year period. The normal wage rate for each remaining individual was then defined as

$$\overline{W} = \frac{1}{n} \sum_{i=1}^{n} W_i$$

where W_i represents a quarterly wage rate, and n for any given individual would be $2 \geq n \geq 0$.

For those individuals who did not have a constructed wage rate, a predicted wage rate was used. This was obtained by regressing $\overline{W}$ on selected characteristics using those individuals for whom a $\overline{W}$ was calculated. The characteristic variables, which explained 30 percent of the variation in $\overline{W}$, were age, education, average earnings in the year prior to the experiment, dummy variables, a dummy health variable, and two race–education interaction terms. Each individual for whom a $\overline{W}$ was not calculated and for whom the characteristic variables were available was then assigned the $\overline{W}$ which was predicted from the regression. Since the reason why most of these individuals did not have a $\overline{W}$ was that they did not work, the predicted wage rate probably overestimates the potential normal wage of the individual. However, the predicted wage enables us to include the individual in the analysis and is a better guess than, say, the mean wage rate. This procedure allowed wage rates to be constructed for 968 family heads.

Table 3.3 Labor-Supply Response of Husbands' Coefficients, Three Primary Models

Independent Variable	Coefficients (Hours per Week)		
	I	II	III
Q	−1.11942**		−13.2258
	(0.62166)		(8.2207)
Q^2		−0.55964**	
		(0.29506)	
EQ			−1.7173
			(1.5610)
AQ			0.64380
			(0.43629)
A^2Q			−0.007843
			(0.005543)
H_0	−0.80394**	−0.80359**	−0.80087**
	(0.03064)	(0.03064)	(0.03072)
$1/\bar{W}$	3.1835	4.9963	3.4827
	(6.4735)	(6.6456)	(6.4821)
A	0.95020**	0.95133**	0.39839
	(0.37424)	(0.37414)	(0.54497)
A^2	−0.011792**	−0.011817**	−0.004902
	(0.004851)	(0.004849)	(0.007133)
L	−5.7097†	−5.6694†	−5.5571†
	(1.3413)	(1.3410)	(1.3427)
E	1.8514	−1.8631	3.0967**
	(1.1523)	(1.1520)	(1.1529)
P	0.28171**	0.28122**	0.27857**
	(0.04064)	(0.04063)	(0.04071)
C_1	0.4983	0.4960	0.4394
	(1.4653)	(1.4643)	(1.4693)
C_2	2.0367	2.0561	1.9913
	(1.3654)	(1.3653)	(1.3672)
C_3	1.2470	1.2782	1.1843
	(1.4396)	(1.4396)	(1.4424)
Constant	−5.8725	−6.7946	4.2714
	(7.8711)	(7.8696)	(10.6391)
R^2	.4800	.4803	.4829

NOTE: Standard errors are in parentheses. Sample size is 799. For definition of independent variables, see text.
** Significant at the 5 percent level, one-tailed test.
† Significant at the 5 percent level, two-tailed test.

combination of their statistical properties and theoretical notions as to their importance in conditioning work behavior.

The most significant control variable is H_0, initial work effort.[11] The other variables entered as controls are the individual's normal wage rate, $1/\overline{W}$; the age and age squared of the husband, A and A^2; two dummy health variables, L (where $L = 1$ if the husband had a health problem which currently limited his work effort, 0 otherwise) and L_m ($L_m = 1$ if information on the husband's health was missing, 0 otherwise); two education dummy variables, E (where $E = 1$ if the husband completed high school, 0 otherwise) and E_m (where $E_m = 1$ if information on the husband's education was missing, 0 otherwise); the weeks worked by the husband in the year prior to the experiment, P; and three site dummy variables, C_1, C_2, C_3.

Several control variables and one experimental interaction are not significant, and their coefficients are excluded from the table in some of the regressions. The coefficients of three of these, L_m, E_m, and (in regression III) $E_m Q$, are not presented in the table because the variables are included in the regression solely for the purpose of maximizing the number of observations which could be included in the sample without contaminating the results. The three site variables, none of which is significant, are nevertheless included in the regression to control for that part of the labor-supply response which is due to city differences. Likewise, the variable $1/\overline{W}$, whose coefficient is also insignificant, is included as a control variable because it interacts with the experimental parameters in the construction of Q; it is also necessary to remove the independent contribution from the experimental variables. The same is true for A and A^2 in regression III.

The difference in the three regressions is the way in which the experimental effect is specified. In regression I only Q is entered; Q^2 is entered into the second regression and this formulation actually explained the variation in H slightly better than Q. Both the coefficients of Q and Q^2 indicate that there was a statistically significant decrease in the work effort of husbands in response to the program. Regression III contains an educational-treatment and two age-treatment interaction terms. While not significant at the generally accepted 5 percent level, this regression is presented because the standard theory of human capital suggests that age and education variables will condition the response to a transfer program like the negative income tax.

---

[11] Several functional forms were used to represent H_0, including a second degree polynomial, dummy variables, and a linear spline function. None were more significant than the simple H_0.

Table 3.4 Estimated Hours Response for Illustrative Values of the Treatment (Q), by Plan

	Guarantee Rate			
	50	75	100	125
Values of Q				
Tax rate 30	−0.44	−0.66	(−0.88)	(−1.10)
50	−0.62	−0.93	−1.24	−1.54
70	(−1.02)	−1.54	−2.06	(−2.57)
Percentage hours response proportional to Q (equation I)[a]				
Tax rate 30	−1.42	−2.14	(−2.85)	(−3.56)
50	−1.99	−2.99	−3.99	−4.99
70	(−3.32)	−4.99	−6.65	(−8.31)
Percentage hours response proportional to Q^2 (equation II)[a]				
Tax rate 30	−0.31	−1.07	(−1.25)	(−1.96)
50	−0.62	−1.50	−2.47	−3.85
70	(−1.70)	−3.85	−6.85	(−10.70)

NOTE: For definition of Q, see text. These values are calculated for a male head with average wage rates of $2.67 per hour. For a head with low wages, say $1.60, the values of Q and the linear response should be multiplied by 1.67 (the quadratic response by 2.78). For a "high wage" family head, say $3.50 per hour, the comparable factors are .76 and .58. Numbers in parentheses are extrapolations to combinations not used in the experiment.

[a] Average preenrollment hours, 34.67, is used as the base for the percentage calculations.

The actual F-statistic of the set of experimental variables in regression III is 1.74; and the F-statistic for the addition of the three interaction terms is only 1.09. The 5 percent significance levels for these two tests are 2.37 and 2.60, respectively. However, it should be noted that this test does not allow for our a priori knowledge of the theoretical signs of the coefficients, which human capital theory can be used to predict as follows:[12]

$$\partial^2 \Delta H / \partial Q \partial A > 0 \text{ and } \partial^2 \Delta H / [\partial Q \partial (A^2)] < 0.$$

Table 3.4 provides an array of illustrative values for the experimental variable Q, along with the estimated response in terms of hours per week as implied by the equations I and II from Table 3.3. The response be-

---

[12] This is derived from the notion that time spent in self-investment is more competitive with work for younger men, and leisure time is more competitive for older men. For a given Q, middle-aged men would be less sensitive to changes in the effective wage rate because they have less opportunity to use their time in other pursuits. Also, some people maintain that younger people are easily alienated from work. If this is true, the income effect of the program would act in a similar way for both young and old workers, which would reinforce our a priori notions as to the signs of the age coefficients.

comes substantial for combinations of high tax rates, high guarantees, and low normal wage ratios, as required by the form specified for Q. It is notable that the equally well fitting quadratic formulation yields a more modest response around the mean levels of wages, guarantees, and tax rates.

The elasticities implied by the estimates are

$$\eta_{H \cdot G} = -1.120/H \text{ and}$$
$$\eta_{H \cdot t} = \eta_{H \cdot G}*t/(1-t).$$

For equation II the elasticity formula is the same except that the elasticities are proportional to Q^2. This is because $dH/dQ = 1.12$ in equation I and $1.12Q$ in equation II. It is clear that only for extreme values do these elasticities exceed one in absolute value. Of course, if the tax rate is allowed to approach 100 percent, the elasticities become large without limit.

Table 3.5 gives the predicted labor-supply response, measured in hours per week, for alternative values of Q, A, and E. The two middle values of Q, 1.44 and 2.06, represent the mean Q for the experimental group and the Q for a family receiving a basic subsidy equal to the poverty level whose head earns \$1.60 an hour and whose earnings are taxed at a 50 percent rate. The figures in parentheses are the responses expressed as a percentage of initial work effort, $\hat{H}_0$, where, for a particular age and education, $\hat{H}_0 = 17.54 + 0.93A - 0.01A^2 + 2.42E$. This formula is derived from the regression of H_0 on A, A^2, E, and E_m. For all ages and education levels, $H_0 = 34.74$.

The first two rows contain the change in work effort independent of age and education. These figures are derived, respectively, from the first and second regressions. At the mean treatment level, the first regression indicates a response of 4.65 percent, with the 95 percent confidence interval bounded by -0.419 and 9.71 percent.

The remaining rows in Table 3.5 give the response estimated by equation III at three different age levels and for those who completed and did not complete high school. Some of the values for particular age and education categories are extreme in the sense that they extrapolate to values where the sample is very sparse. Eighty percent of the sample husbands are between the ages of twenty-six and fifty, 79 percent did not complete high school, and 89 percent of the experimental families show Q values smaller than 2. A majority, 54 percent of the experimental group, fall within all three of the boundaries.

These estimates imply that for the modal group around age forty without a high school diploma and given an "average" size treatment, the response is miniscule. It becomes more consequential for heads that are distinctly younger or older, or have a high school education. It would be

Table 3.5 Predicted Hours Response, for Selected Treatment (Q) Levels, by Age and Education

	Estimate of Mean Hours Worked at Preenrollment	Response in Hours per Week (Percentage Change in Parentheses)			
		$Q = 1.00$	$Q = 1.44$	$Q = 2.06$	$Q = 3.00$
Equation I	34.67	−1.12 (−3.23)	−1.61 (−4.65)	−2.31 (−6.65)	−3.36 (−9.69)
Equation II	34.67	−0.56 (−1.62)	−1.16 (−3.35)	−2.38 (−6.85)	−5.04 (−14.53)
Equation III					
High school dropouts					
25 years old	33.15	−2.03 (−6.13)	−2.93 (−8.83)	−4.19 (−12.63)	−6.10 (−18.40)
41 years old	35.07	−0.01 (0)	−0.02 (−0.00)	−0.03 (−0.00)	−0.04 (−0.00)
50 years old	33.25	−0.64 (−1.92)	−0.93 (−2.80)	−1.33 (−4.00)	−1.93 (−5.80)
High school graduates					
25 years old	35.57	−3.75 (−10.54)	−5.40 (−15.18)	−7.73 (−21.72)	−11.25 (−31.63)
41 years old	37.49	−2.38 (−6.34)	−3.42 (−9.12)	−4.89 (−13.05)	−7.13 (−19.01)
50 years old	35.67	−2.36 (−6.62)	−3.40 (−9.53)	−4.86 (−13.62)	−7.08 (−19.85)

hazardous to draw strong conclusions from these results because of the large errors of estimate, but the patterns are not implausible.

In the process of deriving the equations in Table 3.4, a variety of other variables were tested as control and interaction terms. The coefficients of the ethnic origin, family size, number of children, and initial labor-force-participation variables—and their respective treatment interaction terms—were all insignificant once H_0, A, and A^2 were entered into the model. Nor did initial hours worked, site, or welfare variables interact with the treatment variable to explain a significant portion of the response. Many of these variables were entered using a variety of functional forms, including polynomials, logs, and linear spline functions.

Validation of Q

The variable Q is derived from a rather restrictive theory. The primary results do not allow the vector $\mathbf{B}_1$ to be conditioned by Q, nor does the model allow for an experimental response which is independent of Q. Finally, the effects of tax rate and guarantee are not independent. In light of these restrictions, a variety of regressions were run to test the appropriateness of Q.

Several variables were entered to allow for a nonlinear response to Q. Table 3.6 presents the statistics associated with entering several alternative experimental variable combinations. The variable Q_A is based on the absolute basic guarantee for a particular family size rather than the relative guarantee, which is standardized for family size. It performed slightly worse than Q. The relationship between Q_A and Q_A^2 was also similar to that between Q and Q^2. When Q^2 was tried both alone and with Q, Q^2 performed better than Q, but Q^2 was not significant when entered in addition to Q.

A final test of the appropriateness of Q was made by taking every combination of the experimental parameters, G and t, which are present in Q, and entering them along with Q. This was done to test whether the restrictive formulation of Q generated by the theoretical model failed to capture a significant portion of the influence of the experimental parameters. Table 3.6 presents the appropriate statistics for entering, one by one, each of the variables, G, $1/(1-t)$, G/W, $G/(1-t)$, and $1/W(1-t)$, with Q. Also presented are several groups of these variables which, when entered along with Q, had a relatively high F-level.

The results indicate that none of the variables enter significantly at the 5 percent level once Q is added to the regression. Some combinations, especially $1/(1-t)$ and $G/(1-t)$, do enter at a nontrivial level. The variable $G/(1-t)$, or $Q\overline{W}$, did slightly better than Q when entered as the sole

Table 3.6 Statistics Associated with Entering Alternative Experimental Combinations

Experimental Variables	t-Statistic for Entering Q	F-Statistic for Adding All Experimental Variables	F-Statistic for Adding All Experimental Variables Other Than Q When Q Is Entered
Q	1.80	3.24 (3.85)	—
Q^2	—	3.60 (3.85)	—
Q_A	—	2.50 (3.85)	—
Q_A^2	—	2.77 (3.85)	—
Q, Q^2	0.09	1.80 (3.00)	0.36 (3.85)
T	—	1.72 (3.85)	
Q, T	1.27	1.66 (3.00)	0.08 (3.85)
Q, g	2.05	2.62 (3.00)	2.09 (3.85)
$Q, 1/(1-t)$	0.28	1.81 (3.00)	0.39 (3.85)
$Q, G/(1-t)$	1.78	2.67 (3.00)	2.09 (3.85)
$Q, G/W$	1.58	2.09 (3.00)	0.94 (3.85)
$Q, 1/W(1-t)$	0.42	2.45 (3.00)	1.65 (3.85)
$Q, G, G/(1-t)$	1.78	2.04 (2.61)	1.43 (3.00)
$Q, X/(1-t), G/(1-t)$	1.79	2.37 (2.61)	1.93 (3.00)
$Q, G/(1-t), G/\overline{W}$	2.02	2.00 (2.61)	1.51 (3.00)
$Q, G/(1-t), 1/\overline{W}(1-t)$	1.12	2.35 (2.61)	1.90 (3.00)
$Q, G, 1/(1-t), G/(1-t), G/\overline{W}, 1/\overline{W}(1-t)$	1.04	1.31 (2.10)	0.92 (2.22)

NOTE: Numbers in parentheses are F-levels needed for significance.

variable. It was, however, excluded from being presented in the primary results on theoretical grounds, because it was far from being significant when included in addition to Q. Future investigation should explore further the possibility that the response to Q will be conditioned by the level of $\overline{W}$.

The Pattern of Adjustment

In the foregoing analysis, an average of the seventh through tenth quarters was chosen to make the period long enough to capture much of the labor-supply adjustment and yet exclude any response which anticipates its termination. An examination of the adjustment pattern yields additional information that can be used to interpret the results thus obtained, although it does not, of course, provide an adequate test of the extent of termination effects.

To get a picture of the adjustment path, the response model was applied to twelve different time periods in order to measure the cumulative response to the program at quarterly intervals. The twelve dependent variables, ΔH_i, are defined as

$$\Delta H_i = H_i - H_0, \quad i = 1, \ldots, 12$$

where H_i denotes the hours worked in the ith quarter, and H_0 is the hours worked at preenrollment.

As the experiment progressed, a number of families dropped out. Thus, the usable sample declined from one quarter to the next. In order to determine the effect of attrition, if any, on the labor-supply response, the adjustment-path regressions were run on both a continuous sample, which included only observations where the husband was interviewed in every quarter, and a full usable sample that included all observations usable in any given quarter. Estimates of the coefficients of Q for all quarterly interviews and for both samples are reported in Table 3.7.

The results indicate that most of the response had taken place after two years. However, the irregular pattern also suggests interaction of seasonal factors with the treatment. Estimates of the decrease for the second and third quarters in the first two years are successively smaller in the continuous sample. Thus, if we compare like quarters (every fourth quarter), the decrease in labor supply with respect to Q does not level off until the middle of the third year. The evidence, therefore, does not support the notion that the adjustment took place entirely in the first two years. There is no unambiguous pattern in the differences between the continuous sample and the full usable sample. In the first year the response is greater for the full sample, but in the second year it is some-

Table 3.7 **The Pattern of Adjustment of Response as Measured by Coefficients of Q**

Quarter	Q Coefficients from Continuous Sample ($N = 697$)	Q Coefficients from Full Usable Sample
1	−0.12	−0.65 ($N = 878$)
2	+0.18	+0.31 ($N = 873$)
3	+0.43	−0.47 ($N = 867$)
4	−0.94	−1.25 ($N = 872$)
5	−1.17	−0.47 ($N = 855$)
6	−0.59	−0.64 ($N = 852$)
7	−0.38	−0.29 ($N = 843$)
8	−1.83	−1.36 ($N = 843$)
9	−0.74	−1.00 ($N = 824$)
10	−0.93	−1.03 ($N = 799$)
11	+0.07	+0.47 ($N = 784$)
12	−0.35	−0.86 ($N = 767$)

what smaller. Given that the differences are small relative to the standard errors, sample attrition does not seem to affect the results in a systematic manner.

Concluding Remarks

The results obtained in this section, which are strictly constrained by the form of a simple utility maximization model, appear to be both consistent with that theory and consistent with previous empirical research in indicating quite a modest response to an income subsidy. The supply elasticities of husbands appear to be small except for those who are very young, very old, or have very low wage rates.

The form, Q, of the variable used for measuring the experimental response forces a substantially magnified response to high tax rates, but it should be recalled that extensive testing of alternatives, as well as the theoretical rationale, supports the choice of Q. The one alternative that showed some statistical superiority had the same properties with respect to tax rate variation. Consequently, while the predominant response was modest, there is no support here for the proposition that very high tax rates would not reduce work effort.

The time pattern of response is quite irregular and disappointing from the perspective of attempting to discover a smooth adjustment pattern. But, at the same time, the comparative movements of the continuous and full samples yield some assurance that attrition has not grossly distorted the results.

3. LABOR-SUPPLY RESPONSE DISAGGREGATED BY TIME AND ETHNIC GROUP

This section returns to a more descriptive and exploratory approach to the experimental data, extending the simple comparisons made in the introductory section and providing a basis for the more elaborate econometric efforts in the following section.

The estimated differentials shown in Table 3.2 do not make any distinction among the eight different experimental plans. The next display of results attempts a crude representation of differences related to "generosity" of the treatment. Figure 3.1 shows the relation between net benefits and income (both normalized by the poverty level) for the eight experimental combinations. The vertical lines indicate the limits of the observations at preenrollment—the upper one by design, the lower by availability. The average level of normalized income is around 1.2 for the husband–wife sample, and the mode and median are even higher. Hence, there are three natural groupings of plans according to how much they would pay an "average" experimental family. The top three (125–50, 100–50, 75–30) are denoted *High*. The next three (100–70, 75–50, and 50–30) pay distinctly less over the relevant range and are called *Medium*. The final two (75–70 and 50–50) pay almost nothing over most of the range and are called *Low*. They are, moreover, heavily dominated by public-assistance support levels over most of the experimental period. Subsequently, the Low group will be deleted from the analysis of male-head response on the grounds that some 90 percent of experimental fami-

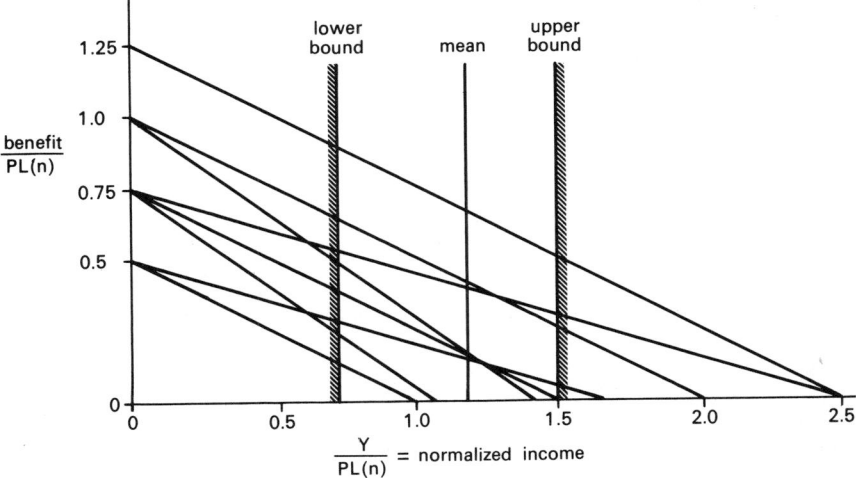

Figure 3.1 Relationship of net benefits to income in the range of sample observations.

lies on these two plans are either on welfare or have income above the breakeven point. While their behavior may be of interest, it is not likely to tell us much about the response to experimental stimuli. Table 3.8 shows how the sample of continuous husband–wife families used here is distributed over this aggregation of experimental plans.

In addition, a more efficient method of control is introduced that makes use of the normal wage-rate and normal family-income variables explained in Chapter 2. A standard form has been adopted that provides a substantial degree of flexibility in the relation of labor-supply variables—participation, hours, employment—to the more traditional determinants of labor supply. This function $S_c(\hat{Y}, \hat{W}, PL)$ is specified as follows:

$$S_c(\ldots) = c_1\hat{Y}/PL(n) + c_2\hat{W} + c_3/\hat{W} + c_4\hat{Y}/\hat{W},$$

where $\hat{Y}$ and $\hat{W}$ are constructed variables denoting normal income and normal wage, respectively. In the first term, the "normal" income variable is normalized by dividing by the poverty level, $PL(n)$. That is, a "welfare" ratio is used. The second and third terms allow for a nonlinear wage-rate effect, and the fourth term allows for an interaction between wage rates and income. We have

$$\partial S_c/\partial \hat{Y} = c_1/PL(n) + c_4/\hat{W}$$

and

$$\partial S_c/\partial \hat{W} = c_2 - (1/\hat{W}^2)(c_3 + c_4\hat{Y})$$

so that the normal income derivative varies both with need, as measured by $PL(\cdot)$, and wage rate. The normal wage rate derivative varies both with wage rate and with normal income.

This function, along with linear terms in preenrollment hours and weeks employed in base year, provided a substantial reduction in the variance of the experimental response, and in cases where the latter ap-

Table 3.8 Distribution of Sample Families, by Plan "Generosity" and Ethnicity

	All	Control	Experimental	Plan		
				High	Medium	Low
White	310 (100)	129 (42)	181 (58)	88 (28)	58 (19)	35 (11)
Black	234 (100)	83 (35)	151 (65)	68 (29)	50 (22)	33 (14)
Spanish-speaking	149 (100)	56 (38)	93 (62)	44 (30)	37 (24)	12 (8)
Total	693 (100)	268 (39)	425 (61)	200 (29)	145 (21)	80 (11)

NOTE: Percentages in parentheses.

LABOR-SUPPLY RESPONSE OF HUSBANDS 79

proached significance showed basically the same pattern of response. Consequently, the coefficients displayed in Table 3.9 have been derived from regressions using S_c and the preexperimental values as the basic control variables and experimental variables defined for the Low, Medium, and High plan groupings explained above—formulated as dummy variables.

We find in this table that nineteen out of 144 individual response coefficients are significant at a 10 percent level or better. This is slightly more than a random data set would provide. Of the joint tests in the last two columns, five out of forty-eight are significant for the test of a null response, and only two out of forty-eight reject the hypothesis of no generosity effect.

In spite of the scarcity of significant results, it may be useful to review the ones that do appear. It will be noted that four of the significant F_3 tests and twelve of the significant coefficients are found for earnings. Nearly all these are positive and are not explainable in terms of similar significant positive responses in hours worked. White males during the third year show significant effects on differences in employment, hours, and earnings. The results show a relatively low participation rate for the white Low group and a relatively high unemployment experience for all three groups, which is reflected as lowered earnings and hours relative to the control group. Only in the case of the Low group does there seem to be a consistent pattern of decreased supply across the whole period. The Spanish-speaking sample displays only one significant coefficient—an excess of hours worked in the Low group in the third year. For blacks (except for the earnings results) the only significant result is the sharp contrast in participation rates between the Low and Medium groups in the third year.

Finally, the three-group classification of plans by generosity was separately estimated for families whose preenrollment income was less than 120 percent of the poverty line and for those whose preenrollment income was greater. This was done to provide a preliminary view of possible interactions between the experimental treatment and the income or earning capacity of the family and its male head. Table 3.10 shows the sample distribution between the two classes and underscores the fact that the experimental design did not assign equal proportions of the sample to each negative income tax plan and each income stratum. Again, forty-eight separate regressions were estimated. In each one, the same control variables were used as in Table 3.9, but this time the base and the three experimental differentials were allowed to have different values for the two strata of normalized preenrollment income. Testing the ninety-six sets of experimental differentials produced eleven rejections of the null hy-

Table 3.9 Experimental Response according to Plan "Generosity" for Four Indicators of Labor Supply, by Ethnicity and Time Period

			Plan					
	Quarters	Base	Low	Medium	High	F_3	F_2	R^2
Labor force participation (percentage)								
White	1–4	95.8	−1.3	1.5	4.5*	1.64	1.63	.40
	5–8	97.7	−3.8	−2.6	2.3	1.59	2.36*	.33
	9–12	94.4	−4.1	−0.7	3.9	1.59	2.31	.28
	3–10	96.9	−2.8	−1.2	2.9	1.39	2.04	.37
Black	1–4	98.3	1.8	0.7	−1.0	0.23	0.34	.25
	5–8	97.8	−3.3	2.0	2.7	1.03	1.43	.26
	9–12	99.3	−5.8	5.7	−0.8	2.05	3.08**	.26
	3–10	97.5	−2.0	2.6	1.5	0.65	0.87	.28
Spanish-speaking	1–4	99.0	3.0	0.4	−0.1	0.19	0.27	.22
	5–8	100.6	1.9	−0.2	0.3	0.09	0.12	.30
	9–12	99.3	1.9	2.2	−0.8	0.42	0.59	.22
	3–10	99.6	2.4	0.0	0.1	0.13	0.18	.29
Employment (percentage)								
White	1–4	92.5	−1.7	0.2	2.6	0.52	0.67	.45
	5–8	92.5	−6.7*	−4.3	0.1	1.52	1.66	.47
	9–12	87.6	−9.6**	−4.7	−3.0	1.52	0.86	.37
	3–10	91.6	−6.3*	−4.2	−0.1	1.55	1.60	.50
Black	1–4	94.0	3.1	3.1	3.5	0.50	0.01	.41
	5–8	93.9	0.1	−0.9	2.1	0.22	0.30	.37
	9–12	92.9	1.1	2.2	2.7	0.15	0.04	.42
	3–10	92.6	1.7	1.6	2.7	0.26	0.06	.44

Spanish-speaking	1–4	96.6	0.1	–3.8	–2.5	0.40	0.23	.31
	5–8	95.7	3.2	–3.6	–0.6	0.35	0.47	.33
	9–12	97.0	8.1	2.3	–1.8	0.74	1.08	.42
	3–10	95.7	4.9	–2.9	–0.5	0.58	0.83	.42
Hours (per week)								
White	1–4	37.2	1.4	–1.0	–1.0	0.73	0.99	.56
	5–8	35.8	–3.9*	–1.5	–0.9	1.33	1.05	.49
	9–12	35.2	–2.5	–4.4**	–3.2**	2.48*	0.34	.47
	3–10	36.2	–2.7	–2.1	–1.3	1.29	0.37	.58
Black	1–4	36.4	3.0	2.5	1.9	1.05	0.15	.43
	5–8	35.7	1.5	0.8	1.1	0.26	0.06	.51
	9–12	36.5	1.3	0.7	1.8	0.34	0.13	.47
	3–10	35.7	2.1	1.2	1.3	0.60	0.12	.56
Spanish-speaking	1–4	37.5	–2.7	–0.8	–1.9	0.53	0.26	.38
	5–8	37.8	2.3	–0.6	–0.3	0.30	0.44	.44
	9–12	37.7	5.6*	1.9	0.9	1.19	1.15	.47
	3–10	37.4	3.1	–0.2	0.1	0.65	0.95	.54
Earnings (dollars per week)								
White	1–4	93.0	10.4**	1.1	2.2	1.72	1.81	.63
	5–8	93.8	–6.0	–3.1	–0.5	0.63	0.61	.68
	9–12	88.4	–4.5	–13.4***	–5.8	2.51*	1.32	.61
	3–10	92.9	–3.4	–4.3	–0.6	0.67	0.58	.75
Black	1–4	95.5	8.7	11.2**	8.6*	2.24**	0.15	.52
	5–8	92.3	16.8***	10.1**	9.6**	3.54**	0.82	.60
	9–12	95.8	14.7**	8.2	9.3*	1.80	0.39	.54
	3–10	92.5	16.3***	9.8**	9.6***	5.02***	1.09	.68

(*continued*)

Table 3.9 (continued)

			Plan				
Quarters	Base	Low	Medium	High	F_3	F_2	R^2

Spanish-speaking

Quarters	Base	Low	Medium	High	F_3	F_2	R^2
1–4	96.3	−9.6	2.4	2.5	1.28	1.87	.63
5–8	94.7	1.3	−2.9	0.5	0.18	0.26	.59
9–12	94.4	9.6	1.2	4.9	0.76	0.63	.64
3–10	93.9	3.4	−1.3	3.5	0.62	0.77	.73

NOTE: From regressions controlling on S_c [$\hat{Y}$, $\hat{W}$, $PL(n)$], and preexperiment values for hours per week and weeks per year. The base is for head with $\hat{Y} = \$100$, $\hat{W} = \$2.50$, $PL(n) = \$80$, who was working forty hours per week at preenrollment and had worked fifty weeks the previous year. F_3 is the F-statistic for the null hypothesis that all three experimental coefficients are zero. That is, all experimental group means are the same as the base. F_2 is the F-statistic for the null hypothesis that all three experimental coefficients are the *same*. That is, there is no variation by plan generosity.
* Significant at the 10 percent level.
** Significant at the 5 percent level.
*** Significant at the 1 percent level.

Table 3.10 **Distribution of Sample by Welfare Ratio at Preenrollment**

	Ethnicity			Plan				
	White	Black	Spanish-speaking	Control	Low	Medium	High	Total
Welfare ratio < 1.2	148	140	95	141	43	94	95	383
Welfare ratio ≥ 1.2	162	94	54	127	27	51	105	310
Total	310	234	149	268	80	145	200	693
Percentage < 1.2	47.7	59.8	63.4	52.6	53.8	64.8	47.5	55.3

pothesis of zero response at the 5 percent level. Rather than showing all the estimates, Table 3.11 displays only the significant ones, along with some adjacent estimates to provide a context for interpretation.

The results observed earlier for white husbands appear to be concentrated in the lower-income stratum and to be characterized by a sharp contrast between the Low group, with negative deviations, and the High group, with much larger positive ones. The only other significant experimental effect for the lower-income stratum is for black husbands in the third year. The Low experimental group shows a negative response in participation in the third year—the effect is notably stronger than for the middle two years. The positive differentials for black earnings here are shown to be concentrated in the upper-income stratum. They are particularly strong for the Low experimental group and, as before, are not paralleled by such high positive deviations in hours. Only in the first year are there significant positive effects in hours. A significant negative differential in earnings appears for the high-stratum Spanish-speaking sample in the first year. It contrasts sharply both with the differentials for other levels of generosity and with the outcome for the same group in the middle two years of the experiment.

From this overview, several conclusions may be suggested. First, and most important, significant overall and simply measured responses to experimental plans are very few. Rejection of the null hypothesis of no experimental effect occurs barely more often than would be the case with random data, although the interactions with income stratum show some promise. The significant results are particularly scarce in the middle year and middle two years, where the most reliable estimates of the response might be expected. In view of this, one must conclude that the effects, if any, are too small or subtle to be discovered by these simple models.

Second, the reasons for suspecting the reliability of the earnings measurements are reinforced here by the frequent inconsistencies between the signs or significance of response in terms of hours and in terms of

Table 3.11 Selected Differentials from Family Income Classification at Preenrollment, by Ethnicity and Time Period

			Plan					
	Quarters	Base	Low	Medium	High	F_3	F_2	R^2
White (welfare ratio < 1.2)								
Participation (percentage)	1–4	97.1	−1.3	3.2	11.5	4.11***	4.41**	.41
	5–8	99.6	−3.4	−0.3	7.0	2.13*	3.01*	.34
	9–12	94.1	−3.2	3.5	10.3	2.78**	3.25**	.30
	3–10	98.1	−2.2	1.6	8.8	2.94**	3.60**	.39
Employment (percentage)	1–4	94.8	−1.1	5.5	13.0	4.04***	3.83**	.47
	5–8	95.3	−5.5	1.1	7.8	2.13*	3.01*	.48
	9–12	88.9	−6.5	−0.7	3.0	0.64	0.94	.38
	3–10	94.0	−4.6	1.3	7.4	1.98	2.75*	.51
Black (welfare ratio < 1.2)								
Participation (percentage)	9–12	102.5	−12.6	4.3	−3.4	3.17**	4.45**	.28
	3–10	97.7	−3.3	3.1	4.0	1.26	1.66	.29
Black (welfare ratio > 1.2)								
Hours (per week)	1–4	33.9	11.3	5.6	2.7	3.78**	2.77*	.46
	5–8	33.4	4.0	2.2	0.6	0.56	0.51	.51
	9–12	33.3	7.8	1.6	1.8	1.18	1.09	.48
	3–10	33.7	6.1	3.2	0.1	1.85	2.06	.58
Earnings (dollars per week)	1–4	86.7	21.0	25.8	16.0	4.54***	0.76	.53
	5–8	83.5	24.5	19.6	13.6	3.37**	0.67	.61
	9–12	86.1	34.8	9.7	11.9	2.77**	1.89	.55
	3–10	84.9	26.5	18.7	11.9	5.07***	1.64	.68
Spanish-speaking (welfare ratio > 1.2)								
Hours (per week)	1–4	36.9	−7.9	−1.7	1.1	1.30	1.91	.41
	3–10	34.7	7.2	2.4	3.3	1.35	0.63	.55
Earnings (dollars per week)	1–4	95.0	−23.9	6.5	7.9	3.25**	4.61**	.65
	3–10	87.0	9.4	5.3	13.1	1.90	0.61	.74

NOTE: For notes see Table 3.9.

earnings. For this reason, the subsequent analysis of the husband's response will be limited to participation, employment, and hours. To the extent that the measured earning-rate changes are real rather than spurious, any supply response in hours will be understated (if the substitution elasticity is positive), and the disincentive effect overstated.

Third, the Low experimental group contains a relatively small number of families and is, moreover, suspect as a reflection of experimental response because it is heavily contaminated with welfare recipients and/or families with income above the breakeven point. Consequently, for the subsequent analysis, in which the possibility of more subtle and structured responses is explored, the two Low experimental subgroups, 50–50 and 75–70, will be eliminated from the sample. The behavior of these families may shed light on the response to welfare and on the effect of being above the breakeven point but, as was mentioned earlier, it can offer little useful evidence for the effect of either positive benefit payments or the high marginal tax rates that affect persons below their breakeven point. No additional efforts are made in the next section to allow for the effect of welfare participation on the possible eligibility of some families for alternative income subsidies, so the results displayed should be interpreted with that qualification in mind.[13]

The apparent differences in both experimental and control behavior among the ethnic groups have persisted in the results reviewed above. Statistical tests were carried out, and these rejected the hypothesis of homogeneity. Consequently, the next section will proceed to analyze the three ethnic divisions separately, despite the serious loss of statistical precision.

The instability of measured response (deriving mostly from random sampling error) displayed for the three groups of experimental plans should be taken as an adequate reason for not undertaking a plan-by-plan analysis.

4. LABOR-SUPPLY RESPONSES AS MEDIATED BY EARNING CAPACITY

A more flexible and complex form for measuring experimental response is developed in this section and then applied to data on labor force participation, employment, and hours from the sample of continuous husband–wife families reduced by the exclusion of the families assigned to the two low-benefit plans. The primary objective is to increase the ability of the relationship between income and the plan breakeven level to condition the response to the experimental treatments. As before, the strategy is to use a "control" function to explain as much as possible of the commonly determined variation for both control and experimental observations. To this is added a response function, the purpose of which is to capture the systematic net deviations for the experimental units. The control function used for this part of the analysis is similar in spirit to the ones

---

[13] See Garfinkel (forthcoming) and Avery (forthcoming) for detailed analyses of this source of contamination.

used in the previous section. It will be specified below, but first it is necessary to specify a different functional form for the response to the experimental treatment. Following this econometric specification, its application to the labor-supply components will be reported.

A New Specification of the Response Function

The asymmetrical nature of the benefit schedule and the associated marginal tax rates suggest that the response to the treatment ought to vanish at some level of earning. Presumably this vanishing point would be above the breakeven level. To capture this notion a variable, θ, was constructed to embody the assumption that a male head who is more than twenty hours' worth of work above the breakeven point is "immune" from the effects of the experimental treatment and can be regarded as equivalent to a control observation. This variable, therefore, is equal to zero for control observations and for those experimental observations that could forego twenty or more hours of work at wage $\hat{W}$ without falling below their breakeven income. Otherwise it is defined as

$$\theta_{iT} = (M_i + 20\hat{W}_{iT} - \hat{Y}_{iT})/10\hat{W}_{iT}$$

where

$M_i = G_i P(n_{it})/t_i$ is the (dollar) breakeven level for the ith household, given its assigned G_i and t_i, and the poverty level $PL(n)$ appropriate for its size, n;
$\hat{W}_{iT}$ = the "normal" wage for the ith male head at time T;
$\hat{Y}_{iT}$ = the "normal" income for the ith family at time T.

The last two components are, again, the constructed variables mentioned above. The variable, θ, will be equal to 2 for an observation with $\hat{Y}$ precisely at the breakeven level, and takes on higher positive values for cases that are below the breakeven level.

In addition to providing an index of distance from a response "vanishing point," this variable is scaled in terms of (tens of) hours. It is proposed that such a measure has greater comparability on an interpersonal basis than would the simple dollar amount of the gap. The "normal" components are used here, however, to avoid the introduction of a possible response in income or wage rates into the explanatory variables.

Clearly θ depends on the guarantee and tax rates as well as upon income and wage rates; and it requires some care to interpret the response associated with θ and different levels of G and t. One cannot hold θ constant for a given person and vary G and t freely.

To provide some acquaintance with the level and range of θ, Table 3.12

Table 3.12 Means and Standard Deviations of θ (Income Relative to Breakeven)

	Quarters			
	1–4	5–8	9–12	3–10
White (N = 146)				
Mean	5.08	4.84	4.18	4.78
Standard deviation	3.33	3.42	3.40	3.41
Black (N = 118)				
Mean	5.18	5.24	5.55	5.28
Standard deviation	2.72	2.63	2.60	2.65
Spanish-speaking (N = 81)				
Mean	5.38	5.33	5.22	5.31
Standard deviation	2.70	2.66	2.56	2.63

NOTE: For definition of θ, see text.

shows the means and standard deviations for the three ethnic groups and for four time intervals. The two Low experimental groups have been deleted from this table for reasons given earlier. A mean of 5 and a standard deviation of 3 are good round numbers to describe the distribution of θ. The whites show a smaller mean and declining trend, but have more variation. The means for blacks show a rising trend and have a variance similar to that of the Spanish-speaking group. The latter's mean displays a weak tendency to decline.

The response function used with θ is a six-parameter, homogeneous-in-θ function as follows:

$$X = (\alpha_{11} + \alpha_{12}S_2 + \alpha_{13}S_3)\theta + (\alpha_{21} + \alpha_{22}S_2 + \alpha_{23}S_3)\theta^2,$$

where $S_2 = G - .75$ and $S_3 = t - .5$ are the linear spline terms in G and t explained in Chapter 2. Hence, the response is constrained to zero for $\theta = 0$ and is a quadratic function of θ for any given values of G and t. The quadratic coefficients are, however, linear functions of G and t. The coefficients α_{11} and α_{21} give the coefficients for θ and θ^2 directly when $G = .75$ and $t = .5$. Alternative combinations of G and t can be generated using appropriate values for S_2 and S_3.

The constraint of homogeneity was tested (by introducing a constant in X) and was rejected less often than the test level would imply. The constraint of linear forms for the coefficients of θ was not tested directly, but previous attempts to get consistent nonlinear patterns across the variation in G and t have been unsuccessful and, moreover, the magnitude of apparent response is so small that six parameters already seem an excessive burden to place on the systematic variation. The quadratic terms have generally proven to be an important part of the function whenever there is a substantial response, so it does not appear advisable to drop that part of the function. Finally, considering that G and t are also present in θ, the overall function is not linear in these variables. (The consideration of the form of this function's derivatives will be explored below at greater length.)

With this introduction of a new variable, it is now possible to specify the model to be used here. Once again averages of four or eight quarterly observations are used. In the case of the participation and employment variables, this means that the variables are limited to the 0–1 interval. Some observations, however, are not at the limits; hence, this variable measures the fraction of the quarterly interviews at which the husbands were employed or participating in the labor force. This averaging procedure provides a partial remedy for the econometric problem of dealing with a binary variable as the dependent variable. That is, while the observations are still limited to the 0–1 interval, they are not all at one limit or the other as is the case before averaging. (This is not claimed as a complete solution to the problem, but it does serve to alleviate it.) The sample size is reduced because the Low group was deleted from the analysis.

The control subfunction is relatively long, some seventeen variables plus a constant. It consists basically of S_c, the nonlinear function of normal income and normal wages (four variables), preexperimental values of hours per week and weeks per year (two variables), linear spline representations for age and education (five variables), numbers of adults and children (two variables), health status averaged from quarters 2 and 6 (two variables), and finally, linear introduction of the parts of normal income and wage rates that derive from the estimated relation and exclude the time-persistent deviation of an individual from that relation.

In combination, these variables explain a substantial amount of the variation in participation and related labor-supply variables. The R^2s range from 40 to 50 percent for participation and even higher for employment and hours. The focus here is on refining the control–experimental comparisons and on securing a substantial level of homogeneity in the comparison among plan groups—hence a certain amount of redundancy in the control function and the rather profligate use of degrees of freedom to provide an inclusive basis for controlling nonexperimental factors.[14] One specimen regression is shown in full in Table 3.13. The means for the variables in the experimental segment shown in the third column are the unconditional means. The means for these white experimental units can

---

[14] The specification of certain variables, such as normal income and wages, would also require more work if the objective were to secure results on the general supply response to variation in price and income directly.

Table 3.13 **Specimen Regression Estimates for White Husbands' Labor Force Participation, Averaged over Quarters 3–10**

Variables	Coefficient	Standard Error	Mean of Variable
I. Control segment			
Preenrollment values			
Hours (0)	.074	.064	36.2
Weeks worked (0)	.501	.087	45.4
Normal wage and income			
$\hat{Y}/PL(n)$	3.477	5.880	1.28
$\hat{W}$	2.677	2.498	2.51
$1/\hat{W}$	11.421	20.470	.43
$\hat{Y}/\hat{W}$	.214	.182	40.6
$(\hat{Y} - \bar{d}_y)/PL$	2.637	5.091	1.18
$\hat{W} - \bar{d}_w$	4.414	4.481	2.44
Age			
A (in years)	-1.716	2.059	39.46
$\text{Max}(A - 25, 0)$	1.638	2.119	14.54
$\text{Max}(A - 45, 0)$	$-.955$	.526	1.40
Education			
E (in years)	$-.755$	1.179	10.05
$\text{Max}(E - 8, 0)$	$-.096$	1.476	2.29
Family size			
No. of adults	-1.346	1.627	2.56
No. of children	.192	.852	3.28
Health			
H_1	-5.142	4.270	.20
H_2	-4.868	5.559	.22
Constant	88.006	53.385	1.00
II. Experimental segment			
θ	.773	1.776	2.54
θ^2	$-.143$	.290	18.31
$S_2\theta$	.008	3.401	.64
$S_2\theta^2$	.243	.560	5.33
$S_3\theta$	2.955	8.095	$-.09$
$S_3\theta^2$	$-.635$	1.409	$-.83$
XH_1	-3.439	5.994	.17
XH_2	2.715	5.692	.12
R^2	.417		

NOTE: This is the full regression from which the top section of Table 3.14 is calculated.

be obtained by multiplying by a factor of 1.98 since the controls all have zero values. The same regression form has been used to obtain the estimates in Tables 3.14, 3.16, 3.17, 3.18, 3.21, 3.22, and 3.23, but only the experimental response parts of the regression estimates are shown.

Table 3.14 **Experimental Response in Husbands' Labor Force Participation as Conditioned by θ, Central Two Years, by Ethnicity**

	Coefficients of			Points on Response Curve		
	θ	θ^2	$\theta^* = -(\alpha_1/\alpha_2)$	$\theta = 2$	$\theta = 5$	$\theta = 8$
White						
75–50	.773	−.143	5.4	1.0	0.3	−3.0
.25S_2	.002	.061	−0.03	0.2	1.5	3.9
.20S_3	.591	−.127	4.7	0.7	−0.2	−3.4
75–30	.182	−.016	11.4	0.3	0.5	0.4
100–50	.775	−.082	9.5	1.2	1.8	1.0
100–70	1.366	−.209	6.5	1.9	1.6	−2.4
$F_8(X) = .43$, $F_2(t) = .11$, $F_2(G) = .44$, $F_3(\theta^2) = .09$, $F_4(G, t) = .46$, $R^2 = .417$, $\sigma_u = 14.7$						
Black						
75–50	1.862	−.258	7.2	2.7	2.9	−1.6
.25S_2	−.611	.105	5.8	−0.8	−0.4	1.8
.20S_3	1.451	−.265	5.5	1.8	0.6	−5.4
75–30	.411	.007	−58.7	0.9	2.2	3.7
100–50	.251	−.153	8.2	1.9	2.4	0.2
100–70	2.702	−.418	6.5	3.7	3.0	−5.1
$F_8(X) = .84$, $F_2(t) = .63$, $F_2(G) = .36$, $F_3(\theta^2) = .45$, $F_4(G, t) = .35$, $R^2 = .441$, $\sigma_u = 13.8$						
Spanish-speaking						
75–50	6.375	−1.451	4.4	6.9	−4.4	−41.9
.25S_2	−2.823	0.670	4.2	−3.0	2.6	20.3
.20S_3	4.289	−1.300	3.3	3.4	−11.1	−48.9
75–30	2.086	−0.151	13.8	3.6	6.7	7.0
100–50	3.552	−0.781	4.5	4.0	−1.8	−21.6
100–70	7.841	−2.081	3.8	7.4	−12.8	−70.5
$F_8(X) = 3.81^{***}$, $F_2(t) = 13.06^{***}$, $F_2(G) = 9.85^{***}$, $F_3(\theta^2) = .653^{***}$, $F_4(G, t) = 6.99^{***}$, $R^2 = .521$, $\sigma_u = 11.0$						

NOTE: Null hypotheses for tests are as follows. Test $F_8(X)$: no experimental response including health interaction; $F_2(t)$: $\alpha_{13} = \alpha_{23} = 0$; $F_2(G)$: $\alpha_{12} = \alpha_{22} = 0$; $F_3(\theta)$: $\alpha_{21} = \alpha_{22} = \alpha_{23} = 0$; $F_4(G, t)$: $\alpha_{12} = \alpha_{22} = \alpha_{13} = \alpha_{23} = 0$.
*** Statistically significant at the 1 percent level.

Response in Terms of Labor Force Participation

Table 3.14 displays the estimated response functions from three different regressions. The first row of each panel provides the estimates of χ_{11} and χ_{21}—coefficients of θ and θ^2 for $G = .75$, $t = .50$. These are followed by θ^*, which is the value at which the response changes sign (usually from positive to negative). The last three elements are points on the response curve corresponding to $\theta = 2$, $\theta = 5$, and $\theta = 8$. These values correspond to the value at the breakeven point at the overall mean of

θ, and at one standard deviation beyond the mean. It must be remembered, however, that different ranges of θ are relevant for the different G and t combinations. If the breakeven level is low relative to the wage rate, it may be impossible to have a value of θ as high as 7 or 8.

For interpreting the results, it may be useful to show how the distribution of θ is related to the breakeven level. Table 3.15 shows the mean, standard deviation, and ninety-fifth percentile value (assuming normality) for the three categories of breakeven. A value of 8 for a low-breakeven plan such as 100–70 or 75–50 is clearly outside the range of observation, but it is close to the mean for a high-breakeven plan such as 75–30 or 125–50.

The second row of Table 3.14 provides the estimated values for α_{12} and α_{22}, which have been multiplied by .25 to yield the increments needed to raise or lower G to one of the actual plans. Similarly, the third row contains α_{13} and α_{23} multiplied by .2. The next three rows show the net coefficients for the 75–30, 100–50 and 100–70 plans, respectively, and can be seen to be sums of combinations of the first three rows. Finally, the bottom of each panel shows the F-statistics for relevant tests on the whole and various parts of the experimental response.

There are no significant effects for whites or blacks in terms of participation averaged over the third through tenth quarters. For the Spanish-speaking, there are strongly significant effects in all aspects of the response. Despite the nonsignificance of the white and black estimates, it is interesting that the same general pattern of signs for the α's is found as for the Spanish-speaking. The effects are milder, however, and show a small disincentive for whites (2 or 3 percentage points) only for the highest values of θ. The black results are also positive over most of the relevant range of θ. The Spanish-speaking group shows small positive response at the breakeven level ($\theta = 2$) and a sharply falling rate for high θ's. As mentioned before, the very large negative entries for $\theta = 8$ on plans 75–50 and 100–70 have to be dismissed as out of range, and even for the 100–50 plan, $\theta = 8$ is close to the limit.

Table 3.16 shows estimates for the Spanish-speaking sample for the three separate years. (Since there were no significant effects for whites or

Table 3.15 **Distribution of θ for Different Breakeven Levels**

Breakeven Index	Number of Cases	Mean	Standard Deviation	95th Percentile
1.42–1.67	145	3.41	1.84	6.44
2.0	44	4.47	2.26	8.19
2.5	156	6.71	3.17	11.92
All	345	5.07	3.00	10.01

Table 3.16 **Experimental Response in Husbands' Labor Force Participation as Conditioned by θ, Spanish-speaking, All Three Years**

	Coefficients of			Points on Response Curve		
	θ	θ^2	$\theta^* = -(\alpha_1/\alpha_2)$	$\theta = 2$	$\theta = 5$	$\theta = 8$
Year 1 (quarters 1–4)						
75–50	3.741	−.893	4.2	3.9	−3.6	−27.2
.25S_2	−1.706	.426	4.0	−1.7	2.1	13.6
.20S_1	2.753	−.828	3.3	2.2	−6.9	−31.0
75–30	.988	−.065	15.2	1.7	3.3	3.7
100–50	2.035	−.467	4.4	2.2	−1.5	−13.6
100–70	4.788	−1.295	3.7	4.4	−8.4	−44.6

$F_8(X) = 2.21^{**}$, $F_2(t) = 5.97^{***}$, $F_2(G) = 5.03^{***}$, $F_3(\theta^2) = 2.92^{**}$, $F_4(G, t) = 3.06^{**}$, $R^2 = .446$, $\sigma_u = 11.8$.

Year 2 (quarters 5–8)						
75–50	6.126	−1.379	4.4	6.6	−3.8	−39.2
.25S_2	−2.991	.664	4.5	−3.3	1.6	18.6
.20S_3	4.034	−1.255	3.2	3.0	−11.2	−48.0
75–30	2.092	−.124	16.9	3.7	7.4	8.8
100–50	3.135	−.715	4.4	3.4	−2.2	−20.7
100–70	7.169	−1.970	3.6	6.5	−13.4	−68.7

$F_8(X) = 3.38^{***}$, $F_2(t) = 10.36^{***}$, $F_2(G) = 7.27^{***}$, $F_3(\theta^2) = 4.96^{***}$, $F_4(G, t) = 6.16^{***}$, $R^2 = .512$, $\sigma_u = 11.9$.

Year 3 (quarters 9–12)						
75–50	5.093	−.964	5.3	6.3	1.4	−21.0
.25S_2	−1.693	.366	4.6	−1.9	0.7	9.9
.20S_1	3.289	−.740	4.4	3.6	−2.1	−21.0
75–30	1.804	−.224	8.1	2.7	3.4	0.1
100–50	3.400	−.598	5.7	4.4	2.0	−11.1
100–70	6.689	−1.338	5.0	8.0	0.0	−32.1

$F_8(X) = 1.18$, $F_2(t) = 2.00$, $F_2(G) = 1.75$, $F_3(\theta^2) = 2.26^*$, $F_4(G, t) = 1.00$, $R^2 = .361$, $\sigma_u = 12.8$.

NOTE: See note to Table 3.14 for null hypotheses of tests.
* Significant at the 10 percent level.
** Significant at the 5 percent level.
*** Significant at the 1 percent level.

blacks, comparable tables are not shown.) Only the first two years show significance here, with the second showing the strong results found for the middle two years. The last year, again, displays a similar pattern, but shows much weaker precision in the estimates.

It should be noted that the value of the response function at the relevant mean value for θ is almost always positive. Moreover, for blacks it is positive even at the appropriate ninety-fifth percentile value for θ. Negative values show up mainly in the Spanish-speaking subsample, and even then only for θ above the mean and for the higher levels of tax rate and guarantee.

To conclude, then, the interaction of income capacity in the form of θ does seem to provide a sensible pattern of response. But it does not, when applied to labor force participation, evoke either substantial labor-supply disincentive estimates or statistically significant relationships across the three ethnic groups.

Employment and Unemployment Responses

Regressions strictly parallel to the participation regressions were carried out on average employment (that is, the proportion of quarterly interviews during a period in which the male head reports being employed the previous week). Before examining the results, it is useful to review how, in experimental data, employment may show a different response from the one found for labor force participation.

The familiar labor force data derive time series of unemployment as the difference between participation and employment. When this gap changes, it is crudely interpreted as the result of some movement in participation (regarded as a supply indicator) and in employment (regarded as a demand index). Indeed, for males the gap (that is, the level of unemployment) is usually interpreted as reflecting almost entirely a change in demand—the supply or "offer" of labor being considered quite stable for prime-age male heads of household.

In the present analysis, where we are concerned with the contrasts between control and experimental families, this identification of the two variables with supply and demand, respectively, is not appropriate. Here both groups to be compared are operating in the same labor market and, except for some variables that can be controlled statistically, both groups are presumably equally attractive to employers. While labor-market demand conditions may affect the response to experimental treatments as those conditions vary over time and space, they should not be called upon to explain contrasts either between controls and experimental units or among different experimental groups. Consequently, the employment variable, being an answer to a more concrete question (Were you employed last week?), may provide a more direct indication of the response to the treatments than the answers to a question about work-seeking activities. Labor-supply reductions may take the form of reduced intensity of search or lower tolerance for undesirable job characteristics (including pay)—both of which would appear as employment reductions *without* a change in participation, the nominal "supply" variable.

Consider now the results for employment in Tables 3.17 and 3.18. The basic patterns are very much the same as for participation, only somewhat larger and more significant. The white and black regressions on the two-year averages remain insignificant (although there are some signs of significance for whites). For blacks, the *positive* responses found for participation are even more positive in the case of employment. For the white and Spanish-speaking groups, the range of θ values producing negative response has been widened. These effects can perhaps be seen more clearly in Table 3.19, which shows the unemployment rates as a function of θ. Estimates are shown for three plans, 75–30, 100–50, and 100–70,

Table 3.17 Experimental Response in Husbands' Employment as Conditioned by θ, Central Two Years, by Ethnicity

	Coefficients of			Points on Response Curve		
	θ	θ^2	$\theta^* = -(\alpha_1/\alpha_2)$	$\theta = 2$	$\theta = 5$	$\theta = 8$
White						
75–50	1.742	−.408	4.3	1.9	−1.5	−12.2
$.25S_2$	−.617	.198	3.1	−.4	1.9	7.7
$.20S_3$	.960	−.287	3.3	.8	−2.4	−10.7
75–30	.782	−.121	6.5	1.0	.9	−1.5
100–50	1.125	−.210	5.4	1.4	.4	−4.4
100–70	2.085	−.497	4.2	2.2	−2.0	−15.1
$F_8(X) = 1.03, F_2(t) = .50, F_2(G) = 1.02, F_3(\theta^2) = 1.15, F_4(G, t) = 1.33, R^2 = .492, \sigma_u = 18.7$						
Black						
75–50	1.961	−.098	20.0	3.5	7.4	9.4
$.25S_2$	−.083	−.010	−8.3	−.2	−.7	−1.3
$.20S_3$	1.353	−.194	7.0	1.9	1.9	−1.6
75–50	.608	.096	−6.3	1.6	5.4	11.0
100–50	1.878	−.108	17.4	3.3	6.7	8.1
100–70	3.231	−.302	10.6	5.2	8.5	6.3
$F_8(X) = 0.87, F_2(t) = 0.24, F_2(G) = 0.45, F_3(\theta^2) = 0.35, F_4(G, t) = 0.36, R^2 = .540, \sigma_u = 17.4$						
Spanish-speaking						
75–50	6.987	−2.147	3.3	5.4	−18.7	−81.5
$.25S_2$	−2.975	.970	3.1	−2.1	9.4	38.3
$.20S_3$	5.168	−1.947	2.7	2.5	−22.8	−83.3
75–30	1.819	−.200	9.1	2.8	4.1	1.8
100–50	4.012	−1.177	3.4	3.3	−9.4	−43.2
100–70	9.180	−3.124	2.9	5.9	−32.2	−126.5
$F_8(X) = 5.79^{***}, F_2(t) = 19.72^{***}, F_2(G) = 15.79^{***}, F_3(\theta^2) = 7.20^{***}, F_4(G, t) = 9.86^{***}, R^2 = .638, \sigma_u = 15.6$						

NOTE: See note to Table 3.14 for null hypotheses of tests.
*** Significant at the 1 percent level.

Table 3.18 **Experimental Response in Husbands' Employment as Conditioned by θ, Spanish-speaking, All Three Years**

	Coefficients of			Points on Response Curve		
	θ	θ^2	$\theta^* = -(\alpha_1/\alpha_2)$	$\theta = 2$	$\theta = 5$	$\theta = 8$
Year 1 (quarters 1–4)						
75–50	4.177	−1.424	2.9	2.7	−14.7	−57.7
.25S_2	−2.644	.733	3.6	−2.4	5.1	25.8
.20S_3	4.397	−1.323	3.3	3.5	−11.1	−49.5
75–30	−.220	−.101	−1.8	−.8	3.6	−8.2
100–50	1.533	−.691	2.2	.3	−9.6	−32.0
100–70	5.930	−2.014	2.9	3.8	−20.7	−81.5
$F_8(X) = 3.80^{***}$, $F_2(t) = 9.23^{***}$, $F_2(G) = 10.99^{***}$, $F_3(\theta^2) = 4.73^{***}$, $F_4(G, t) = 5.60^{***}$, $R^2 = .565$, $\sigma_u = 15.1$						
Year 2 (quarters 5–8)						
75–50	5.228	−2.024	2.6	2.4	−24.5	−87.7
.25S_2	−2.793	.956	2.9	−1.8	9.9	38.8
.20S_3	3.840	−1.842	2.1	.3	−26.9	−87.2
75–30	1.388	−.182	7.0	2.0	2.4	−.5
100–50	2.435	−1.068	2.3	.6	−14.5	−48.9
100–70	6.275	−2.910	2.2	.9	−41.4	−136.0
$F_8(X) = 4.52^{***}$, $F_2(t) = 13.90^{***}$, $F_2(G) = 9.77^{***}$, $F_3(\theta^2) = 3.89^{***}$, $F_4(G, t) = 6.98^{***}$, $R^2 = .546$, $\sigma_u = 19.6$						
Year 3 (quarters 9–12)						
75–50	12.128	−2.471	4.9	14.4	−1.1	−61.1
.25S_2	−4.760	1.138	4.2	−5.0	4.7	34.8
.20S_3	7.708	−1.900	4.1	7.8	−9.0	−59.9
75–30	4.420	−.571	7.7	6.6	7.8	−1.2
100–50	7.368	−1.333	5.5	9.4	3.5	−26.4
100–70	15.076	−3.233	4.7	17.2	−5.4	−86.3
$F_8(X) = 2.84^{***}$, $F_2(t) = 6.15^{***}$, $F_2(G) = 8.22^{***}$, $F_3(\theta^2) = 6.04^{***}$, $F_4(G, t) = 4.37^{***}$, $R^2 = .570$, $\sigma_u = 19.6$						

NOTE: See note to Table 3.14 for null hypotheses of tests.
*** Significant at the 1 percent level.

which have breakeven points at 2.5, 2.0, and 1.43, respectively. The response is shown at the mean and the ninety-fifth percentile of θ for the appropriate breakeven category, as well as for the fixed values 2, 5, and 8. The Spanish-speaking group shows substantially increased unemployment at higher values of θ. The whites are similar qualitatively, but show smaller increases. The blacks, along with the (insignificantly) higher participation rates, show reduced unemployment rates as well—with stronger effects estimated for the poorest (large θ) cases. Probably the best summary number on employment is that of the "central" plan,

Table 3.19 **Experimental Response in Husbands' Unemployment as Related to θ and Plan, by Ethnicity, Various Time Periods**

	θ = Mean	θ = 95th Percentile	θ = 2	θ = 5	θ = 8
White (quarters 3–10)					
75–30	.7	7.7	−.8	−.4	1.9
100–50	1.0	5.7	−.2	1.4	5.4
100–70	.9	7.2	−.3	3.6	12.7
Black (quarters 3–10)					
75–30	−5.3	−14.9	−.8	−3.2	−7.3
100–50	−3.7	−8.2	−1.4	−4.3	−7.9
100–70	−3.1	−8.1	−1.5	−5.5	−11.7
Spanish-speaking (quarters 3–10)					
75–30	4.0	10.1	.7	2.6	5.3
100–50	5.9	22.9	.7	7.6	21.7
100–70	7.5	34.2	1.5	19.4	56.0
Spanish-speaking (quarters 1–4)					
75–30	9.7	19.5	2.6	6.9	12.0
100–50	6.8	19.2	1.9	8.1	18.4
100–70	4.4	22.1	.6	12.3	36.9
Spanish-speaking (quarters 5–8)					
75–30	7.3	16.6	1.6	5.0	9.3
100–50	10.3	29.5	2.8	12.3	28.2
100–70	13.9	44.2	5.5	28.0	67.3
Spanish-speaking (quarters 9–12)					
75–30	−2.0	18.0	−3.8	−4.4	1.3
100–50	−3.0	16.9	−5.0	−1.5	15.3
100–75	−6.6	24.0	−9.2	5.4	54.2

100–50, evaluated at $\theta = 4.5$, where we find a negligible effect for whites (0.8), a curious positive effect for blacks (6.3), and a negative effect for Spanish-speaking (-5.4), which becomes sharply more negative at higher values of θ.

It may be useful at this point to see how the experimentally induced changes in income and net wages have affected the labor supply in terms of more traditional income and substitution (or price) coefficients. To carry this out, some derivation is required as well as a choice of what point(s) on the nonlinear schedules to evaluate. The experimental response part of the function can be written

$$X(G, t, \theta),$$

where $\theta(G, t, \hat{Y}, \hat{W}, n)$ and the form of the X and θ functions are as specified in equations (3.4) and (3.5). Interest here attaches to derivatives

LABOR-SUPPLY RESPONSE OF HUSBANDS

of X with respect to G and/or t, treating $\hat{Y}$, $\hat{W}$, and n as fixed parameters to be given some prototypical value.

Starting with X, the following may be obtained from its total differential:

$$\frac{dX}{dG} = X'_G + X'_t \frac{dt}{DG} + X'_\theta \frac{d\theta}{dG}$$

and

$$\frac{dX}{dt} = X'_t + X'_G \frac{dG}{dt} + X'_\theta \frac{d\theta}{dt}$$

where the X' are the partial derivatives:

$$X'_G = \alpha_{12}\theta + \alpha_{22}\theta^2$$
$$X'_t = \alpha_{13}\theta + \alpha_{23}\theta^2$$
$$X'_\theta = (\alpha_{11} + \alpha_{12}S_2 + \alpha_{13}S_3) + 2(\alpha_{21} + \alpha_{22}S_2 + \alpha_{23}S_3)\theta.$$

In these terms one may first examine a simple income effect, namely,

$$\left.\frac{dX}{dG}\right|_{dt=0} = X'_G + X'_\theta \frac{d\theta}{dG} = X'_G + X'_\theta \frac{PL(n)}{10t\hat{W}}.$$

A natural interest attaches to another derivative which requires compensating movement in G and t to maintain constancy in the breakeven level, $M = G/t$. Since θ is fixed when M is fixed and $dt = (t/G)dG$, we have

$$\left.\frac{dX}{dG}\right|_{dM=0} = X'_G + \frac{t}{G} X'_t.$$

The counterpart to an uncompensated "price effect" is here obtained as

$$\left.\frac{dX}{dt}\right|_{dG=0} = X'_t + X'_\theta \frac{d\theta}{dt} = X'_t - X'_\theta \frac{PL(n)M}{10t\hat{W}}.$$

Finally, the compensated price change or substitution effect can be obtained as the derivative, under the constraint that net benefits, B, remain constant,

$$\left.\frac{dX}{dt}\right|_{dB=0} = X'_t + X'_G \frac{\hat{Y}}{PL(n)} - X'_\theta \left(\frac{PL(n)G - t\hat{Y}}{10t^2\hat{W}}\right).$$

To obtain numerical estimates of these derivatives, it is necessary to specify an experimental plan and specific values of n (or PL), $\hat{W}$, and $\hat{Y}$. The 100–50 plan is close to the centroid of the curtailed sample (actually the means are $G = 94$ and $t = 48$), and will be used as the point of interest in the experimental space. Hence, $S_2 = .25$ and $S_3 = 0$. The values $PL(n) = \$80$, $\hat{Y} = 100$, and $W = 2.5$ were also selected as typical of a modal experimental husband's situation. The family size is slightly larger than six to produce a poverty line at $80 a week. Given the plan, the breakeven level is $160 a week and, consequently, $\theta = 4.4$. For this case, then, one may directly calculate the values of the partial derivative at $\theta = 4.4$, $S_2 = .25$, $S_3 = 0$; and combine these to form

$$\left.\frac{dX}{dG}\right|_{t=.5} = X'_G + 6.4X'_\theta$$

$$\left.\frac{dX}{dG}\right|_{M=2} = X'_G + .5X'_t$$

$$\left.\frac{dX}{dt}\right|_{G=1} = X'_t - 12.8X'_\theta$$

and

$$\left.\frac{dX}{dt}\right|_{B=30} = X'_t + 1.25X'_G - 4.8X'_\theta.$$

Table 3.20 displays estimates of these derivatives, along with the partial derivatives from which they are combined. A second set is also shown for a poorer archetype with wage rate, $\hat{W} = \$2$, and income, $\hat{Y} = 80$. For this case $\theta = 6$. It will be noted that the only set of derivatives with signs consistent with conventional theory and magnitudes large enough to be interesting is for the Spanish-speaking group. This should not be surprising, given that their response was the only one which achieved significance in the present analysis. Even there, however, the effect is not terribly large—a change in the guarantee rate from 1.00 to 1.05 (that is, an increase of 5 percent of the poverty line along with a tax increase to maintain the same breakeven) would, by these estimates, reduce a Spanish-speaking head's employment by less than $1\frac{1}{2}$ percentage points at the $2 wage level. If he were earning $2.50, the reduction would be only half as large.

Part of the response does appear to come from higher unemployment. This seems to be true both for whites and Spanish-speaking, where the apparent response is reduced employment from both sources, and for the blacks, where there is an apparent increase in employment from higher participation and lower unemployment. The only significant results are for the Spanish-speaking, however, and this argues against attempts at interpreting the contrasts provided by the other groups.

Table 3.20 Derivatives of Experimental Response in Husbands' Employment for Two Levels of θ, from Regressions for Central Two Years

	Typical ($\theta = 4.4$)			Poorer ($\theta = 6$)		
	White	Black	Spanish-speaking	White	Black	Spanish-speaking
$X(\theta)$	0.88	6.17	−5.13	−.81	7.38	−18.30
$X'_\theta(\theta)$	−.723	.928	−6.346	−1.395	.582	−10.112
$X'_G(\theta)$	4.474	−2.235	22.757	13.704	−3.432	68.28
$X'_t(\theta)$	−6.662	10.987	−74.774	−22.860	5.670	−195.42
$\left.\dfrac{dX}{dG}\right|_{dt=0}$	−.15	3.70	−17.86	2.54	1.22	−12.62
$\left.\dfrac{dX}{dG}\right|_{dM=0}$	1.14	3.26	−14.63	2.27	−.60	−29.43
$\left.\dfrac{dX}{dt}\right|_{dG=0}$	2.59	−.89	6.45	−.54	−3.641	−33.63
$\left.\dfrac{dX}{dt}\right|_{dB=0}$	2.40	3.74	−15.87	2.00	−2.42	−46.24

Responses in Hours Worked Conditional and Unconditional upon Employment

Given the reasons for doubt about the reliability of earnings comparisons between experimentals and control observations, hours worked is the final comparison that will be used to detect experimental response. One can consider either hours worked in the relevant survey week without regard to employment status or, alternatively, hours worked for only those who are employed. The former will be considered first and should be regarded as combining the effects found earlier with any adjustment in work levels for workers who are employed. It provides an estimate of the total response in work effort and will be proportional to the change in earnings if wage rates are independent of or exogenous to the choices made by individuals. If there is an endogenous wage-rate response to the experimental treatment, however, the equivalence is destroyed.

Tables 3.21 through 3.23 show, in a now familiar format, the estimated response functions for hours. Separate tables are displayed for the three ethnic groups; and, for each group, the estimates are shown for averages over the central two years followed by separate estimates for each of the last two years. As before, the variables are averages of quarterly observations on the variables. The same relatively elaborate control function is

Table 3.21 **Experimental Response in Husbands' Hours Worked per Week as Conditioned by θ, Whites, Central Two Years and Last Two Years**

	Coefficients of			Points on Response Curve		
	θ	θ^2	$\theta^* = -(\alpha_1/\alpha_2)$	$\theta = 2$	$\theta = 5$	$\theta = 8$
Quarters 3–10						
75–50	.064	−.187	.3	−.6	−4.4	−11.5
.25S_2	−.046	.089	.5	.3	2.0	5.3
.20S_3	.345	−.144	2.4	.1	−1.9	−6.5
75–30	−.281	−.043	−6.5	−.7	−2.5	−5.0
100–50	.018	−.098	.2	−.4	−2.4	−6.1
100–70	.363	−.242	1.5	−.2	−4.2	−12.6
$F_8(X) = 2.40^{**}, F_2(t) = .95, F_3(G) = 2.57^*, F_3(\theta^2) = .86, F_4(G, t) = 2.58^{**}, R^2 = .637, \sigma_u = 8.2$						
Quarters 5–8						
75–50	.547	−.261	2.1	0.0	−3.8	−12.3
.25S_2	−.245	.126	1.9	0.0	1.9	6.1
.20S_3	.442	−.190	2.3	0.1	−2.5	−8.6
75–30	.105	−.071	1.5	−.1	−1.2	−3.7
100–50	.302	−.135	2.2	.1	−1.9	−6.2
100–70	.744	−.325	2.3	.2	−4.4	−14.8
$F_8(X) = 1.81^*, F_2(t) = 1.30, F_2(G) = 2.43^*, F_3(\theta^2) = 1.70, F_4(G, t) = 2.61^{**}, R^2 = .554, \sigma_u = 9.7$						
Quarters 9–12						
75–50	.080	−.498	.2	−1.8	−12.1	−31.2
.25S_2	−.230	.235	1.0	.5	4.7	13.2
.20S_3	1.568	−.522	3.0	1.0	−5.2	−20.9
75–30	−1.488	.024	62.0	−2.9	−6.8	−10.4
100–50	−.150	−.263	−.6	−1.4	−7.3	−18.0
100–70	1.418	−.785	1.8	−.3	−12.5	−38.9
$F_8(X) = 3.52^{***}, F_2(t) = 3.70^{**}, F_2(G) = 6.26^{***}, F_3(\theta^2) = 1.49, F_4(G, t) = 3.26^{**}, R^2 = .534, \sigma_u = 10.7$						

NOTE: See note to Table 3.14 for null hypotheses of tests.
* Significant at the 10 percent level.
** Significant at the 5 percent level.
*** Significant at the 1 percent level.

used to provide the baseline for measuring experimental responses. It should be noted that preenrollment hours is among the control variables and, as a consequence, one may regard the response as an increment to the *change* in hours from preenrollment levels, as well as components to be added to the current *level* for control families. Tests were carried out to see if the preenrollment level of hours should also be one of the variables that conditions response (that is, interacts with the treatment variable).

Table 3.22 Experimental Response in Husbands' Hours Worked per Week as Conditioned by θ, Blacks, Central Two Years and Last Two Years

	Coefficients of			Points on Response Curve		
	θ	θ^2	$\theta^* = -(\alpha_1/\alpha_2)$	$\theta = 2$	$\theta = 5$	$\theta = 8$
Quarters 3–10						
75–50	1.877	−.230	8.1	2.8	3.6	.3
.25S_2	−.564	.100	5.6	−.7	−.3	1.9
.20S_3	1.482	−.260	5.7	1.9	.9	−4.8
75–30	.395	.030	−13.2	.9	2.7	5.1
100–50	1.313	−.130	10.1	2.1	3.3	2.1
100–70	2.795	−.390	7.2	4.0	4.2	−2.6

$F_8(X) = 1.28$, $F_2(t) = 2.07$, $F_2(G) = 1.16$, $F_3(\theta^2) = 1.41$, $F_4(G, t) = 1.07$, $R^2 = .658$, $\sigma_u = 7.4$

Quarters 5–8						
75–50	1.566	−.195	8.0	2.4	3.0	.5
.25S_2	−.336	.073	4.6	−.4	.1	2.0
.20S_3	1.799	−.332	5.4	2.3	.7	−6.9
75–30	−.233	.137	1.7	.1	2.3	6.9
100–50	1.230	−.122	10.1	2.0	3.1	2.0
100–70	3.029	−.454	6.7	4.2	3.8	−4.8

$F_8(X) = 1.69$, $F_2(t) = 2.49^*$, $F_2(G) = .53$, $F_3(\theta^2) = 1.83$, $F_4(G, t) = 1.61$, $R^2 = .589$, $\sigma_u = 8.8$

Quarters 9–12						
75–50	3.442	−.502	6.8	4.9	4.7	4.6
.25S_2	−1.486	.260	5.7	−1.9	−.9	4.8
.20S_3	2.047	−.394	5.2	2.5	.4	−8.8
75–30	1.395	−.108	12.9	2.4	4.3	4.2
100–50	1.956	−.242	8.1	2.9	3.7	.2
100–70	4.003	−.636	6.3	5.5	4.1	−8.7

$F_8(X) = 1.61$, $F_2(t) = 2.88^*$, $F_2(G) = 4.35^{**}$, $F_3(\theta^2) = 2.98^{**}$, $F_4(G, t) = 2.23^*$, $R^2 = .569$, $\sigma_u = 10.5$

NOTE: See note to Table 3.14 for null hypotheses of tests.
* Significant at the 10 percent level.
** Significant at the 5 percent level.

The null hypothesis was accepted, and hence the response function was maintained in the same form as for participation and employment.

The estimated response is significant for whites for the first time. It is once more insignificant for blacks in the central period, but shows some significant parts in the last year. And the Spanish-speaking again show a significant patterned response. The qualitative nature of the response for the whites is the same as for the Spanish-speaking—negative and increasing with θ over the relevant range. The apparent response is, however, smaller for the whites in the middle year or middle two-year period. The black response curves are, as before, positive over most of the relevant

Table 3.23 Experimental Response in Husbands' Hours Worked per Week as Conditioned by θ, Spanish-speaking, Central Two Years and Last Two Years

	Coefficients of			Points on Response Curve		
	θ	θ^2	$\theta^* = -(\alpha_1/\alpha_2)$	$\theta = 2$	$\theta = 5$	$\theta = 8$
Quarters 3–10						
75–50	1.781	−6.15	2.9	1.1	−6.5	−25.1
.25S_2	−.748	.282	2.7	−.4	3.3	12.1
.20S_3	1.242	−.544	2.3	.3	−7.4	−24.9
75–30	.539	−.071	7.6	.8	.9	−.2
100–50	1.033	−.333	3.1	.7	−3.2	−13.0
100–70	2.275	−.877	2.6	1.0	−10.6	−37.9

$F_8(X) = 3.10^{***}$, $F_2(t) = 10.33^{***}$, $F_2(G) = 8.87^{***}$, $F_3(\theta^2) = 3.28^{**}$, $F_4(G, t) = 5.29$, $R^2 = .687$, $\sigma_u = 6.6$

Quarters 5–8						
75–50	.809	−.565	1.4	−.6	−10.1	−29.7
.25S_2	−.617	.280	2.2	−.1	3.9	13.0
.20S_3	1.300	−.592	2.2	.3	−8.3	−27.4
75–30	−.500	.027	18.5	−.9	−1.8	−2.3
100–50	.192	−.285	.7	−.8	−6.2	−16.7
100–70	1.501	−.877	1.7	−.5	−14.4	−44.1

$F_8(X) = 2.92^{***}$, $F_2(t) = 6.75^{***}$, $F_2(G) = 5.59^{***}$, $F_3(\theta^2) = 1.92$, $F_4(G, t) = 3.42^{**}$, $R^2 = .576$, $\sigma_u = 8.8$

Quarters 9–12						
75–50	4.508	−.896	5.0	5.4	.1	−21.3
.25S_2	−1.199	.370	3.2	−.9	3.2	14.1
.20S_3	3.045	−.719	4.2	3.2	−2.8	−21.7
75–30	1.463	−.177	8.3	2.2	2.9	.4
100–50	3.309	−.526	6.3	4.5	3.4	−7.2
100–70	6.354	−1.245	5.1	7.7	.6	−28.8

$F_8(X) = 2.46^{**}$, $F_2(t) = 4.62^{**}$, $F_2(G) = 6.86^{***}$, $F_3(\theta^2) = 4.23^{***}$, $F_4(G, t) = 4.02^{*}$, $R^2 = .620$, $\sigma_u = 8.3$

NOTE: See note to Table 3.14 for null hypotheses of tests.
* Significant at the 10 percent level.
** Significant at the 5 percent level.
*** Significant at the 1 percent level.

range although they do, in general, become smaller with increasing θ—particularly in the last year where several of the tests are significant.

Table 3.24 provides what may be a more convenient summary of the estimates. It evaluates the response for each of the six combinations of guarantee and tax rate, arranged in order of increasing breakeven levels for the three intervals, three races, and two levels of θ. The lower level

Table 3.24 Estimated Response in Hours Worked per Week Derived from Smoothed Response Surface, by Plan Generosity, All Three Years

Quarter	Response at Mean of $\theta\|M$			Response at 95th Percentile of $\theta\|M$		
	White	Black	Spanish-speaking	White	Black	Spanish-speaking
100–70 ($M = 1.43$)						
3–10	−1.6	5.0	−2.4	−7.6	1.9	−21.4
5–8	−1.2	5.1	−5.0	−8.6	0.8	−26.3
9–12	−4.3	6.3	7.2	−23.1	−0.4	−10.3
75–50 ($M = 1.50$)						
3–10	−1.9	3.7	−1.1	−7.2	2.6	−13.8
5–8	−1.2	3.1	−3.8	−7.2	2.0	−18.0
9–12	−5.5	5.9	5.0	−19.9	1.5	−7.8
50–30 ($M = 1.67$)						
3–10	−2.3	2.5	0.3	−6.9	3.3	−6.2
5–8	−1.1	1.1	−2.5	−5.8	3.3	−9.6
9–12	−6.7	5.5	2.7	−16.7	3.4	−5.4
100–50 ($M = 2.00$)						
3–10	−1.9	3.2	−2.1	−6.4	2.0	−13.9
5–8	−1.4	3.1	−4.9	−6.6	1.9	−17.6
9–12	−6.0	3.9	4.2	−18.9	−0.2	−8.2
125–50 ($M = 2.50$)						
3–10	−0.6	3.7	−0.4	−1.6	4.7	−3.8
5–8	−0.0	3.8	−3.1	−.6	3.7	−5.8
9–12	−3.8	4.0	7.1	−8.5	8.1	3.0
75–30 ($M = 2.50$)						
3–10	−3.8	4.0	0.4	−9.4	8.9	−3.6
5–8	−2.5	4.6	−2.1	−8.8	16.6	−2.1
9–12	−8.9	4.5	1.9	−14.3	1.3	−7.7

NOTE: Values of θ used for mean and ninety-fifth percentile are, respectively: 3.4, 6.4 for the first three plans; 4.5, 8.2 for the fourth plan; 6.7, 11.9 for the last two plans.

(first three columns) is the average θ for the appropriate breakeven level. The second is the estimated ninety-fifth percentile for θ given the breakeven level (derived as the mean + 1.65 times the standard deviation).

Taking the 100–50 plan as a pivotal example, one can note for whites a reduction of nearly two hours at the mean value of $\theta = 4.5$, ranging to $-6\frac{1}{2}$ at the extreme value. A smaller mean response is shown in the middle year, but a greater curvature produces a larger differential at $\theta = 8.2$. Taking thirty-five hours as an average level of work effort, this corresponds to a 4 to 5 percent reduction in the middle of the experiment; for the very poor, however, the reduction reaches toward 20 percent.

For blacks, there is an increase of two or three hours, which is not statistically significant. This would represent 6 to 8 percent of average hours, or a larger fraction of their average preenrollment value of thirty-two hours.

The Spanish-speaking show a reduction of about the same as whites at mean θ, but they have a more rapidly declining curve for higher values of θ. At the 100–50 plan, the range of response runs from minus two to minus thirteen hours or 4 to 40 percent. In the final year, the Spanish-speaking group shows substantial positive differentials for low and moderate levels of θ. It will be recalled from the previous section that the Spanish-speakers displayed lower-than-average unemployment in this range during the first year.

Higher tax rates appear to produce a slightly greater disincentive for Spanish-speakers, but less for whites; larger guarantees seem to provide less disincentive at higher levels, but more at lower ones. There is not, despite the statistical significance of patterns for whites and Spanish-speakers, a clear and consistent pattern across these groups.

The new element here is the emergence of a significant disincentive for the white sample. Since there was no significant response in participation and employment, we must expect that whites have adjusted their hours within the same levels of employment. This issue was explored using only the observations at quarters in which the husbands reported being employed. (Some may have zero hours, however, if they are on temporary layoff or are sick.) Here the model was altered to use the entire pool of panel data from quarters 1–12. For the three ethnic groups—white, black, and Spanish-speaking—there were, respectively, 12.6 percent, 14.6 percent, and 11.7 percent reductions in the sample on account of nonemployment. The remaining observations were used to fit a variance component regression model which utilized splines to capture the time variation in response and key control parameters.

The control model is quite elaborate and, beyond specifying its content and giving a brief rationale, it will not be discussed further. The basic objective (as before) is to provide as sensible and complete a set of controls as possible, so that the experimental response can be interpreted as a ceteris paribus partial relation. Eight parameters are used to provide a constant and coefficient of preenrollment hours. Each of these parameters varies continuously according to a cubic spline in experimental time, q. Three more define a periodic spline in months within years to allow for seasonal variation. A six-parameter, nonlinear function of normal income and normal wage rate is used, which is identical to the one used for the averaged regressions.[15] Finally, two parameters are allowed to control for the presence of ill health.

---

[15] This consists of S_c (see page 78) and two terms in predicted wages and income, excluding the time-persistent component.

The response function is simply related to the function used for the cross sections of averaged data. Two things are changed: the α_{22} and α_{23} terms are set equal to zero, that is, tax and guarantee do not interact with θ^2; and the remaining coefficients are continuous functions of time, through the multiplication of the corresponding variables by the terms of a cubic spline with "knots" at quarters 0, 4, 8, and 12. Hence we may write the experimental response as

$$X(G, t, \theta) = [\alpha_{11}(q) + \alpha_{12}(q)S_2 + \alpha_{13}(q)S_3]\theta + \alpha_{21}(q)\theta^2,$$

where q is experimental time in quarters, and the ordinates of $\alpha \ldots (q)$ at the knots 0, 4, 8, 12 are directly estimated. As before, two health interaction terms are included to isolate the comparison between healthy husbands.

Table 3.25 again shows the full details of a specimen regression on the data pooled over time. The variables which interact with the cubic spline are shown separately—the base value is for preenrollment time as an extrapolation from the curve fitted to quarters 1–12. To get the ordinate of the spline interactions at quarters 4, 8, or 12 simply add the appropriate increment. Other quarters can be calculated using the appropriately weighted sum of the "knot" values.[16]

The estimated response coefficients are shown in the first four rows of Table 3.26 for each of the ethnicities and at quarters 4, 8, and 12.[17] Subsequent rows show the response in hours $X(\theta)$ for appropriate mean and ninety-fifth percentile points, and the linear coefficients of θ modified to correspond to three additional guarantee–tax combinations. At the bottom are the relevant test and summary statistics from the three regressions. The expression, $F_{16}(X)$, is the overall test for the significance of $X(g, t, \theta)$; $F_4(t)$ tests for absence of a tax-rate coefficient, $\alpha_{13}(q)$; $F_4(G)$ corresponds to $\alpha_{12}(q)$; $F_8(t, G)$ combines the previous two hypotheses; and $F_4(\theta^2)$ tests the hypothesis that $\alpha_{21}(q) = 0$. Besides R^2 and the estimated standard deviations of residuals, $\hat{\sigma}_u$, the intraclass correlation $\hat{\rho}$ is shown for the two components of the residual. The separate component standard deviations—$\hat{\sigma}_\lambda$ for the time-persistent component and $\hat{\sigma}_\nu$ for the transient or "noise" component—are also indicated.

The expected emergence of a response for whites in terms of hours per week for employed males is evidenced here. Whites are the only group that shows a significant response—the blacks, once again, display a small and nonsignificant positive estimated response. The Spanish-speaking group is very similar to the blacks in this case. They show smaller but sta-

---

[16] See Chapter 14 for a detailed technical treatment of splines.

[17] Quarter 0 is not shown because it does not represent a fit to preenrollment data—it is, rather, an extrapolation from the curve fitted to the data in the first few quarters.

Table 3.25 Coefficients of Specimen Regression for Husbands' Hours Worked per Week Conditional on Employment, Whites, Quarters 1–12 (Pooled Data, Variance Components Estimation Procedure)

	Base Value $q=0$	Variables Interacting with Spline in Experimental Time			Variables Constrained to Time-Constant Effects			
		Increment Ordinates						
		$q=4$	$q=8$	$q=12$				
Constant	15.28	5.69	4.58	8.86	Seasonal spline	$m=0, 12$	0	
Hours at preenrollment	.165	−.133	−.115	−.164		$m=3$	−1.67	(.90)
	(.067)	(.078)	(.064)	(.078)				
θ	−1.833	1.568	.515	−.893		$m=6$	.46	(.63)
	(.736)	(.852)	(.693)	(.952)				
θ^2	−.020	−.056	−.011	.039		$m=9$	−1.00	(.95)
	(.048)	(.055)	(.045)	(.061)				
θS_2	2.897	−1.818	−.380	.325	Wage and income	$\hat{Y}/PL(n)$	3.57	(1.67)
	(.442)	(1.726)	(1.399)	(1.945)		$\hat{W}$	−.213	

θS_3	−5.801	4.508	2.457	−2.854
	(3.429)	(4.081)	(3.323)	(4.708)
$1/\hat{W}$	(1.004)
	25.51
	(6.98)
$\hat{Y}/\hat{W}$	.0805
	(.0471)
$(\hat{Y} - dy)/PL(n)$	−3.79
	(1.30)
$\hat{W} - d_w$	2.424
	(1.494)
Health	
H_1	−2.28
	(1.76)
H_2	−4.80
	(1.98)
$H_1 S_1$	0.0
	(2.31)
$H_2 S_1$	3.94
	(2.52)

NOTE: $R^2 = .059$ (weighted); $R_2 = .155$ (unweighted); $\hat{\sigma} = 12.12$; $n = 2886$; $\hat{\rho} = .168$; $F_{37,2848} = 4.78$. Estimated standard errors are in parentheses.

Table 3.26 Experimental Response in Husbands' Hours Worked per Week Conditional on Employment, by Ethnicity, Quarters 4, 8, and 12 (Pooled Data, Variance Components Estimation Procedure)

	White			Black			Spanish-speaking		
	4	8	12	4	8	12	4	8	12
α_{21}	−.076	−.031	.019	.086	−.008	.093	−.005	−.104	−.148
$\alpha_{12}*.25$	.269	.629	.805	−.091	−.051	.126	−.101	.311	.349
$\alpha_{13}*.20$	−.259	−.669	−1.731	.035	−.034	−.108	.118	−.109	.014
$\alpha_t(75$–$50)$	−.264	−1.318	−2.727	−.210	.303	−.613	.151	.688	1.043
$X(3.4)$	−1.7	−4.8	−9.1	0.3	0.9	−1.0	−.5	1.1	1.8
$X(6.4)$	−4.7	−9.7	−16.7	2.2	1.6	−0.1	0.8	0.2	0.6
$\alpha_t(100$–$50)$	.003	−.690	−1.922	−.301	.252	−.487	.050	.999	1.392
$X(4.5)$	−1.5	−3.7	−8.3	0.4	1.0	−0.3	0.1	2.4	3.3
$X(8.2)$	−5.1	−7.7	−14.5	3.3	1.5	2.2	0.1	1.2	1.5
$\alpha_t(75$–$30)$	−.005	−.649	−.996	−.245	.337	−.505	.033	.797	1.029
$X(6.7)$	−3.4	−5.7	−5.8	2.2	1.9	0.8	0.0	0.7	0.3
$X(11.9)$	−10.7	−12.1	−9.2	9.3	2.9	7.1	−0.3	−5.2	−8.6
$\alpha_t(125$–$50)$	.274	−.060	−1.117	−.392	.201	−.361	−.051	1.310	1.741
$X(6.7)$	−1.5	−1.8	−6.6	1.2	1.0	1.8	−0.6	4.1	5.0
$X(11.9)$	−7.5	−5.1	−10.6	7.5	1.3	8.9	−1.3	0.9	−0.2
Test and summary statistics	$F_{16}(X) = 3.15$*** $F_4(t) = 2.64$** $F_4(G) = 3.65$*** $F_8(t, G) = 2.28$** $F_4(\theta^2) = 3.11$**	$R^2 = .059$ $\hat{\sigma}_u = 12.1$ $\hat{\rho} = .17$ $\hat{\sigma}_\lambda = 5.0$ $\hat{\sigma}_\nu = 11.1$		$F_{16}(X) = .84$ $F_4(t) = .13$ $F_4(G) = .39$ $F_8(t, G) = .24$ $F_4(\theta^2) = 1.02$	$R^2 = .039$ $\hat{\sigma}_u = 11.2$ $\hat{\rho} = .100$ $\hat{\sigma}_\lambda = 3.5$ $\hat{\sigma}_\nu = 10.6$		$F_{16}(X) = 1.21$ $F_4(t) = .06$ $F_4(G) = 1.38$ $F_8(t, G) = 1.40$ $F_4(\theta^2) = 1.65$	$R^2 = .071$ $\hat{\sigma}_u = 10.2$ $\hat{\rho} = .050$ $\hat{\sigma}_\lambda = 2.3$ $\hat{\sigma}_\nu = 10.0$	

NOTE: $F_{16}(X)$ is the overall test for the significance of $X(g, t, \theta)$; $F_4(t)$ tests for the significance of a tax-rate coefficient, $\alpha_{13}(q)$; $F_4(G)$ corresponds to $\alpha_{12}(q)$; $F_8(t, G)$ combines the previous two hypotheses; and $F_4(\theta^2)$ tests the hypothesis that $\alpha_{21}(q) = 0$. The estimated standard deviation of residuals is $\hat{\sigma}_u$; $\hat{\rho}$ is the intraclass correlation of the two components of the residual. The separate component standard deviations are as follows: $\hat{\sigma}_\lambda$ is the time-persistent component, and $\hat{\sigma}_\nu$ is the transient or "noise" component.

* Significant at the 10 percent level.
** Significant at the 5 percent level.
*** Significant at the 1 percent level

tistically more reliable responses that are often positive. The white response is significant in all of its parts—particularly strongly in the guarantee (less than 1 percent) and in the curvature parameters. It should be noted that these tests are all joint tests for one or more sets of four spline ordinates. The ordinates determine a continuous function in q, and the null hypothesis is that the time-varying function is zero at *all* points—rejection does not assure that it is significantly different from zero at all points, only that it is different from a constant function at zero.

The R^2s are small relative to the ones obtained for the averaged data. That is both because there is relatively less systematic variation in hours for employed persons and also because much of the noise component is averaged out in the previous regressions. If, for example, the variance of γ_{it} were reduced to $\frac{1}{8}$ of its estimated value when two-year averages are used, the corresponding R^2 would be about .18 and the residual standard deviation would be halved. It may be worthy of note that the noise components have relatively similar variances among the ethnic groups, but that the distributions of the γ components have quite different dispersion.

As for the nature of the responses displayed by white employed husbands, it should be noted that the tax coefficient of θ increases sharply from the fourth quarter to the twelfth. Much of the substantial apparent disincentive shows up for tax rates greater than 50 percent and at the end of the experiment. The more moderate reductions at quarters 4 and 8, however, show a tendency to become large for the poorest (large θ) observations.

The appearance of responses in the form of hours differentials for employed whites raises an obvious question about how these adjustments are made. Overtime work is sometimes an optional choice, and if it is voluntary it presents one obvious way for lowered incentive to manifest itself. While no thorough analysis of the overtime data has been made, one simple exercise was carried out on a binary variable denoting the presence of overtime work during the survey week. This variable was used as the dependent variable in regressions identical to the ones reported in Table 3.9, except that the response was allowed to be nonhomogeneous in θ, and also to vary with preenrollment levels of weekly hours. The results for whites showed substantial excess proclivity for experimental husbands to work overtime at the low values of θ (at and around the breakeven level), but this proclivity declined quite rapidly to negative values at the higher end of the θ distribution. A sharp increase at quarter 12 in the magnitude of the tax-rate coefficient appeared in the overtime regression which parallels the one noted in Table 3.24. The evidence is therefore consistent with the notion that overtime is one category of work effort that is more readily adjusted and one that apparently is exercised by the white subsample.

The derivatives of selected response functions for hours are shown in Table 3.27. The evaluations are at the same points as those used for the employment functions in Table 3.20. In the average regression for the central two years, only the Spanish-speaking display the expected pattern of signs. There is, however, a negative income effect for blacks at the lower wage level. Consider the value for the (compensated) substitution coefficient for low-wage Spanish-speaking of -14.3. If one multiplies that by $-0.5/34 = -.015$ to get an elasticity measure equal to 0.2, one can conclude that a 5 percent change in the tax rate (equivalent to a 5 percent change in net wages) would produce a 1 percent change in total hours. That is not an inconsequential response, but neither is it extremely large relative to current notions about these elasticities. The elasticity is much smaller at the higher wage rate and is, of course, positive for the other two ethnicities. For whites, the conditional hours regression produces a more plausible set of derivatives (or elasticities) when evaluated at the twelfth quarter (see Table 3.28). The middle period, however, shows results quite consistent with the unconditional hours results shown in Table 3.27.

5. CONCLUSIONS AND INTERPRETATIONS

What can be concluded from the extensive analysis in this chapter about the labor supply of male family heads? The evidence is most consistent with the notion that there is a small, perhaps negligible, response

Table 3.27 **Derivatives of Experimental Response in Husbands' Hours Worked per Week for Two Levels of θ, by Ethnicity, Central Two Years**

	Typical ($\theta = 4.4$)			Poorer ($\theta = 6$)		
	White	Black	Spanish-speaking	White	Black	Spanish-speaking
$X(\theta)$	1.82	3.26	-1.90	-3.42	3.19	-5.79
$X'_\theta(\theta)$	$-.844$	.169	-1.897	-1.158	$-.247$	-2.963
$X'_G(\theta)$	6.082	-2.182	8.673	11.710	.864	22.656
$X'_t(\theta)$	-6.349	7.436	-25.335	-15.570	-2.340	-60.660
$\left.\frac{dX}{dG}\right|_{dt=0}$	.680	-1.00	-3.4468	2.446	-1.112	-1.048
$\left.\frac{dX}{dG}\right|_{dM=0}$	2.908	1.536	-3.994	3.925	$-.306$	-7.674
$\left.\frac{dX}{dt}\right|_{dG=0}$	4.454	5.273	-1.053	2.958	1.612	-13.252
$\left.\frac{dX}{dt}\right|_{dB=0}$	5.305	3.893	-5.388	5.404	.500	-14.300

Table 3.28 Derivatives of Experimental Response in Husbands' Hours Worked per Week for Two Levels of θ, Conditional on Employment, Quarters 4, 8, and 12

	Typical ($\theta = 4.4$)			Poorer ($\theta = 6$)		
	4	8	12	4	8	12
$X(\theta)$	−1.45	−3.64	−8.09	−2.70	−5.26	−10.85
$X'_\theta(\theta)$	−.661	−.964	−1.756	−.903	−1.063	−1.695
$X'_G(\theta)$	4.734	11.070	14.168	6.456	15.096	19.320
$X'_t(\theta)$	−5.698	−14.718	−38.08	−7.770	−20.070	−5.1930
$\left.\dfrac{dX}{dG}\right\|_{dM=0}$	1.885	3.711	−4.872	2.571	5.061	−6.645
$\left.\dfrac{dX}{dt}\right\|_{dG=0}$	2.763	−2.379	−15.603	6.678	−3.062	−24.81
$\left.\dfrac{dX}{dt}\right\|_{dB=0}$	3.392	3.746	−11.941	5.91	3.530	−19.050

on the part of such persons (a) if their wage rate is at least as high as the mean in this deliberately chosen, low-income sample ($2.50 per hour), (b) if they are of median age, and (c) if they are assigned to a moderate negative income tax plan, again within the context of this experiment. Those who have distinctly substandard wages, or who have been assigned to the highest levels of subsidization or tax rates, or who are markedly younger or older than average, have shown some tendency to reduce their labor supply by a significant amount. Even for these "extremes," however, the evidence does not indicate drastic reductions. Within the limits of experimental variation and the geographical limits of our samples—drawn from New Jersey and Pennsylvania urban areas—the elasticities appear to be quite small, even at the boundaries.

It may be useful to work through an example for a very poor white family head assigned to a plan providing an income guarantee of 100 percent of poverty, or $80 per week for a family of six. Assume further that the family was assigned to a 50 percent tax rate. An extremely poor family of this type, in terms of our sample, would have a normal income of $67 per week and the family head would earn at $1.50 per hour. This would imply a θ greater than 8, that the head would be more than 60 hours short of the breakeven level ($160). The benefit, before any reduction in work effort, would amount to $46.50 per week. In other words, a 70 percent increase in income and the existence of the experimental tax rate would reduce the net wage rate to $.75 per hour. According to the estimates in the preceding section, this male family head would, on average during the middle two years, work 6.4 hours less per week. That is, he would "spend" about 10 percent ($4.80) of that preresponse benefit on increased leisure.

After his response, the family would have 62 percent or nearly $42 per week more to spend on other items, including the "leisure" of the wife responsible for a family of 6. This is the nature of the labor-supply responses at the extreme of low earning power.

What findings support this conclusion? First, it will be remembered that the crudest comparisons between the central and experimental groups disclosed fewer significant differences than could normally be expected using purely random data. Moreover, the observed differences were small in absolute terms. Second, constrained estimates detected a significant response for the complete sample pooled over ethnic groups but also showed modest responses except for extreme situations. Age and education patterns in response, while not statistically significant, suggested that most of the response was at the extremes of age and in the small group of high school graduates. Third, the simple descriptive model applied to ethnic groups, time segments, and alternative labor-supply measures failed to disclose any consistent pattern of response and found few statistically significant differences among major groups receiving different treatments or having different earning capacities.

Finally, the analysis using θ displayed a consistent and sometimes significant tendency for the reduction in labor supply to accelerate among family heads with high θ values (that is, the poorest families), given the tax and guarantee. These are, of course, those who have the lowest wage rates or largest responsibilities relative to family income. The complex experimental function did not always display statistical significance but, when it did, the patterns displayed income and substitution effects of the expected sign but still of very moderate size.

The apparent ethnic differences which led to separate estimation remain largely unexplained. The fragmentation of the sample has seriously reduced the precision of individual estimates, but, as the findings for the Spanish-speaking group show, it is not impossible for significant, plausible, but moderate response patterns to be estimated. For the non-Spanish-speaking white group there were significant effects for hours, again modest and with plausible signs. The major puzzle remains for the black sample, where nonsignificant positive responses showed up for almost all the indicators of labor supply. Clearly this anomalous pattern of behavior requires further study than has been possible in this instance. The lack of significance, combined with the theoretical presumption of a reduction in desired labor supply, could yield a verdict of no effect for blacks. That conclusion itself is not very satisfying. What is there in "blackness" that might incline their behavior away from the so-called "rational" pattern expected and confirmed for the other groups?

One possible rationalization is that blacks may indeed respond about the same as others in terms of their equilibrium or preferred labor supply, but because of discrimination for jobs, extra jobs, or overtime, they are not able to achieve their desired level of work. Hence, the effect of the experiment for them may have been to bring their actual labor supply closer to a reduced equilibrium level with essentially no change in observed labor supply.[18]

While this explanation is admittedly ad hoc, as are most appeals to disequilibrium conditions, the fact that blacks had distinctly lower levels of employment and hours per week for employed heads relative to whites (both Spanish-speaking and non-Spanish-speaking) does lend some support to it. This line of reasoning also suggests how an income subsidy would affect behavior in periods of high general unemployment. If we assume that reduced labor demand forces many workers below their equilibrium level of work—and that is certainly the conventional assumption—then the observed response to the disincentive of a negative income tax will be correspondingly reduced. Any reduction in their desired level of work will be obscured by their inability to work as much as they would like.

If, of course, the disincentive were strong enough to induce complete withdrawal from the labor market, the demand constraints which keep workers from working as much as they want would not be a problem. But if there is one clear result from the analysis above, it is that complete withdrawal is not a major problem within the range of disincentives provided by this experiment. Despite the many remaining questions and anomalies there is simply no basis here for expecting large and drastic reductions in work from income subsidies with reasonable tax rates and guarantees.

REFERENCES

Avery, R. Forthcoming. The effects of welfare on experimental response. In *The New Jersey income-maintenance experiment*. Vol. 3. *Expenditures, health, and social behavior; and the quality of the evidence,* ed. H. W. Watts and A. Rees. New York: Academic Press.

Becker, G. S. 1965. A theory of the allocation of time. *Economic Journal* 85:493–517.

———. 1967. The allocation of time and goods over time. Mimeographed. Chicago: University of Chicago Department of Economics.

Cain, G. C., and Watts, H. W. 1973. *Income maintenance and labor supply: Econometric studies*. Institute for Research on Poverty Monograph Series. New York: Academic Press.

[18] This explanation was suggested by Professor Martin Bronfenbrenner in correspondence with Professor Albert Rees. He has kindly given permission to cite it here.

Garfinkel, I. Forthcoming. The effects of welfare on experimental response. In *The New Jersey income-maintenance experiment*. Vol. 3. *Expenditures, health, and social behavior; and the quality of the evidence*, ed. H. W. Watts and A. Rees. New York: Academic Press.

Goldberger, A. S. 1964. *Econometric theory*. New York: Wiley.

―――. 1967. Functional form and utility: A review of consumer demand theory. Systems Formulation, Methodology, and Policy Workshop Paper no. 6703. Madison: Social Systems Research Institute, University of Wisconsin.

Green, C. 1967. *Negative income taxes and the poverty problem*. Washington, D.C.: Brookings Institution.

Horner, D. 1972. The impact of negative taxation on the work effort of low income, male headed families. Ph.D. dissertation, University of Wisconsin, Madison.

Watts, H. W. 1969. Graduated work incentives: An experiment in negative taxation. *American Economic Review* 59:463–472.

―――. 1971. Midexperiment report on basic labor-supply response. Discussion Paper no. 98-71. Madison: Institute for Research on Poverty, University of Wisconsin.

Watts, H. W., and Mamer, J. Forthcoming. The problem of a spurious wage-rate response. In *The New Jersey income-maintenance experiment*. Vol. 3. *Expenditures, health, and social behavior; and the quality of the evidence*, ed. H. W. Watts and A. Rees. New York: Academic Press.

4 Labor-supply response of wives

Glen G. Cain
Walter Nicholson
Charles Mallar
Judith Wooldridge

The analysis of the employment experience of married women in the experiment provides a critical test of the work disincentive hypothesis—principally because married women exhibit more flexibility in market-work decisions than husbands, and there are more institutional arrangements to accommodate the short-term and part-time work associated with this flexibility. Let us briefly summarize our principal findings before discussing in more detail the reasons for the importance of this group and our methods of analysis.

1. SUMMARY OF RESULTS

In comparison with the amount of time spent in market work when the experiment began, the work time during the three years of the experiment increased for wives in the control group, and for wives in the experimental group first declined and then increased. This finding is illustrated in Table 4.1, which shows the changes in labor-force-participation rates over the three-year period. It should be noted that the lower level of participation for control wives at the beginning of the experiment is partially

Table 4.1 **Labor-Force-Participation Rates at Preenrollment and for Each Year (Percentages)**

	Preenrollment	First Year	Second Year	Third Year
Experimental wives (N = 450)	16.0	14.0	15.2	18.0
Control wives (N = 292)	13.4	16.3	16.5	18.5

SOURCE: Table 4.2.
NOTE: The observations are the survey week at preenrollment and, for each experimental year, are averages for the four survey weeks of the appropriate year.

explained by the sample stratification design, which allocated more of the families in the lowest income stratum to the control group. Earnings by wives were included in the measure of family income for this allocation.

The change in labor supply during the experiment was generally less for the wives in the experimental group than for those in the control group. Regression estimates of the work disincentive, analyzed in detail later in this chapter, show that differences in labor force participation between experimental and control wives are usually significant, but that differences in hours worked per week are usually not. Differences in earnings are generally similar to those for hours worked. The measured disincentive effects are greater during the first two years of the experiment, although the effects are consistently statistically significant only for the first year. The differences are smallest for the third year and are not statistically significant.

Among the nine different experimental plans—viewing the control group as one plan—the differences in labor supply are neither consistently significant nor consistently in agreement with the theoretically predicted direction of effect. Specifically, the average work experience was sometimes greater for wives in some of the more generous plans (those providing larger transfer payments) and in plans where the implicit tax rate on earnings was highest. Nevertheless, there was a general tendency for higher income guarantees (and thus eligibility for higher transfer payments) to lead to a larger work reduction. There was virtually no work response to tax rate variation. The expected value of the difference in labor supply—experimental minus control—is consistently less for black and Spanish-speaking wives than for white wives, although these ethnic differences are not always statistically significant.

The remainder of this chapter is divided into five sections. In Section 2 we discuss how the analysis of the work behavior of wives fits into the overall assessment of the experiment. Sections 3 and 4 introduce the basic models for measuring the work behavior of wives and present the statistical findings. Section 5 includes further analyses that check for various possible criticisms and qualifications regarding the statistical results of the basic models. The final section offers an interpretation of the findings.[1]

2. THE SPECIAL IMPORTANCE OF THE WORK BEHAVIOR OF MARRIED WOMEN

The importance of analyzing the labor-supply response of wives in the experiment rests on two arguments. First, if a nationwide income-maintenance law were to cover low-income, husband–wife families, wives can be expected to reduce their employment and earnings to a greater extent than do their husbands. Wives in low-income families are not working much in the first place, however, and thus even a sizable percentage reduction might (in terms of total hours reduced per year) be less than a smaller percentage reduction in work by husbands. Nevertheless, changes in the labor supply of wives are economically important in view of the upward trend in labor force participation among married women. Second, the labor-supply response of wives may be a particularly sensitive test of the effects of income maintenance in the context of a short-duration experiment. These two arguments are discussed in turn.

Long-Run Effects of Income Maintenance on Work by Wives

A reduction in market work by women, especially wives, in response to a program of income supplements is suggested by the widely held view that work decisions of wives are more discretionary than those of husbands. For social as well as economic reasons, wives face less constrained choices than do male heads of families regarding entering the labor force and working at full-time jobs. Of course, the other side of the coin is the presumed obligation of the wife to take responsibility for work in the home, particularly child care. This is not to deny that under various conditions of financial stress the wife may be compelled to work to maintain the family's economic viability, but women in families covered by an income-maintenance program would be under less pressure to seek market work.

---

[1] The characteristics of the New Jersey sample of wives and their labor-supply behavioral relationships are compared with other survey data for wives by Nicholson in Watts and Rees (Forthcoming: Chapter 13).

Some wives may be so strongly committed to working either in the home or in the market that no feasible changes in incentives would alter their choices. The question is whether a substantial proportion of wives are "on the margin"—willing and able to enter or leave the labor force when confronted with changes in income and in net wage rates that are large relative to the variation generated by normal market forces.

In the United States as a whole, the evidence is abundant that wives have considerable latitude for varying the amount of their market work:

1. Labor-force-participation rates of married women, husband present, have risen from 24 percent for the survey week in March 1950 to 41 percent in March 1971. During the same period, rates of wives with children under six years of age have increased from 12 percent to 30 percent (U.S. Department of Labor, 1973:165 and 168).
2. Although during the survey week of March 1971 the labor-force-participation rate of wives was 41 percent, about 51 percent of wives worked at some time during 1970 (Waldman and Gover, 1972:A-20).
3. Statistics are not readily available for the percentage of wives who work at some time during their married lives, but probably 80 percent or more do so.[2]
4. Among married women who were working in the survey week in 1971, about 29 percent were working less than full time, that is, less than thirty-five hours a week (Waldman and Gover, 1972:A-12).
5. Among married women who worked during 1970, about 60 percent worked less than a full year. (The 60 percent includes the small number of wives who worked a full year at a part-time job [Waldman and Gover, 1972:A-20].)
6. Evidence from a number of economic studies of the labor-force behavior of married women indicates a positive relation between their labor supply and wage rates, a negative relation with the income of their husbands, and a positive relation to general employment conditions in the market (Bowen and Finegan, 1967).

---

[2] Data for determining a "lifetime" labor-force-participation rate for married women are not readily available. The work history of women at any age prior to a "retirement" age necessarily understates the life time participation rate if there is any possibility that wives who have not worked might work at some time in the future. Data for older wives whose entire labor-force experience (if any) is behind them will understate the experience of younger wives, because of the powerful time trend of more work by wives. In one survey in 1960 of white married women aged 18–39 with husband present, it was found that 71 percent had worked at some time since married, and another 7 percent expected to work in the future (Whelpton, Campbell, and Patterson, 1966:107). Allowing for the trends over time of increasing work by wives, it is likely that 80 to 90 percent of currently married women will have worked at some time after their marriage by the time they reach age sixty.

7. Although the range of income elasticities and substitution (that is, "compensated" wage) elasticities for wives measured in these labor-supply studies is rather wide, the values of 1.0 and −.5 for the substitution and income elasticities, respectively, would not be far from the averages of these measures.[3] Elasticities of this size are quite large relative to the estimates for males, and they testify to the responsiveness of wives' labor supply to changes in prices and incomes.

All the trends noted above would be reinforced by data for the years since 1971, which was used because it was the last year of the experiment.

Wives thus exhibit a good deal of fluidity in labor-force behavior, and they have shown responses to economic incentives that are consistent with the theoretically predicted reduction in labor supply under an income-maintenance plan. It is important to point out, however, that the evidence just discussed pertains to wives in general, not specifically to wives in families that would be eligible to receive payments under an income-maintenance plan. There are several reasons for believing that the behavior of the latter would be different.

First, to receive income-conditioned transfer payments, a family's income must be low and/or a family's size must be large. A family with an employed husband is unlikely to be eligible when the wife is also working. The presence of a large number of children itself indicates a high relative value of the home work activities of the wife and implies a strong commitment to home work. In the experimental sample, less than 20 percent of the wives were working at any survey week before or during the experiment. Such low levels of market work mean simply that there is less "room" for decreases as a response to disincentives than would be the case if participation rates were equal to the national average of around 40 percent.

Second, poor families usually have available some type of public assistance to fall back on if work and earned income are not available or available only under onerous conditions. In particular, Pennsylvania and New Jersey (after 1968) provide public assistance to husband–wife families with dependent children and to unemployed parents. This alternative source of income can be expected to attenuate the disincentive effect of the treatment. Adults in destitute families, who would be forced to work in the absence of any public assistance, need not work; and the alternative of public assistance is obviously more relevant to control families than to

---

[3] See Table 9.2 in Cain and Watts (1973) for a summary of point estimates of income and substitution parameters for females.

treatment families—many of which were covered during the experiment by plans more generous and more accessible than public assistance.

We might point out that the presence of public assistance in the experimental setting interferes with the measuring of income and substitution parameters that might apply to all income strata. Public assistance is not very relevant to middle- and higher-income families; for this reason it is difficult to extrapolate to nonpoor families the experimentally measured income and substitution effects, which are contaminated by the presence of welfare. However, an experiment conducted within a welfare setting may provide an appropriate estimate of the effects of a negative income tax program that coexisted with public assistance.[4]

Third, several characteristics of the home and job environments of low-income families suggest other a priori speculations about the magnitude of the disincentive effect of income-maintenance plans. If available jobs are unattractive, the expected negative wage effect stemming from the increased tax on earnings may be larger than would be the case for wives in middle- and upper-income families. On the other hand, poor families have fewer market goods relative to home goods (including leisure), and this tends to reduce or moderate the work disincentive of income supplements, which permit recipient families to buy more leisure. The amounts of the transfer payments they typically receive are, after all, modest and their incomes still fall short of providing a standard of living enjoyed by middle-income families in the United States.

Short-Run Effects of the Experiment on Work by Wives

The flexibility in labor-force behavior of married women takes on a special importance in studying the labor-supply response in the experiment. The three-year duration is probably the most serious limitation of the experiment as a test of the labor-supply response to legislated (and quasi-permanent) income maintenance. The work behavior of male heads of households is constrained to the extent that they have firm attachments to jobs that require them to work a fixed number of hours per week on a full-year basis. In contrast, the freer options that women have for working less than full time and for working periodically—taking seasonal jobs, working for a period of one, two, or three years or less, and working in a variety of jobs at different times—*permits* wives to show a greater responsiveness to the experimental incentives.

---

[4] The Family Assistance Plan proposed by the Nixon administration would have operated in this manner—a negative income tax for the working poor alongside a modified continuation of the "old" welfare system.

In the New Jersey sample of wives, there was a high prevalence of short-term working arrangements. As Table 4.2 shows, among wives in the 742 husband–wife families who reported for at least eight of the thirteen quarters, the average labor-force-participation rate in the quarterly survey week was 16 percent. However, over the entire experiment, 40 percent of the wives reported being in the labor force during one or more quarters. (The figures for experimentals and controls were lower and higher, respectively, than these averages, but show the same disparity between the average labor-force-participation rates in the survey weeks and the rates over the whole period.) Among the 1031 husband–wife and female-headed families who reported for at least eight of the thirteen quarters, the average labor-force-participation rate in the survey weeks was 19 percent. In contrast, 44 percent of these women were in the labor force for one or more quarters during the three-year experiment. This evidence of considerable mobility regarding labor force participation implies, we suggest, a *potential* responsiveness to the widely varying net wage rates the wives could earn and the varying income supplements their families received.

3. THE STATISTICAL MODEL: GENERAL CONSIDERATIONS

The strategy for the statistical analysis of the experimental data on wives revolves around six major issues.

1. *The measures of the disincentive.* In the analyses presented below, the measures examined will be labor force participation (strictly speaking, the proportion of survey weeks in the labor force), hours of work, and earnings. We do not report the results of the analysis of employment rates, because labor force participation—defined as being either employed or unemployed—provided results similar to those using employment as a measure of labor supply.

2. *The parameterization of the treatment effect.* This will be some combination of the guarantees, implicit tax rates, amounts of transfer payments, and a variety of interaction effects in which the treatment is tested for interactions with various characteristics of the wives.

3. *The time period during which the work behavior is analyzed.* Essentially we have the choice of either the entire three-year period as a way of summarizing the experience, or selected subperiods. Subperiods can show the time pattern of responses, and one or several subperiods may be regarded as particularly representative of the operation of a legislated income-maintenance plan. Thus, the middle two years of the experiment

Table 4.2 Labor-Force-Participation Rates for the Whole Period and by Quarter

	The Three-Year Period	Quarter												
		0	1	2	3	4	5	6	7	8	9	10	11	12
Experimental group														
Number of wives	450	450	448	445	444	448	446	449	446	449	450	447	449	450
Percentage in labor force	38.4	16.0	13.4	13.3	12.8	16.3	14.4	14.9	16.1	15.6	16.9	17.9	19.2	17.8
Control group														
Number of wives	292	292	285	286	289	291	290	290	289	292	291	290	289	292
Percentage in labor force	41.8	13.4	16.1	15.0	17.3	16.8	16.9	16.9	15.9	16.4	18.9	18.6	19.0	17.5
Experimentals plus controls														
Number of wives	742	742	733	731	733	739	736	739	735	741	741	737	738	742
Percentage in labor force	39.8	15.0	14.5	14.0	14.6	16.5	15.4	15.7	16.0	15.9	17.7	18.2	19.1	17.6
Wives plus female heads	1031	936	922	919	989	994	1018	1015	1012	1026	1020	1013	1010	1017
Percentage in labor force	43.6	17.5	17.1	16.3	17.1	18.8	18.7	17.9	19.5	18.3	20.1	19.6	21.3	20.0

NOTE: The sample of wives is the so-called "continuous husband–wife sample," for which usable data exist for at least eight of the thirteen quarters. The number of wives in this table is 742 rather than 693 (which is the number used in the regression analysis to follow) because the latter data set was limited to observations with data for all variables used in the regressions.

might be considered to simulate the "normal" course of a legislated plan because the "start-up" and "wind-down" months of the experiment are ignored.

4. *The specification of independent variables other than the treatment variables.* As already mentioned, a number of characteristics of the wives may be thought to interact with the treatment. In addition, variables suggested by previous research should reduce the unexplained variation in the dependent variable and thereby improve the reliability of the estimates of the treatment effect. These nontreatment variables may also reveal useful information for their own sake. And, finally, including them in the statistical model offers some protection against their possible correlation with the treatment variables.

5. *The handling of missing data.* In the analysis presented below, missing data refer to families who dropped out of the sampling frame of husband–wife, continuously reporting families. Some families attrited, while others experienced family breakups.

6. *The formal statistical model and the estimation techniques.* This chapter presents several versions of two basic models. In the first model, an average measure of the wife's work behavior over an extended period of the experiment is the dependent variable. In the second model the entire thirteen quarters of information are pooled and a "components of variance" analysis is used.

Models of the labor supply of married women have usually been applied at a point in time in which the average or expected behavior of the sample is assumed to represent an equilibrium state. Thus, the current labor force participation or hours worked by the wife (or group of wives) is assumed to be a function of her normal wage-earning capacity, the normal wealth status of her family (in particular, the normal income of the husband), the implicit value of the home productivity of the wife (usually considered a function of the number and ages of the children, among other variables), and a variety of variables controlling for "tastes" or other specific demographic characteristics of the wife or group of wives under study.

A simple illustration of the traditional economic model of labor supply is instructive for an understanding of the statistical models presented below. In recognition of the experimentally induced changes in family incomes and in the net wage rates facing family members, the traditional model appears appropriate in its focus on income and wages. Moreover, the random assignment of families to treatment and control groups justifies ignoring other variables in the model for our pedagogic purpose here.

Let L_n be the labor supply of the wife during the time period, n, of interest, and Y be the equilibrium amount of family income if all family members worked the equilibrium amount of time (L^* for the wife) and if nonlabor income was similarly at its normal level. Let W equal the market rate the wife can earn. Let us assume, for convenience, that W and Y are related to L by a linear, additive model. Ignoring other variables and a stochastic error term, we have $L = a_0 + a_1 W + a_2 Y$. The variable Y is defined as $Y = Y_0 + WL^*$, where Y_0 is the amount of family income from all other sources except the wife's earnings. (In the simple case of a husband–wife family with no other working adults and no nonlabor income, Y_0 would represent the husband's earnings. The absence of *specific* terms for his wage rate and his market labor supply from the general model will be recognized as further simplifying abstractions from reality.) In this linear, additive model, a_1 is the substitution effect, expected to be positive, and a_2 is the income effect, expected to be negative.

A negative income tax will provide transfer payments, P, to families with incomes below the "breakeven level," according to the following formula:

$$P = G - tY, \text{ for } Y < G/t = \text{"breakeven,"}$$

where G is the income guarantee at zero earned income and t is the plan's tax (or offset) rate on family income. Since the net wage the individual faces is now $(1 - t)W$, the first term in the model is $a_1(1 - t)W$. When the transfer payments, P, expressed as $G - t(Y_0 + WL^*)$, are added to the family's income, the wife's labor-supply equation becomes

$$\begin{aligned} L_n &= a_0 + a_1(1 - t)W + a_2[Y_0 + WL^* + G - t(Y_0 + WL^*)] \\ &= a_0 + (a_1 + a_2 L^*)(1 - t)W + a_2[(1 - t)Y_0 + G] \\ &= a_0 + b_1(1 - t)W + a_2[(1 - t)Y_0 + G] \\ &= a_0 + b_1 W - b_1 t W + a_2 Y_0 - a_2 t Y_0 + a_2 G. \end{aligned} \quad (1)$$

Alternatively, we could write the equation in terms of P and t as:

$$L_n = a_0 + b_1 W - a_1 t W + a_2 Y_0 + a_2 P. \quad (2)$$

Since no allowance in the original model was made for differential responses to different *sources* of wage or income changes, it should not be surprising that in equation (1) the coefficients of W and tW are the same except for sign and the coefficients of Y_0, tY_0, and G are also equal in absolute value. In equation (2) the coefficients of Y_0 and P are similarly restricted and, furthermore, $a_2 = (b_1 - a_1)/L^*$. These restrictions are not in any serious sense imposed by theory, but are only reflections of our simplifying assumptions in applying one illustrative theoretical model. In any case, the restrictions can be relaxed and tested with the data.

Another result of the simplifying assumptions made in this pedagogic example is that the effects of t and G are linear. In the experiment, of course, there were eight permissible combinations of the three tax rates and four guarantee levels, and we are prepared to test for nonlinearities in the responses to these programs. Note that families with incomes above the breakeven level will not receive payments or face the experimental tax rates, but their work behavior may well be affected just by their being eligible for payments if their incomes were to decline.

Two other practical considerations may be mentioned briefly at this stage of the discussion of the basic model. First, the parameters of state welfare plans have been ignored, and ways of dealing with this are discussed later in this chapter. Second, traditional sources of data have not yielded satisfactory measures of normal wage, normal income, or "tastes" variables, and we are able to make only modest improvements in the measures of these nonexperimental variables.

There are, of course, several easily measured variables—such as the wife's age and education and the presence of children—which explain some of the variation in the labor-supply behavior of the wife. However, a simple and more powerful device for controlling for the basic determinants of labor supply is to include the preexperiment value of the labor-supply variable as an independent variable. The preexperiment values of labor-supply behavior will partly reflect the effects of the available explanatory variables and, in addition, are assumed to represent all other variables which are not satisfactorily measured, such as the normal income, normal wage, and taste variables.[5] These considerations are represented in equation (3), which is the basic model for the statistical analysis that follows.

$$L_n = F(\mathbf{X}_n, \mathbf{Z}_n, \mathbf{L}_{n-1}, \mathbf{T}_n, \mathbf{T}_n\mathbf{Z}_n) + \epsilon_n \qquad (3)$$

where
- L_n = a measure of labor supply for an individual at experimental time period n;
- $\mathbf{X}$ = a vector of "control" variables which are not presumed to interact with the treatment variables;
- $\mathbf{Z}$ = a vector of "control" variables, including proxies for normal income and wages, which may both interact with the treatment and have separate effects;
- $\mathbf{L}_{n-1}$ = a vector of preexperiment values of the dependent variables;
- $\mathbf{T}$ = a vector of treatment parameters;
- ϵ = a residual term which is assumed to be uncorrelated with the deterministic part of the right-hand side of the model (or, less restrictively, uncorrelated with $\mathbf{T}$ and $\mathbf{TZ}$).

[5] We also used the technique discussed in Chapters 2 and 14, of obtaining a "predicted" income and wage rate of the family members wherein the prediction is based on a regression of observed income and wages on available characteristics, but we do not report the results in this chapter.

4. THE APPLICATION OF THE BASIC MODEL: STATISTICAL RESULTS

The set of observations used in the regression analyses are the 693 households in the continuous husband–wife sample, except where specifically noted. The dependent variables are as follows: (a) the percentage of quarters in which the wife reported being in the labor force for the week surveyed in the respective quarterly interview; (b) the average hours worked by the wife as reported for those survey weeks; (c) average earnings of the wife as reported for those weeks. The first two dependent variables are the main variables reported. In Section 5, we report regressions with all welfare families excluded and regressions excluding all wives who were not in the labor force at any time during the experiment.

Discussion of the Treatment Variables

The treatment effect is specified in several functional forms. The most complete specification we use is nonlinear and involves eight categorical variables that uniquely define each of the eight income-maintenance plans.

One of two simple linear specifications we use involves a dummy variable, T, for experimental status and the guarantee and tax variables scaled as $G - .75$ and $t - .50$. Thus, the plan that guarantees 1.00 times the poverty standard for a given-sized family is assigned the value $G = .25$, and the plan that taxes earnings at 30 percent is assigned the value, $t = -.20$. This specification is written: T, t, G.

The second simple linear parameterization takes into account the zero values of the transfer payments and treatment tax rates for families above the breakeven level of income. It also uses three variables: (1) an experimental dummy; (2) a transfer payment, calculated as what the family would receive if the family's income remained constant at its preenrollment level; and (3) a tax rate, equal to the family's assigned tax rate when its preenrollment income lies below the breakeven level, and zero when its income is at or above the breakeven level. This specification is written: T, P, t'.

These basic formulations were also tried with a number of interactions with personal characteristics of the wives. The following (not all of which appear in the tables that follow) are indicative of the main types of interaction variables used:

BT = interaction of treatment status with black ethnicity
ST = interaction of treatment status with Spanish-speaking ethnicity

$(C < 6)T$ = interaction of treatment status with presence of children under six

$(HE)T$ = interaction of treatment status with husband employed

DT = interaction of treatment status with disability status of the wife or husband.

The two ethnic interactions permit an analysis of a number of hypotheses—some based on previous research and others on conjecture—about different experimental responses by ethnic group. If the treatment effects are in fact different for these groups, the disproportionate number of black and Spanish-speaking families in the sample can be reweighted when making projections for the country as a whole.

The interaction $(C < 6)T$ tests whether the disincentive effect will be stronger for wives with preschool children. The interaction DT is potentially important because the incidence of wives and husbands with health problems and disabilities was relatively high. The interaction variable defined as $(HE)T$ tests whether the labor supply of wives whose husbands are not working is different if they are covered by an income-maintenance plan. Previous studies have found that unemployment of the husband can be expected to have a positive effect on the wife's labor supply. This positive effect should, however, be smaller for wives in the experimental group because the negative income tax payments will make up for part of the income loss that comes from the husbands' unemployment.

The remaining independent variables in the regression models are listed in Table 4.3. They generally represent commonly used predetermined variables. The mean values of these independent variables are listed for the sample comprising the entire twelve quarters of the experiment. (The means for the groups of observations covering quarters 1–4, 5–8, 9–12, and 3–10 are not shown, but are all similar.)

Discussion of Independent Variables Other than Treatment Variables

A thorough analysis of the estimated relationships between the labor-supply variables and the independent variables used as control variables will not be reported in this chapter. Table 4.4 displays a representative set of regression results, and we shall comment briefly on them before discussing the experimental effects in detail. The dependent variable for Table 4.4 is the percent of quarters in the labor force during quarters 3 through 10, and the specification of the treatment is simply T, t, and G (that is, no distinction is made between families below and families above their breakeven income levels). The other independent variables listed

Table 4.3 Statistics of the Independent Variables, Quarters 1–12 Averaged

Variable	Definition	Sample Mean	Sample Standard Deviation
PART	Dummy variable, equals one if the wife is in the labor force	.163	.295
WHMNJ	Dummy variable, equals one if family head is white and they do not live in Scranton	.107	.309
BLTRSC	Dummy variable, equals one if family head is black and they live in either Trenton or Scranton	.059	.236
BLPP	Dummy variable, equals one if family head is black and they live in Paterson–Passaic	.085	.279
BLJC	Dummy variable, equals one if family head is black and they live in Jersey City	.193	.395
SPTRPP	Dummy variable, equals one if family head is Spanish-speaking and they live in either Trenton or Paterson–Passaic	.114	.318
SPJCSC	Dummy variable, equals one if family head is Spanish-speaking and they live in either Jersey City or Scranton	.101	.302
AGE	Wife's age in years	34.974	8.238
AMAX 25	Maximum of AGE-25 and 0	10.254	7.835
AMAX 45	Maximum of AGE-45 and 0	.599	2.021
EDUC	Wife's formal education in years	9.270	2.791
EMAX 8	Maximum of EDUC-8 and 0	1.922	1.658
EDUC 12	Dummy variable, equals one if EDUC is greater than or equal to 12	.263	.440
#K0–1	Number of children in the family between the ages of 0 and 1	.297	.405
#K2–3	Number of children in the family between the ages of 2 and 3	.449	.474
#K4–5	Number of children in the family between the ages of 4 and 5	.541	.507
#K6–15	Number of children in the family between the ages of 6 and 15	2.405	1.656
DIS H	Dummy variable, equals one if the husband has a health disability	.196	.336
DIS W	Dummy variable, equals one if the wife has a health disability	.191	.336
UNINC	Total family non-work-conditioned unearned income	1.754	5.713
#AD1618	Number of adults in the family between the ages of 16 and 18 not including the husband and wife	.375	.576

Table 4.3 (continued)

Variable	Definition	Sample Mean	Sample Standard Deviation
#AD > 18	Number of adults in the family older than 18 not including the husband and wife	.116	.386
AD1618 < 6	Dummy variable, equals one if #AD1618 is greater than 0 and there is a child less than six years old in the family	.129	.276
WEEKS	Number of weeks the wife was employed in the year preceding preenrollment	3.857	10.593
WRKPRE	Dummy variable, equals one if the wife was employed during the pre-enrollment survey week	.120	.325
FAMYXW	Total family earnings in dollars excluding the wife's, for the pre-enrollment survey week	88.746	49.095
T	Dummy variable, equals one for treatment families	.613	.487
t	Treatment tax rate $-.5$	.004	.104
G	Treatment guarantee as a fraction of the poverty level $-.75$	.083	.205

were used, with very few exceptions, in all regressions reported in this chapter.

PREEXPERIMENTAL LABOR-SUPPLY VARIABLES

The variables with the largest t-ratios, in this sense the most "powerful" predictors of labor force participation during the course of the experiment, are (a) whether the wife worked in the prior quarter, and (b) the number of weeks she worked in the year before the experiment began (variables 24 and 23, respectively, in Table 4.4). If the wife worked in the survey week in the preenrollment quarter, her labor-force-participation rate during quarters 3 through 10 is estimated to increase by 37 percentage points, and the t-ratio is nearly 11. For each week worked during the previous year, the wife's labor force participation increases by 0.4 percentage points.

It is instructive to examine the simple correlations among experimental—control status, work during the preenrollment survey week, and work at any time during the previous year. (These correlations are not shown in the table.) Work during the preenrollment survey and treatment

Table 4.4 Representative Regression Results for the Independent Variables, Quarters 3–10 Averaged

Independent Variable	Coefficient	Standard Error	Significance Level
1 WHMNJ	.022	.033	52.07
2 BLTRSC	.154	.043	.04
3 BLPP	.086	.038	1.90
4 BLJC	.007	.028	78.43
5 SPTRPP	−.011	.036	76.68
6 SPJCSC	−.029	.036	42.50
7 AGE	−.035	.013	.84
8 AMAX 25	.036	.014	1.30
9 AMAX 45	−.010	.007	15.32
10 EDUC	.011	.007	16.10
11 EMAX 8	−.018	.015	24.85
12 EDUC 12	.077	.036	3.30
13 #K0–1	−.047	.031	12.55
14 #K2–3	−.059	.033	7.13
15 #K4–5	−.024	.025	33.51
16 #K6–15	.006	.007	41.01
17 DIS H	.036	.030	23.54
18 DIS W	−.071	.029	1.26
19 UNINC	.002	.002	32.37
20 #OAD > 18	.048	.029	10.12
21 #AD1618	−.042	.024	7.98
22 AD1618 < 6	.071	.048	13.81
23 WEEKS	.004	.001	.01
24 WRKPRE	.372	.035	<.01
25 FAMYXW	.000	.000	99.93
26 T	−.018	.021	39.46
27 t	.117	.093	20.67
28 G	−.085	.050	9.12
29 CONSTANT	.937	.328	.42

NOTE: N = 693. Significance levels are stated in percentages and apply to a two-tail test for the probability percentage of a Type I error in rejecting the null hypothesis of no effect. For definitions of variables, see Table 4.3.

status are positively correlated, although the r is small, .056. As noted earlier, the design of the sample called for placing more *relatively* high income families into the treatment status, and wives' earnings were included in family income. That this correlation does not imply that treatment wives were *generally* more likely to work is indicated by the very low correlation between treatment status and work at some time last year: $r = -.003$. There was, however, as might be expected, a strong positive correlation between working last year and working in the survey week: $r = .69$.

SITE–ETHNICITY VARIABLES

The first six variables measure various combinations of the sites of the experiment and ethnic groups. All coefficients should be interpreted in reference to white wives living in Scranton, the omitted category. The hypothesis that all site–ethnicity coefficients are equal to zero is rejected at better than a 99 percent confidence level. As with all significance tests for a set of dummy variables, we used the F-test for the collection of site–ethnicity variables. The labor-force-participation rates of white wives living in the three New Jersey cities were $2\frac{1}{2}$ percentage points higher, but this difference is not statistically significant. The tendency for black wives to work more is clearly evident, a fact which makes the finding of no significant treatment disincentive for black wives all the more impressive. It is not true for black wives, as was apparently the case for black husbands, that the absence of any treatment disincentive can be partly explained by a decline in labor supply on the part of the control group. The Spanish-speaking wives worked somewhat less than white wives, but the differences are not significant. The entire set of site–ethnicity dummy variables was statistically significant at less than a 1 percent level.

AGE-OF-WIFE VARIABLES

The age variables are defined by a linear term, and by linear splines that branch at ages twenty-four and forty-five. Although the set of three age variables is significant at a 2 percent level, the participation rates are fairly flat over the age range between twenty-four and forty-five, but significantly higher for younger wives and significantly lower for older wives.

EDUCATION VARIABLES

Education is specified linearly, with a spline at eight years and a dummy variable at twelve years of schooling. The effect is significant (at the 2 percent level), but the quantitative size is small except for the positive effect measured at twelve years of schooling or more. The relation between labor force participation and schooling is essentially flat below and above twelve years, but the jump at twelve years is large—with the rates practically doubling, from 7 percent at ten years of schooling completed to nearly 14 percent for twelve years. The flat relation below twelve years is not expected, but it may reflect the fact that the major effects of education are already captured in the preexperiment levels of labor supply. Furthermore, the income truncation for this sample and the scarcity of wives with more than twelve years of schooling are two reasons why the flat (slightly negative) relation beyond twelve years does not pose any meaningful conflict with the general finding in the literature of a strong positive relation between work by wives and their education.

PRESENCE OF CHILDREN AND OTHER FAMILY MEMBERS

The effects on labor force participation of having children are negative, as expected. The number of children at ages zero to one, two to three, and four to five has a negative effect, and for some reason the effect is largest for the number of children ages two to three. Perhaps the effect of children aged zero to one is already reflected in the variables measuring the preexperiment labor supply of the wife. The coefficient for children aged six to sixteen is essentially zero. The coefficient for children aged sixteen to eighteen is negative, but this appears offset by the larger positive effect for the interaction of children aged sixteen to eighteen and children under six years of age, although both variables have only moderately low levels of significance. The presence of other adults has a positive effect, which may be interpreted as their representing substitutable home-workers more than substitutable market workers vis-à-vis the wife.

HEALTH VARIABLES

The health terms have the expected effects: health impairment of the wife has a significant negative coefficient, and a health impairment of the husband—which has been shown in other chapters to reduce his employment—has an insignificant positive effect on the wife's work. The available measures of health or disability status are far from perfect. Being based on the interviewees' statements, they may be biased in that persons who are not working, for whatever reason, might claim health problems. Our interpretation of the regression coefficients is correspondingly tentative.[6]

---

[6] If some individuals claimed ill health disability simply as an excuse for not working when they were, in fact, reasonably healthy, the inclusion of such a health variable could attenuate the measured treatment response. If there is a simple correlation between health status and treatment status, however, the failure to include a health measure would also bias the results. In order to overcome these problems and obtain an accurate measure of the extent of health disabilities in our sample, an index was constructed of health disability based on the type, magnitude, and frequency of the illnesses reported. The heads and spouses were classified "unhealthy–mild disability," "unhealthy–serious disability," or "healthy" at the second and sixth quarters, when the probing health questions were asked. Since most of the unhealthy individuals were judged to have a serious health disability and the serious-versus-mild distinction is necessarily arbitrary, this distinction was dropped in the variable used in

It turns out that when health information was obtained at the time of the second quarterly interview, about 20 percent of all wives in husband–wife families had some health disability and 18 percent were "seriously" disabled. Although these figures, especially the latter, seem high, it is reassuring that the percentages were almost the same for experimental and control groups. This was no longer true one year later, at the time of the second health interview, however. For the entire sample, there were still 20 percent disabled, and the percentage seriously disabled had declined a little—to 15.5. The control families, however, showed a slight improvement (17 percent disabled and 14 percent seriously disabled), implying that the experimentals had a relative deterioration in health status.[7]

FAMILY INCOME NOT INCLUDING THE WIFE'S EARNINGS

Two variables are defined to measure conventional income effects in this regression. One is income from nonlabor sources—negligible for poor people except for work-conditioned income, which is excluded. The second is labor earnings from other members of the family (principally the husband's earnings) at the time of preenrollment. These effects are essentially zero, given the presence in the model of preexperiment labor supply variables.

In summary, the relations measured between the control variables and labor supply are weakly compatible with previous research. They significantly reduce the unexplained variance in the dependent variable and thus improve the efficiency of the estimates of the treatment. The R^2 for the regression displayed in Table 4.4 is .32, meaning that a third of the variation is explained. Finally, the independent variables serve to control for the sample stratification that allocated more higher-earnings families to the treatment groups than to the controls. As noted above, these results generally were found throughout our regression analyses. We shall therefore discuss the treatment effects alone in the remainder of the chapter.

---

our analysis here. Our health variable was constructed from this index as follows. (1) If the individual had a health disability at both the second and the sixth quarters, the health variable was assigned a value of 1. (2) If the individual had a health disability at only one of the two quarters, the health variable was assigned a value of $\frac{1}{2}$. (3) If the individual was healthy at both, the health variable was assigned a value of 0. (See Chapter 9 for a detailed discussion of health in relation to labor-supply response.)

[7] This anomaly is pursued in Chapter 9.

Treatment Effects on Labor Force Participation and Hours Worked

Our presentation of treatment effects consists mainly of a series of tables showing the regression coefficients of treatment variables and, at times, the regression-estimated effects of treatment variables calculated at their mean values.

OVERALL EXPERIMENTAL EFFECTS

Table 4.5 shows the effects of the experimental treatment for the central two years of the experiment, quarters 3–10. The first set of columns shows the effect of the treatment when no distinction is made between those below and those above their breakeven points (the first of the two simple linear specifications discussed at the beginning of Section 4). The second set of columns shows the experimental effect when zero values for transfer payments and tax rate are assigned families above their breakeven points (the second of the two simple linear specifications discussed at the beginning of Section 4). Table 4.6 shows analogous results for the whole three years of the experiment.

As was mentioned in the initial summary, the differences in labor force participation between experimentals and controls usually are statistically significant, but differences in hours worked usually are not. The quantitative size of the measured disincentive appears "small" or "moderately large" depending on one's standard of comparison and on the sample subgroup chosen to illustrate the difference. For example, the decrease in labor-force-participation rates for all wives in the experimental group was 3 to 4 percentage points. However, for white wives the difference is a sizable 8 to 9 percentage points, offset by the near-zero differences for black and Spanish-speaking wives. The decrease in hours was on the order of fifty hours over the year for all treatment group wives, 100 hours for white wives, and near zero for black and Spanish-speaking wives. The decrease in annual earned income among wives (not shown)—either as directly measured or when based on the hours reduction—amounts to around $100 for the sample as a whole, $200 for white wives, and around zero (sometimes even positive) for black and Spanish-speaking wives.

While these measures of reductions in work appear small in absolute size, they amount to sizable percentage reductions, given the very low values of labor supply that characterize wives in this sample of poor families. A decrease of fifty hours, for example, amounts to a 20 percent decrease relative to the average annual total of around 250 hours per year that was observed for the control group wives during the course of the

Table 4.5 Labor-Supply Response of Wives, Regression Results, Quarters 3–10

	T, G, t Specification				T, P, t' Specification			
	All	White	Black	Spanish-speaking	All	White	Black	Spanish-speaking
Labor-force-participation rate[a]								
Linear specification	−.043 (8)				−.034 (6)			
Interaction with ethnicity[b]	−.040 (11)	−.094 (<1)	.002 (11)	.005 (29)	−.027 (<1)	−.081 (9)	−.002 (3)	.047 (5)
Hours per week[c]								
Linear specification	−.94 (22)				−.75 (16)			
Interaction with ethnicity[b]	−.76 (48)	−1.94 (7)	.51 (26)	−.80 (78)	−.61 (2)	−1.82 (28)	.60 (1)	.05 (21)

NOTE: The T, G, t specification includes an experimental dummy; and attributes their assigned guarantee and tax rate, scaled as $G - .75$ and $t - .5$, to all experimentals. The T, P, t' specification denotes experimental status by an experimental dummy; but only attributes guarantee and tax-rate values to families below their breakeven at preenrollment (those above breakeven are assigned the same zero values for transfer payment and tax rate as controls). The numbers in parentheses are F-tests. For "all," these are F-tests on the collection of variables that define the treatment in the context of a full regression which includes all other independent variables. The F-test for the white subgroup applies to the three treatment variables and tests for an overall effect significantly different from zero. For the other two ethnic groups, the significance levels are with respect to differences from the white subgroup—*not* to a zero ethnic treatment effect. The F-test significance levels shown in parentheses are the probability percentages that we are making the Type I error of rejecting the null hypothesis that all treatment coefficients are equal to zero.

[a] Control group mean = .17.
[b] "All" here is a weighted average of the three ethnic effects.
[c] Control group mean = 3.83.

Table 4.6 Labor-Supply Response of Wives, Regression Results, Quarters 1–12

	T, G, t Specification				T, P, t' Specification			
	All	White	Black	Spanish-speaking	All	White	Black	Spanish-speaking
Labor-force-participation rate[a]								
Linear specification	−.040				−.031			
	(12)				(11)			
Interaction with ethnicity[b]	−.031	−.086	.002	.009	−.010	−.075	.025	.071
	(14)	(<1)	(12)	(26)	(1)	(10)	(3)	(4)
Hours per week[c]								
Linear specification	−1.02				−.88			
	(12)				(19)			
Interaction with ethnicity[b]	−.90	−2.02	.20	−.54	−.90	−1.94	.33	−.65
	(33)	(5)	(26)	(60)	(1)	(17)	(<1)	(14)

NOTE: The treatment specifications and the F-statistics in parentheses are described in the note to Table 4.5.
[a] Control group mean = .17.
[b] "All" here is a weighted average of the three ethnic effects.
[c] Control group mean = 3.86.

experiment. This 20 percent reduction in hours was similar to the percentage reductions in labor-force-participation rates and earnings.

ALL TREATMENT PLANS

Tables 4.7 through 4.10 show the estimated effects on labor force participation and hours worked for each of the eight experimental plans, with and without an interaction term for ethnicity and treatment status, for four periods of the experiment. Table 4.7 shows the central two years of the experiment (quarters 3–10). Tables 4.8 through 4.10 show the years of the experiment separately. The control variables shown in Table 4.4 were used in the regressions reported in these tables. The reference group for all the coefficient entries is the control group of wives. Each table shows results for all wives in the experimental group and then for white wives in the experimental group. Estimates for experimental wives in the other two ethnic groups may be obtained by adding the ethnicity–treatment interaction coefficient listed at the bottom of the appropriate table.

These tables bear out two conclusions stated in the Section 1 summary. There are no significant effects among the eight treatment plans, and even the signs of the effects do not always agree with our theoretical expectations. Thus, not all cells show negative responses—even for white wives, for whom the overall response was most consistently negative. Not all families, of course, should be expected to be sensitive to the plans. In addition to "random" shocks from a variety of sources that will divert wives and other family members from responding to the treatment, some families became eligible for and received benefits from public assistance. During these periods they received no benefits from their experimental plan. Other families had incomes above the breakeven level; and the guarantee and tax rates may not have had any relevance.

Among the plans with the same guarantee level, the effect of higher tax rates is often positive, but here the theoretically expected sign is inherently ambiguous. Because the amount of transfer payments declines as the tax rate increases, holding family income and family size constant, the negative effect on the labor supply of the higher tax rate is offset by the stimulus to work from reduced payments. Apparently the income effect dominates. In results reported in later tables we in fact show a negative tax rate effect when the amount of transfer payment income is held constant. This negative effect is quantitatively small, however, and insignificant.

It is noteworthy that the theoretical expectation of a negative income effect is supported when the guarantee is examined. The experimental plans have been arranged in Tables 4.7 through 4.10 to facilitate compari-

Table 4.7 Labor-Supply Response for Each Experimental Plan, Including Ethnicity Interactions, Quarters 3–10

	Experimental Plan (Guarantee–Tax Rate)							F-test Significance Level (Percentage)
	50–30	75–30	50–50	75–50	100–50	125–50	75–70	100–70	
Labor-force participation[a]									
All wives	.008	−.033	.006	−.017	−.063	−.065	.009	−.024	(53)
White wives[b]	−.032	−.074	−.038	−.059	−.103	−.104	−.030	−.064	(41)
Hours worked per week[c]									
All wives	−.62	−1.27	.82	−.26	−1.36	−1.30	.62	−.54	(77)
White wives[d]	−1.44	−2.12	−.01	−1.04	−2.11	−2.03	−.21	−1.33	(77)

NOTE: The F-test significance level is the probability percentage that we are making the Type I error of rejecting the null hypothesis that all coefficients are equal to zero.

[a] Control group mean = .163.
[b] The ethnicity–treatment interaction shift coefficient is .069 for blacks and .083 for Spanish-speaking.
[c] Control group mean = 3.83.
[d] The ethnicity–treatment interaction shift coefficient is 1.81 for blacks and .79 for Spanish-speaking.

Table 4.8 Labor-Supply Response for Each Experimental Plan, Including Ethnicity Interactions, Quarters 1–4

	Experimental Plan (Guarantee–Tax Rate)							F-test Significance Level (Percentage)
	50–50	75–30	50–50	75–50	100–50	125–50	75–70	100–70	
Labor-force participation[a]									
All wives	.025	−.079	−.023	−.045	−.032	−.082	−.004	−.036	(12)
White wives[b]	−.002	−.107	−.052	−.073	−.058	−.107	−.027	−.062	(13)
Hours worked per week[c]									
All wives	.08	−2.54	−.32	−.152	−.67	−2.31	.53	−.76	(7)
White wives[d]	−.63	−3.29	−1.09	−2.28	−1.39	−3.01	−.16	−1.51	(10)

NOTE: The F-test significance level is the probability percentage that we are making the Type I error of rejecting the null hypothesis that all coefficients are equal to zero.
[a] Control group mean = .151.
[b] The ethnicity–treatment interaction shift coefficient is .034 for blacks and .077 for Spanish-speaking.
[c] Control group mean = 3.70.
[d] The ethnicity–treatment interaction shift coefficient is 1.14 for blacks and 1.65 for Spanish-speaking.

Table 4.9 Labor-Supply Response for Each Experimental Plan, Including Ethnicity Interactions, Quarters 5–8

	Experimental Plan (Guarantee–Tax Rate)								F-test Significance Level (Percentage)
	50–50	75–30	50–50	75–50	100–50	125–50	75–70	100–70	
Labor-force participation[a]									
All wives	−.015	−.018	.038	−.013	−.059	−.066	−.008	−.013	(54)
White wives[b]	−.049	−.054	.000	−.024	−.095	−.101	−.042	−.050	(51)
Hours worked per week[c]									
All wives	−1.63	−.43	1.29	.59	−.54	−1.10	.39	−.16	(86)
White wives[d]	−2.39	−1.23	.44	−.20	−1.32	−2.61	−.47	−.94	(81)

NOTE: The F-test significance level is the probability percentage that we are making the Type I error of rejecting the null hypothesis that all coefficients are equal to zero.

[a] Control group mean = .157.
[b] The ethnicity–treatment interaction shift coefficient is .061 for blacks and .077 for Spanish-speaking.
[c] Control group mean = 3.56.
[d] The ethnicity–treatment interaction shift coefficient is 2.13 for blacks and .40 for Spanish-speaking.

Table 4.10 Labor-Supply Response for Each Experimental Plan, Including Ethnicity Interactions, Quarters 9–12

	Experimental Plant (Guarantee–Tax Rate)							F-test Significance Level (Percentage)
	50–50	75–30	50–50	75–50	100–50	125–50	75–70	100–70	
Labor-force participation[a]									
All wives	−.001	−.050	−.020	−.018	−.064	−.028	.026	.012	(85)
White wives[b]	−.047	−.099	−.072	.068	−.112	−.075	−.020	−.037	(68)
Hours worked per week[c]									
All wives	−1.88	−1.87	.44	−.51	−2.09	−.99	.26	.40	(75)
White wives[d]	−2.64	−2.66	−.38	−1.30	−2.86	−1.75	−.49	−.37	(82)

NOTE: The F-test significance level is the probability percentage that we are making the Type I error of rejecting the null hypothesis that all coefficients are equal to zero.

[a] Control group mean = .182.
[b] The ethnicity–treatment interaction shift coefficient is .092 for blacks and .086 for Spanish-speaking.
[c] Control group mean = 4.32.
[d] The ethnicity–treatment interaction shift coefficient is 1.54 for blacks and 1.24 for Spanish-speaking.

son of different guarantees holding the tax rate constant. Such an examination reveals quite a consistent negative relation between labor supply and the size of the guarantee.

To the extent that we adhered to a prior belief about the magnitude of the tax rate effects, we expected them to dominate income effects on the basis of the following presumptions:

1. That income effects are biased down and substitution effects are biased up in a short-duration experiment[8]
2. That among wives and other "secondary" workers in husband–wife families substitution effects are larger than income effects in elasticity terms—an empirical proposition based on previous research[9]
3. That among poor families substitution effects dominate income effects—although this presumption usually refers to the effects of *increases* in wage rates and not to tax-induced decreases. (The familiar textbook discussion of the "backward-bending" supply curve of labor often shows a forward sloping segment at low wage levels, implying that the negative income effect is dominant only at middle and upper ranges of wage rates.)

We should be reminded, however, that the specification of the eight treatment variables in these tables is not even close to being statistically significant. The null hypothesis that all eight coefficients are zero cannot be rejected, except for the first year of the experiment, and even there the significance level is between 7 and 13 percent.

TREATMENT EFFECTS MEASURED BY THREE VARIABLES, T, t, AND G

The three-variable parameterization of the treatment imposes the same marginal tax *effect* across the four assigned rates: 0 (for the control group), .3, .5, and .7. Similarly, the same guarantee *effect* is imposed over the five values of the guarantee as a fraction of the poverty line: 0 (for controls), .50, .75, 1.00, and 1.25. A discontinuity in the level of labor-supply response as between treatment and control groups is allowed for by means of the treatment-status dummy variable.

One advantage of this parameterization is its economy. It permits simple linear effects to measure the tax-rate and guarantee variables. One

---

[8] See Metcalf's discussion of this issue in Watts and Rees (forthcoming: Chapter 16) for a discussion of this presumption.

[9] For a discussion of this proposition and the evidence to support it see Chapter 9, and especially Tables 9.1 and 9.2, of Cain and Watts (1973).

can argue that the plans are sufficiently difficult to understand—particularly given changes in family size, fluctuations in income above and below breakeven, and welfare—that accurate qualitative responses and approximately accurate quantitative measures are better achieved by a simpler functional form. A single anomalous cell value may be "corrected" by averaging it with better-behaved adjacent cells. In the previous specification, each plan was represented by a single cell value, independent of other cells; but in a three-year experiment it is perhaps unrealistic to expect to measure consistent and systematic responses to eight plans by a relatively small sample per plan.

A disadvantage of this three-variable parameterization is that it retains the assumption that families (or wives) in the experimental group are expected to respond to positive tax and guarantee variables even when they are above the breakeven level of income. Although we are keenly interested in knowing whether families above the breakeven level will respond, their behavior may cloud the interpretation of tax and guarantee effects.

Regressions for quarters 3–10 are shown in Tables 4.11 through 4.14—Table 4.11 for all wives, and Tables 4.12 through 4.14 for each ethnic group, in which each treatment variable is allowed to interact with ethnicity.[10]

Several findings are brought out in these tables. The disincentive observed for all wives (Table 4.11) is primarily attributable to white wives and stems mainly from the guarantee (or income) effect. The experimental dummy variable is also negative, but is never statistically significant in these tables. The tax effect is usually positive, but the "pure" tax effect obtained after neutralizing the income effect is sometimes negative and always quantitatively small.

The treatment interaction coefficients for black and Spanish-speaking wives are seldom statistically significantly different from those for their white counterparts, and their estimated responses are near zero. The disincentive with respect to labor-force-participation rates is more statistically significant than hours. The disincentive effects for white wives for each of the three years are similar (not shown) although a larger statistical significance is achieved for the first year. For black and Spanish-speaking wives, the treatment effects are positive as often as negative for the last two years of the experiment (also not shown), but none of the interaction treatment variables are jointly statistically significant relative to the additive treatment variables, T, t, and G, which reflect the white group.

[10] Similar regressions for the whole experimental period are reported in Watts and Rees (1973: Chapter BIIIa).

Table 4.11 Labor-Supply Regression Coefficients and Predicted Effects by Plan, All Wives, Quarters 3–10

	Labor-Force Participation[a]		Hours Worked per Week[b]	
	Coefficient	Significance	Coefficient	Significance
Treatment variable				
T	−.015	(50)	−.31	(65)
t	.087	(38)	3.97	(18)
G	−.112	(4)	−2.51	(12)
$t + G$	−.025		1.46	
T, t, G		(8)		(22)
	Predicted Effects by Experimental Plan			
Experimental plan				
50–30	−.004		−.47	
50–50	.013		.32	
75–30	−.032		−1.10	
75–50	−.015		−.31	
75–70	.002		.48	
100–50	−.043		−.94	
100–70	−.026		−.15	
125–50	−.071		−1.57	

NOTE: T = treatment dummy; t = tax rate assigned to the experimental families, scaled as $t - .5$; G = guarantee level assigned to the experimental families, scaled as $G - .75$; $t + G$ = the pure or compensated tax effect. Since t includes a positive tax effect (inducing more labor supply) and a negative income effect, adding the G effect to t isolates the "pure" tax effect.

Significance levels in parentheses refer to the probability percentage that we are making the Type I error of rejecting the null hypotheses that the individual variables $T, t,$ and G are zero or that (in the last row) all three coefficients are equal to zero.

[a] Control group mean = .163.
[b] Control group mean = 3.83.

TREATMENT EFFECTS MEASURED BY THREE VARIABLES, T, P, AND t'

In this specification of the treatment variables, shown in Tables 4.15, 4.16, and 4.17, treatment families with incomes above the breakeven level are assigned the same zero values of transfer payment, P, and tax rate, t', as controls and are distinguished from the controls only by an experimental dummy, T. This model of behavior may be described briefly as one in which only families with incomes below the breakeven level at the beginning of the experiment are assumed to respond to treatment payments and, implicitly, the guarantee. The experimental dummy allows

Table 4.12 Labor-Supply Regression Coefficients and Predicted Effects by Plan, White Wives, Quarters 3–10

	Labor-Force Participation[a]		Hours Worked per Week[b]	
	Coefficient	Significance	Coefficient	Significance
Treatment variable				
T	−.037	(27)	−.65	(51)
t	.150	(29)	4.58	(32)
G	−.229	(1)	−5.16	(3)
$t + G$	−.070		−.58	
T, t, G		(1)		(7)
All		(11)		(48)
Predicted Effects by Experimental Plan				
Experimental plan				
50–30	−.012		−.28	
50–50	.020		.64	
75–30	−.069		−1.57	
75–50	−.037		−.65	
75–70	−.005		.27	
100–50	−.094		−1.94	
100–70	−.062		−1.02	
125–50	−.151		−3.23	

NOTE: See note to Table 4.11.
[a] Control group mean = .163.
[b] Control group mean = 3.83.

this restriction on the behavior of the above-breakeven families to be relaxed with respect to the general status of being experimentals, but not with respect to the specific treatment parameters. Such a sharp discontinuity in response at the breakeven level is not realistic, but it has the virtue of simplicity. (At the end of this section we discuss the effects of relaxing this restriction and permitting the T, t, and G effects to interact with the "distance" from the breakeven level of income.)

The assumption of no response above the breakeven level is contingent upon the current measure of income being a good representation of families' "normal" or "expected" income. In fact, we do not have reliable information about their expected incomes, and our use of the preenrollment value of income is justified mainly on grounds of expediency. Preenrollment income is, of course, unaffected by the experiment, and is specific to the individual family. We also tried a model (not shown) in which we used the treatment family's "predicted" income (predicted on the basis of

Table 4.13 **Labor-Supply Regression Coefficients and Predicted Effects by Plan, Black Wives, Quarters 3–10**

	Labor-Force Participation[a]		Hours Worked per Week[b]	
	Coefficient	Significance	Coefficient	Significance
Treatment–ethnicity interactions				
BT	−.001	(47)	.39	(49)
Bt	−.003	(46)	3.60	(88)
BG	.001	(5)	.47	(13)
"Pure" tax effect, Bt + BG	.008		4.07	
B(T, t, G)		(11)		(26)
All		(11)		(48)

	Predicted Effects by Experimental Plan	
Experimental plan		
50–30	−.004	−.45
50–50	−.004	.27
75–30	−.001	−.33
75–50	−.001	.39
75–70	−.001	1.11
100–50	.002	.51
100–70	.002	1.23
125–50	.005	.63

NOTE: See note to Table 4.11.
[a] Control group mean = .163.
[b] Control group mean = 3.83.

preexperiment variables) to determine a P value, but our results were similar to those shown below.[11]

Although the T, P, t' specification (shown in Tables 4.15, 4.16, and 4.17 for two measures of labor supply and several time periods) achieves about the same results as the specification of $T, t,$ and G, the differences are worth mentioning. First, the quantitative estimates of the disincentive are slightly smaller for T, P, t'; second, the statistical significance is slightly greater. As in the earlier specifications, the effect on labor force participation is statistically significant, but the effect on hours is not. In the regressions with all wives (no ethnic interactions) shown in Table 4.15, the treatment effects taken as a whole are significant at the 11 percent level or lower for all periods except quarters 9–12.

[11] Regressions using this predicted income series are reported in Watts and Rees (1973: Chapter BIIIa).

Table 4.14 Labor-Supply Regression Coefficients and Predicted Effects by Plan, Spanish-speaking Wives, Quarters 3–10

	Labor-Force Participation[a]		Hours Worked per Week[b]	
	Coefficient	Significance	Coefficient	Significance
Treatment–ethnicity interactions				
ST	.054	(36)	−.51	(94)
St	.088	(79)	2.63	(81)
SG	−.049	(21)	−1.15	(36)
"Pure" tax effect, St + SG	.039		1.48	
S(T, t, G)		(29)		(79)
All		(11)		(48)
Predicted Effects by Experimental Plan				
Experimental plan				
50–30	−.013		−.75	
50–50	.029		−.22	
75–30	−.001		−1.04	
75–50	.017		−.51	
75–70	.035		.02	
100–50	.005		−.80	
100–70	.023		−.27	
125–50	−.007		−1.09	

NOTE: See note to Table 4.11.
[a] Control group mean = .163.
[b] Control group mean = 3.83.

The ethnic breakdown shown in Tables 4.16 and 4.17 produces much greater statistical significance. This is not surprising, since the ethnic interactions reveal a sizable disincentive for white wives and, by contrast, near-zero or positive labor-supply responses for black and Spanish-speaking wives. In Table 4.15 we see that the "average" disincentives for all wives at the thirty, fifty, and seventy tax plans amount to 15, 20, and 25 percent reductions in labor force participation during quarters 3–10, and slightly less over the whole period (quarters 1–12). Note that a decline of −.03 represents a 20 percent reduction on a base level of labor force participation of .15. "Average" refers to the labor-supply reduction predicted for each tax plan when the family is assigned the mean transfer payment received by all experimental families. The average payment actually differs according to tax plan and ethnic group, but a single mean

Table 4.15 Coefficients of Treatment Variables and Predicted Effects, by Experimental Status and Payment Level and Tax Rate below Breakeven, Various Time Periods

		Coefficients of Treatment Variables				Predicted Effects by Tax Rate[a]		
	Quarters	T	P	t'	Joint Significance	30	50	70
Labor force participation	3–10	.014 (65)	−.027 (8)	−.042 (50)	(6)	−.026	−.034	−.042
	1–12	.004 (90)	−.026 (9)	−.018 (76)	(11)	−.027	−.031	−.035
	1–4	−.012 (69)	−.035 (3)	.002 (97)	(1)	−.046	−.046	−.046
	5–8	.024 (47)	−.032 (7)	−.040 (55)	(10)	−.020	−.028	−.036
	9–12	.004 (91)	−.010 (59)	−.035 (63)	(67)	−.017	−.024	−.031
Hours worked per week	3–10	.64 (50)	−.75 (14)	−.140 (46)	(16)	−.53	−.81	−1.09
	1–12	.19 (83)	−.64 (18)	−.86 (62)	(19)	−.71	−.88	−1.05
	1–4	−.52 (54)	−.90 (5)	.34 (84)	(2)	1.32	−1.25	−1.19
	5–8	1.00 (32)	−.71 (18)	−1.48 (46)	(29)	−.15	−.45	−.75
	9–12	.24 (84)	−.25 (69)	−2.04 (38)	(47)	−.62	−1.03	−1.44

NOTE: T = treatment dummy; P = weekly transfer payment based on preenrollment income; t' = tax rate if preenrollment income was below breakeven, zero otherwise. The coefficient of P in the table is the regression coefficient of P multiplied by the $27 overall sample mean value of P. Tax rate effect estimates are the sum of the coefficients of T and P (evaluated at the overall sample mean), plus the coefficient of t' multiplied by the appropriate tax rate. Significance levels are in parentheses.

[a] These effects are predicted using the coefficients of the treatment variables.

Table 4.16 Coefficients of Treatment Variables and Predicted Effects, by Experimental Status and Payment Level and Tax Rate below Breakeven, with Ethnicity Interactions, Quarters 3–10

	Coefficients of Treatment Variables				Predicted Effects by Tax Rate[a]			
	T	P	t'	Joint Significance	30	50	70	Joint Significance
Labor force participation								
White	−.047 (29)	−.003 (88)	−.063 (48)	(9)	−.069	−.081	−.094	(<1)
Black	.102 (3)	−.065 (2)	−.078 (91)	(3)	.014	−.002	−.018	(<1)
Spanish-speaking	.050 (24)	−.079 (2)	.151 (18)	(5)	.021	.047	.057	(<1)
Hours worked per week								
White	−.46 (74)	.15 (79)	−3.03 (26)	(28)	−1.22	−1.83	−2.43	(2)
Black	3.16 (8)	−2.23 (<1)	−.67 (55)	(1)	.73	.59	.46	(2)
Spanish-speaking	.34 (75)	−1.89 (5)	3.20 (20)	(17)	−.69	.05	.69	(1)

NOTE: T = treatment dummy; P = weekly transfer payment based on preenrollment income; t' = tax rate if preenrollment income was below breakeven, zero otherwise. The coefficient of P in the table is the regression coefficient of P multiplied by the $27 overall sample mean value of P. (The values of P for each ethnic group were not used in calculating the ethnic responses.) Tax rate effect estimates are the sum of the coefficients of T and P (evaluated at the overall sample mean), plus the coefficient of t' multiplied by the appropriate tax rate. Significance levels are in parentheses. The joint significance levels are for all nine treatment–ethnicity interaction variables.

[a] These effects are predicted using the coefficients of the treatment variables.

Table 4.17 Coefficients of Treatment Variables and Predicted Effects, by Experimental Status and Payment Level and Tax Rate below Breakeven, with Ethnicity Interactions, Quarters 1–12

	Coefficients of Treatment Variables				Predicted Effects by Tax Rate[a]			
	T	P	t'	Joint Significance	30	50	70	Joint Significance
Labor-force participation								
White	−.047	−.001	−.054	(10)	−.064	−.075	−.086	(1)
	(26)	(97)	(52)					
Black	.088	−.064	.003	(3)	.025	.026	.026	(1)
	(4)	(1)	(98)					
Spanish-speaking	.026	−.075	.186	(4)	.007	.004	.081	(1)
	(36)	(3)	(11)					
Hours worked per week								
White	−.61	.27	−3.20	(17)	−1.30	−1.94	−2.54	(1)
	(63)	(63)	(20)					
Black	2.57	−2.20	−.05	(7)	.35	.34	.34	(1)
	(10)	(<1)	(40)					
Spanish-speaking	.12	−1.64	4.67	(14)	−.10	.86	1.81	(1)
	(96)	(6)	(8)					

NOTE: T = treatment dummy; P = weekly transfer payment based on preenrollment income; t' = tax rate if preenrollment income was below breakeven, zero otherwise. The coefficient of P in the table is the regression coefficient of P multiplied by the $27 overall sample mean value of P. (The values of P for each ethnic group were not used in calculating the ethnic responses.) Tax rate effect estimates are the sum of the coefficients of T and P (evaluated at the overall sample mean), plus the coefficient of t' multiplied by the appropriate tax rate. Significance levels are in parentheses. The joint significance levels are for all nine treatment–ethnicity interaction variables.

[a] These effects are predicted using the coefficients of the treatment variables.

value is used to achieve standardization. The average reduction in hours for the three tax plans is somewhat larger, but these are not statistically significant except for quarters 1–4. The reduction predicted for white wives in Tables 4.16 and 4.17 is quite large, however, around 50 percent in both participation and hours for both periods. For black and Spanish-speaking wives, the changes in labor supply are more often positive than negative.

The coefficient of the amount of transfer payment, P, is consistently the most significant treatment variable, which agrees with the finding of greater significance of the G treatment variable in previous tables. However, the t' effect (unlike the t effect) is almost always negative, which implies that the "pure" or compensated tax effect has the theoretically expected negative sign, a result that was not clearly shown by the earlier formulation. For all wives together (Table 4.15) the experimental dummy, T, is never significant. When ethnicity is taken into account (Tables 4.16 and 4.17), T is significant for black wives, and the effect is positive and large: 10 percentage points for the central two years and 9 percentage points over the whole period. This positive T effect for black wives is, however, offset by a P effect that is large and negative; so their overall predicted response to coverage by the plans was close to zero.

Treatment Effects on Earnings

The regression results with earnings as a dependent variable closely parallel the regression analyses with labor force participation and hours as dependent variables. The treatment effect is negative and, measured as a percentage reduction, is about the same size as for hours or labor force participation. The statistical significance of this negative treatment effect on earnings is somewhat less than was found for labor force participation and about the same as in the regressions with hours as the dependent variable.

Earnings are defined as reported earnings during the survey week and may be assumed to represent the product of a wage rate times the number of hours worked in the survey week. Any treatment effect on earnings that is not already measured in the effect on hours must stem, aside from errors in the data, from an effect on wage rates. There is no strong theoretical presumption for a treatment effect on wage rates; plausible arguments may be advanced for both positive and negative effects.

On the one hand, coverage by an income-maintenance plan may have a positive effect on the wage rate a person earns in the long run as a consequence of increased investments in human capital stimulated by the added income. Even in a short-run situation like the three-year experiment, the income transfers and income security afforded may permit the recipient—particularly a secondary worker in a family—to search longer and more effectively for jobs that pay more, have higher fringe benefits, and offer other advantages. On the other hand, participation in an income-maintenance plan may induce a negative effect on wage rates because the need for money is lessened. Thus, recipients may choose jobs that offer nonpecuniary advantages, such as more pleasant work, *at the cost of a lower wage*—assuming such jobs are accessible. Consider, for example, jobs in which the pay is based strictly on output. Workers covered by a negative income tax who are paid on a piece-work basis might well work with less intensity and effort, since any loss in earnings is partly offset by income supplements. Such examples of a negative "treatment" effect on earnings are interesting because they show how the effect on "labor supply" might show up not in fewer hours or quantity of effort but rather in less intensity or "quality" of effort. Nevertheless, we believe that there is, on balance, less theoretical justification for observing a treatment effect on earnings than on hours worked or labor force participation. In addition, there is reason to believe, as we have already seen, that earnings were measured less accurately than hours or labor force participation.

During the experiment, most wives reported zero earnings in any given survey week. However, earnings per week, averaged over the entire experiment, is nonzero for 40 percent of the wives—who worked at some time during the experiment. Overall, the mean amount of earnings reported for a survey week for those who worked was $8.16, implying an average wage rate of $2.13 per hour.

In the interest of economizing on the presentation of regression results, we show the regressions for all wives only, for quarters 3–10, and for two specifications of the treatment effects. A set of accompanying results for hours shows the similarity of the treatment effects for these two dependent variables. The coefficients, significances, estimated effects, and percentage changes are reported. It should be noted that two preexperiment labor-supply variables were used in these regressions. In regression I, the wife's labor force status during the week prior to enrollment in the experiment is the control for her preexperiment labor supply; in regression II, this control is provided by a dummy variable defined as 1 if the wife worked either during the year before *or* during that preenrollment week.

As shown in Table 4.18, the effect of the treatment variables on earnings is similar to their effect on hours worked. In regression I for the T, P, t' specification, the percentage reduction in earnings and hours is 22 to 24 percent for the 50 percent tax plan with the mean transfer payment. For reasons not clear to us, there are two changes in these same treatment effects, $T, P,$ and t', in regression II. The statistical significance of the

Table 4.18 **Earnings and Hours Worked Regressions, Coefficients of Treatment Variables for Two Measures of Preexperimental Labor Supply, Two Treatment Specifications, Quarters 3–10**

	T	P	t'	Joint Significance	T	G	t	Joint Significance
Dollar earnings per week[a]								
I. Wives working at preenrollment	1.97 (24)	-1.30 (27)	-4.94 (36)	(15)	-.23 (88)	-7.30 (5)	5.43 (44)	(21)
II. Wives working at preenrollment or year before	3.56 (10)	-1.89 (9)	-5.21 (25)	(6)	.85 (58)	-8.49 (3)	6.49 (36)	(16)
Hours per week[b]								
I. Wives working at preenrollment	.70 (46)	-.66 (16)	-1.94 (31)	(10)	-.39 (56)	-2.37 (15)	2.61 (39)	(31)
II. Wives working at preenrollment or year before	1.38 (15)	-.92 (6)	-2.07 (29)	(4)	.06 (93)	-2.87 (8)	3.04 (32)	(31)

NOTE: For the difference between the two treatment specifications, see note to Table 4.5. Significance levels are in parentheses.
[a] Control group mean = 8.16 dollars.
[b] Control group mean = 3.83 hours.

treatment effects is much higher, but the percentage reduction is shown to be lower—12 percent for earnings and 15 percent for hours. As with previous regression results for the T, t, G and T, P, t' specifications, the predicted effects for each plan could be calculated and displayed, but this does not seem necessary at this point.

The Effects of Other Interactions with the Experimental Treatment

As noted earlier in this chapter, a great many personal and family characteristics can be expected to interact with the experimental treatments in affecting labor supply. Ethnicity has already been given a good deal of attention. Here we report (without showing tables) the results of the treatment interactions with the presence of preschool children, with the health status of the wife and husband, and with the employment status of the husband.

Of these, only the husband's health status showed a statistically significant effect. The health status of the wife was insignificant in its treatment interaction on the wife's labor supply, and the coefficient had an unexpected sign; unhealthy wives worked more if they were in the treatment group than if they were in the control group. The presence of children under six also had the "wrong" sign in its treatment interaction, but the coefficient was small and statistically insignificant. Clearly, a priori expectations were that the combination of income supplements and high marginal tax rates on earnings would encourage wives with poor health and with preschool children to stay home. These expectations were not upheld. The treatment interaction with the husband's employment status had no consistent effect on the wife's labor supply, although the theoretical prediction is that the pro-work effect of the income loss (stemming from the husband's unemployment) should be less for the treatment group because increased transfer payments will cushion the impact of the income loss.

5. ADDITIONAL RESULTS USING VARIOUS OTHER SAMPLES AND MODELS

In this section we take some initial steps in the extended effort necessary to test the robustness of the basic findings presented above. First we test whether the intrusion of the welfare system and subsequent "loss" of both treatment and control families to the public assistance rolls have distorted our findings about the effect of the experiment. Our expectation is that the presence of welfare families in our sample should produce a downward bias in the measured disincentive effect. Second, we test whether a statistically significant disincentive with respect to hours shows up if we pool the cross-sectional observations over time and if we eliminate from our sample those wives who report the modal value of zero hours worked.

Regression Results Excluding Welfare Recipients

The inclusion of welfare families may be expected to understate the disincentive of the income-maintenance plan for the following reason. Nonworking families among both experimental and control groups are potentially eligible for, and have a potential incentive to apply for and receive, public assistance. However, nonworking experimental families, particularly those in the generous plans, may well forego public assistance which probably carries some stigma and involves some transaction costs. Such experimental families will not be working much and yet are not on welfare. Families in the control group, with similar tastes and under similar circumstances, do not have this favorable alternative to welfare. A systematic selection mechanism between experimental and control families is at work, therefore, allocating more control families that earn and work the least onto the welfare rolls. This selection process is revealed in our data, but it turns out not to be pronounced. The nonwelfare sample had only a slightly larger fraction of experimental families than did the original sample (65.8 percent versus 61.3 percent).

By eliminating welfare families, defined as families receiving welfare payments for more than two quarters, we expect to eliminate disportionately more of the nonworking control families than of the nonworking treatment families. For this reason we expected to see a larger treatment disincentive. This larger disincentive appeared in our data, but its size was also inconsequential. Moreover, the treatment effect was more *positive* among the sample of black wives.[12]

After-the-fact rationalizations may be made, but the lack of a stronger treatment disincentive for the nonwelfare sample is both surprising and reassuring with respect to the robustness of the earlier results. Perhaps even in experimental families, the adults who found themselves in a situation where they could not work much, if at all, were likely to apply for the quasi-permanent benefits of welfare (which, let us remember, might include medical and other benefits not provided by the experiment).

Regarding the ethnic differences, it is possible that white families in the

---

[12] Regressions for the nonwelfare families are reported in Watts and Rees (1973: Chapter BIIIa).

control group looked upon themselves as more "permanently poor" than nonwhite controls, that whites were more knowledgeable about obtaining welfare benefits, and that they found it easier to get on welfare than nonwhites. These differences may, of course, reflect the differences in the administration of welfare between Scranton, Pennsylvania, with an almost totally white population, and the three New Jersey sites. Finally, the New Jersey welfare program covering male-headed families was begun after the experiment was under way and sharply cut back before the three-year duration of the experiment had expired. Under these circumstances, we might expect an incomplete adjustment and response to the program.

We conclude that the measurement of the treatment effect with our sample is not sensitive to the inclusion or exclusion of welfare families. This is not to say that the same experimental–control comparisons would have emerged had there been no welfare system. All states, however, have some form of welfare; and the setting in which any legislated negative income tax plan might be administered is also likely to be a setting in which some public assistance alternative is available. For this reason, we believe the results presented in Section 4 for the full sample are more relevant than the results with the nonwelfare sample.

Results Using Pooled Data, Including a Focus on Wives with Some Labor-Force Attachment

The model underlying all the previous regression analyses is based on a single period as a unit of time for which we have one labor-supply observation per wife. The observation is some average measure of labor supply for this time period. An alternative specification, which is briefly presented below, exploits the fact that for each wife we have as many as twelve observations, one for each quarterly interview. The potential number of observations for the full sample of 693 continuously reporting husband–wife families is, therefore, 8316. A great deal more precision can be achieved for the estimated parameters of the labor-supply function, and the time pattern—including treatment–time interactions—can be estimated. Each observation is not, of course, "independent," and an estimation procedure which accounts for the dependence of residuals for each replication per wife is therefore used.

With a larger number of observations available, we are able to estimate a treatment response not only for all wives, but also for the wives who worked at some time during the three-year period. We can then estimate an hours-of-work function that is conditional upon the decision to participate in the labor force. By this means, we avoid having to fit the regression only to a set of observations in which the largest number of wives is those with zero hours worked, and the minority distributed at much lower densities in an irregular pattern over the positive domain.

Our results, shown in Table 4.19, yield no significant treatment effects. The results for wives who worked at least one week are not qualitatively different from those for all wives, and the former are even less statistically significant. We suggest two reasons for this null finding. One may simply be more errors in measurement concerning hours relative to labor force participation. A second is that in this model, the wife's decision about labor supply is exercised after she has chosen to enter the labor force, and she may typically face institutional constraints on her choice of the number of hours to work.

Table 4.19 Effects on Hours Worked for Two Preenrollment Employment Statuses, Pooled Regressions, Quarters 1–12

	All Wives	Wives Employed at Least One Survey Week	Wives Employed at Time of Observation
	Predicted Effects		
Experimental plan			
50–30	−1.14	−1.33	−1.80
50–50	−.15	.25	−1.01
75–30	−1.63	1.94	−1.72
75–50	−.64	−.36	−.93
75–70	.34	1.22	−.14
100–50	−1.13	−.98	−.85
100–70	−.14	.60	−.06
125–50	−1.62	−1.59	−.77
	Regression Coefficients		
Treatment variable			
T	−.64(30)	−.36(82)	−.93(54)
t	4.95(7)	7.90(27)	3.94(57)
G	−1.96(19)	−2.46(57)	.33(94)
$t + G$	2.99	5.44	4.27
T, t, G	(9)	(70)	(87)
Number of cross section units	693	221	205
Number of time periods	12	12	varies across individuals
Number of pooled observations	8316	2652	1124
rho	.485	.368	.396
Control group mean	3.86	12.11	28.58

NOTE: For definitions of T, t, G, and $t + G$ see note to Table 4.11. The model was estimated as a two components of variance model assuming an intraindividual correlation, rho. The independent variables were identical to those used in previous sections, with the addition of three sets of time variables (an experimental-time cubic spline, a calendar-time cubic spline, and a period cubic spline). Significance levels in parentheses.

Interactions between Treatment Variables and Income

An implicit interaction between treatment variables and income was presented earlier for models in which the treatment specification was T, P, and t'. Because the value of the tax rate is "switched off" when the family's preenrollment (or, alternatively, predicted) income is above the breakeven level, the treatment effects interact with income. The disincentive was more significant when this specification was used than with other specifications but, although this is consistent with a larger effect for lower-income families, the only thing it tells us specifically is that families below their breakeven are more affected by the experiment.

More direct evidence of the interaction between treatment effects and income levels was provided by regressions in which the variables T, t, and G were interacted with the fraction that predicted family income is of the family's breakeven level. These interaction specifications were used in two regressions where the proportion of weeks in the labor force (or labor force participation) was the dependent variable. They showed mixed results. In a linear specification, the entire set of interactions was significant at only the 14 percent level, and many of the specific coefficients were difficult to rationalize. Somewhat greater statistical significance was achieved by using quadratic interaction terms that permitted the treatment effect to decrease as income levels approached breakeven. In the quadratic form, the variables for white wives and for black wives were both jointly significant at less than 2 percent levels of significance, and it is noteworthy that the squared terms were significant at the 8 percent level. Finally, all the treatment-interaction variables were jointly significant at the 5 percent level.[13]

6. AN INTERPRETATION OF THE FINDINGS

The basic findings concerning the labor supply of married women in the experiment may be summarized as follows: statistically significant disincentives are shown with respect to labor force participation for white wives, but not for black and Spanish-speaking wives. Hours worked and earnings were also less for the white and Spanish-speaking wives in the treatment group than they were for their control counterparts, but these differences were not statistically significant. There were no significant dif-

---

[13] These results are discussed in more detail in Watts and Rees (1973: Chapter BIIIa). Major attention is given to the treatment–income interaction in Chapter 3 of this volume, on the labor supply of husbands, and Chapter 6, on the labor supply of the family. Further investigation along these lines for the wives would be worthwhile.

ferences in hours or earnings between black experimental and control wives, and the observed difference was usually positive in favor of the experimental group. Whenever significant negative differences occurred in these tests, the size of the reduction was large in percentage terms—amounting to a 30 or 40 percent reduction for white wives. However, the base was so low that the absolute amount of reduction was not large—3 to 6 percentage points in labor force participation rates for white wives, for example. All the negative differences are reflected in the transfer payment component of the treatment. The tax rate effect was never significant, although it was usually negative.

These findings have shown a reasonable degree of stability after several checks for biases.

1. The experimental plans' negative effect on labor supply was about the same whether or not the group of families that went on welfare were included in the statistical analysis. Thus, it is unlikely that the presence of alternative welfare programs made much difference to the study, even though the original design applied to a state, New Jersey, where male-headed families were virtually ineligible for welfare, and where the introduction of such a program soon after the beginning of the experiment threatened to bias downward any disincentive effect.

2. The initial examination of the problem of attrition has not produced evidence that the limited negative treatment effect would have been very different if all the original families were retained, although on a priori grounds we expected attrition to overstate the disincentive, since low-earning families among the treatment group had the most to gain by staying with the experiment.

3. The statistical results about treatment effects have not been shown to be sensitive to various personal and family characteristics, such as the presence of young children in the family, the health status of the adults, the employment status of the husband, or the normal income of the family. Of course, there are many subgroups in the sample that could be defined by combinations of characteristics. Although it is not feasible to test for "all possible" interactions, much more remains to be done to explore interactions that have theoretical and methodological interest.

But even assuming that these and other similar "procedural" challenges to the validity of the experimental results are satisfactorily addressed, a larger question remains: Can the results of the experiment be generalized to apply to the behavior of a broader population of low-income families under a legislated negative income tax?

There are probably two reasons for skepticism. One is the difference between a small-scale, short-duration experiment and a nationwide, permanent plan. The other reason is the difficulty in reconciling our findings with previous economic research on labor supply.

We can ask two different questions about an experiment as a model for the behavior under an actual plan. One is whether the work experience of wives over the three-year period represents the experience of the *first* three years of a legislated plan. The second is whether the three-year experience represents a long-run equilibrium response to a plan that has been in operation for many years. Neither question can be answered with certainty, and the second question is even more problematic than the first.

Despite the relatively low levels of labor force participation by the wives in the sample, there was considerable mobility in and out of the labor force, which leads us to conclude that the short duration of the experiment did not prevent a response by wives during the three years. The pattern of their labor-force behavior and the type of labor market they work in appear to permit market-work adjustments by wives in response to negative income tax plans. Consider the finding of "no response" by black wives: possibly the long-run equilibrium of a permanent plan would reveal a gradual learning process and "legitimation" of the receipt of transfer payments on the one hand, and greater nonmarket uses of time on the other. We do not know.

The experimental findings for wives are in some respects at odds with the nonexperimental research findings. In the experiment, the work disincentive was not consistently significant for different measures of labor supply, the disincentive that was found was apparently restricted to white wives, and the substitution effect of the implicit tax on earnings was never significant. In research using nonexperimental data, significant and fairly large income and substitution effects in the labor-supply functions of wives have been the rule.

Because research with experimentally generated data is so new, our suggestions for reconciling the conflicting results with conventional research must be tentative. It must be said that the income and substitution parameters estimated with nonexperimental data span a wide range, and some of the estimates are, indeed, consistent with near-zero income and substitution effects (Cain and Watts, 1973: Chapter 9). Nevertheless, the average set of estimates for wives is such that reductions in labor force participation, hours, and earnings would be confidently predicted on the basis of the existing estimates of negative income and positive substitution effects. It is important to point out, however, that no empirical study has measured labor-supply responses by the working poor to negative income tax plans. The expectation of a significant labor-supply reduction is based, therefore, on inferences from one type of sample and one type of process by which incomes and wage rates were generated to a somewhat different sample and an entirely different process.

We have come to the conclusion that the quantitative estimates of income and substitution effects have less stability with respect to the processes generating the income and wage variation than previously believed. Even in the studies with nonexperimental data there is reason to believe, and some evidence, that income effects on labor supply will be different depending on the source of the income. Thus, the income and wage effects stemming from negative income tax plans for working poor families may well yield very different responses from those stemming from the normal workings of the market for middle-income groups.

Three characteristics of wives in low-income families would rationalize relatively small estimates of disincentive during a three-year period.

One is their low levels of participation relative to nonpoor wives. Families with working wives are simply less likely to have incomes low enough to be eligible for inclusion in an income-maintenance plan. We should remember that the impact of a negative income tax on the working poor is unidirectional with respect to the theoretically expected labor-supply response. Only negative responses are predicted and, given a lower bound of zero and the already low levels, there is not a great deal of "room" for further downward adjustments. (Of course, this same low level makes for relatively large percentage changes, as we have seen.)

Another characteristic is the fact that low-income, husband–wife families in such relatively high-wage areas as New Jersey and Pennsylvania have incomes that fluctuate around the breakeven levels, rather than around very low or zero levels. Because these husband–wife families do not normally have incomes low enough to make them eligible for larger transfer payments, the saliency or relevance of the income-maintenance plan is reduced and so, therefore, is the plan's theoretically expected disincentive. A further explanation for a weak disincentive is the likelihood that these low-income families place such a high marginal utility on income (relative to nonmarket activities) that the wives, as well as the husbands, will work when the opportunities arise, even in the face of a low net wage. Again, perhaps a long-run equilibrium response would be different. The "long run," however, is also associated with rising real wages, which serve to diminish the saliency of the tax and guarantee parameters that take effect only when family income drops below breakeven levels.

Finally, the existence of alternative welfare plans does serve to support the lowest stratum of poor families, who are least able to function in the competitive labor market. The remaining strata of families above this level exhibit, almost by definition, a greater capacity for work and earnings. The latter are not, therefore, so likely to show pronounced differences in time spent at work—at least the extreme of zero work is unlikely.

Let us recapitulate our suggestions for why the labor-supply function may be relatively inelastic for poor families: the tendency for impermanence of the families' eligibility status, the prevailing low levels of labor supply, the low tradeoff between any work reduction (greater "leisure") and lower money income, and the alternative of public assistance for those whose labor-supply change is extreme in a negative direction.

Many of us engaged in the analysis of this experiment arrive at some of these conclusions with a good deal of reluctance. We had not, ourselves, suspected that the estimated income and wage parameters from an income maintenance plan would be very different from those measured in previous research. The conclusion, that we need more elaborate models which take account of specific sources and processes of the price and income variation in our data, is not appealing. If carried to extremes it implies that "each case is different"—which defeats our objective of establishing generalizable empirical regularities in behavior. This is, of course, only one interpretation. The most strongly competing alternative is that experiments are inappropriate representations of new conditions which affect the economy as a whole. Resolving these questions deserves a good deal of our attention in the immediate future.

REFERENCES

Bowen, W. G., and Finegan, T. A. 1967. *The economics of labor force participation*. Princeton: Princeton University Press.

Cain, G. G., and Watts, H. W. 1973. *Income maintenance and labor supply: Econometric studies*. Institute for Research on Poverty Monograph Series. New York: Academic Press.

U.S. Department of Labor. 1973. *Manpower report of the president*. Washington, D.C.: Government Printing Office.

Waldman, E., and Gover, Kathryn R. 1972. *Marital and family characteristics of the labor force*. Special Labor Force Report 144 (reprint 2798). Washington, D.C.: U.S. Department of Labor, Bureau of Labor Statistics.

Watts, H. W., and Rees, A., eds. 1973. The New Jersey–Pennsylvania graduated work incentive experiment final report. Madison: Institute for Research on Poverty.

Watts, H. W., and Rees, A., eds. Forthcoming. *The New Jersey income-maintenance experiment*. Vol. 3. *Expenditures, health, and social behavior; and the quality of the evidence*. New York: Academic Press.

Whelpton, K; Campbell, A; and Patterson, J. E. 1966. *Fertility and family planning in the United States*. Princeton: Princeton University Press.

5 The educational and labor-supply responses of young adults in experimental families

Charles D. Mallar

The potential educational and labor-supply responses of children whose parental families would be eligible to receive transfer payments under an income-maintenance program are extremely important from a public policy point of view. If these children augment their investments in future earning capacity by increasing the quality and quantity of their formal educational attainments, the potential costs of such programs in terms of possible work reductions by their parents would be partially or even entirely offset by the direct plus intergenerational benefits from education. The reductions in work effort found among the parents in the experiment—as measured by standard labor-supply variables such as earnings, hours, and labor force participation—were quantitatively small. Therefore, any experimental–control group differential in children's educational attainment attributable to this temporary transfer program is a crucial factor in assessing the desirability of implementing a similar program on a national scale. Youths are also an important group for testing work disincentive hypotheses, since they tend to have more flexible work arrangements and weaker labor-force attachment.

When we are attempting to predict the educational and labor-supply responses of children to a legislated, and hence quasi-permanent, income-maintenance program with data from a limited-duration experiment, the teenage population becomes a particularly relevant group for analysis. Children in their upper teens have the capacity to respond to the receipt of such income subsidies by adjusting their consumption of education and their labor-force-participation behavior. They have nearly the same incentives to adjust their productive activities in a short-run experiment as they would in a legislated program. These young adults will have surpassed the maximum age requirement of compulsory education,[1] and prima facie evidence suggests that whether or not to complete high school is a crucial decision for teenagers from low-income families.[2] The existence of a typically generous welfare system in the experimental sites can be expected to weaken the economic stimuli of the experimental negative income tax plans compared to such a program on a national scale.[3] The short-run nature of the experiment, in contrast, will in no way deter young adult members of experimental families from attaining the full increase in lifetime earnings afforded by using these temporary income subsidies to increase their investment in human capital. Quite the contrary, since the transfer program is of limited duration, investments in future earning capacity become more attractive. Of course, lags and adjustments and short-run constraints on the quantity of education supplied may reduce the observed educational response.

Section 1 of this chapter gives a brief presentation of the theoretical and statistical models of analysis; Sections 2, 3, and 4, respectively, give empirical results for educational attainment, labor supply, and activity rates. Section 5 concludes the chapter with brief summary remarks and an interpretation of the policy implications of the results. In the interest of brevity, lengthy arguments and complex results will be greatly condensed. Ample citations will be given, so that the interested reader can consult more fully developed presentations.

---

[1] The compulsory education law in New Jersey requires attendance in a certified school up to age sixteen, while a similar Pennsylvania law requires such attendance up to age seventeen.

[2] The mean high school completion rate for young adults from low-income families in large northern urban areas, for instance, is only slightly greater than 50 percent (as evidenced by the sample mean for our control group). On a similar note, Jaffe and Adams (1969) found that senior-year dropouts are most likely to come from families with low socioeconomic status.

[3] See Mallar (1974: Chapter 2) for a discussion of the implications of this problem for the educational and labor-supply responses of young adults.

1. METHODOLOGICAL CONSIDERATIONS

Theoretical Models

The usual theoretical model of labor supply assumes a decision-making unit that has as its objective the maximization of a utility function monotonically increasing with respect to leisure and a composite consumption bundle.[4] Furthermore, the effects on individuals' demand for leisure from changes in their own wages are typically decomposed into substitution effects (that is, income-compensated price effects) and income effects. The substitution effect of a wage change is negative and the income effect is positive, under the assumption that leisure is a normal good.

For adult members of families covered by a negative income tax, the price of leisure would effectively be lowered relative to the price of the composite consumption bundle. That is, the real wage rate is decreased by the amount of the implicit tax rate (the rate at which the payment is reduced as earnings increase). Similarly, for families with ex ante income below the breakeven level, family income would be increased by the amount of the transfer payment. Since the direct income effect associated with the implementation of a negative income tax would outweigh the income effect of the wage change, both the total income effect and the substitution effect of the tax rate work in the direction of increasing the demand for leisure. One implication of this model, therefore, is the unambiguous prediction that implementation of such a program would cause persons from low-income families to consume more leisure or, the obverse, supply less labor.

This neoclassical model has two significant defects with respect to the current investigation (in addition to the fact that it must be modified for states that already have categorical transfer programs with high implicit tax rates). The first basic problem with the traditional labor-supply model is that the implicit heterogeneity of the good, leisure, obscures crucial productive activities—such as time spent investing in human capital and time allocated to nonmarket production. A second related problem concerns the static nature of this traditional model, which prohibits us from incorporating the time dynamics of human capital investment.

---

[4] This is the model underlying, at least implicitly, the empirical research in one of the most recent and exhaustive nonexperimental studies of the labor-supply effect of income maintenance (Cain and Watts, 1973); and it has been the accepted theoretical model for economic analyses of labor supply since Lionel Robbins' classic article (1930). Problems associated with family dynamics and individual labor-supply decisions made in a family context are ignored in this chapter. The labor-supply model is presumed to be applicable to individuals.

The inappropriateness of including the diverse potential uses of time not spent in the labor market within a single category when studying the labor-supply behavior of young adults is usually alluded to. For instance, the suggestion is often made that youths' labor supply is more price elastic than that of male heads of households because of larger substitution effects, which are, in turn, a consequence of the assumed better non-market alternatives to labor supply available to young adults and the more flexible labor-supply response permitted by the less constrained institutional arrangements typically associated with youths' employment. This type of analysis leads to the prediction that the labor-supply disincentive effects of a negative income tax would be larger for teenagers than for their fathers. Since the conclusion of larger disincentive effects for young adults is based on their having larger substitution effects, this difference could even be exaggerated in a limited-duration experiment, where the generally accepted theory suggests that income effects will be attenuated and substitution effects magnified as compared to a permanent program (Metcalf, forthcoming).

This cursory approach of appending qualifications to the standard labor-supply model is fundamentally inadequate for our purposes from both theoretical and public policy points of view. We need to focus on the effects of income maintenance on young adults' incentives and abilities to invest in their own education. From a purely theoretical viewpoint, we are interested in explaining the effects of economic variables such as prices and income on individuals' allocations of their fixed amounts of time over several distinct periods to major productive activities—such as market production, nonmarket production, and human capital investment. Similarly, from a public policy point of view, we are interested in how young adults allocated their time among these productive activities—viewing teenagers who allocate zero time to all three activities as, in a certain sense, societal "dropouts." In addition to the question of labor-supply disincentives for young adults, we seek answers to two crucial questions: What would be the effects on educational attainment for the relevant population if a universal income-maintenance program such as a negative income tax were instituted? How would these educational effects interact with the hypothesized labor-supply disincentives for young adults?

In previous research, a simple two-period utility maximization model for young adults has been developed that incorporates school activity and elementary human capital theory into the standard work–leisure model.[5]

---

[5] For more details on the theoretical arguments involved, plus a mathematical exposition of this model and its implications, see Mallar (1975: Chapter 2).

This two-period, work–leisure–education model overcomes some of the inherent limitations of the usual work–leisure model with respect to answering the important questions set forth above. The assumption of only two time periods in this model is relatively innocuous and is utilized merely to simplify the exposition. The practice of including as separate productive activities only time spent participating in the labor market and time spent in formal education programs—while all other activities are subsumed under a broad leisure category—is still, in contrast, somewhat arbitrary and deficient. This work–leisure–education model, however, does permit more meaningful analyses than the usual work–leisure model which includes educational activities within the leisure category. The level of abstraction embodied in the work–leisure–education model allows us to focus on the most important economic decisions faced by teenagers in low-income families—whether or not to continue their formal education and whether or not to enter the labor force. Since the outcomes of these decisions are directly observable, this abstraction also brings the theoretical model into conformity with practical data limitations.

One complication arising with the work–leisure–education model is that the predicted overall effects of the implementation of a negative income tax are no longer qualitatively unambiguous. Under such a program, both the real price (opportunity costs) of leisure and the real price (opportunity costs) of education decline. Assume that leisure time and time spent in school are substitutes. The net income effect of a negative income tax and the own-substitution effect associated with the implicit tax still imply a decrease in the labor-supply incentives of young adults. However, the work–leisure–education model suggests that there would be an offset to the resultant increase in the consumption of leisure because of the cross-substitution effects associated with the simultaneous decline in the price of education. A similar conclusion follows for the consumption of education by young adults. The positive impact of the negative income tax on education from the fall in the price of education and the increase in income would be offset by the cross-substitution effects associated with the simultaneous decline in the price of leisure.

Theoretical derivations of quantitative estimates of the own-substitution effects of changes in the prices of education and leisure, and estimates of these effects based on previous research, are both extremely tenuous. It is thus difficult to compare the relative magnitudes of own-substitution effects in this instance. The overall effects of changes in youths' wage rates on their labor supply appear to be quite small in any case. There is reason to believe, however, that under an income-maintenance program the positive effects on education would be stronger than the disincentive effects with respect to labor supply for teenagers, since the income effects on the consumption of education are likely to be larger than those for labor supply.

When we justifiably relax any assumptions of perfect capital markets and zero direct costs of education, increased income may enable young adults in low-income families to overcome such market imperfections, thus increasing the observed income effects on the consumption of education. Previous research findings seem to support the view that there are large income effects for school enrollment and negligible income effects on labor supply. While Lerman (1970) found a significant income effect for high school enrollment at all income levels and a significant income effect for college enrollment among young adults from high-income families, several studies of young adults' labor supply find (at most) negligible income effects on labor supply.[6]

In conclusion, a reasonable theoretical model, in conjunction with empirical estimates derived from nonexperimental data sources (data generated from processes inherently different from instituting a broad new income-maintenance program), leads us to expect an increase in the consumption of education that is likely to be larger in magnitude than the corresponding reduction in labor supply for young adults. This, in turn, leads us to expect that, on balance, young adults from experimental families will consume slightly less leisure and spend more time in productive activities than those from control families.

Statistical Models

We shall, for the most part, be working with qualitative dependent variables that are dichotomous in nature; an appropriate approach is, therefore, to utilize a probability model. In most instances the least squares methodology associated with the so-called linear probability model will suffice, since for large numbers of observations, the resulting estimators will be approximately consistent within a broad range. In the current context, however, the superiority of maximum likelihood estimators of the parameters within a probit framework has been established (Mallar, 1975: Chapters 3, 5, and Appendix B). Therefore, except for Table 5.2 and the first part of Table 5.4—where we are dealing with more continuous dependent variables and hence use ordinary least squares—the statistical methodology underlying the empirical results presented is the maximum likelihood estimation of a probit probability model.

---

[6] For documentation of the empirical findings summarized above, the interested reader should refer to the Hall and Boskin articles in Cain and Watts (1973), Bowen and Finegan (1965 and 1969), Korbel (1966), Lerman (1970), and Waldeman and Olsen (1968).

In addition to the necessary parameterization of the treatment—which contains a tax variable, a guarantee variable, and a treatment dummy variable—a number of other exogenous explanatory variables are used in the estimation process, yielding a rather elaborate control function. These latter independent variables include representations of youths' family, individual, and environmental characteristics plus a constant term. More specifically, in addition to families' experimental treatment statuses and a constant term, variables were added to account for differences among youths in the following characteristics: (1) their families' city of residence, ethnicity, number of adults, number of children, and normal preenrollment income; (2) their parents' age, education, and health status; and (3) their own age and sex. As a consequence of including control variables concomitant with the treatment variables (assuming our functional form is correct), both the adjusted means and associated adjusted experimental minus control-group differentials presented in Tables 5.1 and 5.2, and the treatment coefficients presented in Tables 5.3 through 5.5, can be interpreted as applicable to experimental and control groups that have identical compositions in terms of these control variables.[7]

While the effects of changes in these control variables are interesting in their own right, and most have, in fact, been explored in some form in previous research endeavors, our main concern in this chapter is to obtain precise estimates of the treatment parameters. Therefore, this control function is designed to protect against any systematic experimental–control differences that may have survived the randomization process. Upon close examination, this control function may appear to be somewhat wasteful in terms of degrees of freedom. The strategy is to maximize the precision of the estimators of the treatment parameters while at the same time guarding against any possible biases by incorporating in the control function differences in sample characteristics that affect our dependent variables.

2. THE EDUCATIONAL RESPONSE

Any welfare-reform proposal that attempts to rectify the inequities between the working and nonworking poor in the current distribution of income transfers, by permitting universal (as opposed to categorical) participation, risks declining real output and increasing transfer payments among those who are offered benefits (for example, the working poor) be-

---

[7] For more details of the statistical methodology, variable construction, and an analysis of the estimated coefficients for the control variables see Mallar (1975: Chapter 3).

cause of hypothesized labor-supply disincentives. The evidence from the New Jersey experiment suggests that these labor-supply disincentives are not as strong as popularly perceived. It is, nevertheless, important to find out to what extent, if any, these quantitatively small reductions in real output and increases in transfer payments will be offset in the future, as children from recipient families respond to incentives to augment their investments in human capital. The conclusions we arrived at via our theoretical model were not unambiguous, since teenagers from treatment families simultaneously have incentives to increase their consumption of leisure. However, statistical inferences from nonexperimental data are consistent with predictions of increases in educational attainment that could offset labor-supply reductions of the magnitude found in the experiment.

Both the current discussion and the previous section have implicitly assumed that individuals can enhance their productivity, and hence enlarge their potential lifetime earnings, by increasing their investments in human capital via formal education and related activities. Before moving on to a discussion of our empirical results, we need to focus some attention on two recent challenges to this traditional assumption.

First, proponents of the so-called screening hypothesis suggest that, while it is indeed true that empirically we should expect to find that market wages are a monotonically increasing function of educational attainment, the accepted causal explanation is wrong. According to this view, potential lifetime earnings increase with education, not only because of enhanced productivity, but also because the formal education process systematically excludes both people with inferior innate abilities and members of groups that are discriminated against, both of whom would receive lower market wages in any case. The advocates of this hypothesis contend that job-specific training provides a more effective means of increasing individuals' productivity. Empirically, it is difficult to differentiate between the screening hypothesis and an assumption of productivity enhancement, since the implications are observationally equivalent. In either case, if a negative income tax program gives rise to an increase in educational attainments among children of recipients, the potential lifetime incomes of these youths will be enlarged and, ceteris paribus, the amount of transfer payments needed to maintain such a negative income tax system in the next generation should be reduced.

The second challenge to the traditional view questions the efficacy of formal education with respect to enhancing potential lifetime earnings. This skeptical opinion stems from a careful reappraisal of formal education in general, and compensatory education programs in particular, as a means for redistributing opportunity and, ultimately, income in the

United States. The perception that youths from low-income families were chronically underinvesting in their human capital (because of market failures relating primarily to a lack of the collateral necessary for obtaining loans and an inequitable initial distribution of income), and that these market failures were self-perpetuating, led to a host of educational programs in the early 1960s. The principal objective of these programs was to break the so-called "cycle of poverty" by enhancing the potential lifetime earnings of children from poor families through increases in the quantity and quality of their formal education and job-related vocational training.

The general conclusions of several independent evaluations of some or all of these programs suggest that promoting increased educational attainment is, for the most part, an inefficient means of alleviating poverty and attaining a more egalitarian distribution of income, in the sense that the costs tend to outweigh the benefits.[8] It does *not* follow from these results, however, that we should qualify our theoretical conclusion that the potential lifetime earnings of children from recipient families would be enlarged under a negative income tax program as a consequence of induced increases in their educational attainment. In fact, one of the most convincing explanations of the small benefit–cost ratios observed is the low level of parental income itself. In the absence of an income-maintenance program to relieve the underlying deprivation, educational programs may require large outlays in order to obtain even modest gains. The theoretical foundation, along with the evidence from nonexperimental data, establishes a strong expectation that a negative income tax program would lead to an increase in the consumption of education among children from working-poor families who become eligible for benefits under such a system. Furthermore, this increase in education would in turn enlarge the potential lifetime earnings of these children and hence reduce the quantity of future transfers needed to maintain a given program.

The sample of youths used for this analysis consists of appropriate age subgroups (specified in the tables themselves) of those who were members of the 693 continuous husband–wife families at preenrollment and were related to the husband as either daughter, son, stepdaughter, stepson, foster daughter, or foster son—with the exception of those for whom we have insufficient data because they formed a separate reporting unit during the experiment and then attrited.

The best available data relating to youths' educational attainment from the New Jersey experiment are (1) the levels of completed education

---

[8] See Ribich (1968) for a judicious application of cost–benefit analysis to several of these educational programs. It should be noted that these investigations concentrate solely on the redistributional aspects, ignoring possible external and unquantifiable benefits of such programs.

obtainable from the family composition survey administered simultaneously with the twelfth quarterly interview at the end of the experiment; and (2) the school enrollment data gathered at the first, fifth, and ninth quarters—the only quarters when the surveys were administered during the normal academic year for all four sites. These data, however, are effectively limited to formal education and are not likely to include either vocational or other kinds of job-specific training. Differences between the education consumption of young adults whose families are enrolled in one of the eight experimental-treatment plans and the education consumption of those in the control group should be more easily discernible when working with the levels of completed education at the end of the experiment rather than school enrollment information from a particular point in time—since the data on completed education will contain some cumulative effects and less random variation or "noise" than an individual cross section of current activities.

Tables 5.1 and 5.2 present both the raw sample differentials and mean-adjusted differentials for the treatment plan means minus the control group mean for the probability of completing high school and the level of completed education, respectively. As predicted by our theoretical model, in conformity with our a priori expectations based on nonexperimental evidence, young adults whose families are covered by the experiment do tend to consume more education than those in the control group. Although the in-depth examination of these results in the discussion below does uncover one troublesome anomaly, the collective response is quite large in magnitude and highly significant.

The sample utilized in Tables 5.1 and 5.2, youths who were nineteen or twenty years old at the conclusion of the experiment, was chosen for two reasons. (1) These youths would normally graduate from high school during the middle two years of the experiment. The treatment stimuli should thus most closely approximate those of permanent programs and enable us to eliminate initial and termination responses with respect to high school completion that may be unrepresentative of the potential response to a permanent program. (2) Youths who are eighteen at the end of the experiment are excluded because they are likely to induce spurious intercity differences in response resulting from the timing of the surveys across sites.

The estimation of the probability of college attendance, given high school completion, obviously necessitates a slightly older sample; as a consequence, the empirical results for college attendance exhibited in Table 5.3 are based on a sample of youths between twenty and twenty-two at the end of the experiment. The other results in Tables 5.3 through 5.5—quarterly results for school enrollment, labor force participation,

Table 5.1 Differentials in Probability of High School Completion for Youths, by Plan

	Experimental Plan (Guarantee–Tax Rate)							
	125–50	100–50	100–70	75–30	75–50	75–70	50–30	50–50
Plan mean	.318	.636	.800	.625	.600	.857	.400	.750
Differential	−.260	.058	.222	.047	.022	.279	−.178	.172
Adjusted plan mean	.407	.650	.955	.380	.843	.990	.624	.948
Adjusted differential	−.113	.130	.435	−.140	.323	.470	.104	.428

Control group mean = .578
Adjusted control group mean = .520
Significance level of equation = < 1%
N = 138

NOTE: The sample for this table consists of youths aged 19–20 at the end of the experiment. The adjusted means are derived from the maximum likelihood estimation of a probit equation containing a three-variable parameterization of the treatment (see note to Table 5.3 for details) plus seventeen variables controlling for youths' family, individual, and environmental characteristics and a constant term.

The coefficients for all treatment variables are statistically significant—individually at less than the 2 percent level for two-tailed tests and jointly at less than the 1 percent level.

Table 5.2 Differentials in Years of Schooling Attained for Youths, by Plan

	Experimental Plan (Guarantee–Tax Rate)								
	125–50	100–50	100–70	75–30	75–50	75–70	50–30	50–50
Plan mean	10.68	11.55	12.00	11.50	11.80	12.29	11.00	11.75
Differential	−.39	.48	.93	.43	.73	1.22	−.07	.68
Adjusted plan mean	10.96	11.36	12.11	11.01	11.76	12.50	11.41	12.16
Adjusted differential	−.03	.37	1.12	.02	.77	1.51	.42	1.17
Control group mean = 11.07								
Adjusted control group mean = 10.99								
R^2 = .282								
N = 138								

NOTE: The sample for this table consists of youths aged 19–20 at the end of the experiment. The adjusted means are derived from a multiple ordinary least squares regression equation containing a three-variable parameterization of the treatment (see note to Table 5.3 for details) plus seventeen variables controlling for youths' family, individual, and environmental characteristics and a constant term.

The coefficients for all treatment variables are statistically significant both individually and jointly at less than the 5 percent level.

and activity rates—focus on the critical last two years of high school, when compulsory education laws are no longer applicable and both a priori expectations and the experience of our control group imply that school dropout rates will be high. Therefore, these cross-section estimates utilize samples of young adults who were either seventeen or eighteen years old at the time of the survey.

A priori reasoning suggests that the educational response to a negative income tax is likely to be larger among youths from single-parent families. The decision was made to concentrate on young adults from husband–wife continuous families, however, both because husband–wife families are the primary public policy focus of the New Jersey experiment and because this focus leads to severe limitations on the number of single-parent families available for analysis in the New Jersey data. Youths who have completed fewer than six years of education are also excluded from the analyses of completed education (Tables 5.1 and 5.2 plus the first part of Table 5.3), because they are presumed either to be miscoded or else to have such low literacy levels that it is unreasonable to expect them to be influenced by a short-duration experiment.

As can be seen from Table 5.1, teenagers whose parents are enrolled in one of the medium generosity plans are, on average, 25–50 percent more likely to complete their high school education than are corresponding young adults in the control group. Similarly, in Table 5.2 we observe that by age nineteen to twenty they have completed, on average, from one-half to a whole year more of formal education after receiving negative income tax payments for only three years. The mean-adjusted differentials tend to be more positive than the unadjusted differentials, especially with respect to the probability of completing high school. This is because the youths whose parents are enrolled in experimental plans have smaller normal family incomes, their parents have completed less formal education, and they have other socioeconomic characteristics similarly lower than those of their counterparts in the control group—all of which would give rise to lower educational attainment among those in the experimental group in the absence of the treatment. In other words, the measured response is somewhat larger when we attain a ceteris paribus comparison than under a gross comparison.

Although we cannot with the later results for labor-supply and activity rates, we are able here to distinguish significant differences by plan in educational response. The tax effect is surprisingly large and significant, given the limited effective variation in tax rates.[9] This strong, positive tax

---

[9] This stems from the fact that most families enrolled in the two plans with the 70 percent tax rates were either eligible for more generous welfare programs or else had normal incomes near or above breakeven level (that is, the income level at which the negative income payments ceased) for their plan.

Table 5.3 Treatment Response in Educational Activity of Youths, Predicted Marginal Effects Evaluated at Appropriate Probabilities

	Probability				
	.3	.4	.5	.6	.7
Completing high school[a]					
Treatment dummy**	.332	.369	.381	.369	.322
Tax rate***	.456	.506	.523	.506	.456
Guarantee***	−.216	−.240	−.248	−.240	−.216
Mean of dependent variable = .565					
Significance level of equation = < 1%					
N = 138					
College attendance, given high school graduation[b]					
Treatment dummy	.236	.262	.271	.262	.236
Tax rate	−.138	−.154	−.159	−.154	−.138
Guarantee	.044	.049	.051	.049	.044
Mean of dependent variable = .238					
Significance level of equation = < 10%					
N = 80					
Attending school, first quarter[c]					
Treatment dummy	.106	.118	.122	.118	.106
Tax rate	.040	.045	.046	.045	.040
Guarantee*	.122	.135	.139	.135	.122
Mean of dependent variable = .527					
Significance level of equation = < 20%					
N = 91					
Attending school, fifth quarter[d]					
Treatment dummy	.118	.131	.136	.131	.118
Tax rate	.108	.120	.124	.120	.108
Guarantee	−.090	−.100	−.103	−.100	−.090
Mean of dependent variable = .513					
Significance level of equation = < 10%					
N = 113					
Attending school, ninth quarter[e]					
Treatment dummy	−.007	−.007	−.008	−.007	−.007
Tax rate	.058	.064	.066	.064	.058
Guarantee	.027	.030	.031	.030	.027
Mean of dependent variable = .500					
Significance level of equation = < 1%					
N = 113					

NOTE: These estimates are derived from the maximum likelihood estimation of a probit equation containing a three-variable parameterization of the treatment plus seventeen variables controlling for youths' family, individual, and environmental characteristics and a constant term. (1) The first treatment variable is a treatment dummy. (2) The tax variable is equal to $t - .5$, so that the treatment dummy represents a 50 percent tax rate. These marginal effects are scaled to reflect an increase in the tax rate of 20 percent. (3) The guarantee variable is equal to $G - .75$, so that the treatment dummy represents a 75 percent effect implies that own-substitution effects are more powerful than we had anticipated.

The one anomalous finding pertains to the signs of the coefficients of the guarantee variables underlying both Tables 5.1 and 5.2. It turns out that this negative guarantee effect is concentrated in the 125–50 plan (the most generous of all the plans), and there is some evidence that it is a spurious sample phenomenon (Mallar, 1975: Chapter 3). Nevertheless, the statistical significance of this coefficient for both the probability of finishing high school and the level of completed education is quite disturbing. This negative guarantee effect, however, is neither as large in magnitude nor as statistically significant for the level of completed education as it is for the probability of finishing high school. Furthermore, neither the results for college attendance nor the quarterly school enrollment results provide any support for negative guarantee effects, as is obvious from Table 5.3.

Although we are unable to distinguish among plans, the overall treatment response with respect to the conditional probability of attending college, given high school completion, is positive, extremely large in magnitude, and nearly statistically significant despite the relatively small number of degrees of freedom. If we combine the estimated response for the probability of completing high school with the estimated response for the conditional probability of attending college, given high school completion, the predicted marginal probability of attending college for young adults from families on medium generosity plans will, on the average, be more than twice as large as that for comparable youths from the control group.

The school enrollment responses, as anticipated, are not as significant as those for completed education. The findings from the three quarters for which we have relatively complete school enrollment information, however, are generally supportive of our a priori expectations and the results previously discussed. A brief examination of the bottom three panels of Table 5.3 reveals estimates of overall positive responses and positive tax

---

guarantee. These marginal effects are scaled to reflect an increase in the guarantee rate of 25 percent.
[a] Sample is youths aged nineteen to twenty at conclusion of the experiment.
[b] Sample is high school graduates aged twenty to twenty-two at conclusion of the experiment. The control function contained an additional variable to capture differences in age.
[c] Sample is youths aged seventeen to eighteen at first quarter.
[d] Sample is youths aged seventeen to eighteen at fifth quarter.
[e] Sample is youths aged seventeen to eighteen at ninth quarter.
* Statistically significant at the 10 percent level.
** Statistically significant at the 5 percent level.
*** Statistically significant at the 1 percent level.

effects, as before. As mentioned above, however, these quarterly school enrollment results are more compatible with our a priori expectations of positive guarantee effects than the estimates either for the probability of finishing high school or for the level of completed education.

Finally, a number of interactions between variables in the control functions and the variables in the treatment parameterization were tested, but the null hypothesis of zero effect could not usually be rejected. Treatment interactions with youths' ethnicity, sex, and age at the end of the experiment, along with interactions with their parents' health statuses, were also tested. Only ethnicity, in a few instances, demonstrated even marginal significance, black youths having a slightly more positive estimated experimental response than whites, and youths from Spanish-speaking families having a more negative one.

3. THE LABOR-SUPPLY RESPONSE

The labor-supply response of young adults from experimental families provides a critical test of the work disincentive hypothesis, since they have both the flexibility to reduce their work effort in the short run and the means to accommodate such reductions in their labor supply through the typical patterns of teenage employment. In addition, the labor-supply response of children could potentially be a large component of any measured family response. The policy ramifications of children reducing their work effort in their adolescent years while simultaneously consuming more education are extremely different from those of parents reducing their labor supply in order to consume more leisure.[10]

The labor-supply disincentive for young adults is in fact likely to be magnified in a short-duration experiment. Recall that in the earlier discussion of the usual qualifications to the work–leisure model for young adults it was suggested that own-substitution effects are likely to be both relatively large for youths and exaggerated in a limited-duration experiment as compared to a permanent program, so that youths' labor-supply responses tend to be larger in a limited-duration experiment than they would be under a permanent program. Furthermore, since the labor-supply responses of teenagers in husband–wife families may be viewed as, in some sense, secondary to the family, we need to interject additional realism into our theoretical models by considering the implications of pos-

---

[10] This is misleading to the extent that the heads of working poor households are also likely to spend at least some of any additional time away from the labor market in human capital investment activities and nonmarket production.

sible interperson cross-substitution effects. To the extent that teenagers' mothers and fathers do not alter their labor-supply behavior after being enrolled in one of the eight experimental plans as much as they would under a similar but permanent program (possibly because of the prohibitive costs of overcoming institutional constraints, given the short-run nature of this experiment), we might again expect that these youths' labor-supply responses would be magnified compared to those under a permanent program (presuming, of course, that the labor supply of teenagers and that of their parents are substitutes). Previous studies of the labor-supply behavior of teenagers (Bowen and Finegan, 1969; and Lerman, 1970) have concluded that these "added worker" type of effects are for the most part negligible for young adults. These findings can be attributed at least in part, however, to demand-related phenomena and to increased nonmarket production among youths (i.e., more work in the home) as their mothers respond to these "added worker" stimuli.

In Table 5.4, results are presented for the labor-supply responses of young adults averaged over the middle two years of the experiment for four measures of labor supply. This sample includes youths who were either sixteen or seventeen years old at preenrollment and hence either nineteen or twenty at the end of the experiment. Quarterly results for the probability of labor force participation (utilizing the same sample as in the bottom three panels of Table 5.3) are exhibited in Table 5.5. As expected, young adults whose families are covered by experimental plans do tend to

Table 5.4 Treatment Response in Labor-Supply Activity of Youths, Predicted Marginal Effects in Middle Two Years

	Labor Force Participation	Hours	Earnings	Employment
Average weekly labor supply				
Treatment dummy	−.014	−3.59	−8.72*	−.099
Tax rate	−.008	−1.87	−5.10	−.077
Guarantee	−.031	−0.29	−1.08	−.020
Mean of dependent variable	.586	9.47	18.74	.322
R^2	.384	.402	.374	.437
N = 109				

NOTE: The sample for this table consists of youths aged sixteen to seventeen at preenrollment. Variables are averaged over those quarters for which valid data exist. These estimates are derived from multiple ordinary least squares regression equations containing the three-variable parameterization of the treatment (see note to Table 5.3 for details) plus eighteen variables controlling for youths' family, individual, and environmental characteristics and a constant term.

* Statistically significant at the 10 percent level.

Table 5.5 Treatment Response in Labor Force Participation of Youths, Predicted Marginal Effects Evaluated at Appropriate Probabilities

	Probability				
	.3	.4	.5	.6	.7
First quarter[a]					
Treatment dummy**	−.316	−.351	−.362	−.351	−.316
Tax rate	.055	.061	.063	.061	.055
Guarantee	−.040	−.044	−.046	−.044	−.040
Mean of dependent variable = .407					
Significance level of equation = < 15%					
N = 91					
Fifth quarter[b]					
Treatment dummy	−.040	−.004	−.046	−.044	−.040
Tax rate	−.098	−.109	−.113	−.109	−.098
Guarantee	−.004	−.005	−.005	−.005	−.004
Mean of dependent variable = .575					
Significance level of equation = < 30%					
N = 113					
Ninth quarter[c]					
Treatment dummy	.029	.032	.033	.032	.029
Tax rate	−.006	−.007	−.007	−.007	−.006
Guarantee	−.069	−.076	−.079	−.076	−.069
Mean of dependent variable = .500					
Significance level of equation = < 1%					
N = 148					

NOTE: These estimates are derived from the maximum likelihood estimation of a probit equation containing the three-variable parameterization of the treatment (see note to Table 5.3 for details) plus seventeen variables controlling for youths' family, individual, and environmental characteristics and a constant term.
[a] Sample consists of youths aged seventeen to eighteen at first quarter.
[b] Sample consists of youths aged seventeen to eighteen at fifth quarter.
[c] Sample consists of youths aged seventeen to eighteen at ninth quarter.
** Statistically significant at the 5 percent level.

respond with reduced work effort with respect to all four measures of labor supply and for all periods of experimental time. The overall predicted responses, as well as the estimated tax and guarantee effects, are negative and of a large enough magnitude to account for most of the differentials in hours and earnings found between the predicted family response (detailed in Chapter 6) and the sum of husband and wife responses (discussed in Chapters 3 and 4). The results in Tables 5.4 and 5.5 are, for the most part, consistent with each other. The data averaged over the middle two years of the experiment probably provide the best summary measure of the labor-supply response for youths, as discussed in earlier chapters. The averaging process should also reduce the random variation or "noise," as compared to an individual cross section of observations. Even the estimated effects for the averaged data, however, achieve only marginal levels of statistical significance.

At least part of this failure to achieve more statistically significant results can be attributed to sample size restrictions and the resultant inability to investigate potential disparities among groups adequately. It is conceivable, for example, that few of the determinants of teenage labor supply maintain constant effects across ethnic and sex groups, so that merely appending ethnicity and sex variables to our control function is inherently inadequate. As a rough test of this, a number of interactions between variables in the control functions and the variables in the treatment parameterization were again tested, with outcomes similar to those discussed in the previous section with respect to young adults' educational response. Once more, only ethnicity ever exhibited even a marginal level of statistical significance. When the response is permitted to vary among ethnic groups in this instance, however, youths from Spanish-speaking experimental families tend to demonstrate smaller (that is, more positive) estimated labor-supply response differentials, while the work reductions among teenagers from both black and white treatment families are slightly stronger than those reported in Tables 5.4 and 5.5.

In conclusion, these findings for young adults conform very well with the results in Chapters 3 and 4 for each of their parents, and the results in Chapter 6 for the family aggregates. Youths' reductions in hours and earnings are large enough to explain most of the predicted differentials between total family responses and their parents' responses, especially if a portion of these effects is extrapolated to siblings whose ages are just beyond the narrow range included in this study. Similarly, the estimated work disincentives appear largest for those ethnicities (black and white youths) where the predicted total family response diverged most from the parents' response.

4. ACTIVITY RATES AND SIMULTANEOUS MODELS

The estimated treatment response with respect to the probability that youths are active—where an active youth is defined as one who is either enrolled in school or participating in the labor force or both—provides a useful summary measure. The activity response shows whether or not we should expect any dramatic shifts in the amount of time teenagers devote

Table 5.6 **Treatment Response in Education and/or Labor-Force Activity of Youths, Predicted Marginal Effects Evaluated at Appropriate Probabilities**

	Probability				
	.75	.80	.85	.90	.95
First quarter					
Treatment dummy	−.159	−.140	−.117	−.088	−.052
Tax rate	.128	.113	.094	.071	.042
Guarantee	.011	.009	.008	.006	.003
Mean of dependent variable = .813					
Significance level of equation = < 2%					
N = 91					
Fifth quarter					
Treatment dummy	.210	.185	.154	.116	.068
Tax rate	−.303	−.267	−.223	−.168	−.099
Guarantee	.089	.078	.065	.049	.029
Mean of dependent variable = .894					
Significance level of equation = < 2%					
N = 113					
Ninth quarter					
Treatment dummy	.224	.197	.164	.124	.073
Tax Rate	.166	.146	.121	.091	.054
Guarantee	−.056	−.049	−.041	−.031	−.018
Mean of dependent variable = .858					
Significance level of equation = < 5%					
N = 148					

NOTE: The sample for this table consists of youths aged seventeen and eighteen at the appropriate quarter. These estimates are derived from the maximum likelihood estimation of a probit equation containing the three-variable parameterization of the treatment (see note to Table 5.3 for details); plus seventeen variables controlling for youths' family, individual, and environmental characteristics and a constant term.

to productive activities if a universal income-maintenance program such as a negative income tax is instituted.[11]

As can be seen from Table 5.6, the overall activity response among children from experimental families is not very significant, and we are, in effect, unable to distinguish among the various plans. While we are uni-

[11] Previous research (Mallar, 1973) has analyzed this activity response and the educational and labor-supply responses of youths, conditional on being active, in great detail. While the previous research explores youths' activity responses in much more detail than the summary presentation below, the empirical model underlying this earlier research somewhat naively assumes a recursive decision-making process for young adults. It was assumed that these youths decide first whether or not to become active, and then, conditional on this decision being positive, they decide whether to enroll in school and/or participate in the labor force.

formly unable to reject the null hypothesis of zero experimental response at any reasonable level of statistical significance, it is noteworthy that the response becomes more positive with the length of treatment. Teenagers from experimental families are initially slightly less active than their counterparts in the control group but, by the ninth quarter, the estimated response differential is positive and large in magnitude for all plans. Assuming an initial adjustment lag of moderate length, one plausible explanation for this observation is that youths in the control group have a predisposition toward being active that is not captured by the control function, so that an improved ceteris paribus comparison would show a more positive activity response among youths from experimental families.

Finally, an appropriate econometric methodology for estimating a simultaneous model with limited dependent variables has been developed and allows us to explore the obvious simultaneity between young adults' decisions about whether or not to continue formal schooling and whether or not to enter the labor force.[12] Despite some serious data limitations, one important policy result is attained from such an investigation. While the estimated direct educational response is nearly the same as the total educational response, the labor-supply reduction among youths from experimental families appears to have been not a direct effect of the treatment but, rather, an indirect response resulting from the increased incentives to invest in education.

5. CONCLUSIONS

The usual predictions of the effects of implementing a negative income tax program with respect to declining real output and increasing transfer payments must be modified in the long run when we incorporate human capital investment activities directly into the work–leisure model for young adults. Our findings, while not entirely conclusive, should be encouraging for the proponents of universal income-maintenance legislation. Given the restriction of our samples to youths from working poor families with both parents present and residing in northern urban poverty tracts, and given the limited experimental stimuli, the children from experimental families exhibit surprisingly large increases in educational attainment vis-à-vis those in the control group. Moreover, this educational response among youths is large enough to easily offset potential costs of

---

[12] See Mallar (1975: Chapter 5) for a complete development of this statistical methodology and a more thorough discussion and presentation of the applicable empirical findings.

income-maintenance programs caused by work reductions among their parents of the size found in the New Jersey experiment.

Most of the observed differential between the predicted total labor-supply response for families and the sum of the predicted labor-supply responses for husbands and wives can be accounted for by the labor-supply reductions found among these young adults. The increases in school enrollment, however, more than offset these reductions in labor force participation, so that youths from treatment families were, if anything, more likely to be engaged in productive activities than their counterparts in the control group. Furthermore, there is empirical support for attributing these reductions in work effort among teenagers to the increased tendency to invest in human capital through increased education—but not vice versa.

REFERENCES

Bowen, W. G., and Finegan, T. A. 1965. Labor force participation and unemployment. In *Employment policy and the labor market,* ed. A. M. Ross, pp. 138–145. Berkeley and Los Angeles: University of California Press.

Bowen, W. G., and Finegan, T. A. 1969. *The economics of labor force participation.* Princeton: Princeton University Press.

Cain, G. C., and Watts, H. W. 1973. *Income maintenance and labor supply: Econometric studies.* New York: Academic Press.

Jaffe, A. J., and Adams, W. 1969. *American higher education in transition.* Bureau of Applied Social Research. New York: Columbia University Press.

Korbel, J. 1966. Labor force entry and attachment of young people. *Journal of the American Statistical Association* 61:117–127.

Lerman, R. I. 1970. An analysis of labor force participation, school activity, and employment rates. Ph.D. dissertation, University of Wisconsin, Madison.

Mallar, C. D. 1973. School enrollment and labor force participation among young adults. Final Report of the Graduated Work Incentive Experiment in New Jersey and Pennsylvania, part B, Chapter 4. Madison: Institute for Research on Poverty, University of Wisconsin.

―――. 1975. The effects of income maintenance on the productive activities of young adults. Ph.D. dissertation, University of Wisconsin, Madison.

Metcalf, C. D. Forthcoming. Predicting the effects of a permanent program from a limited duration experiment. In *The New Jersey income-maintenance experiment.* Vol. 3. *Expenditures, health, and social behavior; and the quality of the evidence,* ed. H. W. Watts and A. Rees. New York: Academic Press.

Ribich, T. I. 1968. *Education and poverty.* Washington, D.C.: Brookings Institution.

Robbins, L. 1930. On the elasticity of demand for income in terms of effort. *Economica* 10:123–129.

Waldeman, E., and Olsen, C. 1968. *Unemployment in the American family.* Special Labor Force Report no. 99. Washington, D.C.: U.S. Department of Labor, Bureau of Labor Statistics.

6 Family labor-supply response in the new jersey experiment

Robinson G. Hollister
Charles E. Metcalf

Under income-maintenance programs like the negative income tax tested in the New Jersey experiment, cash benefits are determined on the basis of family income and family size. It is natural, therefore, that the labor-supply response of the family as a whole, as well as the response of individual family members, should be of direct policy interest. This chapter is thus concerned with family labor-supply response.

Recent economic literature includes numerous theoretical and empirical studies of the labor-supply decisions of individuals and of families.[1] Most recently, considerable emphasis has been put on the interdependence of decisions among various family members. Secondary workers are likely to make decisions about their level of work effort in light of the earnings opportunities of the primary earner, and vice versa. And this interdependence of work decisions is likely to be reinforced by the rules of income-maintenance programs like those tested in the experiment.

One logical procedure would be the estimation of a multiple equation model of family behavior, with a separate equation predicting the labor supply of each household member (Ashenfelter and Heckman, 1974).

---

[1] For a list of the most salient studies, see the bibliography in Cain and Watts (1973).

Properly specified, such a model would account not only for the interdependent structure of such decisions, but for possible cross-equation coefficient restrictions and correlations among stochastic estimation error terms. Thus a "full-information" econometric estimation procedure would be called for.

When applying this type of model to the problem of estimating *total* family labor supply, one would presumably predict hours for each family member and then aggregate the predicted responses. This approach puts considerable weight both on estimation procedure and on the theoretical specification of the functional form of the structural equations.

Further, where hours are the dependent labor-supply variable, there remains the question of how to weight the various family members' hours changes when attempting to translate to national costs. One way to weight them would be to multiply by the observed or predicted wage rate of each member.[2] But there is the additional question of whether the labor-supply response might also involve wage-rate changes. If wage rates are endogenous, the procedure for estimating structural models becomes even more complex; simultaneously determined wage equations must be included.

The labor-supply responses of individual family members reported in Chapters 3, 4, and 5 were independently estimated by limited information methods and were not generated by a coordinated structural model. When we augment these factors by the possibility of specification error in any complicated structural model, it can no longer be presumed that aggregate family responses are best estimated by summing the predicted responses of individual family members. An alternative approach, that of estimating family labor-supply responses with a single stochastic equation, undoubtedly involves specification error (unless the appropriate reduced form could be derived from a fuller model) and conceals much structural information. Yet a case can be made for the contention that a single equation approach provides the most accurate assessment of the effects of experimental plan parameters on aggregate totals.[3]

While future research will probably increasingly use interdependent models of individual behavioral responses, we believe that the presentation of single equation estimates of family labor supply may reveal useful

---

[2] On the issue of the advantages and disadvantages of using predicted versus observed wages, see Cain and Watts (1973:358–361).

[3] A similar debate has involved the use of large, structural econometric models of the U.S. economy to predict broad aggregates such as gross national product. Many econometricians argue that, given our current expertise, broad aggregates are best estimated by relatively simple models.

information. In this chapter, therefore, we limit our approach to single equation models.

For measures of labor-supply response, we have chosen to focus solely on total family earnings and total family hours. A total family weekly earnings measure provides a straightforward way of weighting the importance of individual family members to get the total family response. It also provides the most direct translation of the family response into the national cost implications.

We also use total family hours worked per week as a response variable, for two reasons. First, as already indicated, there are reasons to suspect the reliability of reported earnings differences between the experimental and control groups. The data are consistent with the hypothesis that initially some experimentals and some controls reported net rather than gross earnings, but that the experimentals learned more rapidly than did the controls that the correct amount to report to the experiment was gross earnings. To the extent that this was in fact the case, the higher hourly earnings observed for the experimental group was purely a reporting phenomenon. A second reason for reporting results using hours as a response variable is that traditional economic theory has emphasized hours as the choice variable by which work effort is adjusted, and many empirical studies have focused primarily on hours of work as an indicator of labor supply.

This chapter is divided into four sections, each progressively more complex in its treatment of experimental responses. Section 1 presents our basic experimental findings in the context of a simple model, while Section 2 considers differential responses by plan characteristics. In Section 3 we consider the interaction of experimental response with the level of normal income and investigate some methodological problems implicit in our method of estimating normal income. In Section 4 we examine the extent to which these interactions vary across plan parameters and by breakeven status.

1. BASIC EXPERIMENTAL RESPONSE

In this section we present the first of several models focusing on family labor-supply responses to the experiment. In Tables 6.1 through 6.4 we summarize the basic earnings and hours data to be analyzed, for each quarter from preenrollment through the twelfth. The sample reported and used throughout this study is the basic sample of 693 continuous husband–wife families.

Several comments can be made with respect to the reported data. First,

Table 6.1 Unadjusted Mean Earnings and Labor Supply, Continuous Husband–Wife Sample, Preenrollment through Twelfth Quarter

	Quarter												
	0	1	2	3	4	5	6	7	8	9	10	11	12
Weekly earnings (dollars)													
Experimentals	95	103	103	115	112	112	111	115	116	122	120	127	130
Controls	95	100	102	108	109	115	110	114	119	124	122	129	141
Weekly hours worked													
Experimentals	40.6	39.7	38.3	42.1	39.8	39.0	39.1	39.8	38.9	40.9	39.0	41.5	42.0
Controls	41.0	42.9	40.4	43.1	44.2	44.5	41.8	42.0	43.1	44.6	43.5	44.4	48.2

NOTE: The sample for this table consists of 425 experimental families and 268 controls.

Table 6.2 Unadjusted Mean Earnings and Labor Supply, White Families, Preenrollment through Twelfth Quarter

	Quarter												
	0	1	2	3	4	5	6	7	8	9	10	11	12
Weekly earnings (dollars)													
Experimentals	100	101	102	111	112	112	111	115	118	120	119	130	141
Controls	98	101	105	110	112	116	120	119	137	137	133	144	163
Weekly hours worked													
Experimentals	42.3	39.8	37.5	40.7	40.8	39.2	40.3	40.9	39.6	41.2	39.8	43.8	45.8
Controls	42.2	42.9	44.0	43.8	45.7	45.2	46.2	43.9	48.3	49.9	47.8	49.6	56.1

NOTE: The sample for this table consists of 181 experimentals and 129 controls.

Table 6.3 Unadjusted Mean Earnings and Labor Supply, Black Families, Preenrollment through Twelfth Quarter

	Quarter												
	0	1	2	3	4	5	6	7	8	9	10	11	12
Weekly earnings (dollars)													
Experimentals	94	106	112	122	119	120	120	120	121	127	125	132	127
Controls	90	99	101	105	108	115	102	104	95	107	112	106	112
Weekly hours worked													
Experimentals	40.3	39.7	42.4	44.7	40.7	39.8	40.4	39.4	39.5	41.6	38.6	40.5	39.4
Controls	36.2	41.5	35.3	42.0	43.1	44.8	37.5	37.8	36.0	37.9	38.5	35.5	37.4

NOTE: The sample for this table consists of 151 experimentals and 83 controls.

Table 6.4 Unadjusted Mean Earnings and Labor Supply, Spanish-speaking Families, Preenrollment through Twelfth Quarter

	Quarter												
	0	1	2	3	4	5	6	7	8	9	10	11	12
Weekly earnings (dollars)													
Experimentals	86	101	89	110	98	100	96	106	105	117	112	112	113
Controls	94	99	99	104	102	111	95	114	111	118	111	125	130
Weekly hours worked													
Experimentals	37.8	39.6	33.1	40.6	36.3	37.1	34.5	38.3	36.3	39.3	38.2	38.7	38.2
Controls	43.9	45.1	39.6	43.0	42.2	42.5	37.5	43.8	41.2	41.7	40.4	45.0	44.9

NOTE: The sample for this table consists of 93 experimentals and 56 controls.

while, for the total of all three ethnic groups, the mean earnings and hours variables are quite similar at preenrollment (quarter 0) for both experimental and control groups, there are considerable differences for the black and Spanish-speaking sub-samples. This suggests the need for some sort of control variables to correct for any initial experimental–control differentials. Furthermore, analyses of various labor-supply models used in this chapter and elsewhere indicate that the labor-supply response is significantly different among ethnic groups. Each group is thus examined separately.

Second, it has frequently been argued that responses for the early quarters may be affected by initial adjustment problems, and that in the last few quarters the responses may be distorted by anticipation of the end of the experiment. The data are suggestive of this interpretation, particularly at the end of the experiment. Therefore, except for the first four descriptive tables, we concentrate our analysis on responses during the middle two years of the experiment (quarters 3 through 10).

Our next step is to derive summary measures of the basic experimental differentials in response to the negative income tax plans under which experimentals operated. What we look at in the rest of this section is the simple experimental differential, averaged across all members of the experimental group. There is no attempt to distinguish responses according to difference in the various negative income tax plans.

The regression models used to generate these results are as follows:

$$Y_{ij} = b_0 + b_1 \hat{Y}_{ij} + b_2 \hat{Y}_{ij}^2 + b_3(Q-4)_{ij} + b_4(Q-6)_{ij} \\ + b_5(Q-8)_{ij} + b_6 Spring_{ij} + b_7 Summer_{ij} + b_8 Fall_{ij} \\ + b_9 EXP_i + e_{ij} \qquad (1)$$

where

Y_{ij} = total family earnings for family i in the jth quarter
$\hat{Y}_{ij}$ = a proxy control variable for total family earnings
$(Q-4)_{ij}$ = maximum of quarter $j-4$ and zero, where Q_{ij} is the quarter of observation for the ith family
$(Q-6)_{ij}$ = maximum of quarter $j-6$ and zero, where Q_{ij} is the quarter of observation for the ith family
$(Q-8)_{ij}$ = maximum of quarter $j-8$ and zero, where Q_{ij} is the quarter of observation for the ith family
$Spring_{ij}$ = 1 if observation ij was in Spring, zero otherwise
$Summer_{ij}$ = 1 if observation ij was in Summer, zero otherwise
$Fall_{ij}$ = 1 if observation ij was in Fall, zero otherwise
EXP_i = 1 if observation is in experimental group, zero otherwise

and

$$H_{ij} = b_0 + b_1\hat{Y}_{ij} + b_2\hat{Y}_{ij}^2 + b_3(Q - 4) + b_4(Q - 6) + b_5(Q - 8) \\ + b_6 Spring_{ij} + b_7 Summer_{ij} + b_8 Fall_{ij} + b_9 EXP_i + e_{ij} \quad (2)$$

where
H_{ij} is total family hours for family i in the jth quarter.

Several observations can be made about these models. First, the three variables involving Q form a linear time spline to allow for differences across quarters. Second, the seasonality dummies are entered to take account of seasonal variations that reappear over the time period. Third, both models use the same set of independent variables, but the dependent variable is total family income in model (1) and total family hours in model (2). (Total family income and family earnings are used synonymously in this chapter.)

Further, it has already been noted that control variables are necessary in the labor-supply models, for two basic reasons: to control statistically for any nonrandom differences in preenrollment values of these labor-supply measures, and to improve the efficiency of the estimate of the experimental differential by reducing the standard error of estimate. Several ways of approaching the problem of control variables are available to us. Though we will discuss the choice among these alternatives in greater detail below, a few comments are appropriate here. First, one could include a whole group of demographic characteristics as control variables. However, since one includes variables that are assumed to be related to labor supply, it would seem more straightforward to use a single labor-supply variable. One cannot use the contemporaneous labor-supply variable itself, however, since that is what we examine for labor-supply response. A variable is needed which may be presumed exogenous to the experimental treatment—that is, a proxy variable for what the labor supply of the family would have been in the *absence* of the experimental treatment.

There are three approaches to developing such a proxy variable for labor supply. Since they are conceptually different, we have carried out similar estimates using each of the three proxy control variables. One obvious variable exogenous to the experimental treatment is the preenrollment value of the labor-supply variable. A limitation of this variable is, however, that it does not incorporate information about nonexperimentally induced trends in earnings due to seasonality, changes in the labor market, and so on, that are subsequent to enrollment.

A second proxy variable can be constructed using the information on the control group as a measure of such changes. An equation can be estimated relating earnings over the course of the experiment to such factors as demographic characteristics, time, and seasonality. With the equation estimated on control group data, coefficients can then be applied to the values for both experimental and control group numbers to produce a predicted proxy value for each observation in each time period. This variable can be presumed exogenous because the estimating equation is based on control group data unaffected by the experimental treatment. We describe the variable developed in this fashion as a control-based proxy variable. (Details of its derivation can be found in the Appendix to this chapter.)

A third proxy variable is constructed in a similar fashion but uses information on both controls and experimentals. Endogenous experimental effects are separated out by including an additive function of experimental parameters in the specification and then subtracting the value for this function from the predicting values to obtain a proxy variable. This is the procedure used by Watts to develop a proxy variable for total family earnings.[4] Therefore, where this proxy is used for the control variable, we label it the Watts proxy.[5]

We estimated equations (1) and (2) three times for each ethnic subgroup, each of the three sets of runs using a different proxy for the $\hat{Y}$ and $\hat{Y}^2$ variables in the model. The results, tabulated in Tables 6.5 through 6.7, are based on the pooled quarterly sample and were estimated by the error components variant of generalized least squares.[6]

In Table 6.5, for whites, we find that all three models yield a significant negative experimental differential. The preenrollment and control-based proxies both give reductions of $14 per week in total family earnings—a reduction of about 11 percent in what earnings would have been in the absence of the experiment. Both obtain about a 1 percent significance level. The Watts specification yields a somewhat smaller response for total family earnings and a significance level of about 7 percent.

For total family hours, the preenrollment and control-based specifications yield an experimental differential of 7.5 hours, or about a 16 percent reduction in what hours would have been without the experiment. The significance level for both of these is better than 1 percent. The Watts

[4] The detailed description of this procedure is provided in Chapter 13.

[5] In what follows, when we use Watts' estimate, we do *not* include the value of the average deviation from predicted income for each family. We feel that the use of an error components model with a family-specific component mitigates much of the benefit of including the average deviation. Furthermore, its inclusion artificially inflates global test statistics for the regression and amplifies potential problems resulting from specification error. With respect to the comparative bias discussion in Section 3, the results are not sensitive to whether or not the average deviation is included.

[6] For a description of the error components method used, see Chapter 13.

Table 6.5 Labor-Supply Differentials for Three Proxy Control Variable Specifications, White Families, Quarters 3–10 Pooled

	Proxy Control Variable Specifications		
	Preenrollment	Control Based	Watts
Family earnings			
Differential (dollars per week)	−14.5	−14.1	−10.4
t-statistic	(−2.51)	(−2.59)	(−1.83)
Differential (percentage of control mean)	−11.7	−11.4	−8.4
R^2	.1277	.1904	.1356
Family hours			
Differential (hours per week)	−7.5	−7.5	−6.3
t-statistic	(−3.47)	(−3.66)	(−3.01)
Differential (percentage of control mean)	−16.0	−16.0	−13.5
R^2	.0704	.1291	.1094

NOTE: Number of observations = 2475. Results are estimated from regression functions equivalent to equations (1) and (2).

specification yields a response estimate lower by 6.3 hours or 13 percent. The significance level here is also better than 1 percent.

In Table 6.6, for blacks, we find somewhat greater variability. All of them yield *positive* experimental differentials for earnings, but only the control-based specification is significant at better than the 10 percent level. For total family hours, none of the model specifications yields a sizable or significant experimental differential. We will comment further on these results in subsequent sections.

In Table 6.7, for the Spanish-speaking, the various specifications yield somewhat different estimates of the experimental differentials, but none of the estimates approaches significance, even at the 10 percent level.

The results reported in Tables 6.5 through 6.7, as noted above, were based on pooled samples of quarterly observations and estimated by generalized least squares error components. Estimates were also calculated by averaging family observations across time and then using ordinary least squares to estimate the model. Since the time and seasonal components are averaged out, these elements can be omitted from the labor-supply models in estimation. Thus, the averaged models estimated were

$$Y_{ij} = b_0 + b_1 \hat{Y}_{ij} + b_2 \hat{Y}_{ij}^2 + b_3 EXP_i + e_{ij} \qquad (3)$$

$$H_{ij} = b_0 + b_1 \hat{Y}_{ij} + b_2 \hat{Y}_{ij}^2 + b_3 EXP_i + e_{ij}. \qquad (4)$$

Table 6.6 **Labor-Supply Differentials for Three Proxy Control Variable Specifications, Black Families, Quarters 3–10 Pooled**

	Proxy Control Variable Specifications		
	Preenrollment	Control Based	Watts
Family earnings			
Differential (dollars per week)	9.6	12.1	10.3
t-statistic	(1.44)	(1.99)	(1.64)
Differential (percentage of control means)	8.8	11.0	9.4
R^2	.1050	.1719	.1599
Family hours			
Differential (hours per week)	−0.81	0.16	−0.40
t-statistic	(−0.34)	(0.08)	(−0.18)
Differential (percentage of control means)	−2.0	0.04	−0.1
R^2	.0899	.1874	.1448

NOTE: Number of observations = 1862. Results are estimated from regression functions equivalent to equations (1) and (2).

Table 6.7 **Labor-Supply Differentials for Three Proxy Control Variable Specifications, Spanish-speaking Families, Quarters 3–10 Pooled**

	Proxy Control Variable Specifications		
	Preenrollment	Control Based	Watts
Family earnings			
Differential (dollars per week)	−1.4	4.4	4.7
t-statistic	(−0.21)	(0.69)	(0.71)
Differential (percentage of control mean)	−1.4	4.4	4.7
R^2	.0966	.1085	.0891
Family hours			
Differential (hours per week)	−3.33	−1.65	−1.26
t-statistic	(−1.52)	(−0.74)	(−0.57)
Differential (percentage of control mean)	−8.8	−4.4	−3.3
R^2	.0613	.0699	.0760

NOTE: Number of observations = 1178. Results estimated from regression functions equivalent to equations (1) and (2).

The results of these estimates, again using each of the three proxies, are reported in Tables 6.8 through 6.10. We will note only a few features of these results as compared to those of Tables 6.5 through 6.7. For whites, the magnitude of the estimated responses is somewhat smaller in the averaged than in the pooled. The earnings response is significant at the 5 percent level only for the control-based specification. For white family hours, all the responses are significant at the 5 percent level or better, though their magnitude is somewhat smaller than those of the pooled results. For black and Spanish-speaking families, none of the responses is significant for either averaged or pooled estimates.

Most of the subsequent models reported in this chapter were run both on pooled samples, using generalized least squares error-components methods, and on the averaged sample with ordinary least squares. Only the results using the former techniques are reported in the rest of the chapter, however, because the results were similar whichever method was used, but the pooled results often obtained higher significance levels because of the greater data richness afforded by the pooling technique.

2. LOOKING FOR RESPONSE DIFFERENCES AMONG EXPERIMENTAL PLANS

We have considered the average experimental response to the income-guarantee plans in terms of the average response of the experi-

Table 6.8 Labor-Supply Differentials for Three Proxy Control Variable Specifications, White Families, Quarters 3–10 Averaged

	Proxy Control Variable Specifications		
	Preenrollment	Control Based	Watts
Family earnings			
Differential (dollars per week)	−9.0	−9.9	−7.6
t-statistic	(−1.63)	(−1.94)	(−1.4)
Differential (percentage of control mean)	−7.2	−8.0	−6.1
R^2	.1896	.3001	.2322
Family hours			
Differential (hours per week)	−6.00	−6.41	−5.78
t-statistic	(−2.94)	(−3.33)	(−2.94)
Differential (percentage of control mean)	−12.8	−13.7	−12.4
R^2	.1129	.2105	.1778

NOTE: Number of observations = 310. Results estimated from regression functions equivalent to equations (3) and (4).

Table 6.9 **Labor-Supply Differentials for Three Proxy Control Variable Specifications, Black Families, Quarters 3–10 Averaged**

	Proxy Control Variable Specifications		
	Preenrollment	Control Based	Watts
Family earnings			
Differential (dollars per week)	11.4	12.1	10.6
t-statistic	(1.69)	(2.01)	(1.68)
Differential (percentage of control mean)	10.4	11.0	9.7
R^2	.1653	.3216	.2568
Family hours			
Differential (hours per week)	−0.26	0.25	−0.22
t-statistic	(−0.11)	(0.12)	(−0.09)
Differential (percentage of control mean)	−0.6	0.6	−0.5
R^2	.1363	.3456	.2269

NOTE: Number of observations = 234. Results estimated from regression functions equivalent to equations (3) and (4).

Table 6.10 **Labor-Supply Differentials for Three Proxy Control Variable Specifications, Spanish-speaking Families, Quarters 3–10 Averaged**

	Proxy Control Variable Specifications		
	Preenrollment	Control Based	Watts
Family earnings			
Differential (dollars per week)	1.45	6.26	4.35
t-statistic	(0.23)	(0.98)	(0.66)
Differential (percentage of control mean)	1.4	6.3	4.4
R^2	.1582	.1961	.1374
Family hours			
Differential (hours per week)	−2.50	−1.19	−1.47
t-statistic	(−1.15)	(−0.55)	(−0.67)
Differential (percentage of control mean)	−6.6	−3.1	−3.9
R^2	.1135	.1428	.1326

NOTE: Number of observations = 149. Results are estimated from regression functions equivalent to equations (3) and (4).

mentals taken as a group. However, the experimentals had eight different income guarantee plans, representing different combinations of the basic guarantee, G, and the marginal tax rate on income, t. It is important, therefore, to seek to determine the extent to which differences in these basic parameters, G and t, elicited different responses among the experimentals. For this purpose the models described in equations (1) and (2) were augmented as follows:[7]

$$Y = b_0 + b_1\hat{Y} + B_2\hat{Y}^2 + b_3(Q - 4) + b_4(Q - 6) + b_5(Q - 8)$$
$$+ b_6 Spring + b_7 Summer + b_8 Fall + b_9 EXP + b_{10}(G - 1.0) \quad (5)$$
$$+ b_{11}(t - .5) + e$$
$$H = b_0 + b_1\hat{H} + b_2\hat{H}^2 + b_3(Q - 4) + b_4(Q - 6) + b_5(Q - 8)$$
$$+ b_6 Spring + b_7 Summer + b_8 Fall + b_9 EXP + b_{10}(G - 1.0) \quad (6)$$
$$+ b_{11}(t - .5) + e$$

where

$$\hat{Y} = \hat{Y}_{CB}$$
$$\hat{H} = \hat{H}_{CB}$$

$(G - 1.0)$ = guarantee for the experimental family i, in terms of the ratio of the dollar guarantee to the poverty line for their family size, minus 1; 0 for control families

$(t - .5)$ = rate of reduction of benefits per dollar of income (marginal tax rate) for experimental family i minus 0.5; 0 for control families

and other variables are as defined for (1) above.

Note that the various experimental plans have been parameterized in terms of a linear spline.[8] These variables operate in an additive fashion, all experimentals having a value of 1 for *EXP* and those on plans with $G \neq 1$ and/or $t \neq .5$ having additive, nonzero values for these variables. Thus, if there are no differences in response among plans, these additive terms, $(G - 1.0)$ and $(t - .5)$, will be statistically insignificant.

We report only those models estimated using the control-based proxy for family earnings and hours as our control variable, since that proxy appeared, in the previous section, to yield the most significant results. (The results with similar models using the other two proxy specifications differed in no significant way.)

Table 6.11 displays the results of the estimates based on models (5) and (6), which can be very quickly summarized. In no case, for either earnings or hours, did the coefficients for $(G - 1.0)$ or $(t - .5)$ obtain statistical significance at even the 10 percent level. On this evidence there appears

---

[7] The ij subscripts are omitted in subsequent equations to make them easier to read.
[8] This parameterization is described in Chapter 2, Section 4.

Table 6.11 Labor-Supply Differentials by Tax Rate and Guarantee Differences, Control-based Proxy Control Variable, Quarters 3–10 Pooled

	Family Earnings (Dollars per Week)	Family Hours (Hours per Week)
Whites (n = 2175)		
Central experimental differential (dollars or hours per week)	−15.73	−8.63
t-statistic	(2.8)	(−4.32)
$G - 1$	−14.26	−3.26
t-statistic	(−1.06)	(−0.69)
$t - .5$	20.69	−4.15
t-statistic	(0.81)	(−0.46)
R^2	.1981	.1808
Blacks (n = 1862)		
Central experimental differential	10.80	−0.34
t-statistic	(1.69)	(−0.16)
$G - 1$	−9.58	−2.37
t-statistic	(−0.63)	(−0.47)
$t - .5$	2.00	−3.31
t-statistic	(0.08)	(−0.36)
R^2	.1720	.2236
Spanish-speaking (n = 1178)		
Central experimental differential	2.38	−2.02
t-statistic	(0.36)	(−0.87)
$G - 1$	−18.31	−6.53
t-statistic	(−1.15)	(−1.18)
$t - .5$	−43.62	−7.60
t-statistic	(−1.40)	(−0.71)
R^2	.1224	.0730

NOTE: Results are estimated from regression functions equivalent to equations (5) and (6). The central differential is at $G = 1.0$, $t = .5$. For other values of G, multiply coefficient by $G - 1.0$ and add to central differential. For other values of t, multiply coefficient by $t - .5$ and add to central differential.

to be no significant difference in response among the experimentals as a result of differences in the guarantee or the marginal tax rate to which they were subjected.

The results of this and the previous section taken together are disconcerting. In the previous section, we found a significant negative experimental differential in total family earnings and hours for whites. For blacks, one model found a significant positive experimental response in earnings. For the Spanish-speaking, we found no statistically significant response in either earnings or hours. Table 6.11 shows no significant differential in response *among* experimentals according to differences in the experimental plan generosity, as measured by parameters G and t.

For the whites, where a sizable overall experimental differential was found, it seems somewhat surprising to find no indication of differences in response according to the rather substantial variation across experimental plans. For blacks, the inconsistencies between the earnings and hours findings are disturbing, and the positive earnings differential is unexpected on the basis of a priori theory. For the Spanish-speaking, the failure to detect any significant response is disappointing, though the small sample size may be an obvious reason. There are good reasons, therefore, to use somewhat more complex models of experimental effects on labor supply to see whether they yield any insights into these problems.

One factor we should take into account is that the response of experimental families may differ according to the level of their earnings capabilities. There are two reasons to suppose this might be the case.

First, and most important, some of the families have normal earnings high enough to place them above the breakeven level for their negative income tax plans. For these families, there is some reason to expect that they will have less, if any, experimental response in terms of changed labor supply. If they remain at their normal earnings level, they would receive no cash benefits and would, therefore, face no experimental tax rate on additional earnings. To the extent this is correct, the overall mean experimental response (as in the models in this and the previous section) will be an average of the above-breakeven families' response, which can be expected to be small, and below-breakeven families with, perhaps, greater experimental response. If above-breakeven families can be separated out, the response of below-breakevens may appear more significantly in the results. This may have an effect not only on the means but also on the estimates of different responses for different levels of G and t. The higher the marginal tax rate, holding the guarantee level constant, the lower the breakeven level of income. Thus, tax rates and the proportion of people on a given plan above their breakeven are positively correlated and, when we do not specifically separate out above-breakeven experimentals, this will tend to attenuate any differences in experimental response according to the level of the tax rate.

A second reason for trying to estimate differences in responses according to the level of earnings capability of the family is simply that such responses may vary according to the level of normal earnings. The underlying income and substitution effects need not be constant across income levels, and economic theory gives us no guidance as to whether and how such effects might vary.

Both these reasons have import for the national cost implications of responses to a national negative income tax because the general population is not uniformly distributed across income levels. Since average responses at each income level are multiplied by the population frequency at that level, when translating into national costs, a small labor-supply response at income levels near and just above breakeven (where the population density is greater) may have larger national cost implications than a big response at low income levels (where the population density is small).

To look for differences in response according to levels of earnings capabilities of experimental families, we want to interact one or more of the experimental variables in our labor-supply models with some measure of family earnings capability. As already noted above in the discussion of possible control variables, such a measure would also have the virtue of being a compact summary indicator of those characteristics of families that are likely to be systematically related to labor supply and therefore might result in systematic differences in response to experimental treatments. Interacting such a summary measure with experimental parameters may allow us to avoid numerous interactions of the experimental variables with special characteristics that we feel might condition response.

However, as noted in our control variable discussion, in using an earnings variable on the right-hand side of a labor-supply equation, we face the problem of endogeneity. Earnings is the measure of, or closely related to, the labor-supply response we use in measuring the experimental differentials. Therefore, we cannot use contemporaneous earnings but must seek a proxy variable which may be presumed to indicate what family earnings (or hours) would have been in the absence of the experimental treatment. We need, therefore, to consider in some detail the relative merits of the three alternative proxy variables for the case when family earnings capabilities are interacted with experimental variables.

3. CONTROL VARIABLES FOR NORMAL EARNINGS WHEN INTERACTED WITH EXPERIMENTAL EFFECTS

The models discussed above all control for the effects of normal earnings as a determinant of labor supply. We now wish to test a further hypothesis—that the strength of experimental responses varies according to the level of normal income. In terms of econometric estimation, such tests require the use of interactions between our normal earnings measures and treatment variables.

Unfortunately, the apparent outcome of such tests is extremely sensitive to the manner in which the earnings proxy has been generated. The fact that several alternative approaches to incorporating earnings measures in labor-supply models have been attempted by analysts in the New Jersey experiment (and compared in this chapter) reflects the concern that each is deficient in one or more respects. In particular, the interaction of income proxies with treatment variables creates more serious hazards for interpretation of the results than has been apparent in our analysis so far. We therefore feel it appropriate to outline certain difficulties associated with each of the three procedures followed here. This section first assesses some general problems associated with these three measures. The results of interacting each earnings proxy with experimental status are then reported. The bias implicit in this procedure for two of the proxies is assessed. Finally, we attempt to quantify the bias associated with the control-group proxy and provide corrected estimates.

General Problems

1. Preenrollment earnings measures, while a poor proxy for *normal* earnings from a theoretical perspective, are often utilized because subsequent experimental status cannot (by definition) influence their values. Such variables are deficient as proxies for normal earnings in a number of respects, however. With intrafamily autocorrelated disturbances over time, the use of lagged measures of dependent variables biases both the primary coefficient estimates and the procedures used to correct for the autocorrelation. Furthermore, the degree of such bias is likely to vary with the length of time between enrollment and the period being evaluated. In addition, preenrollment variables are decreasingly efficient proxies for normal earnings as later experimental periods are examined. Finally, there is some evidence that the use of a preenrollment proxy for designating families as above or below the breakeven point can produce misleading analytic results when interacting breakeven status with other negative income tax parameters. Since preenrollment income contains both a normal and a transitory component, the specification of a breakeven dummy effectively constitutes a grouping procedure that isolates permanent income effects not identified by the preenrollment income variable. If one then proceeds to define a tax-rate effect that occurs only below the breakeven point, the measured response will be confounded by the correlation between the tax rate variable and normal income.[9]

2. The use of normal income equations estimated for the control group to predict corresponding ex-ante measures for the experimental group is intuitively attractive in a number of respects. The availability of several

---

[9] Thus Metcalf (forthcoming) detects tax-rate effects using preenrollment measures as his control variables stronger than those found by other researchers analyzing the experiment.

observations for each family permits an effort at netting out transitory influences not possible with a single preenrollment observation and allows the generation of earnings proxies on a contemporaneous basis with the behavior to be analyzed. Furthermore, the exclusion of experimental families from the estimation procedure provides a set of earnings proxies uncontaminated by actual experimental effects.

This method is similar to that adopted for predicting hypothetical wage rates for nonworkers from an equation estimated with data for workers of similar personal and socioeconomic characteristics (Hall, 1973; Kalacheck and Raines, 1970). The only difference is that such wage-rate estimating procedures suffer from possible self-selection bias (that is, given a set of *measured* characteristics, the nonworkers may be a nonrandom subset), whereas the control group has been selected according to a random process.

Aside from possible econometric problems unrelated to the qualitative formulation of the procedure,[10] the use of this sort of normal earnings proxy poses no special problems for the analysis of experimental responses of the type discussed so far.[11] The only apparent weakness is the loss of sample size and the decrease in efficiency of estimates that results from restricting the income prediction process to the control group.

3. The Watts procedure involves estimating normal income variables across the complete sample of treatment and control observations and employs a host of variables related to the negative income tax treatment to "purge" the estimates of experimental effects. This procedure has not been formally scrutinized, but two potential difficulties have become apparent with the approach as followed thus far. First, to the extent that the treatment variables in the predicted income equation are specified differently from those used in the subsequent analysis, an implied specification error may influence the results. Second, the Watts income proxies were estimated in logarithmic form. Users of the proxies in their absolute form should recognize that they represent *medians* of normal income rather than means, and that the implied error distribution differs from that associated with nonlogarithmic specifications.[12] The clear advantage of the Watts procedure is that purging the data of detectable experimental effects makes it possible to use the full data set in generating normal earnings proxies.

[10] Specification error in the predicting equation, improper inclusion of endogenous right-hand variables, and absence of corrections for autocorrelation are several examples.

[11] Special problems do appear when these proxies are interacted with experimental treatment variables, as we shall see.

[12] Adjustments are available to produce a mean income proxy, but the implicit error distribution remains lognormal rather than normal.

Interactions between Earnings Proxies and Experimental Effects

Tables 6.12 through 6.14 report the effects of interacting the three proxy control variables with experimental status in earnings and hours equations for white, black, and Spanish-speaking families, respectively. Each of the reported regressions takes the general form

$$Y = B_o + B_1\hat{Y} + B_2\hat{Y}^2 + B_3 EXP + B_4 EXP \cdot \hat{Y} + \sum_{5}^{K} B_k X_k + u. \quad (7)$$

Except for the $EXP \cdot \hat{Y}$ interaction term, the specifications parallel those underlying the results reported in Tables 6.5 through 6.7.

The estimates for white family earnings and hours illustrate quite well the general trend of the results. Recall from Table 6.5 that a significant negative effect on both earnings and hours was reported for all three proxy procedures. In Table 6.12, when preenrollment income is used as the proxy, no significant interaction with experimental status occurs in either the earnings or the hours response. The joint effect of the experimental variables remains significant, however.

When the control-based proxy is used, there is a strongly negative in-

Table 6.12 Experimental Interaction with Proxy Income Control Variable ($\hat{Y}$) for Three Proxy Specifications, White Families, Quarters 3–10 Pooled

	Proxy Control Variable Specifications		
	Preenrollment	Control Based	Watts
Family earnings			
Experimental differential (EXP)	−4.5	54.2	14.6
t-statistic	(−0.35)	(3.80)	(1.11)
$EXP \cdot \hat{Y}$	−0.10	−0.54	−0.24
t-statistic	(−0.91)	(−5.30)	(−2.09)
Joint significance (EXP, $EXP \cdot \hat{Y}$)	[2.8]	[.00]	[2.1]
R^2	.1286	.2063	.1533
Family hours			
Experimental differential (EXP)	−6.2	15.8	2.4
t-statistic	(−1.33)	(3.01)	(0.50)
$EXP \cdot \hat{Y}$	−0.01	−0.19	−0.08
t-statistic	(−0.32)	(−4.81)	(−1.98)
Joint significance (EXP, $EXP \cdot \hat{Y}$)	[0.23]	[0.00]	[0.15]
R^2	.0702	.1431	.1103

NOTE: Number of observations = 2475. Results are estimated from regression functions equivalent to equation (7). The earnings differential is in dollars per week. The hours differential is in hours per week.

Table 6.13 **Experimental Interaction with Proxy Income Control Variable ($\hat{Y}$) for Three Proxy Specifications, Black Families, Quarters 3–10 Pooled**

	Proxy Control Variable Specifications		
	Preenrollment	Control Based	Watts
Family earnings			
Experimental differential (*EXP*)	−5.8	72.9	16.2
t-statistic	(−0.44)	(5.25)	(1.03)
EXP · $\hat{Y}$	0.17	−0.56	−0.07
t-statistic	(1.36)	(−4.85)	(−0.41)
Joint significance (*EXP, EXP* · $\hat{Y}$)	[13.9]	[.00]	[24.1]
R^2	.1081	.1897	.1598
Family hours			
Experimental Differential (*EXP*)	−0.55	21.9	6.8
t-statistic	(−0.12)	(4.54)	(1.2)
EXP · $\hat{Y}$	−0.00	−0.20	−0.08
t-statistic	(−0.06)	(−4.98)	(−1.41)
Joint significance (*EXP, EXP* · $\hat{Y}$)	[94.2]	[.00]	[36.2]
R^2	.0894	.2148	.1498

NOTE: Number of observations = 1862. Results are estimated from regression functions equivalent to equation (7). The earnings differential is in dollars per week. The hours differential is in hours per week.

teraction effect, offset by a large positive experimental effect at low income and hours levels. Evaluated at the mean value for the control-based income proxy, the net experimental effects are similar to those obtained in Table 6.5. If these results are to be believed, therefore, a negative income tax produces positive incentives at low-income levels and increasingly powerful disincentive effects at income levels in excess of $100 per week. The Watts normal income proxy also produces significantly negative interaction effects, although the interaction coefficient is only 44 percent as large, for both earnings and hours, as in the control-based case.[13]

The above qualitative results reappear, for black and Spanish-speaking families, in both earnings and hours equations. The control-based income proxy uniformly yields a strong, highly significant negative interaction with experimental status. The Watts measure is consistently negative, although no longer significant.

[13] If adjustment is made for the logarithmic basis of the Watts estimate, the interaction coefficient would be slightly less than 40 percent as large as in the control-based case.

FAMILY LABOR-SUPPLY RESPONSE

Table 6.14 Experimental Interaction with Proxy Income Control Variable ($\hat{Y}$) for Three Proxy Specifications, Spanish-speaking Families, Quarters 3–10 Pooled

	Proxy Control Variable Specifications		
	Preenrollment	Control Based	Watts
Family earnings			
Experimental differential (EXP)	17.7	52.6	4.8
t-statistic	(1.04)	(2.58)	(0.24)
EXP · $\hat{Y}$	−0.21	−0.48	−0.002
t-statistic	(−1.21)	(−2.50)	(−0.01)
Joint significance (EXP, EXP · $\hat{Y}$)	[47.1]	[3.6]	[77.8]
R^2	.0999	.1228	.0883
Family hours			
Experimental differential (EXP)	4.6	16.2	1.35
t-statistic	(0.81)	(2.27)	(0.21)
EXP · $\hat{Y}$	−.08	−0.17	−0.03
t-statistic	(−1.49)	(−2.63)	(−0.41)
Joint significance (EXP, EXP · $\hat{Y}$)	[10.13]	[2.38]	[78.0]
R^2	.0662	.0865	.0759

NOTE: Number of observations = 1178. Results are estimated from regression functions equivalent to equation (7). The earnings differential is in dollars per week. The hours differential is in hours per week.

Interaction Biases with Control-based Instruments

Do the above results provide valid information about the interaction between normal earnings and experimental status, or does the method by which earnings proxies are generated introduce a bias into the interaction coefficient? Jonathan Dickinson argues that the latter is the case in the context of control-based income proxies, where the apparent interaction is strongest.[14]

The fundamental problem created by the use of control-based instruments can be illustrated in the context of a simplified model of the form $Y_1 = \alpha_0 + \delta_0 Y_N + u_1$ for controls, and $Y_2 = \alpha + \delta Y_N + u_2$ for experimentals, where Y_N is true normal income in absence of the experiment and where u_1, u_2 are transitory error components having the conventionally assumed properties. For expository purposes, the true values of α_0 and δ_0

---

[14] Jonathan Dickinson's argument was presented in seminars and discussions at the University of Wisconsin, but it is not available in manuscript form. The discussion which follows is based on derivations independently produced by the authors but investigated subsequent to knowledge of the substance of Dickinson's work.

are regarded as being zero and one, respectively. The model is equivalent to a single equation specification which includes a dummy variable for experimental status, Y_N, and an interaction between Y_N and experimental status.

Unbiased, consistent, and efficient estimates of all coefficients could be obtained by ordinary least squares, if Y_N were directly observable. Since Y_N is not observable but is assumed here to be definable as a linear combination of variables which are observable in the form $Y_N = \Sigma C_k X_k$, a control-based instrument for Y_N can be generated by estimating the regression $Y = \Sigma C_k X_k + u_1$ using ordinary least squares across the control sample. The normal income proxy, $\hat{Y}_N$, can then be defined by the expression $\Sigma \hat{C}_k X_k$, where the $\hat{C}_k$ are sample estimates of the true C_k.

If the simplified model is then reestimated with $\hat{Y}_N$ in place of true Y_N, the estimated values of α_0 and δ_0 will be identically zero and one, respectively. The issue is what happens to the estimated coefficients $\hat{\alpha}$ and $\hat{\delta}$ when the normal income proxy, $\hat{Y}_N$, for experimental families is generated by the control-based regression. Concentrating on $\hat{\delta}$, which corresponds to δ_0 plus the interaction coefficient in the single equation variant of the model, Dickinson finds $\hat{\delta}$ is a *downward-biased* estimate of δ. One form of establishing the reason for this finding can be expressed as follows.

1. $\hat{Y}_N$ is uncorrelated with the true errors in the experimental sample, u_2, since the experimental sample was not used in the estimating process.
2. By construction, $\hat{Y}_N$ is uncorrelated with the *estimated* residuals for the control group, but it is *positively* correlated with the unobserved true errors, u_1. This is because $\hat{Y}_N$ differs from the true Y_N in the control group *only* by virtue of the specific values of u_1 in the drawn control sample.
3. For the full (experimental plus control) sample, $\hat{Y}_N$ is therefore differentially correlated with u_1 and u_2. The interaction term picks up the differential effect, producing a downward bias in $\hat{\delta}$.
4. The mean difference in response between experimentals and controls is determined by the sample means and is unrelated to the choice of income proxy. Thus $\hat{\alpha}$ is biased upward to compensate for the downward bias in $\hat{\delta}$.

The exact magnitude of the bias in $\hat{\delta}$ for small samples cannot be quantified formally, for much the same reason that simultaneous estimation techniques such as two-stage least squares have unknown small sample properties. If, however, we write down the expected value of $\hat{\delta}$ and take the probability limit of those terms which correspond to terms disappearing in the limit for two-stage-least-squares estimators, we obtain the following approximation for the bias:

$$\hat{\delta} = \left[\frac{V}{V + (K/M)\sigma^2}\right] \quad (8)$$

where σ^2 is the true variance of current income, that is $E(u^2)$, V is the variance of true Y_N for the experimental sample, K is the number of X_i variables used to predict $\hat{Y}_N$, and M is the number of control observations. As M approaches infinity, $\hat{\delta}$ approaches δ in the limit. Thus $\hat{\delta}$, while biased, is not an inconsistent estimator of δ.

Quantifying the Bias

The models reported in this chapter are more complex than the above example in two major respects—the basic model specification is more complex and the stochastic term is assumed to have a family-specific error component. Thus no direct translation of equation (8) to a quantified bias measure could be achieved, making it necessary to adopt an empirically based procedure, described as follows.

1. The control group was randomly split into two groups, and separate control-based proxies ($\hat{Y}_1$, $\hat{Y}_2$) were created, using the same estimating equation but generated from the two subsamples. These two groups will be referred to as control-1 and control-2.
2. $\hat{Y}_1$ is uncorrelated with the error terms in the control-2 subsample and the experimental subsample. Thus, if a labor-supply equation is estimated over the latter two subsamples, using $\hat{Y}_1$ as the normal earnings proxy, the estimated interaction term should be unbiased. The resulting estimates are extremely inefficient, however, because of the reduced sample used both to estimate Y_1 and to perform the subsequent analysis.
3. If $\hat{Y}_2$ is used in place of $\hat{Y}_1$ in the same sample, the results would again be biased. Comparison of the two results provides a point estimate of the interaction bias.
4. An alternative bias estimate can be obtained by replicating the procedure with the control-1 subsample combined with the experimental subsample.
5. The two bias estimates produced by steps (3) and (4) are dependent on the sizes of the subsamples and are not directly applicable to analyses based on the full sample. Thus the relation between bias and sample size as expressed in equation (8) was used to project the

two bias estimates to the full sample. The estimates were then averaged.[15]

The comparison, reported in Table 6.15, of results for the control subsamples each combined with the experimental group provides striking confirmation of the Dickinson contention. In every case, the income-experimental interaction is strongly negative when the internal control-based proxy is used, and weakly negative (or positive for Spanish-speaking families) when the external proxy is used. Only for white families is there a sustained negative interaction between normal income and experimental status when the externally based $\hat{Y}_N$ variables are used with the control subsamples.[16] The directly measured bias estimates range from 67 percent to 117 percent of the biased (subsample) $EXP \cdot \hat{Y}$ coefficients.

When the bias measures are projected to the full sample, their relative sizes are substantially reduced—to 43 percent for whites and 52 percent for blacks. Thus, according to the procedures attempted here, there remains a substantial negative interaction between normal earnings and experimental status.

Several comments should be made about the results obtained in this section. First, the bias correction procedures used here are only approximate, and are suspect in that the resulting full-sample adjusted interaction estimates are uniformly larger than the unbiased coefficients obtained from the subsample analyses. Thus further investigations of the bias issue are warranted, and the results to date should be viewed with caution.

Second, the Watts procedure for creating income proxies may be subject to the same bias argument, depending upon the specification of the variables used to purge the measure of experimental effects.[17] The empiri-

---

[15] Equation (8) can be rewritten as

$$\delta - \hat{\delta} \approx \hat{\delta} Z, \text{ where we define } Z = \frac{(K/M)\sigma^2}{V}.$$

Given empirical measures of $(\delta - \hat{\delta})$ and $\hat{\delta}$ for each control subsample, Z was calculated. Holding all other components of Z constant, it was then adjusted to reflect the larger value for M for the full control sample. For earnings, $\hat{\delta}$ was obtained for the full sample by adding one to the biased interaction coefficient, and then utilized with the revised Z to obtain each of two bias estimates. A weighted average of the two estimates was calculated to account for the fact that the two subsamples were not exactly equal in size. For hours, $\hat{\delta}$ was calculated by augmenting the interaction coefficient by the earnings proxy coefficient, adjusted for the presence of the proxy squared in the regression. Only one bias estimate was obtained for the hours equation.

[16] The unbiased $EXP \cdot \hat{Y}$ coefficients for white earnings $(-.2122, -.2061)$ both have t-statistics in the vicinity of -2.

[17] For example, if an experimental status interaction term is included for every possible variable, the control-based results are replicated exactly.

Table 6.15 Estimated Biases for Experimental Interactions with Control-based Proxy Income Control Variable ($\hat{Y}$), Quarters 3–10 Pooled

		$EXP \cdot \hat{Y}$ (Control Subsamples)[a]			$EXP \cdot \hat{Y}$ (Full Sample)		
	Subsample	Biased Coeff.	Unbiased Coeff.	Bias	Observed Coeff.	Projected Bias	Adjusted Coeff.
Family earnings							
White	1	-.644	-.212	.432	-.545[b]	.233	-.312
	2	-.704	-.206	.498	(.103)		
Black	1	-.552	.094	.647	-.561	.291	-.269
	2	-.680	-.157	.523	(.116)		
Spanish-speaking	1	-.842	.075	.916	.477	.422	-.055
	2	-.724	.070	.794	(.192)		
Family hours							
White	2	-.230	-.076	.154	-.186	.080	-.106
					(.039)		
Black	2	-.250	-.043	.207	-.200	.107	-.093
					(.040)		
Spanish-speaking	2	-.253	.037	.290	-.177	.172	-.005
					(.067)		

NOTE: Results are estimated from regression functions equivalent to equation (7). The regressions for the two control subsamples both use the entire experimental group.
[a] For the control subsamples 1, $\hat{Y}_1$ is used for the biased coefficient, $\hat{Y}_2$ for the unbiased coefficient. An analogous procedure was used for the control subsamples 2.
[b] Standard errors are in parentheses.

cal estimates appear to indicate that in this case a similar bias in the Watts estimating procedure did not occur, since the Watts proxy coefficients are closer in order of magnitude to the unbiased coefficients in Table 6.15. One cannot be sure, however, that this would always be the case.

Finally, the problems associated with the use of control-based income proxies documented here do not uniformly detract from their use. The measurement of overall mean experimental effects is not affected. Furthermore, because the proxy estimate is not differentially correlated with subsample error terms *within* the experimental group, one may proceed to analyze *relative* interaction effects by plan characteristics so long as the basic gross interaction measure is discounted. This also implies that we need only make one central bias correction, rather than adjust each possible interaction coefficient.[18]

4. DIFFERENTIAL RESPONSE AMONG INDIVIDUALS, USING INTERACTIONS BETWEEN $\hat{Y}$ AND EXPERIMENTAL VARIABLES

Having discussed the problem of bias in the use of the control-based proxy for earnings, $\hat{Y}_{CB}$, when interacted with experimental variables, we proceed to examine models which incorporate interactions of $\hat{Y}_{CB}$ not only with an experimental status variable but also with other experimental parameters. We argued at the close of Section 3 that the bias in $\hat{Y}_{CB} \cdot EXP$ does *not* carry over to interaction with other experimental variables such as G or t. This means that we can develop a measure of whether families' normal earnings (as predicted by $\hat{Y}_{CB}$) would have been sufficient to place them above the breakeven level of income for their experimental plan. Thus we can differentiate above- and below-breakeven families and look for differential responses among experimentals. The rationale for this approach was briefly spelled out in Section 2.

For these purposes we can extend the model given in equation (7) as follows:

$$Y = b_0 + b_1\hat{Y}_{CB} + b_2\hat{Y}_{CB}^2 + b_3EXP + b_4EXP\ \hat{Y}_{CB} + b_5(G - 1.0)$$
$$+ b_6(G - 1.0)\hat{Y}_{CB} + b_7(t - .5) + b_8(t - .5)\hat{Y}_{CB} + b_9ABV$$
$$+ \Sigma b_kX_k + e$$

where $(G - 1.0)$ and $(t - .5)$ are defined as in equations (5) and (6), Σb_kX_k are the quarterly and seasonal variables defined for equation (1), and

---

[18] Watts has questioned this contention, and it warrants further investigation.

$ABV = 1$ for families for which $Y_{CB} \geq G/t$ (that is, normal earnings above the breakeven level of income), 0 otherwise.

An alternative model, which produced stronger empirical results, involved a somewhat different formulation of the experimental variables. This specification used a payment variable, P, equal to the amount of cash transfer the family would receive under their experimental plan at the predicted value for $\hat{Y}_{CB}$; and a variable, $TNAB$, equal to the tax rate for those with $\hat{Y}_{CB}$ below their breakeven and zero for those above it.[19] The rationale for use of the variable P is that families may focus on the payment they would receive if they did not change their labor supply rather than on the cash payment they would get at zero earnings, namely, the guarantee. The rationale for $TNAB$ is obvious.

The model used is

$$Y = b_0 + b_1\hat{Y}_{CB} + b_2\hat{Y}_{CB}^2 + b_3EXP + b_4EXP\,\hat{Y}_{CB} + b_5P \\ + b_6P\hat{Y}_{CB} + b_7TNAB + b_8TNAB\cdot\hat{Y}_{CB} + \Sigma b_k X_k + e \qquad (9)$$

where $P = \$G - t\hat{Y}_{CB}$, where $\$G$ is G times poverty line for family size i; and $TNAB = t$ when ABV is 0, 0 when ABV is 1.

A similar model was run for hours, with H_{CB} substituted for $\hat{Y}_{CB}$

$$H = b_0 + b_1H_{CB} + b_2H_{CB} + b_3EXP\cdot H_{CB} + b_4P + B_5PH_{CB} \\ + b_6TNAB + b_7TNAB\cdot H_{CB} + \Sigma b_k X_k + e. \qquad (10)$$

Note that in equations (9) and (10) above-breakeven experimentals have values of zero for both P and $TNAB$. Thus this model distinguishes between above- and below-breakeven families as well as among those below breakeven but on different plans.

The results of the formulations expressed in equations (9) and (10) are shown in Tables 6.16 through 6.18. It must be remembered that in these tables the joint significance of the EXP, $EXP\cdot\hat{Y}_{CB}$ set of variables is much overstated because the coefficients reported have not been corrected for bias. However, our interest is focused in these tables on the comparisons *among* experimentals, not on the experimental control differences.

In Table 6.16 we find that for total family earnings the tax variable ($TNAB$) and its interaction with $\hat{Y}_{CB}$ are quite significant. For total family hours, the interactions of the payments variable and the tax variable were not significant, so a more truncated version was run which still utilized the above- and below-breakeven distinction (since P and $TNAB$ are zero for those above breakeven). In this case the $TNAB$ variable is again significant.

---

[19] Joint F-tests for significance of the experimental variables were typically stronger for this formulation.

Table 6.16 Differential Responses among Experimentals by Plan Generosity Relative to Income, White Families, Quarters 3–10 Pooled

	Constant	$EXP \cdot \hat{Y}$ Interaction	Joint Significance
Family earnings			
Experimental differential	109.34	−0.9087	na
Payment variable	−0.2873	0.0027	78.58
Tax-rate variable	−129.86	0.8890	0.24
$R^2 = .2076$			
Family hours			
Experimental differential	28.04	−0.6956	na
Payment variable	−0.0169	–	78.77
Tax-rate variable	−0.9520	–	2.00
$R^2 = .1950$			

NOTE: Number of observations = 2175. Estimated from regression functions equivalent to equation (9) for earnings, and equation (10), with b_5 and b_7 equal to zero, for hours. Payment variable equals the amount a family would receive under their experimental plan at their predicted value for $\hat{Y}$. The tax-rate variable equals the tax rate for those with $\hat{Y}$ below breakeven, and zero for those above. For these calculations, $\hat{Y}$ is the control-based income control proxy.

Table 6.17 Differential Responses among Experimentals by Plan Generosity Relative to Income, Black Families, Quarters 3–10 Pooled

	Constant	$EXP \cdot \hat{Y}$ Interaction	Joint Significance
Family earnings			
Experimental differential	68.37	−0.55	0.37
Payment variable	−0.67	0.0057	23.84
Tax-rate variable	61.90	−0.4127	23.42
$R^2 = .1895$			
Family hours			
Experimental differential	20.89	−0.5189	0.02
Payment variable	−0.1739	0.0045	35.55
Tax-rate variable	13.07	−0.3136	55.70
$R^2 = .2465$			

NOTE: Number of observations = 1862. Estimated from regression functions equivalent to equation (9) for earnings, and equation (10), with b_5 and b_7 set equal to zero, for hours. Payment variable equals the amount a family would receive under their experimental plan at their predicted value for $\hat{Y}$. The tax-rate variable equals the tax rate for those with $\hat{Y}$ below breakeven, and zero for those above. For these calculations, $\hat{Y}$ is the control-based income control proxy.

FAMILY LABOR-SUPPLY RESPONSE

Table 6.18 Differential Responses among Experimentals by Plan Generosity Relative to Income, Spanish-speaking Families, Quarters 3–10 Pooled

	Constant	$EXP \cdot \hat{Y}$ Interaction	Joint Significance
Family earnings			
Experimental differential	86.12	−0.7663	0.00
Payment variable	−1.1016	0.0154	0.6
Tax-rate variable		0.3237	2.3
$R^2 = .1288$			
Family hours			
Experimental differential	40.89	−1.034	1.16
Payment variable	−0.3361	0.0108	9.6
Tax-rate variable		−0.2585	5.54
$R^2 = .0928$			

NOTE: Number of observations = 1178. Estimated from regression functions equivalent to equation (9) for earnings, and equation (10), with b_5 and b_7 set equal to zero, for hours. Payment variable equals the amount a family would receive under their experimental plan at their predicted value for $\hat{Y}$. The tax-rate variable equals the tax rate for those with $\hat{Y}$ below breakeven, and zero for those above. For these calculations, $\hat{Y}$ is the control-based income control proxy.

Alternative versions of these models for whites yield somewhat different results. For this reason, we would not put a great deal of emphasis on the estimates of the order of magnitude of response to tax rates. The results with these models basically demonstrate that there is a differential response among experimentals, particularly between below-breakeven and above-breakeven families.

In Table 6.17, for blacks, we find no evidence of any differential response among experimentals. In Table 6.18, for Spanish-speaking families, we find the *P* and *TNAB* functions are significant both for total family earnings and total family hours. The results for the Spanish-speaking families are somewhat more stable among the slightly different formulations of the model than those for the whites. Still, given the sample size, we feel it would not be wise to put much weight on the exact magnitude of the estimated response to *P* and *TNAB*. The key finding is that there is an indication of differential response among experimentals.

5. CONCLUSIONS

Since the response to the experimental treatment is significantly different according to ethnic group, it is best to review our conclusions group by group.

First, with respect to whites, the results in Section 1 indicated a clear experimental response in terms of reduced earnings and hours. For earnings, the estimated range of percentage reductions was between 6 percent and 11 percent. For hours, the estimated range was 13 percent to 16 percent. The results of Section 3 indicate that even after correction for the bias in the control-based measure, there was an increase in the negative experimental response with increases in normal earnings. The results of Section 4 indicated that among experimentals there was a difference in response, largely between those below their breakeven and those above and probably associated with tax-rate differences. No reliable estimates of the exact magnitude of such differences could be obtained, however. The Section 4 analysis gives us somewhat greater confidence in the findings of Section 1, because of the significant differences found among experimentals on different plans.

Second, with respect to blacks, we find in Section 1 a positive significant differential in earnings but no significant effects in hours. In Section 4 we find no significant differences in response among experimentals.

For the Spanish-speaking, the results of Section 1 show no statistically significant family labor-supply response in earnings or hours. In Section 4, however, we do find significant differences in response among experimentals. Once again the order of magnitude of such differences among experimentals cannot be given much precision, but its existence does suggest an experimental response that varies by negative income tax plan.

We have introduced considerable complexity into the analysis of the family labor-supply response. But we believe this complexity is justified by the importance of the issues outlined at the end of Section 3. The search for differences in response among experimentals is important for a number of issues related to the possible implications of a national plan. Unfortunately—probably primarily because of the limits of sample size resulting from the necessity to analyze separately by ethnic group—we can only conclude that there are reasonable statistical indications that, for the white and the Spanish-speaking subsamples at least, response differences among experimentals are undoubtedly important. Future research may permit more exact specification of the magnitude of these differential responses.

APPENDIX: THE DEVELOPMENT OF CONTROL-BASED ESTIMATES OF NORMAL EARNINGS AND NORMAL HOURS

The control-based normal earnings and normal hours variables were generated by single equation models estimated on the basis of the control-group data for the continuous husband–wife sample for quarters 3–10. The rationale for focusing on earnings and hours is briefly discussed in the introduction to the chapter itself.

Theory gives relatively little guidance as to the appropriate functional form for the reduced form equation for total family earnings or hours. We do have some idea of the types of variables, reflecting personal and family characteristics and local labor-market conditions, which should enter such equations. The usual age, education, health status, and family structure variables were entered, in several cases in nonlinear forms. In addition, we were able to add variables reflecting initial industry and occupation for several categories that contained sizable numbers of the sample. The pooled time-series cross-section nature of our data permitted us to enter both time trend and seasonality variables. Finally, we ran preenrollment values for the dependent variable and interactions of this variable with time since preenrollment. Since our objective was to obtain a proxy for what earnings or hours would have been in the absence of the experimental treatment, these time trend and seasonality elements could be important in improving the performance of the control-based proxy as compared to preenrollment values only. Table A.1 defines the variables included in the regressions estimated on the control group for each ethnic sample.

Since pooled time-series cross-section samples were used, the regressions were estimated by the error components method.

Three separate estimates of each control-based proxy were made. First, the control group was randomly divided in half. The regression equation with identical variables was run separately for each half. These two estimating equations were used to produce proxy control-based variables to be used in labor-supply equations in order to estimate the extent of bias. This procedure is described in Section 3 in the text. A third regression was run for the full control sample to be used in labor-supply equations when corrected for bias (as described in Section 3). The proxies used in Sections 2 and 4, $\hat{Y}_{CB}$ and H_{CB}, are also those based on the regression for the full control sample. All three regression equations used for each proxy included, for each ethnic group, the variables indicated in Table A.1. For example, white total family hours had the same variables when regressed on each half of the white control group as for the white controls as a whole.

ACKNOWLEDGMENTS

We wish to thank Mark Breibart and Lewis Shuster for the considerable computational work they carried out for the study.

Table A.1 Variables for Control-based Proxies: Total Family Earnings and Hours

		White		Black		Spanish-speaking	
		Earnings	Hours	Earnings	Hours	Earnings	Hours
HAGE	age of husband	X	X	X	X	X	X
HAGE − 45	max (0, HAGE − 45)	X	X	X	X	X	X
HED	education of husband	X	X	X	X	X	X
HED − 8	max (0, HED − 8)	C	X	X	X	X	X
TR	dummy variable for Trenton	X	X	X	X	0	0
JC	dummy variable for Jersey City	X	X	X	X	X	X
SC	dummy variable for Scranton	C	C	C	C	0	0
PIP	dummy variable for Paterson–Passaic	C	C	C	C	C	C
FS	family size	X	X	X	X	X	X
NKS	number of children aged 0 to 5	X	X	X	X	X	X
NK 14-17	number of children aged 0 to 14	X	X	X	X	X	X
NAD	number of adults not including husband and wife						
MTH	real time elapsed in months, Aug. 1968 = 0	X	X	X	X	X	X
MTH − 32	max (0, MTH − 32)	X	X	X	X	X	X
WINTER	dummy variable for winter quarter	C	C	C	C	C	C
SPRING	dummy variable for spring quarter	X	X	X	X	X	X
SUMMER	dummy variable for summer quarter	X	X	X	X	X	X
FALL	dummy variable for fall quarter	X	X	X	X	X	X
HDIS	dummy variable for husband disabled	X	X	X	X	X	X
WDIS	dummy variable for wife disabled	X	X	X	X	X	X
PRY	total family earnings at preenrollment	X	0	X	0	X	0
PRY · QTR	PRY times variable for quarters since start of experiment (QTR)	X	0	X	0	X	0
PRY · (QTR − 6)	PRY times max (0, QTR − 6)	X	0	X	0	X	0
PRH	total family hours at preenrollment	0	X	0	X	0	X
PRH · QTR	PRH times QTR variable	0	X	0	X	0	X

Variable	Description							
PRH · (QTR − 6)	PRH times max (0, QTR − 6)	0	X	X	X	0	X	X
UN	dummy variable for union member	X	X	X	X	X	X	X
VA	Verbal ability (number correct responses to Ammons and Ammons Quick Test)		X	X	X	X	X	X
HO	dummy variable for homeowner [a]	X	X	X	X	X	X	X
HV	dollar value of house if owned [a]	X	X	X	0	0	0	0
HINC	husband's industry construction [b]	X	X	X	0	0	0	0
HIMED	husband's industry, durable manufacturing	X	X	X	X	X	X	0
HIMEND	husband's industry, nondurable manufacturing	X	X	X	X	X	X	X
HIRTL	husband's industry, retail trade	X	X	X	X	X	X	X
HISV	husband's industry, services	X	X	X	0	0	0	0
HIGT	husband's industry, government	X	X	X	0	0	0	0
HOGFT	husband's occupation, craftsman	X	X	X	X	X	X	X
HOOPR	husband's occupation, operative	X	X	X	X	X	X	X
HOLBR	husband's occupation, laborer	X	X	X	X	X	X	0
WIMED	wife's industry, durable manufacturing	X	X	X	X	X	0	0
WIMEND	wife's industry, nondurable manufacturing	X	X	X	X	X	0	0
WISV	wife's industry, services	X	X	X	X	X	0	0
WIWSM	wife's industry, unknown but worked since marriage [c]	X	X	X	X	0	0	0
WOOPR	wife's occupation, operative	X	X	X	X	X	X	X
WOSRV	wife's occupation, service worker	X	X	X	0	0	X	X
CONSTANT	(note constant terms include dummy variables marked c)	X	X	X	X	X	X	X

NOTE:

X = variable included in regression

C = variable omitted category, takes value for constant term

0 = variable not in regression.

[a] Three families who owned houses but had no house value were assigned average value for those owning and reporting value ($7123).

[b] Industry and occupation are as reported in preenrollment; if no preenrollment value was given in quarter 1, value was used if available.

[c] If no industry or occupation was reported at preenrollment or quarter 1, then those who worked since marriage are given a value of 1 for this variable.

REFERENCES

Ashenfelter, O., and Heckman, J. 1974. The estimation of income and substitution effects in a model of family labor supply. *Econometrica* 42: 73–85.

Cain, G. C., and Watts, H. W., eds. 1973. *Income maintenance and labor supply.* Institute for Research on Poverty Monograph Series, New York: Academic Press.

Hall, R. E. Wages, income and hours of work in the U.S. labor force. In *Income maintenance and labor supply,* ed. G. C. Cain and H. W. Watts, pp. 102–162. Institute for Research on Poverty Monograph Series. New York: Academic Press.

Kalacheck, E. D., and Raines, F. Q. 1970. Labor supply of lower income workers and the negative income tax. In *Technical studies, the president's commission on income maintenance programs.* Washington, D.C.: U.S. Government Printing Office.

Metcalf, C. Forthcoming. Predicting the effects of permanent programs from a limited duration experiment. In *The New Jersey income-maintenance experiment. Vol. 3. Expenditures, health, and social behavior; and the quality of the evidence,* ed. H. W. Watts and A. Rees. New York: Academic Press.

7 The effect of negative income tax payments on job turnover and unemployment duration

Seymour Spilerman
Richard E. Miller

Adoption of an income-maintenance program would increase an individual's flexibility in scheduling his work activity. The consequences of working fewer hours, earning a lower wage, or being unemployed would be diluted by the availability of transfer payments which partially replace the lost income. Under a negative income tax arrangement, the transfer payments would be accompanied by lower retained earnings from labor. In order that the subsidy be limited to the low-income part of the population, the tax rate for a supported family (that is, one below the breakeven point) must exceed its rate in the "positive" tax system. Nevertheless, in total income—retained earnings plus the subsidy—a family would always be better off under the support program. Classical economic theory suggests that a "disincentive effect" should occur in this circumstance; presented with a negative income tax arrangement the rational low-wage earner will substitute leisure (a subsidized activity) for work effort (whose returns are now taxed at a higher rate).

There are reasons why the disincentive may be small. Since the earnings subsidy would still leave most families with incomes near the poverty level, the attractiveness of exchanging work effort for leisure might not be great. In fact, it is conceivable that, after initial startup adjustments following adoption of a negative income tax program, earnings in many families might actually rise. This would happen if the financial cushion provided by the support payments was used by family members to increase their investments in *expected* income, presumably through additional schooling or otherwise raising their earnings potential. Considering the life cycle locations of family heads in the experiment, it is unlikely that many could increase their earnings potential by returning to school. A more accessible strategy for them would be to change jobs in a way that enhances future earnings. The income support payments would facilitate such job mobility, since they permit an individual to accept a low *initial* wage in a position which has good prospects for salary growth, and to sustain periods of unemployment while seeking this sort of position.

If job change behavior among low-income persons were to conform to the above considerations, then, over the brief duration of the negative income tax experiment, we might find that many subjects whom we judge to be improving *future* earnings are reporting lower *current* earnings after a job change. On the basis of the reported earnings figures, it might be concluded that we have witnessed a work disincentive effect, yet this appraisal would certainly misrepresent the impact of the support payments on family incomes in subsequent years. Despite the short time span of the experiment, it is therefore imperative that we attempt to assess whether the payments have an impact on future salary levels, apart from what can be learned by observing changes in current earnings. To investigate this issue we assign an "expected earnings" figure to the job (occupation–industry combination) held by each male family head at the preenrollment interview and at termination of the experiment. These figures were calculated to represent typical earnings of incumbents in the positions. By analyzing changes in the expected earnings figures, we can estimate the probable impact of a negative income tax on *long-run incomes* in the target population.

We will address this particular question in the context of a more general inquiry into the effect of the negative income tax plans on job change behavior. To structure the analysis in a coherent manner, we proceed systematically, in this chapter and the next, to consider the following contingent issues in sequential fashion:

1. *The rate of job turnover.* This topic concerns whether the provision of support payments, or particular plan parameters, will alter an individual's likelihood of leaving his employer. Related questions concern which individuals exhibit large experimental effects and which sorts of jobs tend to be left with greater frequency.

2. *The extent of unemployment.* Among subjects who made at least one change of employer during the period of the experiment, we investigate

the impact of the tax-plan parameters on duration of unemployment. Again, a related question concerns which individuals remain unemployed for long intervals.

3. *The pattern of reemployment.* Here, we limit attention to male heads who left their preenrollment jobs but are employed at a later time (the eighth quarterly was used for the second observation). With this subsample we inquire into changes in job characteristic scores resulting from the employment transition. Although we have motivated the inquiry of this chapter by a discussion of possible changes in expected earnings, and while this is probably the most important job characteristic for policy purposes, it is not the only work facet individuals may attempt to improve when changing jobs. We therefore examine corollary shifts in occupational status and in expected job satisfaction to ascertain whether the flexibility provided by the support payments is being used to alter these aspects of the work situation. This topic is addressed in the next chapter.

As a subsidiary theme, we explore the possibility of distinct racial and ethnic responses. Formally, ethnicity is just one more individual attribute, like age and education, to be considered in the process of analyzing subject responses to the negative tax payments. However, because of the social significance of this identity, we will perform parallel analyses for each ethnic subsample. There are many descriptions in the sociological literature (Gans, 1969; Moynihan, 1966; Poll, 1962; Duncan and Duncan, 1968; Spilerman and Elesh, 1971) which suggest that ethnicity does, indeed, pattern work attitudes and work behavior.[1] Moreover, the research in Chapter 3 on the labor response of male family heads reports results concerning the experimental impact on wages and hours worked by blacks, Spanish-speaking, and whites, that exhibit persistent ethnic effects despite the presence of controls for the commonly accepted determinants of these factors. For both these reasons, we pay particular attention to the ethnic dimension.

In the next section, preliminary to addressing the question of the experimental impact on job-change behavior, we discuss the analytic procedure that will be used and summarize the observed and expected job character-

---

[1] One prevalent type of explanation invokes the presence of culturally specific values regarding the importance of work and what constitutes a desirable occupation. An alternative kind of explanation for ethnic differences in labor-force characteristics (occupational distribution, rate of occupational mobility) stresses situational factors—discrimination in hiring and promotion; the concentration of ethnic groups in particular cities and neighborhoods where certain industries are located (and the tendency for industries to have technologically determined skill distributions); the historical concentration of ethnics in certain kinds of industries irrespective of residence (for example, Irish in police work, Jews in the apparel trades), with their occupational prospects again determined by the industries' requirements.

istic values of the negative income tax sample at preenrollment. This description serves to introduce the job characteristic variables, and provides a contextual setting for interpreting some of the experimental findings.

1. PRELIMINARY CONSIDERATIONS

Expected Job Characteristics

To investigate the impact of the support payments on job change behavior we must distinguish between the personal attributes and attitudes of individuals in the experiment and the intrinsic characteristics of their jobs (such as typical earnings and expected work satisfaction). One reason for making this distinction was noted in the introduction, where it was indicated that many jobs with prospects for improved earnings provide low initial wage rates. (An example would be apprenticeship programs.) For analogous reasons, it is necessary to differentiate between the work attitudes of participants in the experiment and the attitudes commonly expressed by incumbents in the same jobs. To use the negative income tax subjects as informants about work satisfaction, by contrast, and then explain their job change behavior on the basis of these expressions, would confound evaluations typical of work situations with evaluations derived from the participants' personal reasons for changing jobs. Since our objective is to analyze the effect of the tax plan parameters on transitions among jobs having different intrinsic characteristics, we prefer to employ estimates that are uncontaminated with the subjects' own reasons for movement.

We therefore characterized each job (specified by a 3-digit Census occupation code and a 3-digit industry code) by the attributes of incumbents in the position and by their attitudes toward aspects of the work situation—the job profiles having been constructed from other data sets. Our measures of job characteristics were computed from the 1966 National Longitudinal Survey of Work Experience (commonly known as the Parnes study) and from the 1970 Census 1 percent sample on population characteristics. The Parnes study involved a national sample of males between the ages of forty-five and fifty-nine.[2] From this data file we computed two measures of satisfaction with particular work aspects (job content, financial rewards) and a measure of occupational status (Duncan

---

[2] A second file, covering young males between fourteen and twenty-four, is available but was not used because few persons in this age category would have been employed.

score). These indices were constructed by averaging the values of individuals who held the same job. A more detailed description of the procedure is presented in Appendix A of this chapter.

Although earnings information was available on the Parnes tape and could have been used to compute an expected earnings figure according to the procedure detailed above, this was not done. Since the Parnes sample is a national one, the earnings estimates would have been contaminated with regional and city-size earnings differentials. Using the Parnes figures, a change in expected earnings by an individual in the experiment as a result of a job shift would reflect, partially, the geographic distributions of the two jobs. Instead of using the Parnes data, expected earnings figures were constructed from the 1970 Census of Population 1 percent sample tape for the New York and Newark SMSAs. As a consequence of using the census information, differences in expected earnings among jobs will reflect only the wage differential pattern in what is essentially a single labor market. Other job characteristics obtained from the Census tape relate to average educational attainment and percent black in a position; these two variables, together with the Duncan scores, serve as general indices of the attractiveness of a work situation.[3]

Measures of the Experimental Effect

We employ two formulations of the experimental variables. As our primary specification we utilize three spline variables, described generally in Chapter 2 and formulated in detail in Chapter 12. The first spline ($S1$) provides a contrast between control and experimental subjects at the guarantee level, $G = 75$ percent of the poverty line (for a family of four this equaled \$2475 in 1968), and tax rate, $t = 50$ percent. The coefficient of the second spline ($S2$) reports the slope with respect to a change in guarantee level, while the coefficient of the third spline ($S3$) describes the slope with respect to a change in the tax rate.

The attractiveness of this specification is that it relates subject responses directly to the treatment parameters. However, it is possible that participants are reacting to other aspects of the support payments structure in determining their work effort and that these aspects are not adequately captured by the spline formulation. Indeed, the subjects may have little awareness of the plan parameters and, therefore, may be poor judges of the consequence of changes in work effort for the support they

---

[3] In light of the probable overrepresentation of blacks in "dead end" jobs (positions with little mobility prospects) and the traditional exclusion of blacks from many desirable occupations, the variable "percent black in a position" was used as an indicator of low job attractiveness, and is discussed together with the status measures.

Table 7.1 Characteristics of the Male Family Heads Employed at Preenrollment

	Total Sample	Whites	Blacks	Spanish-speaking
Subject characteristics				
Family income in previous year (dollars)[a]	4188	4232	4374	3924
Head's earnings in previous year (dollars)	4001	4096	4099	3767
Wife's earnings in previous year (dollars)	229	172	318	208
Family size	5.9	5.6	6.5	5.7
Head's education (years)	8.8	10.0	8.8	7.2
Head's age	36.2	38.5	35.4	34.3
Expected values for head's occupation–industry, from the Census[b]				
Average annual earnings (dollars)	7573	7989	7416	7236
Percentage in job with earnings > $6000	68.3	72.1	67.9	64.3
Percentage in job with earnings > $8000	39.0	44.8	37.8	33.3
Percentage black	20.9	19.1	22.5	21.3
Average education (years)	9.6	10.0	9.5	9.4
Proportion stayers (same occupation–industry in 1970 as in 1965)	62.0	62.1	61.2	62.8
Earnings of stayers (dollars)	7868	8272	7767	7494
Earnings of movers (dollars)	7538	7784	7453	7331
Expected values for head's occupation–industry, from the Parnes data[c]				
Duncan status score	19.1	21.5	17.2	18.3
Job satisfaction (content)[d]	174	196	167	158
Job satisfaction (financial)[d]	113	110	116	115
(Number of observations at preenrollment)	(948)	(348)	(305)	(295)

[a] The failure of head's earnings plus wife's earnings to be less than total family income is caused by the earnings figures having been computed from estimates of weeks worked in the year and average weekly earnings by head and wife.

will receive. First of all, many families had stable incomes over much of the two-year interval under consideration; they would have had little experience with the payments adjustment mechanism. Second, the payment calculation for each four-week period was a complex process, with time lags, smoothing of income fluctuations, and year-end rebates and subtractions confusing the relation between a family's earnings and the amount it received from the experiment. For these reasons, we will entertain the possibility that decisions were made by subjects on the assumption of a continuation of *current* support levels, rather than in terms of the benefit which would accrue following a change in work behavior. As an alternate formulation of the experimental parameters, we therefore computed the dollar amount which the experiment is worth to a family, based on its size, negative tax plan, and estimated family income in a period prior to the consideration of a change in job status. This formulation is referred to as *BENEFIT* 1 and is specified by $BENEFIT\ 1 = G_s - tE_f$, where G_s equals the dollar guarantee for a family of size s, t equals the tax rate facing the family, and E_f denotes family income in the year preceding preenrollment.

Occupational Characteristics of the Negative Income Tax Sample at Preenrollment

Information on a number of participant characteristics and on their preenrollment jobs is presented in Table 7.1. In the top portion of the table, sample means are reported for several individual attributes which will be utilized in subsequent analyses. Summarizing the main ethnic patterns: black males in our sample have somewhat higher family earnings than white males, though less education; the higher black family earnings appear to be entirely a consequence of wives' earnings; and Spanish-speaking heads have the lowest incomes and education levels and are slightly younger than the other participants.

The entries for the census and Parnes variables report expected characteristics for the jobs held by male family heads at the time of preenrollment. The expected earnings figures indicate that, based on their occupa-

---

[b] Values assigned to respondents in the negative income tax sample are means over Census individuals with the same occupation and industry codes, or are proportions of individuals in a Census category. Where no Census individual had occupation and industry codes that match an experimental participant's, the Census value for the occupation alone was used.

[c] Values assigned to respondents in the negative income tax sample were computed from Parnes individuals with the same occupation and industry codes, as explained in note (*b*).

[d] Each job aspect score was constructed from several questions. The scores ($\times\ 10^{-3}$) measure the relative frequency with which an aspect was selected by incumbents in the job. (See Appendix A for details.)

tion and industry attachments, white participants should have averaged $7989, while mean earnings by black and Spanish-speaking subjects should have amounted to $7416 and $7236, respectively. These values are in terms of New York and Newark SMSA wage rates in 1970; therefore, only comparisons of relative earnings with analogous statistics for family heads in the experiment are appropriate. Making such comparisons, we find that blacks in the negative income tax sample were doing reasonably well in comparison with whites ($4099 versus $4096), considering the difference in their expected earnings ($7416 versus $7989). Spanish-speaking persons, by contrast, have the lowest expected earnings and the lowest actual earnings.

The principal ethnic patterns in expected job characteristics are the following. Blacks are concentrated in positions with high expected percentage black values; that is, they tend to be employed in the same occupations and industries in communities where the experiment was conducted, as in New York City and Newark. Black and Spanish-speaking heads hold jobs for which the expected earnings differential between stayers in the positions and movers is small relative to the white differential (whites are in jobs in which stayers average $488 more than movers). White family heads are employed in positions with higher Duncan status scores than black or Spanish-speaking subjects. With respect to work attitudes, there is one large interethnic difference, and it indicates that whites are more frequently employed at tasks in which workers express satisfaction with "job content." Comparable means for the Census and Parnes samples are presented in Appendix B, Table 7B.1.

To provide additional detail on the distribution of job characteristics in the negative income tax sample, we report some regression results. We are interested in relating individual attributes to the kinds of positions in which the persons are employed. Job characteristic scores of the family heads at preenrollment were used as dependent variables, the regressors being other characteristics of the individuals: race and ethnicity (dummy variables denoting white, black, and Spanish-speaking), city-site location (four dummy variables), age, education, and family size. To correct for heteroskedasticity in the error term resulting from the various occupation–industry means having been computed from different numbers of persons, generalized least squares was used with $\sqrt{n_i}$ as weights, where n_i equals the number of individuals in occupation–industry i on the Parnes or Census tape.

The results are reported in Table 7.2. The first pair of equations, in which the dependent variable is average earnings in a position, reveals that both blacks and Spanish-speaking persons are concentrated in low-paying jobs, relative to whites in the experiment. For the Spanish-

Dependent Variables[a]	Constant	Trenton	Paterson–Passaic	Jersey City	Black	Spanish-speaking	Education	Age	Family Size	R^2
Census Variables										
Average earnings	8176**	277	616**	173	−638**	−1009**				.042
	(72.09)	(0.91)	(2.39)	(0.69)	(−2.73)	(−4.15)				
Average earnings	7093**	427	768**	254	−604**	−836**	93.7**	2.93	2.92	.050
	(15.88)	(1.40)	(2.95)	(1.01)	(−2.58)	(−3.39)	(3.72)	(.042)	(0.09)	
Jobs > $6000	0.722**	0.011	0.054**	0.022	−0.031*	−0.076**				.039
	(77.33)	(0.44)	(2.54)	(1.06)	(−1.60)	(−3.77)				
Jobs > $6000	0.673**	0.019	0.061**	0.024	−0.033	−0.063**	0.0070**	−0.0011**	0.0038*	.046
	(18.38)	(0.75)	(2.86)	(1.17)	(−1.72)	(−3.14)	(3.37)	(−1.97)	(1.51)	
Jobs > $8000	0.399**	0.015	0.054**	0.022	−0.053**	0.083**	0.0076**	−0.00097	0.0034	.041
	(9.47)	(0.52)	(2.42)	(0.91)	(−2.39)	(−3.56)	(3.22)	(−1.49)	(1.18)	
Percentage black	0.192**	0.010	−0.0013	0.013	0.035**	0.0099	−0.0026*	0.00035	−0.0027	.018
	(7.87)	(0.59)	(−0.09)	(1.00)	(2.76)	(0.74)	(−1.90)	(0.95)	(−1.59)	
Average education	9.06**	0.171	0.654**	0.341**	−0.456**	−0.526**	0.058**	0.0030	0.0179	.047
	(37.09)	(1.02)	(4.59)	(2.48)	(−3.56)	(−3.90)	(4.25)	(0.80)	(1.06)	
Parnes Variables										
Duncan score	20.05**	−1.47	2.14	−0.136	−4.53**	−4.00**	0.171	−0.121**	0.514**	.071
	(8.35)	(−0.94)	(1.49)	(−0.10)	(−3.67)	(−3.15)	(1.36)	(−3.26)	(3.05)	
Job satisfaction (content)	212.4**	−10.4	−15.7	−23.4**	−18.6*	−36.7**	.426	−.548*	3.28**	.021
	(10.37)	(−0.78)	(−1.28)	(−2.00)	(−1.76)	(−3.39)	(0.40)	(−1.72)	(2.28)	
Job satisfaction (financial)	101.1**	0.899	13.0**	7.92	−1.87	−5.56	0.987*	−0.172	0.972	.020
	(9.07)	(0.12)	(1.94)	(1.25)	(−0.33)	(−0.94)	(1.69)	(−0.99)	(1.24)	

NOTE: Selected regressions are presented to depict the main relationships between job characteristics and attributes of participants in the experiment. Entries are unstandardized regression coefficients; t-values are in parentheses. To correct for heteroskedasticity resulting from the various job characteristics' means having been computed from different numbers of persons, the regression equations were transformed as follows: Each observation was multiplied by $\sqrt{n_i}$, where n_i = the number of individuals (in the Census or Parnes file) from which the occupation–industry mean was computed; the term $\sqrt{n_i}$ was introduced as a regressor, and the constant was suppressed. The R^2 values obtained from the least squares' algorithm after this transformation are no longer appropriate for the original regression; the reported values in the last column pertain to the untransformed equations (Kmenta, 1971:249–267).

[a] For more descriptive names of the dependent variables, see Table 7.1.
* Significant at $p < .10$.
** Significant at $p < .05$.

speaking group, low educational attainment and the other controls partially account for its disadvantage in average earnings (the decrease from $1009 to $836); for blacks the portion of the earnings differential that can be attributed to those factors is negligible (the change from $638 to $604). The same pattern emerges with several other job characteristics as dependent variables: percentage of persons with earnings in excess of $6000, percentage with earnings in excess of $8000, percentage black,[4] mean years of education, and occupational status (Duncan score). The ethnic effects in these equations consistently show that, net of the controls for education, age, and family size, the "nonwhite" groups are employed in positions with low expected remuneration and status. Aside from the ethnic effects, the equations indicate that occupational earnings and status decrease with age (significant in two of the six equations), but increase with education (significant in five equations) and with family size (significant in two equations). With regard to the attitudinal measures, black and Spanish-speaking participants tend to be concentrated in jobs where the men in the Parnes sample are less likely to express satisfaction with the work content and with financial return—although the latter effect is not statistically significant.

As a whole, the results are quite consistent with our notions regarding the employment situations of minority group members (thereby serving to validate our job measures), though it is perhaps surprising that in a sample selected for low incomes the effects would be so pronounced. It should also be observed that, with the sole exception of the Duncan status code, the job characteristic scores do not measure the negative income tax participants' own values on the dependent variables. What we have reported, therefore, are patterns in the distribution of types of work situations in this population sample. The ethnic differentials, in particular, must be understood entirely in terms of the process by which jobs of varying desirability are allocated among the groups; to no extent are they attributable to discrimination among persons in the same occupation.

2. THE EFFECT OF THE PAYMENTS ON JOB TURNOVER

The first issue we address concerns whether the support payments affect the amount of job turnover or the pattern of job departures. Subjects might respond to the provision of income support by reducing work effort

---

[4] Note that low percentage black corresponds to high status. Consequently, the coefficients in the percentage black equation, with their signs reversed, indicate the contributions of the respective terms to high status.

and leaving employment. Also, the experimental response via job departures may vary according to individual attributes and characteristics of the work situation—for instance, there may be a tendency under income maintenance to leave only less satisfying positions with greater frequency. Consequently, we consider the possibility of interactions among subject attributes, job characteristics, and the tax plan parameters.

The dependent variable in this inquiry ($JOBCHG$) is a dichotomous term which distinguishes between having changed employers during the course of the experiment and having remained with the same firm. It was coded 1 if, at the eighth quarterly, the subject was no longer employed by the company he worked for at preenrollment; it was scored 0 if he worked for the same firm.[5] Unemployment at the eighth quarterly, contingent upon having been employed at preenrollment, was also treated as a job change. Because we wish to relate job characteristics to departures from employment, this analysis was restricted to male heads who were employed at preenrollment and had valid occupation–industry codes.

Additive Effects

To analyze the effect of the support payments on job departures we initially specified the following model of the determinants of job turnover:

$$JOBCHG = f(\text{race–ethnicity, city site, education, age,} \\ \text{head's earnings, wife's earnings, family size, } EXP). \quad (1)$$

The term race–ethnicity denotes three dummy variables, city-site location is represented by four terms, education is measured by head's years of schooling, the income variables report head's and wife's earnings in the year preceding preenrollment, and family size equals the number of family members at the time of the preenrollment interview. These controls were introduced because they are probable determinants of the job departure rate in this population and because differences in the pattern of attri-

---

[5] There is a statistical problem in using a dummy dependent variable because the assumption of homoskedasticity is no longer valid. The least squares estimators of the regression coefficients will still be unbiased, but their standard errors will be biased and inconsistent. One alternative is to use the two-stage method described in Goldberger (1964:248–50). However, this procedure breaks down for observations in which the estimated values of the dependent variable in the first stage are less than zero or in excess of unity. Alternate methods, such as probit and discriminant analysis, are computationally cumbersome and hardly preferable to ordinary least squares (Ashenfelter, 1969a, quoted in Comay, 1971). Moreover, for a problem similar to ours, Ashenfelter (1969b:644–48) reports that hypothesis tests using ordinary least squares estimates tend to be conservative, in that the true significance levels are apt to be lower.

tion between experimental and control families may have created systematic discrepancies between the groups on these variables.

The variable *EXP* specifies either the spline formulation of the experimental parameters or the *BENEFIT* 1 formulation—the latter having been computed from family income in the year preceding preenrollment. This variable therefore measures the impact of support payments at approximately the annual amount consonant with a subject's preenrollment income on his prospects for making a job departure in the succeeding two years.

In Table 7.3 we report regressions relating individual characteristics to job turnover. The equations are arranged by ethnic category, and within each group both the spline and *BENEFIT* 1 formulations are presented. From the entries in columns (1) and (2) it is apparent that in the total sample age, head's earnings, and family size are all negatively associated with the probability of a job departure, net of the other factors. In both formulations there is also a significant experimental effect; in the spline specification, participation in the experiment and, beyond this, a high guarantee level appear to reduce job turnover (although the individual splines are insignificant), while a high tax rate increases job mobility. Together, these effects suggest that job turnover declines with plan generosity. This interpretation is supported by the results with *BENEFIT* 1 (column 2) wherein it is apparent that large estimated transfer payments are associated with low job turnover.

The separate regressions for the ethnic groups are consistent with the results for the combined sample, though the effects tend to be weaker. In two of the ethnic equations with the *BENEFIT* 1 specification (whites, blacks), the experimental parameter is negatively associated with job turnover ($p < .10$): large transfer payments decrease the frequency of a departure. In the equation for Spanish-speaking persons, the coefficient for *BENEFIT* 1 is not significant, although it has the same sign as the corresponding coefficients in the other ethnic regressions. The joint test for the spline formulation is significant for the Spanish-speaking, with the tax-rate variable largely accounting for the experimental effect, as was the case with the combined sample. There appears to be a considerable tendency for Spanish-speaking persons in the high tax-rate plans to leave their preenrollment employers; with an increase in tax rate equal to .20 (coded 20 in our data) the probability of a job change during the two-year interval under consideration was raised by $(9.379 \times 10^{-3})(20) = .188$ percentage points. In the other ethnic subsamples, the tax-rate parameter is not significant. In no instance, however, does it have the opposite sign.

On the basis of the formulation described by equation (1) we conclude that there is a systematic tendency for high transfer payments to depress job turnover. The precise aspect of the payments structure to which the subjects are responding may be unclear—for whites and blacks it is the dollar amount of the predeparture payment which is significant, for Spanish-speaking heads the tax rate parameter in the spline formulation is significant, while for the combined sample both specifications are significant. Nevertheless, *the results from the two formulations are consistent with the contention that plan generosity depresses the rate of job turnover.*

Interaction Effects

In addition to the additive specification of the experimental parameters (equation [1]), there is reason to suspect the existence of interactions with subject characteristics and with selected job features. For instance, older persons receiving support payments may be even more likely to discontinue working than a combination of the additive effects from these variables would suggest. Similarly, the fact of being employed at an unsatisfying task *and* receiving generous support payments might lead to job departures at a rate which cannot be accounted for by the separate contributions from the two factors. Formally, the interaction model is specified by the equation

$$JOBCHG = f(\text{subject variables}, EXP, \text{job characteristic}, EXP \times V), \quad (2)$$

where the first two terms summarize the independent variables which appear in equation (1), "job characteristic" denotes one of the Census or Parnes variables, and the last term represents the interaction between the experimental parameters and a subject or a job characteristic, V.

Preliminary to discussing the interaction models, we briefly summarize the effects of the job characteristics on the departure probability, when the former are introduced as additive terms in a regression containing the controls enumerated in equation (1). Since the job characteristics affect the experimental response only indirectly, through their presence as additional control variables, they are reported in Appendix B (Table 7B.2). Also, since addition of the job characteristics introduces but minor changes in the coefficients of the other variables in Table 7.3, only the coefficients for the new terms are presented. Finally, because the figures in the two experimental formulations differ by a small extent, the *BENEFIT* 1 specification is not shown.

Very few of the job characteristics in Table 7B.2 are significantly related to the probability of an employment departure. The few that reach significance concern objective characteristics of incumbents in a position rather than attitudes toward the work situation. These associations support our intuitive notions as to what sorts of jobs retain their employees: departures are less likely from positions with high expected earnings and

Table 7.3 Regressions of Job Departure Decision on Subject Characteristics, Additive Effects Model, Two Formulations

Independent Variable	Total Sample		Whites		Blacks[a]		Spanish-speaking[a]	
	Spline	Benefit 1	Spline	Benefit 1	Spline	Benefit 1	Spline	Benefit 1
Constant	1.371**	1.411**	1.743**	1.816**	0.633	0.679	1.451**	1.384**
	(9.79)	(10.04)	(7.68)	(7.97)	(1.42)	(1.53)	(6.52)	(6.19)
Trenton	7.525	6.924	3.051	1.672	48.98	46.89	22.44	19.70
($\times 10^{-2}$)	(0.88)	(0.82)	(0.21)	(0.12)	(1.35)	(1.29)	(1.38)	(1.22)
Paterson–Passaic	1.155	4.875	63.72	62.62	406.2	379.5	−8.929	32.45
($\times 10^{-3}$)	(0.02)	(0.07)	(0.62)	(0.63)	(1.14)	(1.07)	(−0.12)	(0.46)
Jersey City	−4.423	−4.403	−18.70**	−18.75**	—	—	—	—
($\times 10^{-2}$)	(−0.66)	(−0.67)	(−2.18)	(−2.22)				
Black	1.691	1.376	—	—	—	—	—	—
($\times 10^{-2}$)	(0.27)	(0.22)						
Spanish-speaking	2.001	1.455	—	—	—	—	—	—
($\times 10^{-2}$)	(0.30)	(0.22)						
Age	−1.021**	−1.035**	−1.206**	−1.227**	−0.6067	−.6003	−1.117**	−0.940**
($\times 10^{-2}$)	(−4.98)	(−5.05)	(−3.90)	(−3.99)	(−1.55)	(−1.55)	(−2.67)	(−2.26)
Education, head	−1.125	−1.129	−4.572**	−4.796**	−0.0346	0.0371	0.170	0.458
($\times 10^{-2}$)	(−1.54)	(−1.55)	(−3.03)	(−3.21)	(−0.02)	(0.02)	(0.15)	(0.41)
Earnings, head	−7.155**	−8.077**	−7.973**	−8.785**	−2.011	−3.800	−12.80**	−12.35**
($\times 10^{-5}$)	(−4.91)	(−5.41)	(−3.90)	(−4.21)	(−0.69)	(−1.29)	(−4.12)	(−3.88)
Earnings, wife	−2.196	−2.982	−2.562	−2.980	6.479	4.959	−7.015	−7.862
($\times 10^{-5}$)	(−0.54)	(−0.73)	(−0.40)	(−0.47)	(0.84)	(0.64)	(−0.91)	(−1.01)

	(1)	(2)	(3)	(4)	(5)	(6)	(7)	(8)
Family size ($\times 10^{-2}$)	−1.163* (−1.76)	−1.542* (−1.67)	−0.129 (−0.08)	−.0245 (−.016)	−2.914* (−1.84)	−3.105** (−2.04)	−1.073 (−0.55)	−1.320 (−0.69)
Experimental status (spline 1 $\times 10^{-2}$)	−2.505 (−0.59)	—	−1.146 (−0.17)	—	−11.41 (−1.45)	—	5.690 (0.70)	—
Guarantee (spline 2 $\times 10^{-5}$)	−2.903 (−1.27)	—	−2.710 (−0.73)	—	−4.023 (−1.03)	—	−2.725 (−0.59)	—
Tax rate (spline 3 $\times 10^{-3}$)	3.852** (2.18)	—	2.785 (0.97)	—	2.051 (0.67)	—	9.379** (2.60)	—
BENEFIT 1 ($\$$) ($\times 10^{-5}$)	—	−3.920** (−2.32)	—	−4.350* (−1.70)	—	−5.849* (−1.86)	—	−1.881 (−0.58)
R^2	.11	.10	.15	.15	.11	.10	.15	.12
N	749	749	304	304	239	239	206	206
Joint F-test for experimental effects	$F_{3,735} = 2.42$ $p < .065$	$F_{1,737} = 5.41$ $p < .021$	$F_{3,290} = 0.58$ $p < .637$	$F_{1,290} = 2.90$ $p < .090$	$F_{3,226} = 2.01$ $p < .112$	$F_{1,228} = 3.46$ $p < .064$	$F_{3,194} = 2.33$ $p < .075$	$F_{1,196} = 0.34$ $p < .565$
Dependent variable (JOBCHG)								
mean	.47		.43		.46		.53	
s.d.	.50		.50		.50		.50	

NOTE: Entries are unstandardized regression coefficients; t-values are in parentheses. Spline 1 = 1 indicates presence on plan ($G = \$2475$, $t = .50$). The dummy variable for Scranton was deleted from the city effect terms; the variable for whites was deleted from the ethnic terms in the total sample regressions.

[a] Because of the absence of blacks and Spanish-speaking persons in Scranton, the dummy variable for Jersey City was deleted from these regressions.

* Significant at $p < .10$.
** Significant at $p < .05$.

high occupational status. While there are only four significant associations, the pattern of findings with these variables and with the attitudinal measures is very consistent. Considering the total sample and the three ethnic subsamples, there are thirty-two indices of job desirability based upon objective characteristics of the job incumbents (five Census variables plus the Duncan occupational status score) and upon the two evaluations of their work situations. In twenty-five of the thirty-two instances, the results are in accordance with the notion that desirable job characteristics operate to retain employees. It should also be noted that these effects are net of *subject* earnings and education. What we have reported, therefore, concerns the additional impact of the job characteristics per se.

From the perspective of evaluating the effect of the experiment, the interactions between these terms and the experimental parameters hold greater interest. The interactions relate to the question of whether certain kinds of positions experience disproportionate changes in frequency of departure under the support payments. In Table 7.4 we report regression equation parts for the interaction formulation in all instances where there is a significant interaction ($p < .10$) between the experimental variables and a subject or job characteristic.

The most striking finding is that there are exceedingly few significant interactions. Out of a possible 104 (four ethnic categories times two formulations of the experimental parameters times thirteen subject and job characteristics) only six are significant. However, they present a consistent pattern, and we may at least speculate upon an interpretation. Three of the significant interactions involve income variables, and these describe a situation whereby *workers in low remunerative positions*[6] *grow less likely to leave employment as plan generosity increases, while job turnover in high expected earnings contexts is only marginally affected by plan generosity.*

The effects are easier to convey in graphic form, and in Figures 7.1 and 7.2 we plot the job turnover response by whites for positions with different proportions of individuals earning more than the indicated amounts. In Figure 7.1, the contours are net of control group change so that each curve can be compared with the horizontal axis, representing the control group.[7] In Figure 7.2, since *BENEFIT* 1 = 0 does not distin-

---

[6] In the single case of a significant interaction with education (Spanish-speaking sample), the direction of effect is consistent with the earnings variables: subjects with little education have lower rates of job departures when on generous support plans.

[7] The contours were constructed using the spline denoting presence in the experimental group ($S1$), the interaction between $S1$ and V, the guarantee ($S2$) or tax spline ($S3$) (depending on which is significant), and its interaction with V. The deleted experimental parameter is set equal to zero which, in actuality, means $2475 (in the case of $S2$), and a 50 percent tax rate (in the case of $S3$).

Table 7.4 Regression Coefficients for Significant Interactions with Experimental Variables, for Job Departures

Subject or job characteristic, V	V	(Experimental status) $S1 \times 10^{-2}$	(Guarantee) $S2 \times 10^{-5}$	(Tax rate) $S3 \times 10^{-3}$	$S1 \times V \times 10^{-2}$	$S2 \times V \times 10^{-5}$	$S3 \times V \times 10^{-3}$	BENEFIT 1 $\times 10^{-5}$	BEN 1 $\times V \times 10^{-5}$	Joint F-test[a]
1. Total Sample										
Family size ($\times 10^{-2}$)	1.133 (0.76)	24.20** (2.00)	−3.643 (−0.63)	5.996 (1.15)	−4.794** (−2.34)	0.3345 (0.39)	−0.3445 (−0.48)			$F_{3,732} = 2.12$ $p < .096$
2. Whites										
Jobs > $6000 ($\times 10^{-1}$)	−2.214 (−1.35)	23.35 (1.06)	−27.12** (−2.47)	18.68* (1.70)	−32.59 (−1.12)	33.75** (2.37)	−21.45 (−1.48)			$F_{3,286} = 2.42$ $p < .066$
Job satisfaction (content) ($\times 10^{-4}$)	−0.8710 (−0.35)	5.229 (0.50)	−5.245 (−0.96)	13.12** (2.56)	−0.0361 (−0.84)	0.0149 (0.66)	−0.0574** (−2.39)			$F_{3,286} = 2.05$ $p < .099$
Jobs > $8000 ($\times 10^{-1}$)	−3.048** (−2.29)							−10.31** (−2.25)	14.02* (1.65)	$F_{1,290} = 2.70$ $p < .098$
4. Spanish-speaking										
Education, head ($\times 10^{-3}$)	−8.671 (−0.65)							−13.55* (−1.81)	1.706* (1.72)	$F_{1,195} = 2.96$ $p < .086$
Job satisfaction (financial) ($\times 10^{-5}$)	−28.67 (−0.69)							−9.746* (−1.76)	0.0669* (1.75)	$F_{1,194} = 3.06$ $p < .082$

NOTE: The complete equations are specified by the addition of the interaction terms and V (where V is a job characteristic) to the models in Table 7.3. (See text equation [2]). Entries are unstandardized regression coefficients; t-values are in parentheses.

[a] The joint F-tests are for interactions with experimental variables.

* Significant at $p < .10$.
** Significant at $p < .05$.

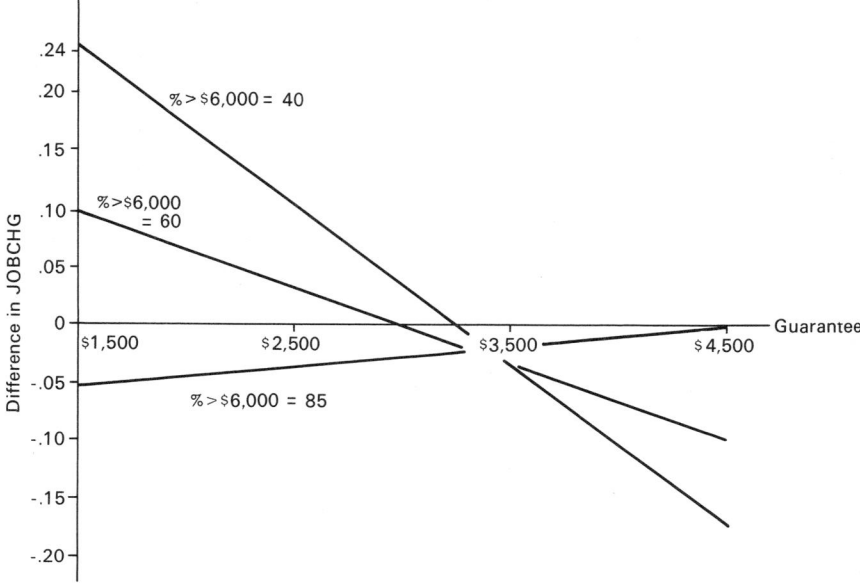

Figure 7.1 Interaction between guarantee level (spline 2) and job characteristic, "percentage with earnings greater than $6000," whites' job departures. The vertical scale indexes differences in the probability of a job departure during 1969–1970. Each contour compares the response by an experimental group population with a comparable control group category (X axis). The vertical scale is adjusted by the additive effect of the spline 1 term and by its interaction with the job characteristic; intercepts correspond to tax rate = .50. Means and standard deviations of the variables are ($3045, $945) for the guarantee level—$3045 corresponds to a spline 2 mean of $570—and (72, 23) for the job characteristic.

guish between the control group and experimentals who are above the breakeven point, the horizontal axis represents a mixture of the two categories. Both figures show that whites who are in jobs in which few individuals report high earnings experience a substantial decrease in turnover as a function of guarantee level (or *BENEFIT* 1 amount), whereas their departure rate from higher-salaried positions shows little response to plan generosity. Much the same pattern is found for Spanish-speaking persons with the related attitudinal variable, "satisfaction with financial return." *Our interpretation of these interactions is that a generous support level, by functioning as an earnings supplement, permits a family head to continue in a low-salaried position. In this sense, possibly, it is considered by subjects as a wage raise.*

From the analyses in this section we conclude that (1) in each ethnic group there is evidence of an additive effect by the negative income tax payments on job departures, with turnover being depressed by plan generosity (as indexed either by high dollar payments or by a low tax rate);

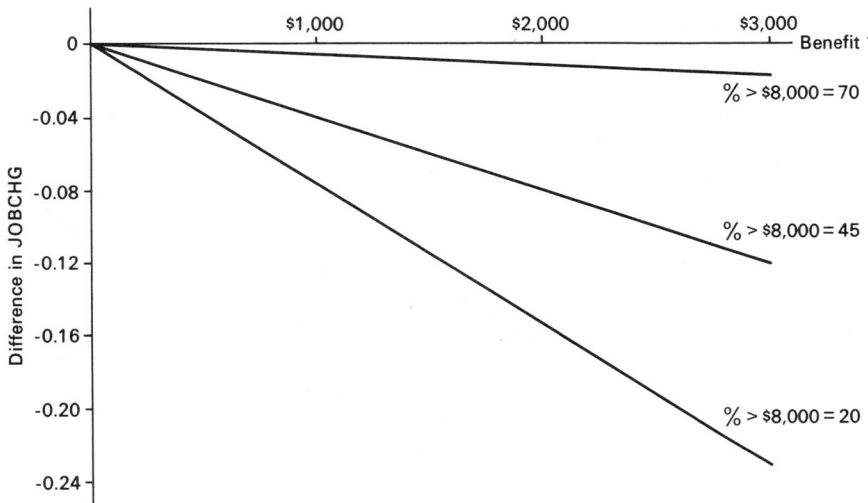

Figure 7.2 Interaction between *BENEFIT* 1 and job characteristic, "percentage with earnings greater than $8000," whites' job departures. The vertical scale indexes differences in the probability of a job departure during 1969–1970. Each contour compares the response of a population category among supported subjects with a comparable subpopulation among unsupported heads (X axis). Means and standard deviations of the variables are ($730, $1084) for *BENEFIT* 1 and (45, 26) for the job characteristic.

and (2) for whites and, to a lesser extent, for Spanish-speaking participants, there is some indication of an interaction between plan generosity and expected earnings, with the result that a disproportionate portion of the overall decrease in turnover among supported heads can be accounted for by lower rates in the less remunerative positions. We hasten to add that, in view of the few significant interactions that were found, the latter finding is exceedingly tentative.

3. THE EFFECTS OF THE PAYMENTS ON DURATION OF UNEMPLOYMENT

We now consider the related question of whether there is an experimental effect on duration of unemployment among those who left their preenrollment positions. An increase in unemployment would be consistent with a disincentive argument, or it could signal a willingness by individuals to seek longer for desirable work situations, since the maintenance payments provide them with greater flexibility to delay employment. We also investigate the possibility of interactions between subject characteristics and the experimental variables; for instance, family heads with working wives *and* on high generosity plans may show more of a tendency to long unemployment intervals than is suggested by the additive effects from these terms.

Additive Effects

The dependent variable in this analysis is number of weeks unemployed in 1969–1970 (*WKSUNEMP*), roughly the initial two years of the experiment. Our independent variables are the same ones which were present in equation (1), subject to the following alteration: the dollar benefit specification of the experimental parameters is now calculated on the assumption that the head is unemployed, rather than in terms of his earnings in the year preceding preenrollment. The reason is that we are analyzing the behavior of subjects who have left their preenrollment jobs and wish to ascertain the effect of the payments amount received by an unemployed head's family on his duration of unemployment. The *BENEFIT* 2 calculation is specified by *BENEFIT* $2 = G_s - tE_w$, where G_s equals the dollar guarantee for a family of size s on plan (G, t), t is the tax rate of the plan, and E_w denotes wife's annual earnings in the year preceding preenrollment. The spline formulation of the negative tax plans is not changed.

The results from the additive specification of the experimental parameters are reported in Table 7.5 for the total sample and for each ethnic group. With respect to the subject characteristics, the most consistent finding is that heads' preenrollment earnings (a measure of earnings potential) is negatively correlated with number of weeks unemployed. The higher a person's earnings, the shorter the unemployment duration (given an employer change) he was likely to experience in the following two years. Family size has a positive effect on unemployment for Spanish-speaking participants and for the combined sample. We have no satisfactory explanation for this result, and can only speculate that in our low-income population very large families may mean extended families with several workers or potential workers reducing family dependence on the head's earnings. Consistent with this interpretation, in the white subsample duration of unemployment is positively related to wife's earnings. Neither effect, however, is systematic across the ethnic groups.

The experimental effects display a consistent pattern of insignificance (joint *F*-test) although the tax rate parameter does attain significance (positive) in the equation for whites. Also, the coefficients for this spline in the other groups have identical signs. There is some possibility, then, that a high tax rate on earnings contributes to long unemployment intervals, although we emphasize that the evidence for such an effect is exceedingly weak.

Interaction Effects

Since we have retained in this analysis only family heads who made a change in employer, we will not examine interactions between job characteristics and the experimental variables. There would be some conceptual difficulty in attempting to explain unemployment duration by reference to characteristics of the previous work situation. We have analyzed interactions between *subject* characteristics and the experimental parameters; factors such as family size, age, and wife's earnings more clearly adhere to an individual under change of employment. (The sole exception is the job characteristic, head's earnings in the preenrollment year, which was retained as an index of his income-producing potential.)

In Table 7.6 we report regression equation parts for the interaction terms in all instances of significant interactions between experimental parameters and the subject characteristics listed in Table 7.5. Out of a possible forty interactions (five subject characteristics times four groups times two specifications of the experimental parameters), six are significant at the level $p < .10$. These divide into three groups: two instances of an interaction with education, two instances of an interaction with wife's earnings (both pairs are significant for whites and the combined sample), and two interactions with head's prior earnings (the alternative formulations of the experimental parameters in the black subsample). In every case the effect pattern within a pair is the same; consequently we discuss only the more highly significant member of each.

The interaction with head's earnings (blacks, Figure 7.3) is consistent with the experimental effects we have already reported concerning job turnover. In discussing Figures 7.1 and 7.2 we noted that (among whites) high plan generosity depresses departures from low-paying positions but has little effect on turnover in more financially rewarding jobs. We interpreted that finding as indicating less need to change employers for financial reasons; in effect the support payments constitute a "raise" in earnings. Similarly, the decrease in unemployment duration as a function of benefit amount among low-earnings-potential blacks (Figure 7.3) may reveal a willingness to accept low-salaried positions because of the maintenance subsidy. We will return to this theme in the next chapter.

The highly significant interaction with wife's earnings (whites, Figure 7.4) describes a situation in which supported heads with supplementary incomes reduce unemployment duration when on low tax-rate plans. One interpretation for this is that, in the context of both high supplementary earnings *and* a low tax rate, there would be less financial pressure on the family head to prolong unemployment until he locates a well-paying position. As the tax rate is raised, the return from wife's earnings declines, and obtaining such a position becomes a matter of greater consequence,

Table 7.5 Regressions of Unemployment Duration on Subject Characteristics, Additive Effects Model, Two Formulations

Independent Variable	Total Sample		Whites		Blacks[a]		Spanish-speaking[a]	
	Spline	Benefit 2	Spline	Benefit 2	Spline	Benefit 2	Spline	Benefit 2
Constant ($\times 10^1$)	2.748** (2.79)	2.793** (2.85)	1.007 (0.59)	1.300 (0.76)	3.206* (1.85)	3.327* (1.95)	3.861** (2.34)	4.009** (2.58)
Trenton	0.2561 (0.04)	0.5189 (0.08)	9.379 (0.93)	2.313 (0.24)	7.233 (1.06)	8.103 (1.24)	−9.098 (−0.87)	−11.15 (−1.09)
Paterson–Passaic	−2.762 (−0.51)	−1.725 (−0.32)	−4.552 (−0.66)	−4.385 (−0.63)	3.939 (0.71)	4.675 (0.87)	1.175 (0.22)	1.921 (0.38)
Jersey City	−5.432 (−1.00)	−5.171 (−0.95)	−7.201 (−0.86)	−5.285 (−0.63)	—	—	—	—
Black	6.545 (1.32)	6.222 (1.25)	—	—	—	—	—	—
Spanish-speaking	3.867 (0.76)	3.444 (0.68)	—	—	—	—	—	—
Age ($\times 10^{-2}$)	0.6995 (0.04)	1.813 (0.12)	17.69 (0.78)	13.87 (0.61)	26.68 (1.03)	25.92 (1.02)	−66.10** (−2.17)	−64.08** (−2.18)
Education, head ($\times 10^{-1}$)	4.138 (0.78)	3.933 (0.74)	9.730 (0.88)	4.464 (0.41)	4.846 (0.51)	5.386 (0.56)	5.720 (0.70)	5.184 (0.64)
Earnings, head ($\times 10^{-3}$)	−5.511** (−5.03)	−5.380** (−4.91)	−1.645 (−0.95)	−1.425 (−0.82)	−7.714** (−3.62)	−7.849** (−3.72)	−7.816** (−3.78)	−7.410** (−3.75)
Earnings, wife ($\times 10^{-3}$)	3.269 (1.11)	3.598 (1.22)	8.776* (1.83)	10.40** (2.17)	3.030 (0.61)	2.326 (0.46)	−0.06031 (0.01)	−0.4941 (−0.08)

Family size	1.863**	1.729**	−0.1516	0.2632	1.694	1.615	4.812**	4.268**
	(2.53)	(2.46)	(−0.12)	(0.22)	(1.45)	(1.46)	(2.93)	(2.80)
Experimental status	2.467	—	−0.3085	—	−1.531	—	7.359	—
(spline 1)	(0.86)		(−0.06)		(−0.28)		(1.27)	
Guarantee	−1.546	—	2.580	—	−3.344	—	−1.597	—
(spline 2 × 10⁻³)	(−0.89)		(0.94)		(−1.12)		(−0.44)	
Tax rate	2.019	—	4.458**	—	1.151	—	2.157	—
(spline 3 × 10⁻¹)	(1.50)		(2.06)		(0.47)		(0.77)	
BENEFIT 2 ($)	—	1.442	—	11.13	—	−16.50	—	18.73
(× 10⁻⁴)		(0.19)		(0.95)		(−1.28)		(1.28)
R^2	.10	.09	.11	.07	.21	.20	.19	.18
N	349	349	131	131	109	109	109	109
Joint F-test for experimental effects	$F_{3,335} = 0.97$	$F_{1,337} = 0.04$	$F_{3,117} = 1.99$	$F_{1,119} = 0.90$	$F_{3,97} = 0.73$	$F_{1,99} = 1.65$	$F_{3,97} = 0.71$	$F_{1,99} = 1.63$
	$p < .411$	$p < .842$	$p < .124$	$p < .343$	$p < 0.542$	$p < .201$	$p < .558$	$p < .207$
Dependent variable (WKSUNEMP)								
mean	22		21		24		23	
s.d.	25		23		25		26	

NOTE: Entries are unstandardized regression coefficients; t-values are in parentheses. Spline 1 = 1 indicates presence on plan ($G = \$2475$, $t = .50$). The dummy variable for Scranton was deleted from the city effect terms; the variable for whites was deleted from the ethnic terms in the total sample regressions.

[a] Because of the absence of blacks and Spanish-speaking persons in Scranton, the dummy variable for Jersey City was deleted from these regressions.

* Significant at $p < .10$.
** Significant at $p < .05$.

Table 7.6 Regression Coefficients for Significant Interactions with Experimental Variables, for Unemployment Duration

Subject Characteristic, V	V	(Experimental status) $S1 \times 10^{-1}$	(Guarantee) $S2 \times 10^{-2}$	(Tax rate) $S3 \times 10^{-1}$	$S1 \times V \times 10^{-2}$	$S2 \times V \times 10^{-6}$	$S3 \times V \times 10^{-4}$	BENEFIT 2 $\times 10^{-3}$	BEN 2 $\times V \times 10^{-6}$	Joint F-test[a]
1. Total Sample										
Education, head ($\times 10^{-1}$)	5.305 (0.75)	130.5 (1.40)	−1.524** (−2.52)	9.209** (2.06)	−127.3 (−1.24)	1574.** (2.35)	−832.1* (−1.68)			$F_{3,332} = 2.27$ $p < .080$
Earnings, wife ($\times 10^{-3}$)	−0.300 (−0.06)	23.51 (0.73)	−0.1609 (−0.89)	0.9747 (0.70)	−0.4614 (−0.55)	2.355 (0.54)	7.100** (2.39)			$F_{3,332} = 2.29$ $p < .078$
2. Whites										
Education, head ($\times 10^{-1}$)	9.297 (0.53)	155.9 (0.68)	−2.325** (−2.30)	17.44 (1.53)	−184.8 (−0.82)	2800.** (2.69)	−1395. (−1.22)			$F_{3,114} = 2.95$ $p < .036$
Earnings, wife ($\times 10^{-3}$)	−2.666 (−0.27)	19.51 (0.38)	0.1380 (0.52)	2.227 (1.02)	−1.901 (−1.27)	17.62** (2.03)	13.19** (2.68)			$F_{3,114} = 4.63$ $p < .004$
3. Blacks										
Earnings, head ($\times 10^{-3}$)	−12.44** (−4.35)	−350.5* (−1.83)	−0.4531 (−0.50)	−8.526 (−0.90)	0.8298* (1.77)	0.0790 (0.04)	2.391 (1.07)			$F_{3,94} = 2.33$ $p < .079$
Earnings, head ($\times 10^{-3}$)	−11.77** (−4.30)							−10.62** (−2.48)	2.089** (2.19)	$F_{1,98} = 4.89$ $p < .031$

NOTE: The complete equations are specified by addition of the interaction terms to the models in Table 7.5. (See text equation [2].) Entries are unstandardized regression coefficients; t-values are in parentheses.

[a] The joint F-tests are for interactions with experimental variables.

* Significant at $p < .10$.
** Significant at $p < .05$.

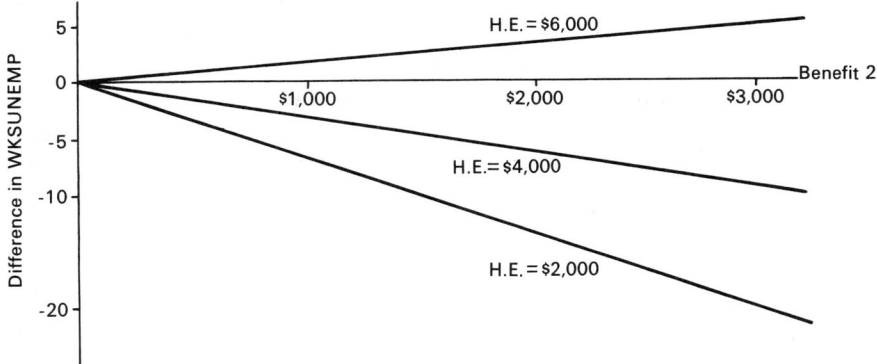

Figure 7.3 Interaction between *BENEFIT* 2 and head's earnings (*H.E.*), blacks' unemployment duration. The vertical scale indexes differences in number of weeks unemployed during 1969–1970. Each contour compares the response of a population category among supported subjects with a comparable subpopulation among unsupported family heads (*X* axis). Means and standard deviations of the variables are ($1875, $1796) for *BENEFIT* 2 and ($4141, $1193) for head's earnings.

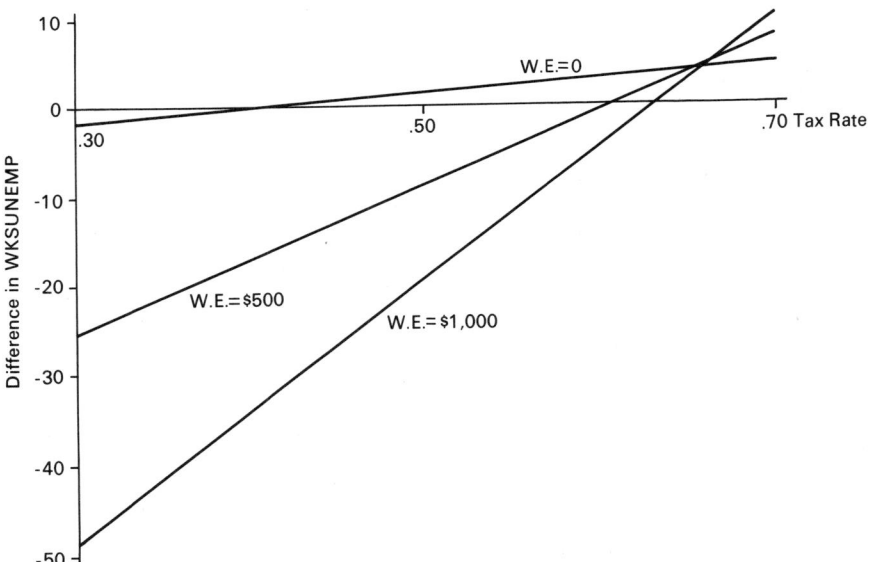

Figure 7.4 Interaction between the tax rate (spline 3) and wife's earnings (*W.E.*), whites' unemployment duration. The vertical scale indexes differences in number of weeks unemployed during 1969–1970. Each contour compares the response by an experimental group population with a comparable control group category (*X* axis). The vertical scale is adjusted by the additive effect of the spline 1 term and by its interaction with wife's earnings; intercepts correspond to guarantee = $2475 (coded zero in the data). The tax rate parameters (.30, .50, .70) were coded (−20, 0, 20) in the regression equations. The mean and standard deviation of wife's earnings are ($144, $448).

generating longer intervals of job seeking. An alternative explanation for the increase in unemployment duration among subjects with high-earning wives, as a function of tax rate, would emphasize greater "dropping out" when the spouse earns a good income and the family head would have to endure a stiff tax rate. One would expect a parallel effect on wife's unemployment duration (or presence in the labor force) but we shall not investigate this possibility here.

Figure 7.5 describes the interaction between the head's educational attainment and guarantee level in the white subsample. The decrease in unemployment among low-education individuals, as a function of plan generosity, is consistent with the preceding discussion concerning the effect of income maintenance on low-earnings subjects, who would be disproportionately represented in the low-education category. At this point we have no satisfactory explanation for the increase in unemployment among persons with high education, although we will argue in the next chapter that the added duration may have been used by many to locate more attractive positions. At the same time, we caution that the sample size in

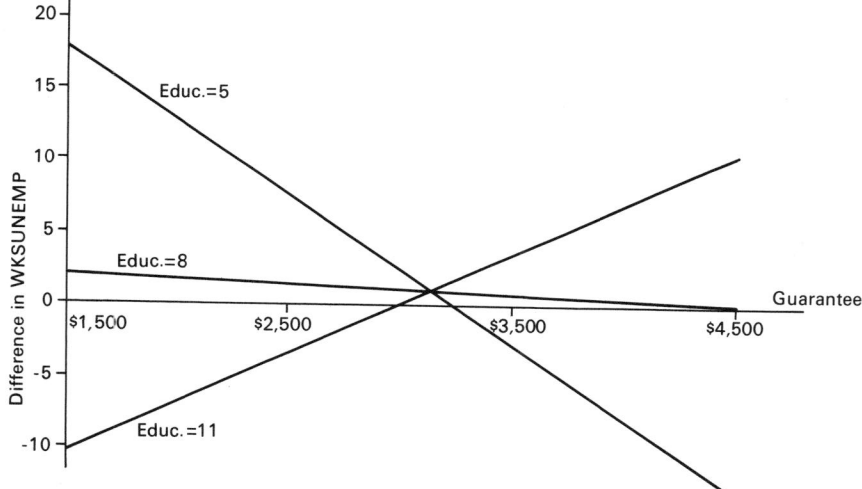

Figure 7.5 Interaction between the guarantee level (spline 2) and head's education, whites' unemployment duration. The vertical scale indexes differences in number of weeks unemployed during 1969–1970. Each contour compares the response by an experimental group population with a comparable control group category (X axis). The vertical scale is adjusted by the additive effect of the spline 1 term and by its interaction with education; intercepts correspond to tax rate = .50. Means and standard deviations of the variables are ($2970, $929) for the guarantee level—$2970 corresponds to a spline 2 mean of $495—and (9.7, 2.1) for head's education.

this analysis is small ($N = 131$), and only about one-quarter of the group completed eleven or more years of schooling.

Our assessment of the impact of the support payments on unemployment duration can be summarized as follows: (1) there is no additive effect, but (2) there is evidence that *low "normal-earnings" individuals (and persons with little education), on generous support plans, reduce their unemployment durations.* In the analysis of job departures in the preceding section, we suggested that the transfer payments may have been interpreted by subjects as a salary increase, permitting them to remain in poorly paying positions. There is now evidence that high plan generosity (particularly when coupled with high supplementary earnings) also produces a reduction in unemployment, possibly because it enables male heads to accept early job offers rather than hold out for better-salaried positions.

We defer a detailed assessment of these findings to the conclusion of the next chapter, because the results on job selection will contribute to our understanding of the negative income tax effects on job departures and unemployment duration. By way of qualifying the present findings, however, we do wish to emphasis two points. First, because of the very few significant interactions, we have not explored the possibility of distinct ethnic responses, but have sought instead to identify consistent patterns across the ethnic groups as a means of establishing "first-order" effects. Second, our analysis is not sufficiently detailed to substantiate the post hoc interpretations we have proposed for many of the findings; verification will require supplementary investigations with the New Jersey data file and—what would be more persuasive—replication of these results using information from other income-maintenance studies now in the field.

APPENDIX A:
CONSTRUCTION OF THE JOB
SATISFACTION MEASURES

The Parnes questionnaire contained an instruction requesting respondents to list three features of their jobs with which they were particularly satisfied. The responses were classified according to a list of twenty-five job aspects; thus the record for an individual consists of up to three "ones" scattered amidst twenty-two or more "zeros."

A common technique for ascertaining underlying dimensions in a list of items, for the purpose of assigning a dimension score to each observation, is to factor analyze the items. However, this procedure is not appropriate when the data consist of a fixed number of selections made from a larger array. For instance, if several questions were to relate to a single satisfaction dimension, an individual would probably choose only one item from the subset, rather than allocate more than one of his limited choices to the same dimension. Consequently, items expected to load on the same factor would not have positive intercorrelations in our data set.

While we could have devised a clustering procedure which incorporates our assumptions as to how the data were generated, time constraints made it advisable simply to group items which appear to tap a common underlying dimension. We constructed two scales in this way, using a portion of the items. Satisfaction with job content is based on five possible responses; satisfaction with financial rewards is based on two items. A job's score on each scale indicates the relative frequency with which its items were chosen by respondents in the job. The specific responses used in constructing the satisfaction scales are

A. Satisfaction with job content:
  1. Liking the kind of work
  2. Job is important, gives satisfaction
  3. Job has variety, is interesting
  4. Job has responsibility
  5. Meet interesting people
B. Satisfaction with financial rewards:
  1. Good wages
  2. Good fringe benefits

APPENDIX B: SUPPLEMENTARY TABLES

Table 7B.1 provides means for the Census and Parnes samples that are comparable to the characteristics, shown in Table 7.1, of the male family heads in the New Jersey–Pennsylvania sample who were employed at preenrollment.

Table 7B.2 shows coefficients measuring the effects of job characteristics on the probability of leaving a job.

Table 7B.1 **Characteristics of the Census and Parnes Samples**

	Total Sample	Whites	Blacks	Spanish-speaking[b]
Census variables[a]				
Average earnings (dollars)	11,084	11,642	7,179	6,969
Percentage in job with earnings > $6000	82.2	85.4	64.6	55.0
Percentage in job with earnings > $8000	64.1	68.8	35.4	29.2
Percentage black	12.0	—	—	10.0
Average education (years)	11.9	12.1	10.7	9.7
Proportion stayers (same occupation–industry in 1970 as in 1965)	67.0	67.6	65.1	60.1
Earnings of stayers (dollars)	11,610	12,174	7,316	7,124
Earnings of movers (dollars)	9,867	10,300	6,845	6,656
(Number of observations in Census sample)	(21,910)	(18,020)	(2,390)	(1,664)
Parnes variables[a]				
Duncan status score	31.1	37.2	18.7	
Job satisfaction (content)[c]	277	324	164	
Job satisfaction (financial)[c]	97	93	106	
(Number of observations in Parnes sample)	(4944)	(3524)	(1420)	

NOTE: Census data are from the 1970 1 percent sample for New York and Newark SMSAs. Parnes data pertain to a national sample, aged 45–59 in 1966. Data are for males.
[a] Entries are means over individuals unless stated otherwise.
[b] Spanish-speaking persons are not identified on the Parnes tape.
[c] Each job aspect score was constructed from several questions. The score ($\times 10^{-3}$) reflects the relative frequency with which the aspect was selected.

Table 7B.2 Coefficients of Job Characteristics, from Additive Regression Models (Spline Formulation), for Job Departures

Job Characteristic, V	(1) Total Sample	(2) Whites	(3) Blacks	(4) Spanish-speaking
Census variables				
Average annual earnings (dollars)($\times 10^{-5}$)	−1.682* (−1.76)	−1.208 (−0.94)	−2.300 (−1.15)	−2.357 (−1.07)
Percent in job with earnings > $6,000 ($\times 10^{-2}$)	−11.58 (−1.59)	−17.87 (−1.53)	−9.114 (−0.66)	−3.780 (−0.28)
Percent in job with earnings > $8,000 ($\times 10^{-2}$)	−11.30 (−1.55)	−17.85* (−1.68)	−1.280 (−0.08)	−7.346 (−0.49)
Percent black ($\times 10^{-2}$)	−8.078 (−0.89)	−9.622 (−0.69)	−13.92 (−0.84)	−1.388 (−0.07)
Average education (years)($\times 10^{-3}$)	−20.98* (−1.71)	4.963 (0.23)	−49.57** (−2.13)	−7.056 (−0.33)
Parnes variables				
Duncan status score ($\times 10^{-4}$)	−13.43 (−0.87)	−5.249 (−0.25)	9.845 (0.28)	−22.54 (−0.69)
Job satisfaction (content) ($\times 10^{-5}$)	−19.09 (−1.62)	−18.86 (−1.14)	−22.40 (−0.90)	−5.651 (−0.24)
Job satisfaction (financial) ($\times 10^{-5}$)	−8.158 (−0.46)	−18.44 (−0.70)	−9.972 (−0.30)	8.490 (0.23)

NOTE: The complete equations are specified by the addition of a job characteristic, V, to the models of Table 7.3. Each coefficient resulted from the estimation of a separate regression. Entries are unstandardized regression coefficients; t-values are in parentheses.
* Significant at $p < .10$.
** Significant at $p < .05$.

REFERENCES

Ashenfelter, O. 1969a. A note on the use of dichotomous dependent variables in multiple regression. Unpublished note circulated at the Industrial Relations Section, Princeton University.

Ashenfelter, O. 1969b. Some statistical difficulties in using dummy dependent variables. In W. G. Bowen and T. A. Finegan, *The economics of labor force participation,* pp. 644–650. Princeton: Princeton University Press.

Comay, Y. 1971. Influences on the migration of Canadian professionals. *Journal of Human Resources* 6:333–344.

Duncan, O. D., and Duncan, B. 1968. Minorities and the process of stratification. *American Sociological Review* 33:356–364.

Goldberger, A. S. 1964. *Econometric theory.* New York: Wiley.

Gans, H. 1969. Culture and class in the study of poverty: An approach to antipoverty research. In *On understanding poverty,* ed. D. P. Moynihan. New York: Basic Books.

Kmenta, J. 1971. *Elements of econometrics.* New York: Macmillan.
Moynihan, D. P. 1966. Employment, income, and the ordeal of the Negro family. In *The Negro American,* ed. T. Parsons and K. Clark. Boston: Beacon Press.
Poll, S. 1962. *The Hasidic community.* New York: Free Press.
Spilerman, S., and Elesh, D. 1971. Alternative conceptions of poverty and their implications for income maintenance. *Social Problems* 18:358–373.

8 The impact of the experiment on job selection

Seymour Spilerman
Richard E. Miller

In the preceding chapter, we investigated the impact of the negative income tax payments on departures from employment and on unemployment duration. The principal findings were that, among subjects in poorly paying positions at the inception of the experiment and among individuals with little education, generous support levels serve to depress job turnover and to reduce the lengths of unemployment intervals. In comparison, among better-educated family heads and subjects in relatively well paying jobs at the time of the preenrollment interview, generous support levels appear to produce an increase in duration of unemployment.

The issue we discuss in this chapter concerns the impact of the tax plans on selection of new positions. We wish to inquire whether supported individuals tend to acquire jobs with certain characteristics and, in particular, whether there is a systematic relation between the plan parameters—guarantee level and tax rate—and features of the entered positions. For instance, are participants on the generous support plans more willing to accept low-salaried positions (since the transfer payments constitute an earnings subsidy), or do they enter high salaried jobs or ones with a steep earnings incline, presumably waiting longer to locate such positions and supporting themselves in the interim with the negative income tax monies? A related question concerns whether individuals with different personal attributes respond in the same manner to the plan parameters.

To address these topics, we use the data file described in the preceding chapter. In particular, we are concerned with changes among *jobs* having particular characteristics (expected income level, satisfaction scores), rather than with the individuals' own values on the job dimensions. In the present analysis, we restrict attention to male heads who changed occupation (retaining the same employer) or changed employers between the preenrollment interview and the eighth quarterly. By way of introduction to the subject, we present in Table 8.1 the job characteristic means for each ethnic group, arranged by experimental and control categories, at preenrollment (Q_0) and at the eighth quarterly (Q_8).

The income measures (average earnings, percentage with earnings > $6000, percentage with earnings > $8000) describe a pattern whereby whites in the experimental group reduce expected earnings when changing jobs, net of adjustments by the control group (compare third and sixth columns). In contrast, supported black and Spanish-speaking heads appear to improve expected earnings, net of the control-group trend. The job status indices (percentage black,[1] average education, Duncan status score), which are correlated with the earnings measures, present much the same pattern: a deterioration in the white score, net of control group change; and an increase in the means for blacks, though no trend for Spanish-speaking persons. With respect to job satisfaction, supported whites again reveal a deterioration, Spanish-speaking an improvement, and blacks no consistent change pattern.

While the job characteristic measures in Table 8.1 exhibit persistent ethnic patterns, these entries have not been adjusted for the many ways in which the control and experimental samples differ, the result, in part, of differential attrition during the period of the study and, in part, of a not entirely random assignment to the treatment plans. To investigate the experimental impact, net of population differences between the groups, we resort to a regression analysis, which permits adjustments to be made for the effects of group differences on key variables.

The job characteristics of the participants at the eighth quarterly were regressed against the experimental parameters and the control variables, the latter including an individual's job-characteristic score at preenrollment. Our model, then, is specified by the equation

$$V_8 = f(\text{race–ethnicity, city site, family size, education,} \\ \text{age, head's earnings, wife's earnings, } V_0, EXP) \quad (1)$$

[1] The reader is reminded that the signs of the percentage black terms must be reversed for consistency of interpretation with the other status terms.

where V_8 and V_0 represent the job characteristic under investigation at the two time points, *EXP* denotes the spline formulation of the experimental parameters, and the other variables are the same ones described in conjunction with equation (1) in Chapter 7. (The earnings variables refer to the preenrollment year and index individual earnings potentials.) The observations in this analysis are male heads who either changed occupations or changed employers between preenrollment and the eighth quarterly.[2]

The *BENEFIT* formulation was not used because of the ambiguity concerning which specification should be associated with those individuals who experienced unemployment intervals of moderate duration. Presumably *BENEFIT* 1 (computed from family earnings in the year preceding preenrollment) would provide a reasonable estimate of a family's subsidy (and its expectations concerning the amount of future payments) where the head acquired a new job while incurring little unemployment. Also, *BENEFIT* 2 (calculated from wife's earnings) would be appropriate for characterizing family payments where the head experienced a long duration of unemployment. Which formulation, however, should be associated with the many individuals who experienced between two and eight weeks of unemployment? We have argued that there is great value in considering alternative specifications of the experimental parameters, since it is unclear, a priori, to which aspect of the payments structure the participants are responding. Unfortunately, the time constraints under which this research was pursued precluded constructing and validating a suitable *BENEFIT*-type measure for individuals with moderate unemployment durations. The results in this chapter are therefore limited to the spline formulation.

1. EARNINGS AND STATUS

In Tables 8.2 through 8.6, we present regression results for the equation (1) specification with the job characteristic (V_8, V_0) varying over the earnings and status measures. In the earnings equations (average earnings, percentage earning > $6000, percentage earning > $8000) the control variables reveal a consistent tendency in all groups except blacks for expected earnings under a job change to deteriorate with age (significant in at least two equations for each ethnic group), and to be "passed on" from one position to the next (V_0 is significant and positive in at least two equations for each group). In the status equations[3] (mean education

---

[2] Because the error term is heteroskedastic, the weighted regression procedure described in Section 1 of Chapter 7 was used.

[3] For the purpose of conserving space, a separate table is not presented for the percentage black measure. In every ethnic group the experimental effect was insignificant (joint *F*-test on the splines).

Table 8.1 Changes in Job Characteristic Means under Employment Transition, by Total Sample and Ethnic Group

	Experimental			Control		
	Q_0	Q_8	$Q_8 - Q_0$	Q_0	Q_8	$Q_8 - Q_0$
			1. Total Sample			
Census variables						
Average annual earnings (dollars)	7289	7650	361	7678	7753	75
Percentage in job with earnings > $6,000	65.17	69.44	4.27	70.66	69.03	−01.63
Percentage in job with earnings > $8,000	35.52	39.63	4.11	39.24	43.89	4.65
Percentage black	19.87	23.59	3.72	20.30	18.48	−1.82
Average education (years)	9.273	9.539	.266	9.746	10.01	.257
Parnes variables						
Duncan status score	19.52	18.77	−.75	18.07	21.43	3.36
Job satisfaction (content)	156.3	162.9	6.6	163.7	179.7	16.0
Job satisfaction (financial)	123.9	143.7	19.8	108.6	123.5	14.9
(Number of observations)	(126)	(126)		(105)	(105)	
			2. Whites			
Census variables						
Average annual earnings (dollars)	8116	7814	−302	8077	8016	−61
Percentage in job with earnings > $6,000	72.39	69.61	−2.78	73.59	73.11	−0.48

Percentage in job with earnings > $8,000	45.97	43.37	−2.60	42.27	47.63	5.36
Percentage black	16.35	21.30	4.95	19.86	15.09	−4.77
Average education (years)	9.779	9.491	−.2880	10.06	10.39	.33
Parnes variables						
Duncan status score	24.61	18.83	−5.78	19.75	24.71	4.96
Job satisfaction (content)	180.3	173.0	−7.3	199.8	216.4	16.6
Job satisfaction (financial)	120.0	135.9	15.9	105.3	131.5	26.2
(Number of observations)	(46)	(46)		(44)	(44)	
3. Blacks						
Census variables						
Average annual earnings (dollars)	6746	7549	803	7526	7790	264
Percentage in job with earnings > $6,000	60.77	69.67	8.90	69.68	70.21	.53
Percentage in job with earnings > $8,000	32.94	39.79	6.85	40.21	47.56	7.35
Percentage black	22.49	21.71	−.78	19.01	20.03	1.02
Average education (years)	9.020	9.482	.462	9.562	9.872	.310
Parnes variables						
Duncan status score	16.58	19.10	2.52	16.38	18.14	1.76
Job satisfaction (content)	151.0	163.6	12.6	133.4	157.8	24.4
Job satisfaction (financial)	124.0	154.7	30.7	99.65	129.9	30.25
(Number of observations)	(40)	(40)		(29)	(29)	

(continued)

Table 8.1 (continued)

	Experimental			Control		
	Q_0	Q_8	$Q_8 - Q_0$	Q_0	Q_8	$Q_8 - Q_0$
			4. *Spanish-speaking*			
Census variables						
Average annual earnings (dollars)	6883	7567	684	7263	7358	95
Percentage in job with earnings > $6,000	61.27	69.03	7.76	67.50	62.34	−5.16
Percentage in job with earnings > $8,000	26.10	35.17	9.07	34.24	35.43	1.19
Percentage black	21.29	28.13	6.84	22.07	21.60	−.47
Average education (years)	8.944	9.650	.706	9.479	9.603	.124
Parnes variables						
Duncan status score	16.60	18.40	1.80	17.28	19.91	2.63
Job satisfaction (content)	134.1	150.4	16.3	141.4	148.9	7.5
Job satisfaction (financial)	128.4	141.7	13.3	121.2	106.7	−14.5
(Number of observations)	(40)	(40)		(32)	(32)	

NOTE: Observations are heads who either changed employers or changed occupations and have valid occupation–industry codes at Q_0 and Q_8.

of job incumbents, Duncan score) education appears to be important for raising status (significant in at least one equation for each group). Also, whites are able to perpetuate occupational rank under a job change (significant, positive V_0) while Spanish-speaking and black heads fail to do so. In passing, we would remark that the lower dependence among blacks of expected earnings on individual attributes and on characteristics of the preceding job, factors which structure career development in other ethnic groups, is a matter warranting further attention.

Our obligation in this research, however, concerns the effect of the payments on the normal process of job change. In this regard, the spline variables in the earnings equations (Tables 8.2 through 8.4) generally show less impact than was noted in Table 8.1, suggesting that a combination of attrition and nonrandom considerations in the initial assignment to treatment plans was partially responsible for the findings in the earlier table. In particular, we now fail to note a positive experimental effect in the black subsample; in fact, the status equations (Tables 8.5 and 8.6) exhibit a consistent pattern whereby blacks transfer to *low-ranking* jobs as plan generosity (high guarantee and low tax rate) is increased. For whites, we continue to find that plan generosity depresses expected earnings (the guarantee spline, $S2$, in Tables 8.2 and 8.4; the tax spline, $S3$, in Table 8.3). However, an interpretation consistent with Table 8.1 is made difficult by the positive spline 1 in one equation (Table 8.2), which suggests that presence on a support plan serves to raise the level of expected earnings, net of the (contrary) effect from plan generosity.

In terms of an overall F-test for an experimental effect, the earnings equations for Spanish-speaking participants do not reach significance. Nevertheless, several of the terms, individually, are significant, and the signs of all nine coefficients in Tables 8.2, 8.3, and 8.4 are consistent with the pattern noted in Table 8.1, namely, that Spanish-speaking participants in the treatment groups raised their expected earnings through job transitions. The spline formulation shows that this effect increases with guarantee level, declines with tax rate, and therefore is largest on high-generosity plans. In regard to status change (Tables 8.5 and 8.6), Spanish-speaking heads show an analogous experimental effect which is now highly significant: they improve job status, as well as expected earnings, as a function of plan generosity.

Interaction Effects

The additive effects models may be obscuring adaptations to the experimental parameters which are contingent upon particular individual attributes. Rather than there being a common response by heads of all ages

Table 8.2 Regression Equations for Job Characteristic, Average Earnings (V_8), Additive Effects Model

Independent Variable	Total Sample	Whites	Blacks[a]	Spanish-speaking[a]
Constant	5388.**	5184.**	7969.**	5590.**
	(5.70)	(3.32)	(5.71)	(4.09)
Trenton	-838.6*	-2412.**	-303.2	-433.9
	(-1.72)	(-2.02)	(-0.73)	(-0.75)
Paterson – Passaic	-1064.**	-1274.*	-590.9	-697.3*
	(-2.62)	(-1.87)	(-1.49)	(-1.97)
Jersey City	-504.1	-693.7	—	—
	(-1.33)	(-1.32)		
Black	568.1	—	—	—
	(1.59)			
Spanish-speaking	35.28	—	—	—
	(0.09)			
Age	-31.47**	-57.75**	10.60	-33.07
	(-2.45)	(-2.78)	(0.51)	(-1.59)
Education	60.11	6.942	115.1*	38.03
	(1.40)	(0.07)	(1.95)	(0.67)
Earnings, head	-0.1260	-0.3424**	-0.1392	0.02962
	(-1.33)	(-2.03)	(-0.90)	(0.15)

Earnings, wife	−0.1156	−0.9790*	0.04326	0.005353
	(−0.53)	(−1.81)	(0.16)	(0.01)
Family size	116.3**	376.4**	−57.10	68.69
	(2.07)	(3.32)	(−0.74)	(0.79)
Average earnings (V_0)	0.4195**	0.5780**	0.006514	0.3086**
	(8.95)	(8.73)	(0.08)	(2.40)
Experimental status (spline 1)	423.5*	961.1**	−197.9	143.9
	(1.77)	(2.22)	(−0.54)	(0.38)
Guarantee (spline 2)	−0.1145	−0.7706**	−0.08419	0.3663
	(−0.82)	(−2.76)	(−0.45)	(1.57)
Tax rate (spline 3)	−4.199	7.523	−8.032	−28.79*
	(−0.44)	(0.39)	(−0.62)	(−1.73)
R^2	.167	.370	.069	.115
N	231	90	69	72
Joint F-test for experimental effects	$F_{3,219} = 1.15$	$F_{3,75} = 2.72$	$F_{3,56} = 0.50$	$F_{3,59} = 1.73$
	$p < .329$	$p < .051$	$p < .682$	$p < .171$
Dependent variable				
mean	7697.	7913.	7650.	7473.
s.d.	1947.	2190.	1649.	1883.

For notes, see Table 8.6.

Table 8.3 Regression Equations for Job Characteristic, Percentage with Earnings > $6000 ($V_8$), Additive Effects Model

Independent Variable	Total Sample	Whites	Blacks[a]	Spanish-speaking[a]
Constant	0.6642**	0.5477**	0.7032**	0.6012**
	(7.68)	(3.91)	(4.65)	(4.01)
Trenton	−0.03951	−0.03309	−0.04278	−0.09195
	(−0.83)	(−0.30)	(−0.82)	(−1.18)
Paterson–Passaic	−0.09799**	−0.08694	−0.05089	−0.09944**
	(−2.47)	(−1.39)	(−1.02)	(−2.05)
Jersey City	−0.02171	−0.01023	—	—
	(−0.58)	(−0.21)		
Black	0.03471	—	—	—
	(0.99)			
Spanish-speaking	−0.03083	—	—	—
	(−0.83)			
Age ($\times 10^{-3}$)	−3.670**	−4.348**	−0.9309	−4.781*
	(−2.92)	(−2.29)	(−0.36)	(−1.71)
Education ($\times 10^{-3}$)	7.198*	20.66**	10.42	−4.151
	(1.69)	(2.12)	(1.39)	(−0.55)
Earnings, head ($\times 10^{-5}$)	1.191	0.4305	0.07550	2.559
	(1.28)	(0.28)	(0.04)	(1.01)
Earnings, wife ($\times 10^{-5}$)	3.839*	0.2976	5.311	1.025
	(1.79)	(0.06)	(1.60)	(0.19)
Family size ($\times 10^{-3}$)	4.482	11.01	−4.499	9.363
	(0.81)	(1.05)	(−0.47)	(0.81)
Earnings > $6000 ($V_0$)	0.1004**	0.1180	0.04497	0.1494*
	(2.47)	(1.30)	(0.73)	(1.71)
Experimental status (spline 1)	0.01696	0.006817	0.01056	0.03349
	(0.72)	(0.17)	(0.24)	(0.66)
Guarantee (spline 2 $\times 10^{-5}$)	−1.668	−2.472	−2.192	4.454
	(−1.22)	(−0.98)	(−0.92)	(1.42)
Tax rate (spline 3 $\times 10^{-3}$)	−0.07893	3.489**	−1.326	−3.347
	(−0.08)	(1.99)	(−0.81)	(−1.50)
R^2	.147	.279	.156	.189
N	231	90	69	72
Joint F-test for experimental effects	$F_{3,219} = 0.543$ $p < .654$	$F_{3,75} = 1.62$ $p < .192$	$F_{3,56} = 0.60$ $p < .619$	$F_{3,59} = 1.64$ $p < .189$
Dependent variable mean	.6926	.7133	.6990	.6606
s.d.	.2392	.2340	.2338	.2503

For notes, see Table 8.6.

Table 8.4 Regression Equations for Job Characteristic, Percent with Earnings > $8000 ($V_8$), Additive Effects Model

Independent Variable	Total Sample	Whites	Blacks[a]	Spanish-speaking[a]
Constant	0.4525**	0.5235**	0.4244**	0.3274**
	(4.81)	(3.34)	(2.61)	(2.14)
Trenton	−0.08780*	−0.07615	−0.04060	−0.1183
	(−1.66)	(−0.62)	(−0.71)	(−1.49)
Paterson–Passaic	−0.1266**	−0.1500**	−0.06912	−0.1013**
	(−2.88)	(−2.12)	(−1.29)	(−2.08)
Jersey City	−0.05355	−0.09609*	—	—
	(−1.30)	(−1.77)		
Black	0.05192	—	—	—
	(1.34)			
Spanish-speaking	−0.02115	—	—	—
	(−0.52)			
Age ($\times 10^{-3}$)	−4.778**	−6.777**	−0.8670	−6.504**
	(−3.43)	(−3.14)	(−0.31)	(−2.29)
Education ($\times 10^{-3}$)	6.381	3.834	12.26	4.065
	(1.35)	(0.36)	(1.51)	(0.53)
Earnings, head ($\times 10^{-6}$)	9.417	−16.47	10.64	22.07
	(0.92)	(−0.96)	(0.51)	(0.88)
Earnings, wife ($\times 10^{-5}$)	2.165	−5.078	4.168	−2.990
	(0.91)	(−0.92)	(1.14)	(−0.54)
Family size	0.007114	0.02918**	−0.007227	0.01004
	(1.17)	(2.49)	(−0.70)	(0.85)
Earnings > $8000 ($V_0$)	0.1883**	0.2581**	0.03849	0.3700**
	(3.99)	(3.47)	(0.45)	(2.96)
Experimental status (spline 1)	0.01764	0.04578	−0.01292	0.01124
	(0.68)	(1.02)	(−0.27)	(0.21)
Guarantee (spline 2 $\times 10^{-5}$)	−2.151	−6.877**	−2.129	5.559*
	(−1.43)	(−2.40)	(−0.84)	(1.74)
Tax rate (spline 3 $\times 10^{-3}$)	−0.6814	1.949	−2.433	−4.483**
	(−0.65)	(0.95)	(−1.38)	(−1.98)
R^2	.141	.222	.178	.194
N	231	90	69	72
Joint F-test for experimental effects	$F_{3,219} = 1.02$ $p < .387$	$F_{3,75} = 2.25$ $p < .089$	$F_{3,56} = 1.20$ $p < .318$	$F_{3,59} = 2.02$ $p < .120$
Dependent variable mean	.4157	.4546	.4306	.3529
s.d.	.2395	.2338	.2341	.2423

For notes, see Table 8.6.

Table 8.5 **Regression Equations for Job Characteristic, Average Education (V_8), Additive Effects Model**

Independent Variable	Total Sample	Whites	Blacks[a]	Spanish-speaking[a]
Constant	8.590**	5.130**	10.11**	7.702**
	(10.57)	(4.05)	(10.60)	(5.60)
Trenton	−0.4892	−0.4770	−0.2843	−2.019**
	(−1.25)	(−0.58)	(−0.97)	(−3.46)
Paterson–Passaic	−0.2233	0.2097	−0.6776**	0.5132
	(−0.69)	(0.45)	(−2.43)	(1.41)
Jersey City	−0.2351	−0.6198*	—	—
	(−0.77)	(−1.73)		
Black	−0.1205	—	—	—
	(−0.42)			
Spanish-speaking	−0.09436	—	—	—
	(−0.32)			
Age	−0.007594	−0.01449	0.01270	0.003505
	(−0.74)	(−0.99)	(0.88)	(0.15)
Education	0.1208**	−0.009624	0.08058*	0.1805**
	(3.52)	(−0.13)	(1.93)	(3.09)
Earnings, head ($\times 10^{-5}$)	−9.546	−13.80	5.935	−7.213
	(−1.26)	(−1.21)	(0.55)	(−0.38)
Earnings, wife ($\times 10^{-5}$)	−5.110	−15.30	33.33*	−80.56**
	(−0.29)	(−0.39)	(1.80)	(−2.00)
Family size	0.08892**	0.1070	0.007235	−0.01477
	(1.97)	(1.34)	(0.13)	(−0.17)
Average education (V_0)	0.06581	0.5820**	−0.1688**	0.07638
	(1.29)	(5.00)	(−3.22)	(0.72)
Experimental status (spline 1)	−0.1766	−0.2636	0.1259	−0.3386
	(−0.92)	(−0.84)	(0.52)	(−0.88)
Guarantee (spline 2 $\times 10^{-4}$)	2.053*	0.8792	−3.163**	13.53**
	(1.82)	(0.46)	(−2.34)	(5.70)
Tax rate (spline 3 $\times 10^{-3}$)	3.520	−7.275	25.41**	−79.25**
	(0.46)	(−0.55)	(2.78)	(−4.65)
R^2	.144	.225	.282	.223
N	231	90	69	72
Joint F-test for experimental effects	$F_{3,219} = 1.37$ $p < .253$	$F_{3,75} = 0.36$ $p < .779$	$F_{3,56} = 4.19$ $p < .010$	$F_{3,59} = 13.57$ $p < .001$
Dependent variable mean	9.751	9.929	9.646	9.629
s.d.	1.554	1.730	1.185	1.630

For notes, see Table 8.6.

Table 8.6 Regression Equations for Job Characteristic, Occupational Status (Duncan) Score (V_8), Additive Effects Model

Independent Variable	Total Sample	Whites	Blacks[a]	Spanish-speaking[a]
Constant	12.20**	−13.11	21.60**	13.12
	(2.04)	(−1.22)	(2.41)	(1.29)
Trenton	−8.744**	−2.326	1.653	−10.06*
	(−2.24)	(−0.23)	(0.44)	(−1.98)
Paterson–Passaic	−5.305	6.046	−4.736	3.852
	(−1.52)	(0.96)	(−1.44)	(1.08)
Jersey City	−5.799**	−9.226**	—	—
	(−1.97)	(−2.67)		
Black	2.858	—	—	—
	(0.95)			
Spanish-speaking	4.476	—	—	—
	(1.38)			
Age	0.05487	0.4065**	0.03401	0.2733
	(0.54)	(2.62)	(0.21)	(1.34)
Education	0.1998	1.722*	−0.2775	1.645**
	(0.54)	(1.97)	(−0.47)	(2.97)
Earnings, head ($\times 10^{-3}$)	−1.155*	−1.644*	0.2651	−1.124
	(−1.66)	(−1.85)	(0.16)	(−0.67)
Earnings, wife ($\times 10^{-3}$)	−3.121*	−13.50**	3.313	−2.757
	(−1.95)	(−4.74)	(1.48)	(−0.50)
Family size	1.054**	1.227*	−0.3869	−0.6652
	(2.12)	(1.70)	(−0.46)	(−0.68)
Duncan status Score (V_0)	0.3163**	0.4228**	0.001343	−0.2356
	(5.18)	(5.64)	(0.01)	(−1.40)
Experimental status (spline 1)	−5.224**	−8.576**	−2.144	−8.878**
	(−2.87)	(−2.80)	(−0.72)	(−2.60)
Guarantee (spline 2 $\times 10^{-3}$)	2.005*	3.858*	−1.912	6.117**
	(1.81)	(1.85)	(−1.08)	(2.70)
Tax rate (spline 3)	0.1445*	0.1164	0.4104**	−0.3859**
	(1.95)	(0.88)	(3.54)	(−2.59)
R^2	.133	.306	.197	.093
N	231	90	69	72
Joint F-test for experimental effects	$F_{3,216} = 5.15$ $p < .002$	$F_{3,75} = 2.92$ $p < .040$	$F_{3,56} = 5.05$ $p < .004$	$F_{3,59} = 3.77$ $p < .015$
Dependent variable mean	19.98	21.70	18.70	19.07
s.d.	12.13	13.47	10.76	11.49

NOTE: To correct for heteroskedasticity resulting from the various job characteristic values having been computed from different numbers of persons, the regression equations were transformed as follows: each observation was multiplied by $\sqrt{n_i}$ where n_i = the number of individuals (in the Census or Parnes file) from which the occupation–industry value was computed. The term $\sqrt{n_i}$ was also introduced as a regressor and the constant was suppressed. The R^2 figures obtained from the least squares algorithm after this transformation and all education levels, older participants, for instance, might adapt differently from younger men, or more educated individuals differently from those with less education. To investigate this possibility, the equations in Tables 8.2 through 8.6 were modified by the inclusion of interaction terms between the spline parameters and the respondent attributes, age and education, and the job characteristic, V_0—these being considered the most easily interpretable of the large number of possible interactions. Formally, this model is specified by

$$V_8 = f(\text{age, education}, V_0, \text{other controls}, EXP, EXP \times V), \quad (2)$$

where "other controls" refers to the variables in equation (1) aside from those listed here, EXP denotes the spline formulation, and V indicates one of the initial three terms in equation (2). Regression equation parts for all cases of significant interactions are presented in Tables 8.7 through 8.10.

The effects in the total sample are a composite of the adjustments by the ethnic groups. To the extent that these groups adapt differently to the treatment parameters, the combined response may be difficult to interpret. This appears to be the case with the earnings interactions. On the other hand, with one exception (average education/average education),[4] the seven significant status interactions reveal a consistent pattern whereby,[5] among supported participants, occupational rank is reduced for older persons, for individuals with little education, and for those initially employed in low-status positions—to some degree the same subjects would be responsible for all three findings (for example, r[age, head's education] $= -.352$). Moreover, the reduction is greater on high guarantee plans. Younger heads, more educated individuals, and ones better situated occupationally at Q_0, exhibit little status change when their responses on the different support plans are averaged. They do, however, show a persistent tendency to transfer to higher-ranked positions as a function of plan generosity.

The interactions are easier to comprehend in graphic form, so we present in Figure 8.1 a plot typical of the status adjustments. As we have described in conjunction with the job turnover graphs, the curves are net of control-group changes so that each contour can be compared with the horizontal axis, representing the control group. For instance, the contour for heads with eleven years of schooling indicates that, at a guarantee

[4] In this notation, the first entry reports the dependent variable, V_8; the second indicates the subject or job characteristic, V, in the interaction term.

[5] This evaluation refers to a computation using $S1$, the interaction between $S1$ and V, $S2$ or $S3$ (depending on which is significant) and its interaction with V. The deleted experimental parameter is set equal to zero which, in actuality, means $2475 (in the case of $S2$) and a 50 percent tax rate (in the case of $S3$).

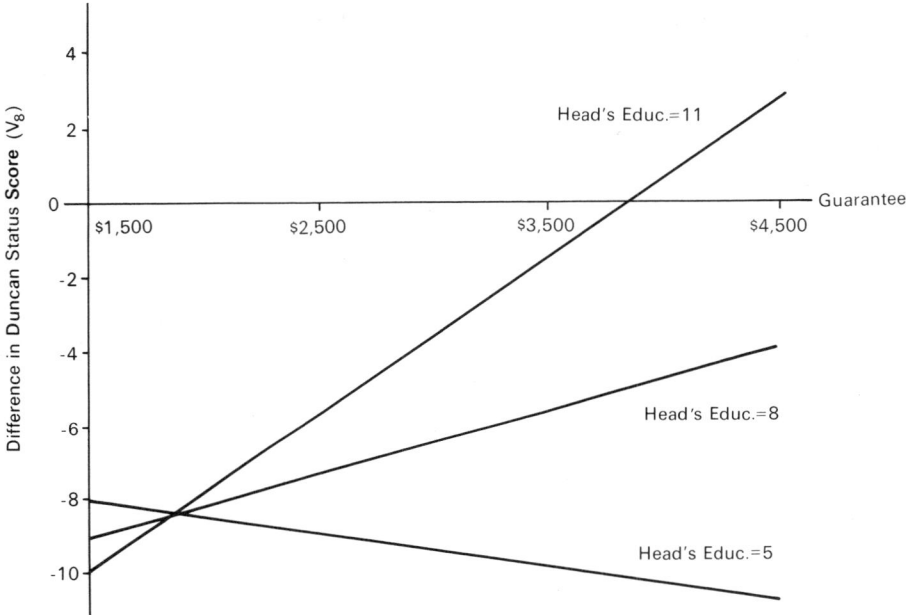

Figure 8.1 Interaction between guarantee level (spline 2) and head's education, in equation for "Duncan status score (V_8)," total sample. Each contour compares the response by an experimental group population with a comparable control group category (X axis). The vertical scale is adjusted by the additive effect of the spline 1 term and by its interaction with education; intercepts correspond to tax rate = .50. Means and standard deviations of the variables are ($2918, $839) for the guarantee level—$2918 corresponds to a spline 2 mean of $443—and (8.8, 2.8) for education.

equal to $1500, status decreased by ten points on the Duncan scale, under a job change, in comparison with comparably educated individuals in the control group. At a guarantee equal to $4500, the status change for supported subjects has increased to a three-point improvement.

Rather than attempt to elucidate the interactions in the total sample at greater length, we turn to comparable analyses of the ethnic subsamples.

---

are no longer appropriate to the original problem; the reported R^2s pertain to the untransformed equations. See Kmenta (1971: 249–267) for technical details. Entries are unstandardized regression coefficients; t-values are in parentheses. Spline 1 = 1 indicates presence on plan (G = $2475, t = .50). The dummy variable for Scranton was deleted from the city effects terms; the variable for whites was deleted from the ethnic terms in the total sample regressions.

[a] Because of the absence of blacks and Spanish-speaking families in Scranton, the dummy variable for Jersey City was deleted from these models.

* Significant at $p < .10$.
** Significant at $p < .05$.

Table 8.7 Regression Coefficients for Significant Interactions with Experimental Variables (Splines), for Employment Transition, Total Sample

Subject or Job Characteristic, V	V	(Experimental status) $S1$	(Guarantee) $S2$	(Tax rate) $S3$	$S1 \times V$	$S2 \times V$	$S3 \times V$	Joint F-test
				V_8 = Average Earnings[a]				
Age	−48.69** (−2.66)	−1739.* (−1.95)	2.218** (3.56)	−2.915 (−0.07)	64.14** (2.49)	−0.0656** (−3.87)	−0.2505 (−0.21)	$F_{3,216} = 6.03$ $p < .001$
				V_8 = Percentage in Jobs with Earnings > \$6000				
Education, head	0.01778** (2.86)	0.1042 (1.32)	4.725×10^{-5} (1.06)	−0.005480* (−1.70)	−0.008763 (−1.05)	-7.063×10^{-6} (−1.47)	0.000605 (1.69)	$F_{3,216} = 2.83$ $p < .040$
				V_8 = Percentage in Jobs with Earnings > \$8000				
Age	−0.005155** (−2.85)	−0.1604 (−1.63)	0.000202** (2.94)	−0.003183 (−0.69)	0.005201* (1.83)	$-6.254 \times 10^{-6**}$ (−3.35)	5.455×10^{-5} (0.42)	$F_{3,216} = 3.95$ $p < .009$
Percentage with earnings > \$8000 (V_0)	0.3095** (3.87)	0.06642 (1.27)	3.85×10^{-6} (0.14)	−0.004438** (−2.33)	−0.09820 (−0.91)	-6.53×10^{-5} (−1.07)	0.009297** (2.31)	$F_{3,216} = 2.93$ $p < .035$
				V_8 = Percentage Black in Occupation–Industry				
Percentage black in occupation–industry (V_0)	0.1351* (1.79)	0.02880 (1.20)	$-4.403 \times 10^{-5**}$ (−3.08)	0.0002854 (0.32)	−0.1353 (−1.44)	0.0002244** (3.38)	−0.004884 (−1.59)	$F_{3,216} = 3.89$ $p < .010$

V_8 = Average Education for Occupation–Industry

Education, head	0.09024* (1.80)	−0.3077 (−0.48)	−0.0003511 (−0.96)	−0.02493 (−0.95)	0.009680 (0.14)	6.34×10^{-5} (1.60)	0.003454 (1.18)	$F_{3,216} = 2.27$ $p < .082$
Age	0.003147 (0.21)	−0.6540 (−0.91)	0.002116** (4.19)	−0.03942 (−1.18)	0.01242 (0.60)	-5.27×10^{-5}** (−3.85)	0.001144 (1.21)	$F_{3,216} = 5.57$ $p < .001$
Average education (V_0)	0.3518** (3.44)	2.589* (1.81)	0.0007928 (1.33)	−0.02094 (−0.34)	−0.2767* (−1.88)	-6.41×10^{-5} (−1.01)	0.002696 (0.40)	$F_{3,216} = 3.80$ $p < .011$
			V_8 = Occupational Status (Duncan) Score					
Education, head	−0.6726 (−1.10)	−11.70 (−1.55)	−0.005288 (−1.44)	0.2793 (1.03)	0.5672 (0.72)	0.0008757** (2.09)	−0.01577 (−0.53)	$F_{3,213} = 2.51$ $p < .060$
Age	0.1881 (1.28)	−7.159 (−1.02)	0.01859** (3.50)	−0.3521 (−1.11)	0.04594 (0.21)	−0.0004727** (−3.15)	0.01417 (1.50)	$F_{3,213} = 4.09$ $p < .008$
Occupational status (Duncan) score (V_0)	0.03338 (0.32)	−6.802* (−1.71)	−0.002804 (−1.32)	0.07414 (0.38)	0.004987 (0.03)	0.0002801** (2.54)	0.002824 (0.29)	$F_{3,213} = 6.10$ $p < .001$
			V_8 = Job Satisfaction (Content)					
Education, head	−5.544 (−1.17)	−92.86 (−1.55)	−0.02304 (−0.80)	1.012 (0.47)	5.552 (0.90)	0.006204* (1.89)	−0.2311 (−0.97)	$F_{3,213} = 2.51$ $p < .060$
Job satisfaction (content) (V_0)	0.2430** (2.94)	−11.65 (−0.50)	0.002055 (0.13)	0.5625 (0.62)	−0.1421 (−1.26)	0.0001363** (2.01)	−0.008317** (−2.26)	$F_{3,213} = 2.32$ $p < .076$
			V_8 = Job Satisfaction (Financial)					
Job satisfaction (financial) (V_0)	0.0399 (0.52)	−18.78 (−1.53)	−0.01970** (−2.70)	1.537** (2.84)	0.05386 (0.61)	0.0001253** (2.64)	−0.009976** (−2.33)	$F_{3,213} = 3.53$ $p < .016$

NOTE: See notes to Table 8.10.
* Significant at $p < .10$.
** Significant at $p < .05$.

Table 8.8 Regression Coefficients for Significant Interactions with Experimental Variables (Splines), for Employment Transition, Whites

Subject or Job Characteristic, V	V	$S1$	$S2$	$S3$	$S1 \times V$	$S2 \times V$	$S3 \times V$	Joint F-test
			V_8 = Percentage in Jobs with Earnings > \$6000[a]					
Percentage with earnings > \$6000 (V_0)	-0.07557 (-0.61)	-0.3551** (-2.33)	7.516×10^{-5} (0.83)	-0.003485 (-0.50)	0.4846** (2.47)	-0.0001380 (-1.19)	0.009387 (1.01)	$F_{3,72} = 2.24$ $p < .091$
			V_8 = Percentage Black in Occupation–Industry					
Education, head	0.01089 (1.34)	-0.1060 (-0.87)	0.0001770** (2.86)	0.003217 (0.41)	0.008401 (0.72)	-1.790×10^{-5}** (-2.86)	-7.557×10^{-5} (-0.10)	$F_{3,72} = 3.12$ $p < .031$
Percentage black in occupation–industry (V_0)	0.03734 (0.29)	-0.04612 (-1.09)	-1.774×10^{-5} (-0.74)	0.003746** (2.17)	0.1186 (0.70)	0.0001896* (1.84)	-0.01001 (-1.56)	$F_{3,72} = 2.28$ $p < .087$
			V_8 = Occupational Status (Duncan) Score					
Age	0.7203** (3.41)	10.59 (0.74)	0.01148 (1.22)	0.08637 (0.13)	-0.5813 (-1.43)	-0.0002255 (-0.88)	0.001089 (0.06)	$F_{3,72} = 2.25$ $p < .090$
Occupational status (Duncan) score (V_0)	0.1473 (1.06)	-16.70** (-2.89)	0.003393 (0.96)	0.7842* (1.78)	0.3442 (1.30)	1.627×10^{-5} (0.11)	-0.03860 (-1.60)	$F_{3,72} = 2.71$ $p < .051$
			V_8 = Job Satisfaction (Financial)					
Education, head	7.025 (1.23)	-40.03 (-0.43)	0.08426* (1.97)	5.711 (1.20)	2.074 (0.23)	-0.009285** (-2.06)	-0.4788 (-1.01)	$F_{3,72} = 2.42$ $p < .072$
Job satisfaction (financial) (V_0)	0.1579 (1.33)	22.55 (0.92)	-0.04425** (-2.88)	1.543* (1.70)	-0.2358 (-1.37)	0.0003090** (2.99)	-0.006028 (-0.90)	$F_{3,72} = 3.16$ $p < .029$

NOTE: See notes to Table 8.10.
* Significant at $p < .10$.
** Significant at $p < .05$.

There are five significant interactions in the white sub-sample,[6] one involving an income measure. It reveals that supported heads in low-earnings positions at Q_0 experience a reduction in expected earnings, while individuals initially in higher-salaried jobs enjoy a modest increase (earnings > $6000/earnings > $6000). Correspondingly, the status interactions indicate that older heads, less educated heads, and heads in low ranked positions at Q_0 lose status under a job change, the reduction generally increasing with plan generosity (Duncan/age; Duncan/Duncan; percentage black/head's education; percentage black/percentage black).[7] Younger persons and those initially in higher ranked positions exhibit little experimental effect when their responses on the various plans are averaged; however, they do show a consistent tendency toward status improvement with plan generosity—high guarantee (Duncan/age; percentage black/head's education), and low tax rate (Duncan/Duncan; percentage black/percentage black). Figures 8.2 and 8.3 provide illustrations of these effects.

There are nine significant interactions in the black subsample. Five are with income measures, and these reveal transitions to higher expected earnings jobs by low education heads in the treatment groups (average earnings/head's education), by heads in low earnings positions at Q_0 (/earnings > $6000/earnings > $6000; earnings > $8000/earnings > $8000; average earnings/average earnings), and by older heads (average earnings/age). In the sole case of significant interactions with plan parameters in an income equation (average earnings/age), the improvement in expected earnings by older subjects appears to decline with plan generosity; it is largest on the low-guarantee and high tax rate plans. Nevertheless, the effect under every support arrangement is still to increase the expected earnings of older and less educated black family heads. In contrast, among younger participants, more educated heads, and those initially in jobs with higher earnings, there is a persistent tendency toward reduced expected earnings. This reduction, though, is generally small and decreases with plan generosity (average earnings/age). Figure 8.4 depicts a typical earnings response pattern in the black subsample.

Four of the status equations for blacks have significant interactions. Unlike the earnings equations, there is little evidence here of an advantage on all tax plans for any education group. With regard to the plan parameters, less educated blacks and those in high percentage black posi-

---

[6] Only the income and status equations are considered at this point. The satisfaction interactions will be discussed in Section 2.

[7] The reader is reminded that when percentage black is the dependent variable the signs of the coefficients must be reversed for consistent interpretation with the other status measures.

Table 8.9 Regression Coefficients for Significant Interactions with Experimental Variables (Splines), for Employment Transition, Blacks

Subject or Job Characteristic, V	V	$S1$	$S2$	$S3$	$S1 \times V$	$S2 \times V$	$S3 \times V$	Joint F-test
				V_8 = Average Earnings[a]				
Education, head	350.0**	3640.**	−0.3324	37.29	−405.9**	0.01938	−5.652	$F_{3,53} = 3.40$
	(3.61)	(2.61)	(−0.47)	(0.85)	(−2.83)	(0.27)	(−1.08)	$p < .024$
Age	−43.56	−5369.**	2.078**	−189.1**	160.7**	−0.06310**	5.176**	$F_{3,53} = 3.95$
	(−1.42)	(−3.43)	(2.11)	(−2.48)	(3.36)	(−2.36)	(2.40)	$p < .013$
Average earnings (V_0)	0.6456**	6358.**	0.001727	49.03	−0.8730**	-1.242×10^{-5}	−0.008073	$F_{3,53} = 7.77$
	(4.27)	(3.75)	(0.00)	(0.77)	(−3.72)	(−0.13)	(−0.86)	$p < .001$
			V_8 = Percentage in Jobs with Earnings > \$6000					
Percentage with earnings > \$6000 (V_0)	0.5428**	0.4396**	-2.261×10^{-5}	−0.0006168	−0.5884**	-9.849×10^{-7}	−0.0006962	$F_{3,53} = 4.67$
	(3.75)	(3.39)	(−0.45)	(−0.19)	(−3.40)	(−0.01)	(−0.15)	$p < .006$
			V_8 = Percentage in Jobs with Earnings > \$8000					
Percentage with earnings > \$8000 (V_0)	0.4922**	0.2635**	-1.666×10^{-5}	−0.001912	−0.6520**	-2.324×10^{-5}	−0.001258	$F_{3,53} = 5.48$
	(3.62)	(2.88)	(−0.37)	(−0.59)	(−3.38)	(−0.20)	(−0.16)	$p < .002$

	V_8 = Percentage Black in Occupation–Industry					
Age	0.003744*	0.2996**	2.354 × 10⁻⁵	0.008387	−0.009897**	−1.966 × 10⁻⁷	−0.0003070**	$F_{3,53}$ = 5.04
	(1.73)	(2.70)	(0.34)	(1.56)	(−2.92)	(−0.11)	(−2.03)	$p < .004$
Percentage black in occupation–industry (V_0)	0.2873**	0.06008	−4.774 × 10⁻⁵**	−0.001025	−0.3108*	0.0003268**	−0.006642	$F_{3,53}$ = 3.97
	(2.56)	(1.60)	(−2.39)	(−0.81)	(−1.97)	(3.19)	(−1.29)	$p < .013$

	V_8 = Average Education for Occupation–Industry							
Average education (V_0)	0.1536	1.921	0.0006023	−0.2794**	−0.1500	−0.0001123	0.03389**	$F_{3,53}$ = 5.41
	(0.96)	(0.98)	(0.83)	(−2.85)	(−0.74)	(−1.45)	(3.13)	$p < .003$

	V_8 = Occupational Status (Duncan) Score							
Education, head	−1.703*	1.147	−0.01743**	0.8651*	−0.4474	0.001744**	−0.05245	$F_{3,53}$ = 2.83
	(−1.69)	(0.08)	(−2.62)	(1.90)	(−0.31)	(2.50)	(−1.04)	$p < .047$

	V_8 = Job Satisfaction (Content)							
Education, head	−3.356	42.53	−0.08279*	4.453	−4.906	0.01190**	−0.4656	$F_{3,53}$ = 2.78
	(−0.54)	(0.47)	(−1.97)	(1.54)	(−0.53)	(2.61)	(−1.46)	$p < .050$
Job satisfaction (content) (V_0)	0.07997	12.64	−0.02078	1.285	−0.1255	0.0002211**	−0.005342	$F_{3,53}$ = 2.37
	(0.50)	(0.38)	(−1.10)	(0.92)	(−0.63)	(2.65)	(−1.05)	$p < .081$

NOTE: See notes to table 8.10.
* Significant at $p < .10$.
** Significant at $p < .05$.

Table 8.10 Regression Coefficients for Significant Interactions with Experimental Variables (Splines), for Employment Transition, Spanish-speaking

Subject or Job Characteristic, V	V	$S1$	$S2$	$S3$	$S1 \times V$	$S2 \times V$	$S3 \times V$	Joint F-test
V_8 = Average Education for Occupation–Industry[a]								
Education, head	0.1630*	0.3273	−0.0009739	−0.01363	−0.07786	0.0003061**	−0.006843	$F_{3,56} = 3.00$
	(1.90)	(0.34)	(−1.12)	(−0.27)	(−0.62)	(2.82)	(−1.16)	$p < .038$
Average education (V_0)	0.09649	3.382	−0.005332**	0.04696	−0.3693	0.0007087**	−0.01257	$F_{3,56} = 3.82$
	(0.60)	(1.50)	(−2.43)	(0.41)	(−1.61)	(3.08)	(−1.06)	$p < .015$
V_8 = Occupation Status (Duncan) Score								
Education, head	2.015**	5.257	−0.009417	0.6294*	−2.036*	0.002166**	−0.1311**	$F_{3,56} = 4.31$
	(2.11)	(0.58)	(−1.38)	(1.82)	(−1.80)	(2.51)	(−3.13)	$p < .008$
Age	−0.4232	−44.48**	0.01424	−1.188**	−1.169**	−0.0002925	−0.02782	$F_{3,56} = 3.72$
	(−1.40)	(−3.46)	(1.18)	(−2.11)	(2.90)	(−0.75)	(1.46)	$p < .017$
Occupational status (Duncan) score (V_0)	−0.1517	−8.027	−0.004913	0.8510**	−0.04275	0.0006879*	−0.06756**	$F_{3,56} = 5.26$
	(−0.83)	(−1.14)	(−0.78)	(2.28)	(−0.12)	(1.87)	(−3.55)	$p < .003$
V_8 = Job Satisfaction (Financial)								
Job satisfaction (financial) (V_0)	−0.2801	−51.84*	−0.03740	1.668	0.6157**	8.453×10^{-5}	−0.003324	$F_{3,56} = 2.77$
	(−1.60)	(−1.87)	(−1.30)	(1.03)	(2.53)	(0.37)	(−0.23)	$p < .050$

NOTE: The complete equations are specified by the addition of the interaction terms to the models of Table 8.2. Entries are unstandardized regression coefficients; t-values are in parentheses. To correct for heteroskedasticity resulting from the job-characteristic values having been computed from different numbers of persons, the regression equations were transformed as follows: each observation was weighted by $\sqrt{n_i}$, where n_i = the number of individuals (in the Census or Parnes files) from which the occupation/industry value was computed. The term $\sqrt{n_i}$ was also introduced as a regressor and the constant was suppressed. See Kmenta (1971: 249–267) for technical details. The joint F-test is for interactions with experimental variables.

[a] Subheadings in Tables 8.7 through 8.10 present dependent variables for the regression equation parts (rows) that follow.

* Significant at $p < .10$.

** Significant at $p < .05$.

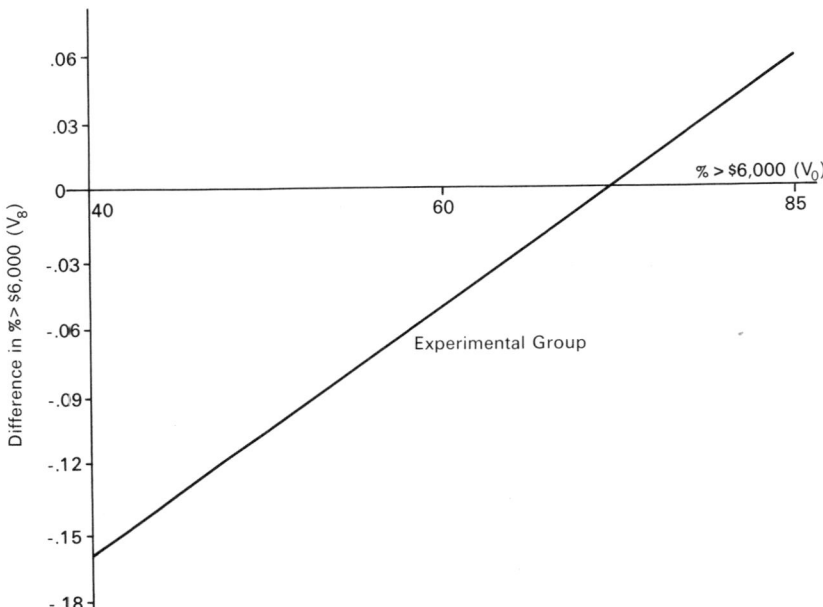

Figure 8.2 Interaction between presence in experimental group (spline 1) and job characteristic, "percentage with earnings greater than $6000 ($V_0$)," in equation for "percentage with earnings greater than $6000 ($V_8$)," white subsample. Contour compares experimental group response with control group change (X axis). The mean and standard deviation of the job characteristic (V_0) are (.72, .21).

tions at Q_0 exhibit a status decline as the guarantee is raised (Duncan/head's education; percentage black/percentage black). The two significant interactions with tax rate (spline 3) are inconsistent. One of them (percentage black/age) shows a status decline (higher percentage black) for older persons as the tax rate is lowered; together with the guarantee spline it is consistent with the earnings interactions—a decline in both status and expected earnings for black heads as a function of plan generosity. The other tax rate interaction (average education/average education) suggests the opposite response, that supported blacks in jobs with low average education improve status when on low tax rate plans. In interpreting the results, we discount this exception, noting that the finding of a status decline with plan generosity is also consistent with the additive effects models for blacks (Tables 8.5 and 8.6). Finally, since more educated heads and younger participants exhibit little response to the treatment parameters, we conclude that the results with the additive models reflect, to a large degree, the adaptations by older heads, less educated heads, and those initially in low-status occupations. Figure 8.5 illustrates the status response pattern.

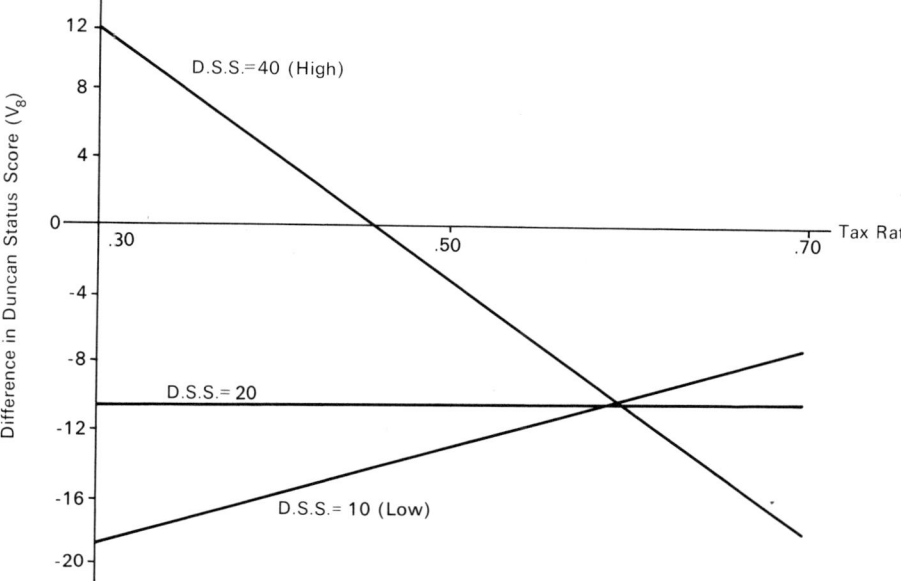

Figure 8.3 Interaction between tax rate (spline 3) and job characteristic, "Duncan status score (V_0)," in equation for "Duncan status score (V_8)," white subsample. Each contour compares the response by an experimental group population with a comparable control group category (X axis). The vertical scale is adjusted by the additive effect of the spline 1 term and by its interaction with V_0; intercepts correspond to guarantee = $2475 (coded zero in our data). The tax-rate parameters (.30, .50, .70) were coded (-20, 0, 20) in the regression equations. The mean and standard deviation of the job characteristic (V_0) are (22.2, 14.9).

There are no significant interactions in the earnings equations for the Spanish-speaking subsample, although five are present in the status models. The evidence regarding the levels of the response contours is inconsistent; in some equations, younger and more educated heads in the experimental group exhibit a status loss irrespective of plan parameters (Duncan/age; Duncan/head's education), but the other models fail to corroborate this effect. With respect to the plan parameters, there is a consistent tendency for more educated subjects and those in positions with high average education at Q_0 to improve status as a function of guarantee amount (average education/head's education; Duncan/head's education; average education/average education), and for educated heads, younger heads, and those initially in high-ranked positions to lose status as the tax rate is raised (Duncan/head's education; Duncan/age; Duncan/Duncan). Thus, younger and more educated Spanish-speaking participants on the generous support plans succeed in elevating job status. Since older heads, those with little education, and those in low-ranked po-

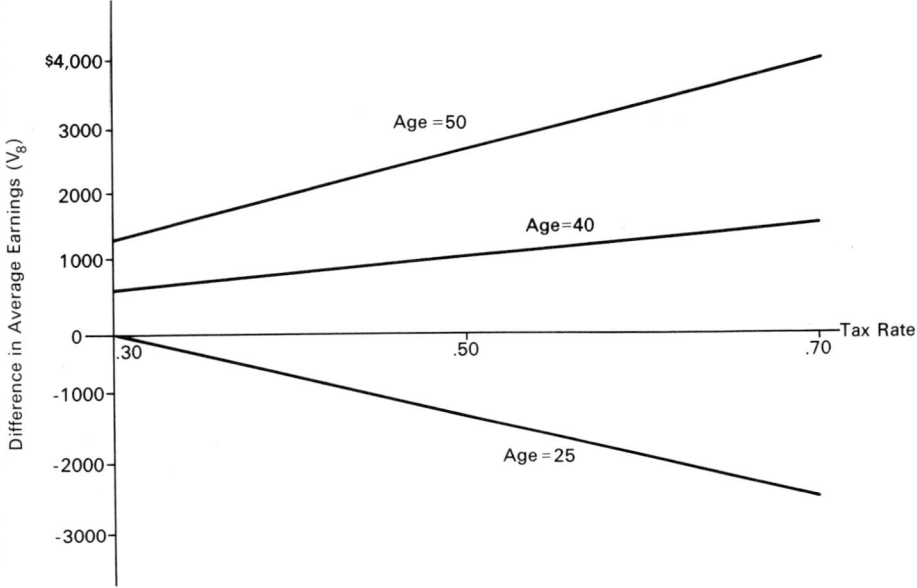

Figure 8.4 Interaction between tax rate (spline 3) and head's age, in equation for "average earnings (V_8)," black subsample. Each contour compares the response by an experimental group population with a comparable control group category. The vertical scale is adjusted by the additive effect of the spline 1 term and by its interaction with head's age; intercepts correspond to guarantee = $2475 (coded zero in our data). The tax-rate parameters (.30, .50, .70) were coded (−20, 0, 20) in the regression equations.

sitions at Q_0 show little response to the plan parameters, the strong tendency in the additive models (Tables 8.5 and 8.6) toward improved status as a function of plan generosity appears to be largely a consequence of the adaptations by younger and more educated subjects. Figure 8.6 is typical of the status adjustments by Spanish-speaking participants.

What does this amount to? First, the interaction models reveal the presence of two categories of respondents: (1) older heads, less educated heads, and heads initially employed in low expected earnings and low-status positions, and (2) participants at the other extremes on these dimensions. With respect to the first category—more disadvantaged individuals with regard to employment—supported whites show a reduction in expected earnings and status under a job change, irrespective of plan parameters; black heads in all treatment groups exhibit an improvement in expected earnings. As a function of the plan parameters, however, the response by both ethnic groups is much the same: *a decline (or less improvement) in earnings and status by older and less educated white and black heads with increasing plan generosity—high guarantee and low tax*

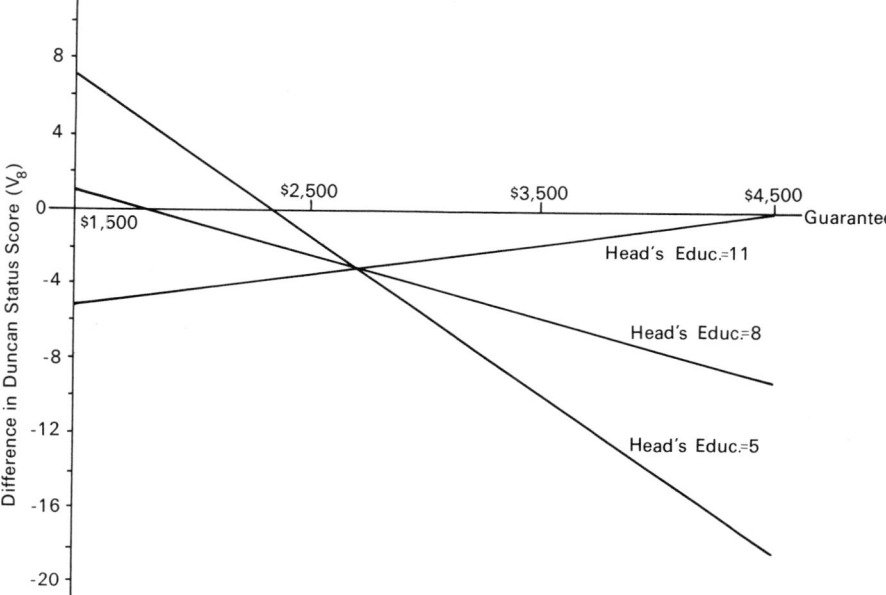

Figure 8.5 Interaction between guarantee level (spline 2) and head's education, in equation for "Duncan status score (V_8)," black subsample. Each contour compares the response by an experimental group population with a comparable control group category (X axis). The vertical scale is adjusted by the additive effect of the spline 1 term and by its interaction with education; intercepts correspond to tax rate = .50. Means and standard deviations of the variables are ($2993, $913) for the guarantee level—$2993 corresponds to a spline 2 mean of $518—and (9.0, 2.7) for education.

rate. Spanish-speaking participants display a weak tendency toward higher earnings on the more generous plans (additive effects models) and little status change.[8]

With respect to the second category—younger, more educated heads and those initially in high-earnings and high-status positions—whites increase expected earnings, irrespective of the plan parameters, while blacks in all treatment groups transfer to lower earnings positions. As a function of the plan parameters, whites acquire higher status and blacks higher earnings (less of a deficit) as plan generosity is raised. Spanish-speaking participants improve earnings slightly (additive effects models), and status considerably, on the more generous support arrangements. *Thus, younger and more educated heads in all three groups show a propensity toward higher earnings and higher status as a function of plan generosity,* although the levels of the response contours vary among the

[8] This statement is based upon the repetition of an experimental effect pattern which does not, however, reach significance in any single equation (Tables 8.2 through 8.4).

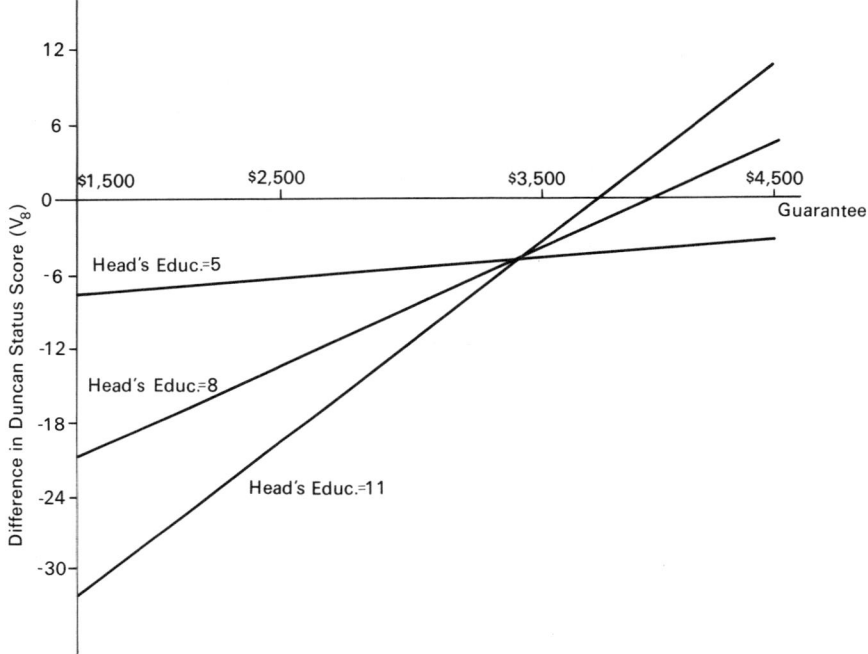

Figure 8.6 Interaction between guarantee level (spline 2) and head's education, in equation for "Duncan status score (V_8)," Spanish-speaking subsample. Each contour compares the response by an experimental group population with a comparable control group category. The vertical scale is adjusted by the additive effect of the spline 1 term and by its interaction with education; intercepts correspond to tax rate = .50. Means and standard deviations of the variables are ($2813, $713) for the guarantee level—$2813 corresponds to a spline 2 mean of $338—and (7.4, 3.0) for education.

ethnic groups—an improvement for whites, a deficit for blacks, no change for the Spanish-speaking.

2. SATISFACTION

We also analyzed a measure of satisfaction with each of two job aspects—work content and financial rewards (wages plus fringe benefits). Because of the very few significant experimental effects in the three ethnic subsamples, instead of attempting to discern distinct ethnic responses, our strategy was to identify common adjustment patterns to the plan parameters which could be substantiated by their recurrence in several equations, much as we proceeded in the analysis of job change and unemployment duration in Chapter 7. Also, because of the problematic character of the satisfaction measures (see Chapter 7, Appendix A), the results in this section are more tentative than those based on the earnings and status measures.

With respect to work content, we find a consistent tendency toward higher satisfaction as a function of plan generosity—high guarantee and low tax rate (additive effects models[9] for the total sample and Spanish-speaking participants). The interaction equations (Tables 8.7 through 8.10) reveal that this improvement is largely accounted for by the adaptation of more educated subjects and those initially in relatively satisfying work situations (total sample—work content/head's education; work content/work content; blacks—work content/head's education; work content/work content). Less educated heads and individuals in jobs with low satisfaction at Q_0 show little response to the plan parameters.

With regard to remuneration, there is evidence of a reduction in satisfaction by individuals receiving support payments, which increases as a function of plan generosity (total sample—additive effects model).[10] The interactions indicate that individuals in low-satisfaction positions at Q_0 are primarily responsible for the decline with plan generosity in the additive model (total sample—financial rewards/financial rewards; whites—financial rewards/financial rewards); better situated family heads show a small improvement, although there are some inconsistencies. In particular, in the Spanish-speaking sample, while subjects in less satisfying jobs at the inception of the study experience a satisfaction loss, and those in more rewarding positions an improvement, these effects are not contingent upon the plan parameters (financial rewards/financial rewards). Also, there is one instance of an interaction (whites—financial rewards/head's education) in which subjects with little education exhibit an *increase* in expected satisfaction as a function of guarantee level.

Thus, among relatively educated and occupationally better situated individuals, satisfaction with work content appears to respond to the plan parameters in much the same way as do expected earnings and job status—all factors improve under job transitions as a function of plan generosity. Our measure of satisfaction with remuneration also behaves in a way largely consistent with the results from the earnings equations: family heads who are poorly situated at Q_0 tend to undergo a reduction in sat-

---

[9] To conserve space we do not display the additive effects models for the satisfaction measures. In the work content equations, based on a joint F-test, the splines were significant for the total sample ($p < .008$)—with coefficients (and t-values) for splines 1, 2, and 3 equal to $-32.3(-2.26)$, $0.28(3.21)$, and $-1.02(-1.76)$, respectively; and for Spanish-speaking heads ($p < .001$)—with coefficients $-51.8(-1.43)$, $.120(4.96)$, and $-6.57(-4.22)$.

[10] In the satisfaction with remuneration equations, the joint F-test for an experimental effect was significant only for the total group ($p < .008$). In consecutive order, the splines (and t-coefficients) are $-18.2(-2.31)$, $-.0044(-0.91)$, $.480(1.51)$.

isfaction with financial rewards, as well as a reduction in expected earnings, with increasing plan generosity; more advantageously positioned individuals show an improvement.

3. CONCLUSIONS

Our objective in this chapter and in Chapter 7 has been to comprehend a large amount of material concerning the effect of the negative income tax parameters on the pattern of job change, rather than to explore specific hypotheses. In the preceding pages we have accorded extensive attention to detail, pointing out inconsistencies and findings which could not be corroborated by other equations, in our desire to be comprehensive and precise. In this concluding section we attempt to construct a forest from the trees, and provide a coherent account of what appear to be the main themes and most persistent results.

We initially divided the content of this topic into three contingent issues—departures from employment, length of unemployment, and changes in job characteristics upon reemployment—so that the impact of the negative income tax parameters could be associated with specific aspects of job mobility. Our first conclusion concerns the locus of influence: we find a consistent experimental effect on job departures, the rate being depressed in all ethnic groups as a function of plan generosity; only a modest impact on duration of unemployment; and a considerable, though complicated, effect on changes in job characteristics, the complexities arising from the fact that the experimental impact operates primarily through interactions with subject and job characteristics.

The most compelling findings concern patterns which reappear in the analyses of the component aspects of job mobility. First, the results in every section hang together in terms of an explanation which distinguishes two categories of individuals. *As a function of plan generosity, we find that older heads, subjects with little education, and those initially in less desirable jobs have especially lower rates of departure from employment; when leaving jobs they experience briefer unemployment durations; and when obtaining new employment they exhibit a decline in expected earnings, occupational status, and expected satisfaction with remuneration.* Our interpretation is that the support payments are viewed by these individuals as an earnings subsidy, enabling them to continue in low-wage positions and to accept such jobs when unemployed, thereby generating shorter unemployment intervals.

Among younger, more educated family heads, and those in better occupations at the start of the study, we find little experimental impact on the job departure rate, some evidence of longer unemployment duration when there is a departure, and considerable evidence of an improvement in expected earnings, occupational status, and expected satisfaction with work content upon reemployment. Whether this improvement is a result of seeking longer for well-paying jobs and attempting to capitalize on better income producing characteristics, or whether these individuals enter positions with low initial wage rates but good prospects for earnings growth, we cannot say. The fact is, though, that presence on a generous support plan contributes to acquiring jobs with higher expected earnings and more desirable work features (status, satisfaction) than comparable individuals in the control group manage to obtain.

The policy implications of these findings are considerable. They suggest that a negative income tax program would function to increase employment stability among family heads who are poorly prepared for competing in the labor market. We find that, rather than displaying a tendency to discontinue working when on generous support plans, these family heads are relieved to some extent of income considerations in making job change decisions, permitting them to settle down in low-wage positions. Correspondingly, the support payments provide family heads who have higher earnings potential with the flexibility to better manage their work careers and improve expected earnings and status through strategic job transitions.[11] Many citizens and policymakers, we believe, will consider these adaptations as socially desirable outcomes.

Superimposed on this dominant theme, there is evidence of distinct ethnic adjustments; but these appear to be second-order effects, modifying the response to the negative income tax parameters by raising or lowering the response contours. In particular, older and less educated whites in the experimental group incur a reduction in expected earnings and status, while younger and better educated family heads from this ethnic category enjoy a status improvement. Thus, among white participants, the levels of the response contours modify the plan parameter effects in a manner which permits a consistent interpretation: presence in the experimental group and high plan generosity (controlling for presence) produce effects in the same direction. This is not the case for blacks, among whom

---

[11] Evidence to support some of our findings may be found in an analysis of the Life History Study, directed by James S. Coleman and Peter Rossi. Reporting on this study, Ornstein (1975a:9) writes that individuals with the fewest labor market resources tend to change jobs less frequently; also, for young men, job changing appears to be a sign of strength, in that it reflects the ability of an individual to find a better work situation. In a second paper, Ornstein (1975b:144) notes that wage increases had the effect of lengthening job duration, and that this effect was greater for blacks (individuals with generally poor labor market resources) than for white workers.

the contribution from presence on a support plan runs counter to the impact of plan generosity. Spanish-speaking family heads differ from both these groups, revealing little modification of the response contours; in this sense their behavior is intermediate between the white and black adaptations. We have no explanation for these ethnic differences, or for the apparent contradiction in the black response, and merely report the findings.

REFERENCES

Kmenta, J. 1971. *Elements of econometrics*. New York: Macmillan.
Ornstein, M. 1975a. Entry into the labor force. Unpublished manuscript (to appear in M. Ornstein, *Entry into the labor force*. New York: Academic Press).
Ornstein, M. 1975b. Social mobility after entry. Unpublished manuscript (to appear in M. Ornstein, *Entry into the labor force*. New York: Academic Press).

part II
Factors modifying the labor-supply response

Introduction

Part II of this volume on the labor-supply response of the New Jersey experiment includes three studies designed to investigate whether certain factors affected the response to the experiment. These three factors are health, social psychological make-up, and level of understanding of the experimental stimulus.

Chapter 9 examines the effects of health. The expectation was that ill health would reduce work effort and, when combined with the effect of the experiment, would further reduce it. That is, we expected that unhealthy husbands and wives in the experimental group would work less than either their unhealthy counterparts in the control group or healthy husbands and wives in the experimental group.

For husbands, our expectations were confirmed. Healthy husbands worked more than unhealthy ones in both experimental and control groups. In addition, the difference in work effort between the healthy and unhealthy was greater for the experimental group than for the control group. For wives, however, our expectations were not confirmed. Health did not, for our sample, show up as having any significant effect on the work effort of wives in the experimental group as compared with the control group. The amount of the benefit did, however, have a somewhat paradoxical effect. Healthy wives in families receiving large checks worked less than healthy wives receiving no check (which included controls *and* experimentals above their breakeven point). But unhealthy wives receiving large benefits worked *more* than unhealthy wives in the low-benefit group. One can speculate that unhealthy wives who choose to work in spite of their disabilities and in spite of transfer payment possibilities have an unusually strong work motivation.

Chapter 10 examines the effect of social pyschological factors on work effort. The hypothesis is the culture of poverty theory—that, controlling for income level, those persons who exhibit certain character traits such as lack of self-esteem, alienation, short time-horizons—will work less than those who are integrated into the major values and institutions of the society.

In contrast to the health hypothesis, there is no evidence that such factors affected the work effort of the New Jersey experiment sample. The lack of results could be due to the short duration of the experiment; however, they could also be due to conceptual inadequacies in predicting the effects of social psychological characteristics on work. The problem of work incentives has only recently been addressed in the sociological literature. No conceptual approach, other than the culture of poverty idea, has so far allowed empirically based predictions about the effects of attitudinal variables on labor supply in an income-maintenance setting.

Chapter 11 addresses the effect of recipient understanding of the experimental stimulus on labor-supply response. The hypothesis here is that unless those in the experimental group understand the negative income tax plan to which they are assigned—that is, understand what happens to their payment as they change the amount they earn—they will not be in a position to respond in a consistent manner to the stimulus. This leads, in turn, to the expectation that the better they understand the stimulus the greater will be the incentive effect.

Information level, by and large, was not found to be associated with labor-supply response. There were, however, two exceptions to this. First, for those who understood the level of their guarantee, work disincentive was greater the higher that guarantee was. Second, those who had experienced low income—and therefore also experienced higher actual payments than others on the same plan—perceived their guarantee more accurately than those with higher incomes. Attempts to interpret these findings, therefore, run into the chicken-and-egg dilemma. Families with expected responses in terms of labor-supply could have arrived at those because they understood the payments system. But they could, alternatively, have come to understand the system because changes in their income circumstances had enabled them to learn from experience. Probably there was some of both.

9 The effects of health on the supply of and returns to labor

David Elesh
M. J. Lefcowitz

That the labor force status of an individual will be affected by his health is an unassailable proposition. It is unassailable, however, because a priori reasoning and casual observation tell us it must be so, not because there is a mass of supporting evidence [Bowen and Finegan, 1969:62].

This chapter focuses on the effects of health on the supply of and returns to labor by household heads and their spouses in the experiment. The question is important because there are strong a priori grounds to suspect that the effects of the experimental payments on the returns to and supply of labor may interact with the workers' health. In addition, some part of the possible differential responses by ethnicity, education, and other variables may ultimately be attributable to associations between health and these factors.

Prior empirical evidence that would support these suspicions is scarce; the best available data—from the National Health Surveys—show that increasing disability is associated with lower incomes and fewer days of work, and that there are related differentials by race; but the data are quite crude and will not support a causal inference.[1] Consequently, we

[1] See also Luft (1972) for an excellent review of the published material.

shall follow the example set by Bowen and Finegan by phrasing our expectations as to the effects of health on experimental response more in terms of existing theory than in terms of existing evidence.

1. HYPOTHESES

From an economic viewpoint, the role of health may be described in terms of a simple labor-supply model based on the general theory of choice. The unit of analysis is defined as the household, made up of individuals whose preference functions are combined to form the aggregate household preferences and whose activities determine its resource base. The household supplies labor by allocating its members' time to work or nonwork (leisure) activities, and the factors affecting this allocation are fourfold: (1) the family's values or preferences; (2) the expected market earning rates of its members; (3) the nonmarket earning rates of its members; and (4) the household's total budget constraint. This last factor is a function of the total number of hours available, the set of prospective market and nonmarket earning rates, any other income the household expects to receive, and the monetary value of the household's salable assets.

Health is related to all four of these factors. Because health is itself socially defined, it clearly plays a role in the family's values. Individuals and groups differ in terms of what they consider symptoms and in terms of the interpretations they place upon them (Mechanic, 1968). Thus, if an individual or group of individuals place a high value on work as such, their labor supply may not be affected by a health condition as much as the labor supply of persons less attached to work as a value. (Conversely, someone who dislikes work may report he is "ill" in order to rationalize not working.[2]) Consequently, unhealthy persons with little attachment to work as such may be more inclined to accept the experimental benefits in lieu of earnings than those who value work more highly.

The effect of health on an individual's earning rate in the market is also clear. Other things equal, as health status declines, the kinds and amounts of work one can do also diminish, typically causing a reduction in wage rates, earnings, or both. Moreover, because certain kinds of work are foreclosed to the person with a disability, periods of unemployment are likely to be more frequent and longer.[3] Some evidence regarding this last

---

[2] For some suggestive evidence on this point, see Cole and Lejeune (1972).

[3] Since *severely disabled* is defined as inability to work regularly or altogether, its relationship to labor force participation and full-time work is definitional. Nevertheless, the persistence of some work attachment (albeit at a low level) among severely disabled men commands attention.

point is available from Bowen and Finegan, who report that 97.5 percent of male household heads with no activity limitation due to a chronic condition were in the labor force, in contrast to 71.5 percent with some activity limitation (Bowen and Finegan, 1969:62).

Similarly, ill health should reduce a person's nonmarket earning rate—albeit probably to a lesser extent. Ill health that inhibits one's ability to work in the labor market may also constrain one's capacity to do housework, care for children, and the like. As in the market, the value placed on housework depends upon the ability to do that work.

Finally, the health status of family members affects the family's total budget constraint in three principal ways. First, other things equal, if one or more family members has a health handicap, the family will have fewer hours per week allocated to work, and family earnings should be reduced correspondingly. Second, if the health condition of the family member or members is sufficiently serious, potential hours of work may be lost not only by the ill, whose work time is reduced, but also by the healthy, who may be forced to work less in order to care for the ill. Indeed, if the healthy cannot both work and care for the unhealthy, they may have to pay someone outside the primary earner's household for such care, which has the effect of lowering the head's effective wage rate. (They may also need to increase hours worked in order to pay for outside care.) Third, if it is the husband who is in ill health, the wife may find it necessary to work in order to support the family. Because women are typically paid a lower wage, this means that family earnings will decline. In sum, we would expect persons and families with activity-limiting health conditions to work and earn less than persons and families without such conditions.

Taking the individual's attachment to work *together* with his health status as determinants of whether the experimental benefits will have a work disincentive effect is important, because there is considerable evidence in the sociological literature that the unhealthy place a high value on work. For example, more than 25 percent of all severely disabled men are in the labor force, although few of them work full time all year. Moreover, over 90 percent of those men with lesser disabilities are in the labor force (Haber, 1970). Thus, although health is an important factor in constraining labor supply, attachment to work is so strong for males as to make its effects relatively small for all but the most severely disabled.

There is also a great deal of evidence that shows these statements to be equally true for the poor and nonpoor. First, studies of motivation or attitudes toward work have found no differences between the poor and nonpoor (Goodwin, 1972). Second, studies of the unemployed poor typically find that they view themselves as inadequate because they view having a good job as important—just like the rest of society. Liebow has put it most dramatically:

> Convinced of their inadequacies, not only do they not seek out those few better-paying jobs which test their resources, but they actively avoid them, gravitating in a mass to the menial routine jobs which offer no challenge—and therefore pose no threat—to the already diminished images they have of themselves [Liebow, 1967:54].

For women, however, employment is less salient. Traditionally, their adult role has been oriented to household management and child care. When they do work outside the home, the motivation is to provide greater resources for household consumption; consequently, their families are less dependent on their earnings. Thus, for the average disabled woman, the earnings of her spouse provides 75 percent of the family's income regardless of the wife's degree of disability; whereas, for a disabled man, spouse's earnings are a much smaller share of family income—at most 30 percent—and it declines as the husband's disability becomes less severe (Swisher, 1966).

Given a lesser attachment to work among women, compared to men, we would expect that disability or poor health would have, relatively, a more negative effect on the work effort of women. Unfortunately, there are few data available to test this hypothesis. One difficulty is that work effort is affected by other factors, also associated with ill health, e.g., age and education. The typical presentation of data on the impact of health status on work does not usually take those other factors into account. In one study that does (Morgan et al., 1962), the data indicate that the health status of wives who are secondary earners has a greater effect on their labor force participation, hours worked, and hourly earnings than does the health status of female primary earners (who are largely women without husbands in the household).

Undoubtedly, this lesser attachment to work for women results from the same societal factors that produce the opposite behavior for men. Work does not—at least not yet—define a woman's role; the value placed on the family puts greater emphasis on her responsibility for household and child management. Hence, when she is ill or disabled, there is no reason, sociologically speaking, for her to resist the work-limiting consequences; this results in the expectation of a greater impact of disability on the woman's work effort in the market compared to a man's.

The discussion so far yields four general points. Health has a direct impact on all indicators of work effort, although labor force participation is the area most affected. Men are strongly attached to work and continue their work effort even with adverse health conditions and small returns for this effort. For women, attachment to work is weaker than for men and is likely to be weakened even more under the stress of poor health.

The differential attachment to work for men and women is in some part a function of social forces—particularly the difference in work for defining male and female roles and the value placed on the family in our society, with the associated differential family role performances for husbands and wives.

From traditional economic theory, we would expect families to substitute the negative income tax payments for earned income, thus reducing their labor-market supply. Briefly, the argument for this disincentive effect on labor supply is that the payments will increase income, and thus families will purchase more leisure (the so-called income effect). At the same time, a negative income tax on earnings decreases the effective wage rate for the worker; and even though the payments fully compensate, in the sense that the family has the same (or higher) income if family members work the same amount, they will find the price of an extra hour of leisure (i.e., the income foregone) substantially reduced (the so-called substitution effect). Presumably, poor health would act as an added disincentive, since some of those who would need to work in spite of their disabilities will be able to work less without sustaining the full cost of that decreased work. For wives with unhealthy husbands, the benefits may mean that they do not need to enter the labor force to help support their families.

Remember, however, that according to sociological and psychological theory, work itself is an important aspect of male identity. Hence, contrary to the economic assumption, leisure may be an inferior good—particularly with respect to the unhealthy heads included in our sample. Such an outcome is not unlikely, since there is no reason to believe that the actual standard of living of low-income families is the level they aspire to. Thus, although we would expect that—to the extent that unhealthy heads worked less than the healthy—the experiment would reinforce that difference, this differential response will be constrained by the abovementioned inducements to work. Given the lesser importance of market work per se for women, except for income-supplementing reasons, the expectation would be that the effect of their health status on response to the experiment would more closely follow classical economic theory.

Finally, we should recall that one criterion for inclusion in the sample was that the family contain one adult with some regular attachment to the labor force. That criterion, in conjunction with the fact that the major effect of ill health is on labor force participation, suggests that we have a sample of families in which the unhealthy male heads typically are highly committed to work. Thus, exclusion of households with a completely disabled male could limit the possible effect of the experiment.

2. METHODOLOGICAL ISSUES

In this section, we consider the question of the kinds and quality of the data on health, the choice of the measure used in the subsequent analysis, and the timing of its measurement. In addition, we shall briefly discuss the measures of labor supply and earnings used here. Following this, we present the variables that must be held constant in order to assess the effects of health on labor supply properly. We then note the differences between the sample analyzed here and that used in most of the studies in this volume. Finally, we discuss the somewhat unusual tabular format used in the bulk of our analysis.

Data on Health

Because of the presumed importance of the effects of health on the response to the experiment, a substantial amount of data was gathered on questions determining health status for the head and spouse of the household. The available data include, for the year prior to the interview, measures of the number of days spent in a hospital, the number of hospital stays, the number of days spent in bed because of illness, and the number of days of work (including housework) lost because of illness. In addition, data are available on the number and types of chronic illnesses either the head or spouse may have had. The range of these data is sufficiently broad for one to feel confident that any reasonable definition of health or ill health can be encompassed within it, and the information is similar to that collected in most other health surveys (indeed, most of the questions on health were adapted from the National Health Survey). It is, however, of somewhat better quality, in that the head and spouse were each asked to report on his or her own health, whereas the more common practice is to ask a single family member to report on the health of the entire household.

The health conditions described by the above measures vary considerably in terms of their utility for the present analysis. For example, the hospital variables have little appeal on conceptual grounds, since individuals may be both seriously and chronically ill without requiring hospitalization. Thus, to use these variables would be to neglect a great deal of serious illness. Moreover, since ill health is a relatively rare event in the entire U.S. population, one must take care not to use a measure which defines a rather rare subgroup among the unhealthy population, and thus produces a sample that is too small to analyze. Since only about 10 percent of the population is hospitalized in a given year (National Center for

Health Statistics, 1973:3), the hospitalization variables would also appear to be inadequate in these terms.

While the number of days in bed and days lost from work because of illness have neither of these problems, they are also not ideal. First, our conception of health status connotes some relative permanence to being healthy, whereas bed days or days lost from work include some temporary disability such as a cold. Moreover, both variables suffer from the fact that, in addition to measuring ill health, they also tap the desire to give a "legitimate" reason for not working or not desiring to work. Thus, the use of either of these variables could produce an overestimate of the "true" amount of ill health.

The final measure, the number of chronic illnesses, is (like the hospitalization variables) deficient in the sense that persons with chronic illnesses are relatively rare: in any given year, only about 12 percent of the population report such conditions (National Center for Health Statistics, 1973:3). On the other hand, unlike the hospitalization variables, it is more likely to have a persistent effect on labor supply.

Construction of Health Variables

Having discussed the deficiencies of our measures of health, we turn now to the problem of whether a more adequate measure can be constructed from a combination of them. This new measure should meet three criteria: first, it should meet the objections leveled at the days-in-bed and days-lost-from-work variables—namely that they include too many people who are not "really" unhealthy but are temporarily ill or are simply giving ill health as an excuse for not working or not desiring to work; second, it should include enough of the sample as unhealthy to make the analysis of the expected interaction between health and the experiment viable; third, the definition of ill health should include most of those actually unhealthy. Obviously, these criteria do not provide us with an absolute definition of health, but any definition of health is necessarily somewhat arbitrary, because health is a continuous dimension with a meaning which may vary from time to time and group to group.

With this caveat and these criteria in mind, we may eliminate the hospitalization variables from further consideration for our measure of ill health. As stated earlier, the chief problem with these variables is that they do not include many who are genuinely unhealthy but who do not require hospitalization; thus these measures do not meet the criteria.

From the remaining three variables, three possible combinations may be constructed. First, days in bed can be combined with days of work lost. Second, days in bed can be combined with number of chronic illnesses. Third, days of work lost can be combined with number of chronic illnesses. The first of these is obviously of little value, since days in bed and days of work lost are conceptually and statistically almost identical (in our data, $r = .92$). Consequently, the choice lies between the latter two combinations; we shall adopt the second of these because of its greater salience to labor supply.

Operational Definition of Health

We constructed our health variable by defining individuals who reported no chronic illnesses and who stated that they missed fewer than fifteen days of work in the year prior to the interview as healthy; all others were defined as unhealthy. The unhealthy, therefore, included all persons who reported a chronic condition or who stated that they had lost at least three work weeks during the preceding year because of illness. Setting the minimum work weeks lost as high as three takes into account the possibility that some individuals may be unhealthy (e.g., susceptible to respiratory ailments), even though there is no specific condition affecting their activities to which they can point, while at the same time purging the work-days-lost variable of people who may on occasion have used ill health as a socially acceptable excuse for not working.

By this definition, 29 to 30 percent of the male heads in our sample and 26 to 27 percent of their spouses were in ill health in each of the years preceding the quarterly interview at which health information was gathered. For the combined time periods in the analysis, the three years of the experiment and the middle two years, unhealthy persons are those categorized as unhealthy in each of the years covered. Thus, persons are classified as unhealthy only if they reported being unhealthy by our criteria during the entire length of the period covered—one year, the middle years, or the entire experimental period, according to which time period is being considered. The result is that the proportion of the sample who are unhealthy during the middle years and over the length of the experiment is less than the percentage in any single year (16 and 10 percent, respectively).

In our earlier report on health and labor-force behavior in the New Jersey experiment,[4] we used a health measure drawn from the second quarterly interview only. At that time, our analyses of the effects of the experimental treatments on health and health care were incomplete; and, given the possibility of such effects, we decided to make our health mea-

---

[4] See Elesh and Lefcowitz in Watts and Rees (1973).

sure as exogenous as possible. But this decision placed us in the curious position of, at times, predicting labor supply and earnings with a health variable measured eighteen months *earlier* and referring to the respondent's health in the period eighteen to thirty months *prior to the measurement*. Clearly, if one wants to know why a respondent's labor supply and earnings drop during a particular period, the appropriate investigation is of his or her health during *that* period, not a time one and one-half years earlier. Consequently, having since found no experimental effects on health,[5] we here use the most contemporaneous measures that we could construct. Because of the lag between the start of the experiment and the first collection of health data, however, the contemporaneity must remain somewhat incomplete. During each of the first-, second-, and third-year analyses, there is only a six-month overlap in the time period; during the total three-year period, there is an overlap of two years. Only during the middle two years is the overlap complete.

Some readers of our earlier report may be greatly upset by this decision because they objected to the definition of our health variable on the grounds that, by including days lost from work because of illness in its construction, we had measures of labor supply on both sides of our regression equation. To them, the decision to make our health measures contemporaneous only compounds our problems.

But we assert that this objection is without merit. Contrary to their belief, there is no definitional relation between the health and the labor-supply measures. The former are based on questions in one to three interviews referring to health during an entire year prior to an interview. The latter are constructed from questions in four to twelve interviews, all of which refer to the week prior to the interview. Obviously, there is no one-to-one relationship between them. If a respondent's labor supply is low, it does not follow that the reason was ill health. Even if the health and labor-supply variables referred to precisely the same time periods, we would argue that the criticism is still invalid. In this instance, one would, in effect, be decomposing the labor-supply variable into its definitional components: work, illness, vacation time, unemployment, etc. The size of effect of each of the nonwork components is problematic, and it is assuredly useful to know how much of the total is due to health.

Measures of the Supply of and Returns to Labor

The measures of labor supply and earnings used in this analysis are the average weekly hours and earnings of the head and spouse during the

---

[5] For an analysis of our evidence on this point, see Lefcowitz and Elesh in Watts and Rees (forthcoming).

experiment and, for spouses, the percentage of quarters employed. The figures reported are totals for all jobs. All overtime work is also included. Thus, the figures represent the totality of a person's labor supply and earnings—the quantities the experiment is expected to affect.

To assess possible variation in the response to the experiment over time, the data are analyzed separately for five time periods: the three-year duration of the experiment; the first, second, and third years separately; and the middle two years. The last period is defined by dropping the first and last six months of the experiment from consideration and its use is predicated, as mentioned in previous chapters, on the assumption that the data from these "end" periods may not represent a "true" response because families may behave differently when the experimental payments have just begun and also when there is a looming prospect of the payments ending. The expectation that the middle two years contain the cleanest and most valid data may, of course, be entirely misplaced; there is no real basis for predicting the lag in the response time. It may be that families have little difficulty in integrating the benefits into their decision making and that their response is almost immediate; or, as many theorists and commentators have argued, the lag may be more than three years. We present our data for five time periods because we take the matter to be an empirical question.

Parameterization of Experimental Plans

Given that there are eight experimental plans combining the four guarantee levels and three tax rates, the problem arises as to how best to estimate the effects of these plans on our dependent variables. Two different approaches are employed here. The first uses the treatment variables formulated as splines in Chapter 2.[6] As no nonlinear or interactive effects were found in our preliminary analyses, we shall report here only the effects of three spline variables. The first is simply a dummy variable, scored one if the family is in the experimental group and zero otherwise. The second tests for variation in the effect of the guarantee levels (around a guarantee of 75 percent of the poverty line). The third tests for variation in the effect of the tax rates (around the middle or 50 percent rate). When the three splines are present together in the same equation, the first measures the effect of the plan with the 75 percent guarantee and 50 percent tax rate, the second and third estimate the effects of deviations from that plan in terms of guarantee and tax rate, respectively.

[6] We shall not attempt to introduce here the theory of splines to those unfamiliar with the technique as we are making only modest use of it. Readers desiring further background on this technique should consult Chapter 14.

The assumption underlying this parameterization is that the families have some genuine understanding of their guarantee levels and tax rates and react to the experiment accordingly. However, whether they actually have such an understanding can be questioned on both empirical and theoretical grounds. On the empirical side, Shore (1970) found that few of the families he surveyed could name their guarantee or tax rate; and, typically, families knew little more than that their payments decreased as their earnings increased. On the theoretical side, these findings lend support to our suspicion that families may respond more readily to the actual payments received than to payments they might potentially receive under their particular experimental plan. In suggesting this, we do not wish to imply any support for the notions of some poverty-culture theorists that the poor are distinguished by a strong present time orientation or an inability to delay gratification, for the evidence on this question is highly moot (Miller, Reissman, and Seagull, 1968). Rather, we suggest that people generally prefer to act in terms of the concrete present—the payments—rather than the abstract future—the potential payments.[7]

Our second approach, therefore, is to formulate the experimental stimulus in terms of payment size. There is a major methodological difficulty in this parameterization—the payments are themselves a function of prior earnings. Since earnings tend to be highly correlated over time, it can be argued that the payments variable used on the right-hand side of an equation would simply be a proxy for the earnings variable on the left-hand side.[8] Thus, if the relationship between payments and earnings is linear, a definitional and negative correlation between the two would exist. To attempt to minimize this defect, we have used only the total of the payments made during the first three months of the experiment. To take account of the possibility that the impact of the payments may occur only after a threshold amount is reached, the payments are expressed as a quadratic in the analysis.

Control Variables

Because the design of the experiment did not randomly assign families to the various experimental plans and because the design was modified

---

[7] We should note, however, that the most generous plans will, in general, make the largest payments. Thus, although families may be explicitly making labor-supply decisions in terms of the size of the benefit checks they receive, they are implicitly reacting to a high guarantee and moderate-to-low tax rate—these being definitional of the most generous plans. (The potential generosity of a plan can also be expressed in terms of its breakeven point, which is expressed as its guarantee level divided by its tax rate.)

[8] However, the correlations are not as high as may be thought; the correlation between the head's average earnings in the first and third years is only .62.

during the year-long periods of screening and enrollment, several variables must be held constant in order to obtain unbiased estimates of the effects of the parameterization. The most important of these is the income stratum of the family. The assignment model, as mentioned above in Chapter 2, was deliberately asymmetrical with regard to family income, with the consequence that the families on the various experimental plans differed in average family income at the beginning of the experiment. Consequently the estimation of unbiased effects requires that this variable be controlled for. Ethnicity and experimental site must also be held constant because continuing efforts were made to achieve an ethnic balance *during* the period of screening and enrollment. As the four experimental sites were brought into the experiment sequentially over a year, this meant that certain ethnic groups were more heavily sampled in some cities than in others. In addition, the welfare status of the family must be controlled for because we are dealing with an experiment rather than a national program, and the experiment exists in a natural setting that includes a welfare program as an alternative to the experiment's benefits.[9]

Several other factors, unrelated to design considerations, have also been controlled in our analysis in order to clarify the effects of the central variables of interest. All these were measured at preenrollment. Because both age and education are well known to affect labor supply and earnings, both are held constant here. Age is expressed as a set of three dummy variables centered around the age category thirty-one to forty because the cross-sectional age–earnings profile peaks at this point for most low-income workers (Rees and Schultz, 1970). The number of earners and the number of dependents (which together sum to family size) are also held constant. Other things equal, we would expect that neither the head nor the spouse would feel as much pressure to work in families where there are two or more earners as they would in single-earner families. On the other hand, the male head of a large family, having more dependents than the head of a small one, is more likely, in general, to feel a greater need to work. His wife probably will be less able to contribute to family income, since the higher cost of child care will increase the value of her housework and tend to restrict her from the labor force. It also seems useful to control for the individual's labor-force-participation history, which we take to be behavioral indication of one's commitment to work as a value. While, if considered by itself, one's past participation may also reflect the lack of a physical or mental disability, the availability of work, and the match of demanded and supplied skill levels, we believe our controls for these factors in terms of our health, city, and education

---

[9] For analysis of the impact of welfare on the experimental response, see Garfinkel in Watts and Rees (forthcoming).

variables permit our interpretation of this variable as indicating commitment to work.

Two variables are unique to the equations for the wives' labor supply and earnings: a variable for whether the wife was pregnant and a variable for whether she had any children under age six. Since there are considerable data indicating that women in either of these statuses work less in the market than the average woman (Bowen and Finegan, 1969:111–114), failure to include these variables would lead to underestimates of wives' labor supply. We also include the husband's health in the spouse's model because there is evidence that wives are likely to work if their husbands are incapacitated (Swisher, 1971).

Finally, the preenrollment values of all the dependent variables were included in their respective equations. The variables in the equation that estimate the effects of the experiment and health on changes in the dependent variables are operationally defined in Appendix A.

The Sample

Our analysis focuses on 732 husband–wife families which were in the experiment "continuously."[10] A continuous husband–wife family was defined as a family with husband and wife present that completed an interview at preenrollment, at the twelfth quarter, and at six of the remaining eleven quarters. In addition, the families had to be husband–wife and present at the second, sixth, and tenth quarters—the quarters at which health data were collected for the head and spouse—and they could have missed no more than two quarters in succession. Thus, families that split up for a period longer than two quarters were considered to have attrited in terms of the above definition and are not represented in the results reported here. The exclusion of family splits is consistent with the major purpose of the experiment, which is to estimate the labor-supply response of male-headed families to the negative income tax; the second exclusion is prompted simply because techniques for estimating the possible biases resulting from attrition have not been fully developed. This sample represents 55 percent of all families originally enrolled.

Format of Tabular Presentation

Since the equations containing the aforementioned variables are rather large and our interest centers on experimental effects, health variables,

---

[10] This sample, while conceptually the same, is larger than the continuous husband–wife sample (693 families) used in earlier chapters (cf. Chapter 2). The data file used here was developed from primary files especially for the study of health, and the effect of various minor differences in criteria for inclusion led to the additional thirty-nine families.

and the interactions of one with the other, we have relegated the complete equations to Appendix B, and present in the text only those results associated with health and the experiment. Moreover, to clarify the effects of the interactions between the experimental plans and health, we present a simple transformation of the coefficients expressing the interactions rather than the coefficients themselves. The purpose of the transformation is to show the interactions as deviations from the effect for that part of the control group in ill health. To understand the nature of this transformation, consider the following hypothetical equation for the interactions between head's health and the three splines:

$$Y = a + b_1 SD + b_2 SG + b_3 ST + b_4 H + b_5 HS1 + b_6 HS2 + b_7 HS3$$

where

SD = dummy spline
SG = guarantee spline
ST = tax spline
H = head's health
$HS1$ = interaction between H and SD
$HS2$ = interaction between H and SG
$HS3$ = interaction between H and ST.

Given this equation, effects of the interaction between experimental status (SD) and head's health can be expressed in terms of four categories:

effect for healthy experimentals = $(b_1 + b_4 + b_5) + SG(b_2 + b_6)$
$\qquad\qquad + ST(b_3 + b_7)$
effect for unhealthy experimentals = $b_1 + b_2 SG + b_3 ST$
effect for healthy controls = b_4
effect for unhealthy controls = 0.

The effects of the interaction between the guarantee level and head's health, net of the effects of the tax rate, can be similarly constructed:

effect of healthy–guarantee = $(b_1 + b_4 + b_5) + SG(b_2 + b_6)$
effect of unhealthy–guarantee = $b_1 + b_2 SG$
effect of healthy controls = b_4
effect of unhealthy controls = 0.

The effect of any particular guarantee level is found by simply evaluating these expressions for SG equal to that value.

Finally, in comparable fashion, we give the expressions for the effects of the interaction between the tax rate and head's health, net of the guarantee levels:

effect of healthy–tax rate = $(b_1 + b_4 + b_5) + ST(b_3 + b_7)$
effect of unhealthy–tax rate = $b_1 + b_3 ST$
effect of healthy controls = b_4
effect of unhealthy controls = 0.

3. LABOR SUPPLY OF HUSBANDS

What is the effect, then, of health of the family head on his labor supply when entered in the model described above? In our presentation of the results, the findings for the whole three-year period of the experiment will be given first. Then the consistency of the findings for separate years of the experiment will be examined.[11]

Effect of Health on Labor Supply over the Full Length of the Experiment

As might be expected, healthy heads in experimental and control groups worked and earned more, on average, than unhealthy heads. More directly bearing on our thesis, however, is the fact that the differences between the estimated average labor supply of healthy and unhealthy heads are larger during the three years of the experiment for experimentals than for controls. Columns 1 and 2 of Table 9.1 present those estimates relative to the unhealthy control heads.[12] Looking at average earnings for family heads, for example, the estimated effect of being healthy is about the same for the control and the experimental group. On the other hand, family heads in the experimental group who were unhealthy earned, on the average, $12.60 *less* than their counterparts in the control group. The difference between healthy and unhealthy heads in average earnings is, moreover, $16.41 for the control group and $29.42 for the experimentals—close to double the difference for the controls. A similar pattern is obtained for average hours. Moreover, the latter estimates are based on statistically significant coefficients for all three relevant health and experimental variables (see Appendix B, Table 9B.1). Thus,

---

[11] In the interests of conserving space, many of the regressions and calculations on which the following sections are based are not presented. Copies can be obtained by specific request from the authors.

[12] The full results of the regression on which this table is based can be found in Appendix B, Table 9B.1. Columns (1) and (2) are derived from model I and the rest of the table from model II for each dependent variable.

Table 9.1 Estimated Effects on Head's Average Labor Supply for the Entire Experiment, Health Status and Experimental Parameters

Labor Supply	Control	Unadjusted for Guarantee and Tax Rate	Experimental Effect						
			Adjusted for Guarantee (Net of Tax Rate) Relative to .75				Adjusted for Tax Rate (Net of Guarantee) Relative to .50		
			-.25	0	.25	.50	-.20	0	.20
Average earnings (dollars per week)									
Healthy	16.41	16.82	21.99	18.89	15.79	12.69	14.71	18.89	23.07
Unhealthy	0	-12.60	-23.66	-15.51	-7.37	.78	-3.36	-15.51	-27.67
Average hours (per week)									
Healthy	5.68	4.12	5.00	4.47	3.95	3.42	3.73	4.47	5.21
Unhealthy	0	-6.31	-9.84	-7.09	-4.34	-1.59	-1.41	-7.09	-12.77

NOTE: These are deviations of the respective subgroups from the estimates for unhealthy controls.

over the three years of the experiment, the average working time of the experimentals—both healthy and unhealthy—declines relative to their controls, but the decline is somewhat greater for the unhealthy.

How are these patterns affected by variations in the guarantee level and tax rate? What we find is that the lower the guarantee, the larger the difference between healthy and unhealthy experimentals; and the higher the tax rate, the smaller the difference (see Table 9.1). For example, at the 125 percent guarantee level, the estimated effect of being healthy and in the experiment relative to the unhealthy controls is an additional $12.69 in average earnings; while unhealthy heads at that guarantee level are estimated to have earned $.78 more on the average than unhealthy controls. Thus, at the highest guarantee level, the healthy–unhealthy difference in average earnings is $11.91, which approximates the $16.41 difference obtained for the control group. At the lowest guarantee level, however, the healthy–unhealthy difference in estimated average earnings is over $45, considerably larger than the difference in the control group. For tax rate, however, the healthy–unhealthy difference in earnings is over $50 at the highest level and $8.07 at the lowest. This pattern is common to both the hours and earnings measures of labor supply. Moreover, the coefficients on which the estimates are based are all statistically significant except for the net tax rate and guarantee effects on earnings (see Appendix B, Table 9B.1).

This convergence emerges from (1) a decline in average labor supply among the healthy and an increase for the unhealthy as the guarantee increases, and (2) an increase in average labor supply for the healthy and a decline for the unhealthy as the tax rate increases. What appears to be happening is that at the highest guarantee level and lowest tax rate, the labor supply of healthy and unhealthy experimental heads is more like that of comparable control heads. At the lowest guarantee level and at highest tax rate, their labor supply is quite different from the controls and has moved in opposite directions from one another. Economic theory suggests that higher guarantees and/or tax rates should result in a diminished labor supply. According to our results, the healthy with respect to tax rate and the unhealthy with respect to guarantee do not conform to that hypothesis.[13]

---

[13] However, because the pattern obtained for the whole sample over the three-year period consistently appeared in other analyses—for various time periods, for welfare and nonwelfare families, when separate regressions were run for each ethnic group—we do not reject completely the possibility that the apparently contradictory results reflect an unexplained behavioral pattern.

*Effect of Health on Labor-Supply Response during
Different Experimental Time Periods*

As indicated in the introductory section, the time duration of the experiment could affect the labor-supply response and, thus, the interaction of health status with that response. To test that possibility, the effects of health and of the experiment on labor supply were calculated separately for each year. The coefficients for these variables and their interactions are presented in Table 9.2. As we can see, the pattern for each single year is similar to that obtained for the entire three-year period (see Appendix B, Table 9B.1). But, when we look at the details, we find that only the net effect of health is significant. For the three-year period, however, the unhealthy were persons classified as ill for all three years. Thus, only the more chronically ill, for whom the experiment provided some financial relief, may have been isolated in Table 9.1. The health variable for each year, on the other hand, includes more than these permanently ill male heads. It categorizes as unhealthy those heads whose illnesses were less continuous. One possibility is that, given the temporary character of the experiment, it may have had less effect on the temporarily ill heads. For the more continuously unhealthy, however, the experiment might have provided a resting period, albeit temporarily, during which they could recoup and/or regroup for the future. One test of this hypothesis is whether focussing on the stable unhealthy—those who were ill during the whole three-year period—will affect the coefficients. This indeed turns out to be the case, as can be seen in Table 9.3. Moreover, the three-year period shows an increasingly negative effect of the experimental–unhealthy in-

Table 9.2 Regression Coefficients for Health Status (Defined for Each Year of the Experiment) and Experimental Parameter, from Equations Estimating Head's Labor Supply in Each Year of the Experiment

	Average Earnings (Dollars per Week)			Average Hours (per Week)		
	Year 1	Year 2	Year 3	Year 1	Year 2	Year 3
Health status	10.518**	6.814	9.307**	4.556**	3.510**	3.633**
In experiment	−2.956	−2.077	−1.860	−1.406	−2.075	−.775
Health–experiment interaction	7.807	−.728	1.399	.717	.851	.300

** Statistically significant at the 5 percent level or better for a one-tailed test.

EFFECTS OF HEALTH ON LABOR SUPPLY

Table 9.3 Estimated Effects of Health Status on Head's Labor Supply for Specified Time Periods (Unhealthy is Defined as Those Who Were Unhealthy for All Three Years)

	Earnings		Hours	
	Control	Experimental	Control	Experimental
First year				
Healthy	19.625	21.700	7.168	6.096
Unhealthy	0	−2.877	0	−2.270
Second year				
Healthy	9.735	8.568	3.881	3.045
Unhealthy	0	−14.251	0	−7.051
Third year				
Healthy	−.051	.096	1.482	1.135
Unhealthy	0	−16.513	0	−4.724

NOTE: These are deviations of the respective subgroups from the estimates for unhealthy controls.

teraction over the three-year period and a reduction in the effect of health.[14]

Given the changing impact of ill health on the labor-supply response and the decrease in that differential response over the time of the experiment, the hypothesis that the middle years—that is, from six months after its inception up to six months before its end—would be the most appropriate time to look at experimental effects does not appear valid. In fact, the experimental–health effects during the middle years are the same as those for the whole three-year period, regardless of how health is defined (the estimated effects for the middle years can be found in Appendix B, Table 9B.2).

Health and Benefit Levels

Experimental benefits, as well as being a function of the experimental parameters, are also related to income. One problem, therefore, in assessing their effect for the duration of the experiment is that they are a consequence as well as a cause of the experimental response. To limit that problem, we have used only payments for the first quarter in our equation. Since these payments correlate ($r = .886$) with payments over the first two years, the earliest payments received appear to be a reasonable indication of benefits over the whole experiment. In addition, the square

---

[14] The decreasing effect of health over time could result from the inclusion in this category of more persons who reported ill health only for the relevant period (altogether healthy in the other years). Regressions to test this possibility produced results identical with Table 9.3.

of the first payment has also been introduced to assess the possibility that families with very high benefits will respond differently from those with more modest payments.

Over the three-year period, benefits do apparently interact with health to affect labor supply. This effect appears to be most pronounced among those families with large payments who are unhealthy (see Appendix B, Table 9B.3). This pattern, however, is statistically significant only for earnings.

The pattern for the three years individually is quite similar. What is more interesting is that the net health coefficient moves closer to zero while the effect of benefits and its interactions with health increase. This pattern is very striking with hours, where all health–benefit coefficients in the third year are significant (see Appendix B, Table 9B.3). These coefficients result in labor-supply estimates which decrease as benefit generosity rises, but at a more rapid rate for the unhealthy as the experiment moved into its second and third years. In Table 9.4, where the estimates for hours are presented at varying payment levels, the difference between healthy and unhealthy in net estimates of hours worked in the first year is greater the lower the payment level, whereas the relationship is just the opposite in the second and third years. The importance of these results is underscored by the fact that many families had very high payments (the mean for this sample of what intact families received was $180.32, but the standard deviation was $250.92).

However, it is possible that these results reflect more accurate reporting or increasing underreporting as families become more familiar

Table 9.4 **Estimated Average Hours Worked per Week by Husband for Each Year of the Experiment, by Benefits and Health Status**

	Benefits		
	None	At the Mean	Mean Plus One Standard Deviation
First year			
Healthy	5.75	4.84	2.79
Unhealthy	0	−.39	−1.07
Second year			
Healthy	3.55	3.17	1.91
Unhealthy	0	−1.11	−3.46
Third year			
Healthy	2.68	2.35	1.80
Unhealthy	0	.11	−1.45

NOTE: These are deviations of the respective subgroups from the estimates for the unhealthy people at a no-benefit level.

with the reporting requirements and benefits of the experiment. That the third-year differences in estimates are smaller, however, is not consistent with this hypothesis.

4. LABOR SUPPLY OF WIFE

What about the wife's health status? Does the interaction of the wife's health with the experiment have effects on her labor supply similar to that of the male head? One of the problems in answering that question is the low level of work effort for wives. For example, only 11.9 percent of the wives in our sample were employed at preenrollment; and during the year prior to the experiment, the mean number of hours worked was about four per week. As can be imagined, the average hours and earnings during the course of the experiment are low, making it difficult to capture any work disincentive in response to the experiment. For that reason, percentage of quarters employed is used as an additional measure of wife's labor supply.

Findings

The health status of wives in interaction both with being in the experiment and with the experimental parameters has, in general, no significant effect on their labor supply for any period of the experiment. Moreover, the direction of such effect as is found is opposite to the predicted one; that is, healthy wives in the experiment work less, relative to healthy wives in the control group, while the unhealthy wives increase their work effort relative to those in the control group. Although the statistical insignificance of the coefficients does not permit any reliance to be placed on the results, the unexpected sign does call for some speculation on factors other than chance. Possibly the lesser attachment to work for women has, on the one hand, already severely restricted the labor supply of unhealthy wives and, on the other, allows healthy wives to decrease their work effort when an alternative source of income is available.

When the effects of health in interaction with experimental benefits are examined, however, a somewhat clearer picture emerges. For the entire three-year period of the study, payments are significantly related to labor supply. The interaction of health and benefits is positive and significant; the interaction between health and the quadratic term, however, is significant and negative, suggesting that healthy wives with very high benefits may withdraw more of their labor supply than either wives in families with low benefits or unhealthy wives (see Appendix B, Table 9B.4).

To obtain some understanding of these effects, we have estimated their impact for wives (1) where there is no benefit (which includes the control group), (2) at the mean benefit for the first quarter ($180.32), and (3) where the first quarter benefit is one standard deviation above the mean ($431.24). These estimates for the whole experimental period can be found in Table 9.5.

As can be seen, where the families' first-quarter payments are at the average, there is a tendency for both healthy and unhealthy wives to decrease their work effort relative to no-benefit wives in the same health status. Where the benefits are one standard deviation above the mean, healthy wives continue to show a dramatic decrease, while there is a corresponding positive increase in the labor supply of unhealthy wives. When we consider that the mean work effort of the wives is low (13.9 percent of experimental quarters employed), these results are even more striking.

The year-by-year coefficients suggest that the observed pattern over the full three years reflects more response in the first year of the experiment than in the second and third years. The estimates for each year, based on the coefficients for hours worked, are presented in Table 9.6. As can be seen, increased benefits among the healthy lead to decreased work, but this relationship becomes weaker over time. Among the unhealthy, large benefits appear to have an effect only in the first year, and that effect is positive. Finally, in the third year the differences among the

Table 9.5 Estimates of Three-Year Labor Supply of Wives, by Benefits and Health Status

	First-Quarter Benefits		
	None	At the Mean	Mean Plus One Standard Deviation
Earnings (*dollars per week*)			
Healthy	2.5857	1.2118	−.4748
Unhealthy	0	−2.2930	.7799
Hours (*per week*)			
Healthy	1.2883	.6498	−.1418
Unhealthy	0	−1.1124	.4337
Percentage of quarters employed			
Healthy	3.8065	1.4577	−1.1276
Unhealthy	0	−3.8034	−.9774

NOTE: These are deviations of the respective subgroups from the estimates for unhealthy wives receiving no benefits (including controls).

Table 9.6 **Estimated Hours Worked per Week by Wives, for Each Experimental Year, by Benefits and Health Status**

	First-Quarter Benefits		
	None	At the Mean	Mean Plus One Standard Deviation
First year			
Healthy	1.62	.78	−.21
Unhealthy	0	−.10	.21
Second year			
Healthy	1.81	1.53	1.23
Unhealthy	0	.00	.01
Third year			
Healthy	−1.26	1.35	−1.48
Unhealthy	0	−.86	−.97

NOTE: These are deviations of the respective subgroups from the estimates for unhealthy wives receiving no benefits (including controls).

healthy and unhealthy get smaller at all benefit levels, relative to years one and two.

The immediate labor-supply response of wives to benefits is consistent with the hypothesis that they have a lesser attachment to work than men, and that when they do work it is motivated largely by a desire to supplement family income. Thus the benefits, by reducing the need to work to supplement income, appear to affect their labor supply at first. As the experiment draws to a close, however, the choice of work versus income supplementation shows work to be more attractive and the effect of benefits is weakened.

The smaller effect on unhealthy wives may be explained similarly. As noted above there is evidence that ill health more severely restricts the labor supply of women than of men. Thus, those unhealthy wives who do work may be more than usually motivated and consequently less affected by an alternative income source. On the other hand, the lesser work effort of unhealthy wives because of their ill health puts a bound on their work disincentive relative to healthy wives. This limit consequently may restrict the possibility for reduction in labor supply in response to payments, and this, therefore, may possibly explain our results.

5. CONCLUSION

This chapter has focussed on the effects of health on the supply of and returns to labor of married men and women in the experiment. Traditional economic theory tells us that families on the experiment can be expected to substitute their benefits for earnings, thus reducing their labor supply. It also suggests that poor health will tend to exacerbate this disincentive because those who work in spite of illness (and therefore for whom the psychic and physical strain of working is greater than for the normal person) will be even more motivated to cut down on work when they do not have to bear the full cost of the reduction. Sociological and psychological theory provides one caveat to that expectation. Work is an important aspect of male identity. Therefore, contrary to economic theory, leisure may be an inferior good—particularly for those men who are unhealthy and who may consequently need to compensate for their lack of health by being more eager to work.

Our results show that for men the expectations of economic theory are borne out when the experiment as such is considered. Healthy husbands of both experimental and control families worked and earned more, on average, than unhealthy husbands. More than this, the differences between the labor supply of the healthy and unhealthy husbands are larger for experimentals than controls. When the experimental effect is looked at separately for each year of the experiment, we find that the pattern of differentials is the same within each year but that the effect of the health is greatest in the first year and decreases thereafter.

For wives, our expectations were not fulfilled. The health status of married women has no significant interaction effect either with being on the experiment or with the specific experimental parameters. The effects of health in interaction with benefit generosity are, however, significant. Average first-quarter payments lead healthy and unhealthy wives to decrease their work effort with respect to their nonbenefit counterparts (including controls). Apparently, very high benefits lead healthy wives to show a greater work disincentive in comparison to healthy wives in the control group and also lead unhealthy wives to work more in comparison to the unhealthy in the no-benefit group. Ill health may be more likely to restrict female labor supply than male in this society, so that those ill wives who continue to work must be more than usually motivated. Alternatively, their work effort may already be so low that further reductions must, by definition, be comparatively small.

APPENDIX A: OPERATIONAL DEFINITIONS OF VARIABLES

Ethnicity
    Black = 1 if black; 0 otherwise.
    Spanish-speaking = 1 if Spanish-speaking; 0 otherwise.

Head's Age
   Under 31 = 1 if under 31; 0 otherwise.
   Over 40 = 1 if over 40; 0 otherwise.
Head's Education = years of school completed.
Site
   Trenton = 1 if resident of Trenton; 0 otherwise.
   Paterson–Passaic = 1 if resident of Paterson–Passaic; 0 otherwise.
   Jersey City = 1 if resident of Jersey City; 0 otherwise.
Preenrollment Year
   Weeks worked by head = number of weeks worked during preenrollment year.
Family Poverty Level
   Under poverty line = 1 if income for year prior to experiment was below poverty line; 0 otherwise.
   Over 1.25 of poverty line = 1 if income for year prior to experiment was over 125 percent of income at poverty line; 0 otherwise.
At Preenrollment
   Value of dependent variable = earnings, hours or wage rates as appropriate.
   Number of earners = coded as the number of adults who reported earning some money (greater than $0.00) last week.
   Number of dependents = the number of earners (as defined above) subtracted from the number of members in the household.
   On welfare = 1 if on welfare; 0 otherwise.
During Experiment
   Welfare experience = percentage of quarters on welfare during time period analyzed.
   Health status = 1 if husband had fewer than two chronic illnesses and missed fewer than seven days of work because of illness; 0 otherwise.
   In experiment = 1 if in experimental group; 0 if in control group.
   Guarantee (relative to 75 percent of poverty line) = $G - .75$, where G is the percent of the poverty line guaranteed.
   Tax rate (relative to a 50 percent tax rate) = $t - .50$, where t is the tax rate.
Interactions
   Health status times experimental status.
   Health status times guarantee.
   Health status times tax rate.
Additional Variables for Wife
   Pregnant = 1 if wife pregnant during time period analyzed; 0 otherwise.

Kids under six = percentage of quarters during the time period analyzed family had children under age six.

Children healthy at $Q2$ = 1 if at second quarter per capita number of children's chronic illnesses is less than one and per capita number of days in bed due to illnesses is less than eleven; 0 otherwise.

Means were supplied for missing data for continuous variables; in the case of dichotomous variables, missing values were assumed to be zero.

APPENDIX B: SUPPLEMENTARY DETAILED TABULATIONS

Table 9B.1 Effects of Health Status and Experiment on Husband's Average Labor Supply over Entire Experiment: Regression Coefficients in Full Equation for Models I and II

	Earnings (Dollars per Week)		Hours per Week	
	I	II	I	II
Constant	23.099	22.124	10.148	10.133
Ethnicity				
Black	−7.023	−7.078	−1.329	−1.426
Spanish-speaking	−2.600	−2.588	−.893	−.782
Head's age				
Under 31	−3.899	−3.478	−1.021	−.929
Over 40	−4.054	−4.279	−.289	−.370
Head's education	1.542**	1.435**	.225	.199
Site				
Trenton	5.374	5.111	−.469	−.230
Paterson–Passaic	3.561	2.029	−.965	−1.170
Jersey City	2.932	2.857	−1.044	−.968
Preenrollment year				
Weeks worked by head	.479**	.489**	.255**	.261**
Family poverty level				
Under poverty line	−7.008**	−5.511	.365	.438
Over 125 percent of poverty line	2.486	4.537	−.985	−.822
At preenrollment				
Value of dependent variable	.302**	.294**	.208**	.205**
Number of earners	−6.114**	−5.578**	−.825	−.656
Number of dependents	3.149**	−3.210**	.414**	.418**
On welfare	1.815	2.264	2.248	2.304
During experiment				
Welfare experience	−32.797**	−32.576**	−9.714**	−9.416**
Health status	16.409**	16.418**	5.680**	5.730
In experiment	−12.601	−15.515**	−6.308**	−7.086**
Guarantee, relative to .75	—	.326	—	.110**
Tax rate, relative to .50	—	−.608	—	−.284
Health status interactions with				
In experiment	13.011	17.983**	4.747**	5.827**
Guarantee, relative to .75	—	−.450**	—	−.131**
Tax rate, relative to .50	—	.817**	—	.321**
Coefficient of determination (corrected)	.381	.385	.352	.358

** Statistically significant at 5 percent level or better for two-tail test, except for health status and experimental variables, where the one-tail test was applied.

Table 9B.2 Estimated Effects on Head's Average Labor Supply for the Middle Two Years of the Experiment, by Health Status and Experimental Parameters

Labor Supply	Control	Unadjusted for Guarantee and Tax Rate	Experimental Effect							
			Adjusted for Guarantee (Net of Tax Rate) Relative to .75				Tax Rate (Net of Guarantee) Relative to .50			
			−.25	0	.25	.50	−.20	0	.20
Average earnings (dollars)										
Healthy	19.85	19.47	28.36	22.81	17.26	11.71	18.28	22.81	27.34
Unhealthy	0	−5.52	−10.89	−5.66	−.4235	4.81	7.47	−5.66	−18.79
Average hours										
Healthy	8.43	6.35	7.38	6.74	6.10	5.47	5.77	6.74	7.71
Unhealthy	0	−2.16	−3.87	−2.28	−.69	.90	2.27	−2.28	−6.83

NOTE: These are deviations from the estimates for the unhealthy controls.

Table 9B.3 Regression Coefficients for Health Status and Experimental Benefits Received, from Equations Estimating Husband's Labor Supply for Years in the Experiment

	Average Earnings (Dollars per Week)				Average Hours per Week			
	All	Year 1	Year 2	Year 3	All	Year 1	Year 2	Year 3
Health status	22.638**	15.890**	5.131	6.094	7.226**	5.745**	3.549	2.680**
Benefits	3.069	2.508	−.035	−6.362**	−.291	.162	.026	−1.984**
Benefits squared	−1.218**	−.552**	−.413	.696**	−.220	−.059	−.119	.237**
Interaction of health with								
Benefits	4.883	−2.000	−2.123	5.613	−.341	−.298	−.524	2.141**
Benefits squared	1.176**	.287	.480	−.674	.222	−.020	.136	−.289**

** Statistically significant at the 5 percent level or better for a one-tail test.

Table 9B.4 **Effect of Health Status and Experiment on Wife's Average Labor Supply over Entire Experiment: Regression Coefficients in Full Equation**

	Earnings (Dollars per Week)	Hours per Week	Percentage of Quarters Employed
Constant	2.273	1.077	5.411
Ethnicity			
Black	−.623	.075	1.506
Spanish-speaking	−2.334	−.711	−.748
Spouse's age			
Under 31	1.437	.574	1.517
Over 40	.797	.624	1.816
Spouse's education	.479	.261**	.707**
Site			
Trenton	8.683**	3.915**	10.545**
Paterson–Passaic	3.810	1.216	−.359
Jersey City	.700	−.216	−4.879
Preenrollment year			
Weeks worked by spouse	.266**	.110**	.430**
Family poverty level			
Under poverty line	−4.213**	−1.361	−2.780
Over 125 percent of poverty line	−2.875	−1.024	−2.471
At preenrollment			
Value of dependent variable	.359**	.351**	36.593**
Number of earners	.008	−.311	−1.805
Number of dependents	.391	.069	.539
On welfare	2.458	.923	1.887
During the experiment			
Pregnant	−3.759**	−1.635**	−6.161**
Children under six	−2.193	−1.292	−2.260
Husband's health	−3.387	−1.333	−4.574
Welfare status	−8.111**	−3.572**	−13.063**
Health status	2.586	1.288	3.807
First payment first year[a]	−5.895	2.901**	−8.101**
First payment first year squared	.874**	.432**	1.133**
Health status interaction with			
First payment first year	4.977	2.475**	6.295**
First payment first year squared	−.843**	−.418**	−1.037**

[a] The coefficients are for each $100 of benefits in the first quarter and $10,000 for the squared term.

** Statistically significant at the 5 percent level or better for two-tail test, except for health status and experimental variables, where the one-tail test was applied.

REFERENCES

Bowen, W. G., and Finegan, T. 1969. *The economics of labor force participation*. Princeton: Princeton University Press.
Cole, S., and Lejeune, R. 1972. Illness and the legitimation of failure. *American Sociological Review* 37: 347–356.
Conlisk, J., and Watts, H. W. 1969. A model for optimizing experimental designs for estimating response surfaces. Proceedings of the Social Statistics Section, pp. 150–156. Washington D.C.: American Statistical Association.
Goodwin, L. 1972. *Do the poor want to work? A social-psychological study of work orientations*. Washington, D.C.: Brookings Institution.
Haber, L. D. 1970. Disability and social planning: Implications of the Social Security Disability Survey. Paper presented at the Annual Meeting of the National Conference on Social Welfare, Chicago.
Liebow, E. 1967. *Tally's corner*. Boston: Little, Brown.
Luft, H. S. 1972. Poverty and health: An empirical investigation of the economic interactions. Ph.D. dissertation, Harvard Center for Community Health, Boston.
Mechanic, D. 1968. *Medical sociology: A selective view*. New York: Free Press.
Miller, S. M.; Riessman, F.; and Seagull, A. 1968. Poverty and self-indulgence: A critique of the nondeferred gratification pattern. In *Poverty in America*, ed. L. A. Ferman, J. L. Kornbluh, and A. Haber, pp. 416–432. Ann Arbor: University of Michigan Press.
Morgan, J. N., et al. 1962. *Income and welfare in the United States*. New York: McGraw Hill.
National Center for Health Statistics (NCHS). 1973. *Current estimation from the health interview survey*. United States-1971, Series 10, Number 79. Washington, D.C.: Government Printing Office.
Rees, A., and Shultz, G. P. 1970. *Workers and wages in an urban labor market*. Chicago: University of Chicago Press.
Shore, A. 1970. Institutional assistance: A study of the negative income tax experiment. Ph.D. dissertation, Princeton University.
Swisher, I. G. 1971. *Sources and size of income of the disabled*. Social Security of the Disabled, Report No. 16. Washington, D.C.: U.S. Government Printing Office.
Watts, H. W., and Rees, A., eds. Forthcoming. *The New Jersey income-maintenance experiment*. Vol. 3. *Expenditures, health, and social behavior; and the quality of the evidence*. New York: Academic Press.

10 Social psychological characteristics and labor-force response of male heads

Sonia Wright

The question to be considered in this chapter is whether certain personality characteristics and orientations toward work interact with experimental status to produce differential labor-supply responses for male heads of households. Although economic theory predicts work disincentives due to a negative income tax plan, sociological and social psychological factors may operate to confound the predictions of the work–leisure choice hypothesis (Cain and Watts, 1973; Spilerman and Elesh, 1971). Values, attitudes, and social psychological traits may differentially affect responses to the program. For example, persons with high mobility aspirations may increase labor force participation as their income maintenance benefits afford more economic flexibility, whereas persons without such aspirations may respond as the simple model predicts. Since it is unlikely that the poverty population is homogeneous in these traits, aggregating experimental effects across a psychologically heterogeneous population may account for the overall lack of significant findings, even though individual variation in experimental response may be present.

The most recent statement about the nature of such attitudinal variables usually omitted from econometric models appears in Cain and Watts:

> The most likely . . . are (1) preferences for work relative to nonwork activities; (2) skills and/or productivity in relevant nonmarket work activities . . . and (3) various unmeasured traits affecting wage, income, and labor supply such as the quality of education, training, work experience, and mental and physical health. The general point about preferences is that personal traits—ambition, the "protestant ethic," a desire to retire in comfort or to leave abundant material goods to one's heirs, a dislike for spending time at home, or any number of other characteristics—could be "causal" to decisions to obtain high wages . . . *and* to work many hours in the market. Clearly, because an income-maintenance program will change the effective wage rates and nonlabor income across all families in the eligible population, the information we are looking for is the partial relationships between wage rates and income on labor supply, holding personal traits constant [Cain and Watts, 1973:355].

The purpose of this analysis is to examine such personal traits and their possible effects on work behavior in the context of the experiment. The first section will discuss the "culture of poverty" hypotheses to be tested. Section 2 describes the sample and model used. Section 3 lays out the results. Section 4 presents a summary and discussion.

1. THE CULTURE OF POVERTY

Social psychological analyses of poverty have suggested that the poor exhibit values, attitudes, characteristics, and behaviors which set them apart from the rest of the society. The lower class is, thus, seen as a distinct subculture, a self-perpetuating way of life which is transmitted from one generation to the next.

The most notable proponent of the culture of poverty view, Oscar Lewis (1966a, 1966b), held that the poor lack integration into the major values and institutions of the society. "The disengagement, the nonintegration, of the poor with respect to the major institutions of society is a crucial element in the culture of poverty" (1966b:21). Prominent traits which allegedly represent the attitudes, values, and character structure of the poor include

> . . . a strong feeling of fatalism, helplessness, dependence, and inferiority, . . . a high incidence of weak ego structures, . . . a strong present time orientation with relatively little disposition to defer gratification and plan for the future, and a high tolerance for psychological pathology of all kinds [1966a:23].

Such views of the poor are not limited to culture of poverty theorists; similar descriptions are found in most theories of lower-class culture. For example, in an essay that specifically addresses work-related issues

SOCIAL PSYCHOLOGICAL CHARACTERISTICS

among lower-class black youth, Himes writes about their exclusion from the work ethos:

> . . . workers who are restricted to the fringes of the occupational structure tend to be excluded from the tenets and rationalizations of the work ethos. They cannot perceive the linkage between effort and advancement. . . . Hard work and extra effort may be a necessary condition of keeping a job. But neither hard work nor self-improvement leads to a promotion. What then is the value of hard work, extra effort, and self-improvement? . . . In spite of the teachings of social institutions and the mass media, they believe that work is simply work, an unpleasant though necessary condition of staying alive. They go to the job in the morning with reluctance and escape from it at day's end with relief [Himes, 1972:387].

Although evidence for the cultural view of poverty is scant and its theoretical and empirical validity have been questioned (for example, Allen, 1970; Goodwin, 1972; Irelan, Moles, and O'Shea, 1969; Johnson and Sanday, 1971; Roach and Gursslin, 1967; Rossi and Blum, 1968; Valentine, 1968), the perspective remains an important rationale for policy judgments. The implications of cultural theories of poverty for income-maintenance programs are clear. Lewis, for example, states:

> By the time children are six or seven they have usually absorbed the basic attitudes and values of their subculture. Thereafter they are psychologically unready to take full advantage of changing conditions or improving opportunities that may develop in their lifetime [1966a:21].

Economic approaches to poverty will prove insufficient. A negative income tax program can be expected to produce work disincentives, but these will be worst among those most integrated into the culture of poverty. Since this group lacks the "right" values and aspirations with regard to work, the security provided by the payments might be sufficient reason for leaving their unvalued jobs. Moreover, the "tangle of pathologies" reputed to constitute the psychological core of the poor can be expected to aggravate the disincentive effect further.

2. SAMPLE AND MODEL

Sample

The sample analyzed in this chapter consists of 869 "continuous" male heads of household. The major differences between this sample and the 693 analyzed for the central labor-supply responses are that the male head did not have to have a spouse present, and the "new controls" are included.[1]

Social Psychological Variables

The quarterly interviews contain several social psychological variables that may affect work behavior. In all, thirty-seven theoretically relevant attitudinal variables were obtained. Most items were measured at least twice, and no single interview contained all the items. Thus, the decision concerning timepoints for inclusion in this analysis was made on the basis of three criteria. First, it was considered important that the items appear as close together as possible in the sequence of quarterly administration because it had been anticipated that many of the traits would themselves show changes resulting from the experiment.[2] The second consideration dealt with the validity of the data—the argument that (a) families would only gradually become adjusted to the program and the options it provides, and (b) their behavior also would be affected by the approaching end of the experiment to the extent that they anticipate it. Thus, only the middle stretch of the experiment would reflect "normal" behavior under a negative income tax program. Third, early quarterlies unfortunately did not contain several variables central to cultural theories of poverty—for example, time orientation and self-esteem.

Data for all items are available in the seventh, eighth, and ninth quarterlies that correspond roughly to the middle year of the experiment. Furthermore, those interviews contain the most recent and complete set of responses to those variables relevant here. Hence, the social psychological, as well as economic, data from these quarterlies were chosen as the focus for this study.[3]

---

[1] For the "new" controls from Trenton and Paterson–Passaic, the three criteria for continuity were adjusted to reflect their late entry into the program. Thus, the preenrollment interview for the Trenton new controls was actually the fifth quarterly and for the Paterson–Passaic new controls the third quarterly. Of the remaining six and eight interviews, respectively, the respondents could miss no more than three or four, respectively, and in neither case could more than two consecutive interviews be missed. Analyses show that including the new controls in the sample does not alter the results, but their inclusion does add stability to the estimates.

[2] Analysis of the social psychological variables as dependent variables is the focus of Middleton and Allen's research (in Watts and Rees, forthcoming).

[3] It must be emphasized that those data were measured at three different times, within a six-month period, and are not truly cross-sectional, although they will be treated as such. Although it may be inappropriate to consider second-year attitudinal measures as independent variables, since they themselves may have been affected by the experiment, detailed analyses of the measures for which earlier data are available show no systematic or signifi-

For the most part, the attitudinal questions were drawn from prior studies. Some items were designed to measure respondents' attitudes toward work, and others were taken from standard personality scales. In many cases, only some of the items from the original scale were used. Moreover, most scales included have been developed and validated on middle-class populations, or occasionally on representative national samples; consequently, little is known about how these measures operate in the context of the poor. When considering a population in which a number of deviant values and attitudes are thought to coalesce into a syndrome or culture of poverty, the designation of items to be treated as measures of particular traits is likely to be highly arbitrary. (See, for example, Irelan, Moles, and O'Shea, 1969.) For these reasons, the available social psychological items were factor analyzed in order to uncover the major dimensions being measured.

A principal components factoring routine extracted twelve factors[4] which were then subjected to a Varimax rotation. The rotated factors account for 52.4 percent of the total variance among the items, and the solution approaches simple structure—the majority of items loading highly on one and only one factor.[5] An examination of the factors revealed eight dimensions that, according to the theory, may be expected to influence work behavior.[6] The dimensions were defined as follows (the items are listed in Appendix A):

Anomy (from McClosky and Schaar, 1965:38–39): This represents the "tendency to perceive the society as normless, morally chaotic, and adrift."

Self-esteem (from Rosenberg, 1965:31): A person with high self-esteem

---

cant differences between controls and experimentals (Wright, 1973b). Furthermore, Middleton and Allen's extensive research on a broader set of social psychological variables (three of which coincide with those used below, namely, anomy, self-esteem, and control of future), also shows no experimental effects.

[4] The computational routine was instructed to stop factoring when the eigenvalue reached one. Thus, by definition, the amount of variation reproduced by the twelve factors equals the total common variance.

[5] Following the usual convention, a factor loading of .30 was taken as high. Although there were five exceptions to the pattern, each of those items loaded highest on factors which have unambiguous interpretation.

[6] Three factors containing disparate items with low intercorrelations were dropped from the analysis. Three items from the Crowne and Marlowe (1964) social desirability scale comprised an additional factor, but separate analyses indicated that social desirability bias was not present in the responses to the attitudinal items under consideration. Hence, no controls or corrections for social desirability bias need to be introduced. A detailed discussion of the above and the factor analysis is available in Wright (1973b).

"respects himself, considers himself worthy, he does not necessarily consider himself worse, he does not feel that he is the ultimate in perfection but, on the contrary, recognizes his limitations and expects to grow and improve."

Personal inefficacy (from Strodbeck, 1958): This implies the lack of ability or willingness to direct the course of one's life. This measure is termed "control of future" by Middleton and Allen in Watts and Rees (forthcoming). The concept has been variously termed powerlessness, internal versus external control of reinforcements, mastery, and fatalism.

Time orientation: This measures present time orientation, that is, a short time perspective.

Work involvement: This represents involvement with or attachment to one's work.

Occupational flexibility: This is taken as the unwillingness of the respondent to avail himself of new occupational opportunities.

Job satisfaction: This is a general measure of overall satisfaction with one's job.

Perception of financial need: This expresses the respondent's sense of adequate family income and is used as a proxy for financial expectations or aspirations.

For each of the measures (except the last one), a summated scale was constructed.[7] Each scale was coded such that high scores correspond to negative responses in the context of poverty culture theories. Thus, high scores on the first two scales indicate high anomy and negative self-esteem, respectively. The item measuring perceptions of financial need was adjusted for family size and, hence, the responses are in dollars per family member.

The first four, then, are measures of detrimental personality characteristics and the other four represent negative work orientations. The expectation is that persons exhibiting any or all of these traits will respond to a negative income tax by showing a reduction in work effort.[8]

---

[7] For a discussion of the technique and properties of summated scales see Edwards (1957). A detailed analysis of the methodological properties of the scales is available in Wright (1973b). In sum, their reliability, computed by Cronbach's alpha, ranges from .67 to .27. The measures do not appear to be distributed significantly differently for the experimental and control groups. Furthermore, as noted in footnote 3, for the scales which were administered at different times, an analysis was performed to determine the possibility of changes in the attitudes over time. Experimentals were not found to be significantly different from the controls.

[8] Detailed discussions of the literature relevant to these social psychological measures and specific hypotheses in relation to work behavior are available in Wright (1973a, 1973b).

SOCIAL PSYCHOLOGICAL CHARACTERISTICS

Dependent Variables

Three standard measures of labor force participation for the week prior to interview administration are used: employment status, total earnings, and total hours worked (each for the male head of household). Following the rationale summarized in Chapter 2 and treated in detail in Chapter 13, the measures were aggregated across calendar years to control for seasonal and labor-market variations. Since the social psychological measures were obtained roughly during the middle year of the experiment and several scales are not available prior to the seventh quarter, data from the first year of the study will not be considered. The middle year, then, or fifth through eighth quarters, is the basis for this analysis, but data from the third year are also shown to determine whether the attitudinal variables predict or condition labor-force behavior, or if their effects extend to the last year. Finally, since it was possible to miss one or more interviews for a given year, each labor-force yearly average (as well as all other variables in the model) was computed for the quarters the respondent was present. The employment measure, then, represents the probability that the respondent was employed given that an interview was conducted (shown as a percentage). Earnings and hours are weekly data, but averaged across four quarters per year.

Independent Variables

The following independent variables are contained in the basic model: stratum, family earnings and family size at preenrollment, the preenrollment value of the dependent variable (meaning, therefore, that the analysis is of changes in the dependent variables relative to their preenrollment values), city, ethnicity, age, marital status, health, family size and number of adults available for work, education, and welfare status. The first three control for the fact that the allocation model (Conlisk and Watts, 1969) did not assign the families to experimental or control groups independently of income, but stratified the families into one of three strata on the basis of permanent income adjusted for family size. Since stratum is a discrete variable which takes only three values, total family earnings reported at the preenrollment interview are also introduced into the model, along with family size. While preenrollment earnings reflect only a temporary measure of income, as opposed to the more permanent one used to determine stratum, they do represent a continuous variable. The city variable is included to control for differences in labor-market conditions in each of the sites, as well as for seasonal labor-market conditions. Ethnicity, age, health, family structure and size, and education are all known to affect labor-force behavior. Finally, welfare status is included, since the experiment occurred in the context of an operating public assistance system.[9]

[9] More precisely, each of the variables was operationalized as follows:

stratum 1 = 1 if at preenrollment the family had income adjusted for family size up to 100 percent of the poverty level, otherwise 0;

stratum 3 = 1 if the family had income adjusted for family size between 125 and 150 percent of the poverty level, otherwise 0;

preenrollment earnings (family's or head's): coded in dollars, taken at fifth and third quarters for Trenton and Paterson–Passaic new controls, respectively;

preenrollment hours: coded in hours, also taken at fifth and third quarters for new controls;

employed at preenrollment = 1 if employed, otherwise 0;

preenrollment family size: number of persons in the household, also taken at fifth and third quarters for new controls;

Trenton = 1 if the respondent lives in Trenton, otherwise 0;

Paterson–Passaic = 1 if the respondent lives in Paterson–Passaic, otherwise 0;

Scranton = 1 if the respondent lives in Scranton, otherwise 0;

black = 1 if the respondent is black, otherwise 0;

Spanish = 1 if the respondent is Spanish-speaking, otherwise 0;

young = 1 if the respondent is less than thirty-five years old, otherwise 0;

old = 1 if the respondent is more than fifty years old, otherwise 0;

married = coded as the proportion of the quarters for which there is an interview during which the male head's wife was present;

healthy = 1 if the respondent has no more than one "long-term illness, disability, or health problem that cuts down or limits" what he can do, which he has had for more than three months, and if he has had no more than six work days in the previous years when he was "unable to go to work because of illness or accident," as reported in the sixth and tenth quarterlies (see Chapter 9).

family size = average number of persons in the household during the second and third years;

number of available adults = average number of persons in the household who are sixteen years or over and are available for work, that is excepting those who are either in school or disabled, and women who have children in the house under six years of age, averaged for each of the two years;

education = number of years of education the male head reported at the first quarterly interview;

welfare = proportion of quarters for which there is an interview during which the respondent received any of five types of public assistance: AFDC, AFDC-UP, Aid to the Disabled, Aid to the Blind, or Aid to the Aged.

Missing data (an interview is available, but data for a particular item or items are missing) were omitted from the computations for all the labor-force variables, but means were imputed for age, education, welfare status, and health. For some of these variables there is a considerable proportion of missing data, and if the observations had been dropped, the sample size would have been drastically reduced. The labor-force variables, on the other hand, were submitted to extensive data cleaning procedures, and a negligible amount of missing data remained which were omitted.

Experimental Parameters

The experimental parameters used in this chapter consist essentially of the linear spline series described in Chapter 2 and treated in detail in Chapter 12. The first spline is a "dummy" variable, coded 1 for the experimental observations and 0 for the controls, which measures an average, experimental effect. The response to guarantee and tax are measured by

spline 2 = spline 1 $(G - .75)$
spline 3 = spline 1 $(t - .50)$.

The 75 percent guarantee level and the 50 percent tax rate were arbitrarily chosen as an origin from which interplan variation is measured. Thus, experimental effects are measured as deviations from the 75–50 plan, and the regression coefficients to be estimated represent the slopes with respect to changes in guarantee and tax from the origin at the 75–50 plan.

The last three spline functions allow nonlinear, but additive, effects of guarantee level and tax rates and are defined as follows:

spline 4 = maximum $(0, t - .50)$
spline 5 = maximum $(0, G - 1.00)$
spline 6 = minimum $(0, G - .75)$

Each allows for changes in the slopes for different intervals or levels of guarantee and tax rates. The coefficients estimated for the fourth through sixth spline functions are interpreted as the changes in the slopes of the regressions above (or below, in the case of the last one) the specified guarantee and tax levels that appear in each of the functions.

3. RESULTS

Culture of poverty theory implies that the poor who exhibit any or most of the negative traits and work attitudes will evidence a work disincentive effect if their incomes are maintained by a negative income tax plan. Put in other terms, the question is whether the social psychological traits interact with experimental status to determine labor supply. The six basic regression models predicting average work activity during the middle and last years of the experiment are examined with the social psychological variables included (as summated scales) both as main effects and as interaction terms with experimental status. Regression coefficients for the interaction terms thus represent the effect of the particular attitudinal variable for persons in the experimental group on the labor-force variables. The results are reported in Table 10.1.

Table 10.1 Social Psychological and Experimental Effects on Labor-Force Activity

	Second Year			Third Year		
Characteristic	Percentage Employed	Average Earnings	Average Hours	Percentage Employed	Average Earnings	Average Hours
I. Characteristic						
Constant	−5.10 (12.61)	−54.08 (19.56)	−6.06 (6.10)	8.45 (14.47)	−29.06 (23.02)	1.87 (6.72)
Stratum 1	.26 (2.42)	−2.84 (3.77)	−.48 (1.18)	−.60 (2.79)	−5.42 (4.47)	−1.26 (1.30)
Stratum 3	1.86 (2.19)	6.89** (3.41)	−.09 (1.06)	4.24** (2.56)	9.20** (4.09)	.77 (1.19)
Preenrollment family earnings	−.07*** (.02)	−.20*** (.05)	−.04*** (.01)	−.06*** (.02)	−.22*** (.06)	−.04*** (.01)
Preenrollment family size	.42 (.92)	1.78 (1.43)	.20 (.45)	1.78** (.95)	4.54*** (1.52)	1.00** (.44)
Employed at preenrollment	30.84*** (2.99)	—	—	27.26*** (3.54)	—	—
Preenrollment earnings	—	.48*** (.05)	—	—	.45*** (.06)	—
Preenrollment hours	—	—	.30*** (.03)	—	—	.27*** (.03)
Trenton	3.47 (3.14)	5.34 (4.89)	2.00 (1.53)	1.12 (3.70)	1.90 (5.91)	−.35 (1.72)
Paterson–Passaic	−.93 (2.37)	−2.57 (3.69)	.52 (1.16)	−1.85 (2.75)	.18 (4.39)	.79 (1.29)
Scranton	−2.47 (3.33)	−2.30 (5.19)	.45 (1.62)	1.14 (3.88)	.52 (6.20)	2.62 (1.81)
Black	−5.48** (2.95)	−7.28 (4.61)	−2.15 (1.44)	−4.41 (3.47)	−8.56 (5.56)	−1.74 (1.62)
Spanish-speaking	−1.74 (3.15)	−1.18 (4.91)	.83 (1.53)	3.52 (3.70)	1.82 (5.90)	2.17 (1.72)

Young	3.10	2.57	1.11	3.86	4.64	1.28
	(2.08)	(3.24)	(1.01)	(2.45)	(3.90)	(1.14)
Old	−4.08	−9.71**	−3.18**	−10.83***	−15.38***	−4.19***
	(2.83)	(4.41)	(1.38)	(3.32)	(5.29)	(1.54)
Married	32.11***	52.48***	13.29***	28.15***	55.83***	12.91***
	(5.80)	(9.03)	(2.82)	(6.02)	(9.60)	(2.80)
Healthy	5.82***	9.30***	4.12***	9.22***	18.20***	6.03***
	(1.85)	(2.89)	(.90)	(2.27)	(3.62)	(1.06)
Family size	2.03**	2.81**	.93**	.20	−.21	−.12
	(.96)	(1.51)	(.47)	(.96)	(1.54)	(.45)
Number of available adults	7.76***	8.44***	3.07***	6.99***	6.92***	2.61***
	(1.42)	(2.23)	(.69)	(1.50)	(2.43)	(.70)
Education	.61**	1.66***	.37**	.59	2.03***	.36**
	(.33)	(.51)	(.16)	(.38)	(.62)	(.18)
Welfare	−22.64***	−37.61***	−10.74***	−22.75***	−37.30***	−10.29***
	(2.86)	(4.46)	(1.39)	(3.38)	(5.43)	(1.58)
Experimental status	9.92	22.57	.60	4.46	17.16	−1.08
	(12.33)	(19.24)	(6.00)	(14.44)	(23.08)	(6.73)
Spline 2	−15.84	−38.88*	−5.90	−16.18	−56.81*	−8.41
	(12.72)	(19.81)	(6.19)	(14.90)	(23.78)	(6.94)
Spline 3	−19.68	36.32	−1.10	13.56	63.95*	13.10
	(16.84)	(26.26)	(8.20)	(19.70)	(31.46)	(9.18)
Spline 4	16.06	−49.53	−4.16	−8.22	−45.57	−9.34
	(26.08)	(40.65)	(12.70)	(30.58)	(48.81)	(14.25)
Spline 5	25.56	37.28	12.78	21.82	81.24*	18.72
	(24.48)	(38.14)	(11.91)	(28.68)	(45.78)	(13.36)
Spline 6	13.97	40.55	5.26	2.48	48.39	2.37
	(20.88)	(32.55)	(10.16)	(24.44)	(39.03)	(11.39)
Anomy	.22	.40	.08	−.33	−.05	−.16
	(.40)	(.63)	(.20)	(.48)	(.76)	(.22)
Negative self-esteem	−.40	.96	.16	.26	.38	.15
	(.86)	(1.34)	(.42)	(1.00)	(1.60)	(.48)

(continued)

Table 10.1 (continued)

	Second Year				Third Year			
	Percentage Employed	Average Earnings	Average Hours		Percentage Employed	Average Earnings	Average Hours	
Personal inefficacy	.30 (.58)	−.07 (.90)	.00 (.28)		.35 (.68)	−1.09 (1.07)	.09 (.31)	
Present time orientation	.24 (.51)	.65 (.79)	.07 (.25)		.32 (.60)	.94 (.95)	.05 (.28)	
Work uninvolvement	.07 (.37)	.14 (.57)	−.04 (.18)		−.77** (.43)	−.88 (.69)	−.33** (.20)	
Occupational inflexibility	.37 (.54)	.13 (.83)	.04 (.26)		1.13** (.63)	.81 (1.00)	.30 (.29)	
Job dissatisfaction	−.31 (.73)	−1.66 (1.13)	−.23 (.35)		−1.14 (.85)	−2.39** (1.36)	−.49 (.40)	
Financial need	.003** (.001)	.007*** (.002)	.002** (.001)		.002 (.002)	.005** (.002)	.001 (.001)	
II. Interactions with experimental status								
Anomy	−.31 (.54)	−.17 (.84)	−.10 (.26)		.20 (.63)	.42 (1.01)	.19 (.30)	
Negative self-esteem	−1.30 (1.13)	−2.65 (1.77)	−.65 (.55)		−1.85 (1.33)	−2.89 (2.12)	−.72 (.62)	
Personal inefficacy	.61 (.76)	.81 (1.18)	.60 (.37)		−.16 (.89)	−.24 (1.42)	.04 (.41)	
Present time orientation	−1.26** (.69)	−2.38** (1.07)	−.58** (.33)		−.82 (.80)	−2.58** (1.28)	−.52 (.38)	
Work uninvolvement	.22 (.48)	.85 (.75)	.16 (.23)		.78 (.56)	1.39 (.90)	.24 (.26)	
Occupational inflexibility	−.18 (.71)	1.35 (1.10)	.28 (.34)		−1.15 (.83)	.48 (1.32)	−.04 (.39)	

Job dissatisfaction	−.98 (.98)	−2.38 (1.51)	−.08 (.47)	−.35 (1.13)	−1.52 (1.81)	.24 (.53)
Financial need	.002 (.002)	.003 (.002)	.001 (.001)	.002 (.002)	.004 (.003)	.001 (.001)
R^2	.357	.425	.344	.305	.374	.306

NOTE: Coefficients are raw regression coefficients. Numbers in parentheses are standard errors.
** One-tailed test significant at the 5 percent level.
*** One-tailed test significant at the 1 percent level.

For the attitudinal variables, the only main effect that is statistically significant and consistent for the three measures of work behavior during the second year of the experiment is the individual's perception of his family's financial need. During the third year, the effect of the variables remains only for earnings; but work uninvolvement reduces both the probability of employment and hours worked, and job dissatisfaction decreases earnings. On the other hand, occupational inflexibility increases the probability of employment.

The relevance of the social psychological results for the poverty-culture thesis can be summarized as follows: First, the large majority of the coefficients (forty out of forty-eight) are not statistically significant. Second, of the four variables which have significant effects, one shows a reversed sign (occupational inflexibility). Third, of those variables which show both significant and consistent influence in the predicted direction, the effects are not striking. Consider, for example, job dissatisfaction. Next to financial need, job dissatisfaction shows the largest effects on work activity. Yet a one-unit increase in job dissatisfaction reduced the probability of employment by 1 percent, reduced average weekly earnings by $2 and reduced the average time worked per week by about thirty minutes (all for the third year and relative to preenrollment). These effects can be compared, for example, to the effects of being over fifty years old: close to 11 percent reduction in employment, $15 less earnings, and about four fewer hours. In short, the evidence suggests that current work activity is far more conditioned by standard economic and sociological variables, such as the person's prior history of labor force participation, ethnicity, family structure and size, health status, education, age, and welfare status.

Table 10.1 also shows that, contrary to predictions, only four of forty-eight interaction terms representing the attitudinal variables by experimental status are statistically significant at the .05 level, all for present time orientation. Experimentals with strong present time orientation were 1 percent less likely to be employed during the second year, earned $2 less per week during both years, and worked about one-half hour less per week the second year than both those in the experimental group with a future time orientation and the controls.[10]

Although obviously lacking strong effects, thirty-one out of the forty-eight interaction terms do have the predicted sign;[11] thus, it is possible that all of them taken together would show a significant effect on work.

---

[10] These data, of course, do *not* mean that the poor in the New Jersey–Pennsylvania sample have a strong present time orientation. Rather, they indicate that those who do have a present time orientation and are also in the experimental group show a disincentive effect. These specific results do conform to the culture-of-poverty predictions.

[11] Their net effects (summing the eight coefficients) for each of the six models are, respectively: -3.20, -4.57, -3.70, -3.35, -4.94, $-.57$.

SOCIAL PSYCHOLOGICAL CHARACTERISTICS

Accordingly, the eight interaction terms were entered into the regressions as a group, stepwise, and joint F-tests were computed. None was statistically significant.[12]

It was anticipated, on the basis of the poverty culture theory, that the poor who are most integrated into the culture of poverty, that is, those who can be characterized as most "pathological," would exhibit a work disincentive effect.[13] Accordingly, three summary measures were developed that combine highly negative responses on several of the social psychological traits.[14] The first, "poverty culture integration," represents those with high scores on at least four of the eight separate scales.[15] This variable was further decomposed into two separate dimensions: "negative personality traits" and negative work orientations.[16] Dummy scores were constructed for each of the variables, and the resulting labor-force regressions are shown in Tables 10.2 and 10.3.

Although the signs of each of the coefficients indicate a disincentive effect, none is statistically significant. It is worth noting, however, that only about 15 percent of this sample (regardless of experimental status) exhibit the highly negative characteristics. It should also be noted that the R^2 for each of these equations is smaller than the ones reported in earlier tables, where the eight separate scales are used instead.

4. SUMMARY AND DISCUSSION

The results of the preceding analysis can be summarized as follows: First, compared with the effects apparent for the basic economic and de-

---

[12] The F-statistics for the six equations are, respectively: .98, 1.74, .99, 1.15, 1.35, .84, all with 8 and 828 degrees of freedom.

[13] Another possibility is that the hypothesized effects will only appear among certain ethnic groups (see, for example, Irelan, Moles, and O'Shea, 1969; Johnson and Sanday, 1971). Although other analyses of labor supply reported in this volume uncovered experimental work effects by ethnicity, none such are indicated by the present attitudinal data. The models which appear in Table 10.1 were run for the three ethnic groups separately and F-tests for equality of coefficients computed. Those F-values are: .98, .96, 1.14, 1.21, 1.24, 1.09, with 76 and 752 degrees of freedom, none statistically significant.

[14] Discussion of those measures, including the criteria for their construction, is again available in Wright (1973b).

[15] $N = 120$, or 13.8 percent of this sample, and 70 or 14.4 percent of experimentals.

[16] The personality measure represents those with high scores on three or more of the following: anomy, negative self-esteem, personal efficacy, and present time orientation. ($N = 137$, or 15.8 percent of this sample, and 74 or 15.2 percent of these experimentals.) The work orientation measure includes those with high scores on two or more of the following: work uninvolvement, occupational inflexibility, job dissatisfaction, and perceptions of low financial need. ($N = 134$, or 15.4 percent of this sample, and 74 or 15.2 percent of these experimentals.)

Table 10.2 Social Psychological and Experimental Effects on Work Activity, High Culture of Poverty Integration

	Second Year			Third Year		
	Percentage Employed	Average Earnings	Average Hours	Percentage Employed	Average Earnings	Average Hours
Constant	19.02 (7.74)	−3.14 (11.96)	4.39 (3.68)	15.33 (8.60)	−12.97 (13.53)	2.97 (3.92)
Stratum 1	−.18 (2.44)	−4.45 (3.87)	−.76 (1.18)	−.50 (2.80)	−6.01 (4.53)	−1.21 (1.30)
Stratum 3	2.20 (2.21)	7.21** (3.50)	−.09 (1.07)	4.50** (2.56)	9.66*** (4.14)	.79 (1.19)
Preenrollment family earnings	−.07*** (.02)	−.18*** (.05)	−.03*** (.01)	−.06*** (.02)	−.21*** (.06)	−.04*** (.01)
Preenrollment family size	1.40 (.89)	3.92*** (1.42)	.68 (.43)	2.10** (.93)	5.63*** (1.51)	1.14*** (.43)
Employed at preenrollment	31.60*** (2.99)	—	—	27.28*** (3.52)	—	—
Preenrollment earnings	—	.49*** (.05)	—	—	.44*** (.06)	—
Preenrollment hours	—	—	.31*** (.03)	—	—	.28*** (.03)
Trenton	2.86 (3.10)	5.32 (4.91)	2.03 (1.50)	2.07 (3.63)	3.94 (5.85)	.22 (1.68)
Paterson–Passaic	−.15 (2.31)	−.28 (3.65)	.85 (1.12)	.20 (2.67)	4.24 (4.29)	1.52 (1.24)
Scranton	−2.35 (3.24)	−.69 (5.16)	.63 (1.57)	3.28 (3.76)	4.60 (6.07)	3.44* (1.74)
Black	−4.13 (2.92)	−5.45 (4.65)	−1.43 (1.42)	−4.28 (3.42)	−8.37 (5.55)	−1.57 (1.59)
Spanish-speaking	−1.31 (3.16)	.10 (5.01)	1.14 (1.53)	3.35 (3.69)	2.08 (5.95)	2.23 (1.71)
Young	2.40 (2.07)	1.16 (3.28)	.79 (1.00)	2.90 (2.42)	3.02 (3.90)	.86 (1.12)

Old	3.16	12.16	3.42			
	(2.81)	(4.46)	(1.36)	(3.28)	(5.29)	(1.52)
Married	20.99***	30.34***	8.19***	21.41***	40.92***	9.70***
	(5.28)	(8.38)	(2.56)	(5.52)	(8.91)	(2.56)
Healthy	6.74***	11.43***	4.49***	9.67***	19.38***	6.32***
	(1.85)	(2.94)	(.90)	(2.26)	(3.65)	(1.05)
Family size	.30	−.96	.10	−.54	−2.28	−.42
	(.86)	(1.38)	(.42)	(.88)	(1.43)	(.41)
Number of available adults	7.92***	8.94***	3.10***	7.16***	7.11***	2.72***
	(1.43)	(2.29)	(.69)	(1.50)	(2.46)	(.70)
Education	.51	1.50***	.32**	.49	1.99***	.31**
	(.33)	(.52)	(.16)	(.38)	(.61)	(.18)
Welfare	−22.87***	−35.25***	−10.33***	−23.22***	−37.91***	−10.37***
	(2.88)	(4.58)	(1.40)	(3.39)	(5.50)	(1.57)
Experimental status	−2.54	8.24**	−1.28	−1.33	7.68	−.87
	(2.90)	(4.61)	(1.41)	(3.38)	(5.46)	(1.57)
Spline 2	−17.16	−43.23**	−6.27	−19.94	−67.54***	−10.62
	(12.89)	(20.44)	(6.25)	(15.01)	(24.22)	(6.96)
Spline 3	−23.13	30.83	−2.75	11.53	59.62**	12.00
	(16.94)	(26.90)	(8.22)	(19.70)	(31.82)	(9.14)
Spline 4	22.36	−41.22	−.99	−3.94	−33.04	−5.49
	(26.04)	(41.34)	(12.64)	(30.34)	(48.98)	(14.08)
Spline 5	31.98	56.66	16.35	29.32	109.65***	24.90**
	(24.64)	(39.10)	(11.96)	(28.71)	(46.36)	(13.32)
Spline 6	15.97	47.15	5.10	9.74	64.08	4.67
	(21.14)	(33.56)	(10.26)	(24.60)	(39.74)	(11.41)
High poverty culture integration	1.63	.16	.64	−4.72	−5.15	−1.60
	(3.74)	(5.94)	(1.82)	(4.36)	(7.04)	(2.02)
High poverty culture integration by experimental status	−6.72	−7.91	−2.00	−3.08	−12.53	−2.57
	(4.91)	(7.79)	(2.38)	(5.72)	(9.23)	(2.65)
R^2	.328	.377	.319	.283	.339	.291

NOTE: Coefficients are raw regression coefficients. Numbers in parentheses are standard errors.
** One-tailed test significant at the 5 percent level.
*** One-tailed test significant at the 1 percent level.

Table 10.3 Social Psychological and Experimental Effects on Work Activity, Negative Personality Traits and Work Ethic

	Second Year			Third Year		
	Percentage Employed	Average Earnings	Average Hours	Percentage Employed	Average Earnings	Average Hours
Constant	19.06	−2.31	4.47	15.89	−10.74	3.29
	(7.77)	(12.01)	(3.70)	(8.65)	(13.62)	(3.94)
Stratum 1	−.27	−4.51	−.77	−.70	−6.39	−1.29
	(2.44)	(3.88)	(1.18)	(2.81)	(4.55)	(1.30)
Stratum 3	2.12	7.18**	−.13	4.55**	9.58**	.81
	(2.21)	(3.51)	(1.07)	(2.58)	(4.16)	(1.19)
Preenrollment family earnings	−.06***	−.19***	−.03***	−.06***	−.21***	−.04***
	(.02)	(.05)	(.01)	(.02)	(.06)	(.01)
Preenrollment family size	1.36	3.87***	.66	2.14**	5.66***	1.15***
	(.89)	(1.42)	(.43)	(.94)	(1.51)	(.43)
Employed at preenrollment	31.59***	—	—	27.30***	—	—
	(3.00)			(3.54)		
Preenrollment earnings	—	.49***	—	—	.45***	—
		(.05)			(.06)	
Preenrollment hours	—	—	.31***	—	—	.28***
			(.03)			(.03)
Trenton	2.71	4.98	1.97	2.04	3.32	.20
	(3.11)	(4.93)	(1.51)	(3.65)	(5.88)	(1.69)
Paterson–Passaic	−.22	−.71	.75	.21	4.20	1.53
	(2.33)	(3.68)	(1.13)	(2.70)	(4.33)	(1.25)
Scranton	−2.46	−.96	.55	3.10	3.99	3.34
	(3.25)	(5.16)	(1.58)	(3.77)	(6.10)	(1.75)
Black	−4.03	−5.40	−1.46	−4.34	−8.55	−1.61
	(2.93)	(4.66)	(1.42)	(3.44)	(5.58)	(1.60)
Spanish-speaking	−1.22	.18	1.13	3.29	1.77	2.18
	(3.17)	(5.03)	(1.54)	(3.71)	(5.98)	(1.72)

Young	2.22	.98	.74	2.88	2.90	.85
	(2.07)	(3.28)	(1.00)	(2.43)	(3.92)	(1.13)
Old	−5.12**	−12.14***	−3.39***	−10.89***	−16.96***	−4.12***
	(2.82)	(4.47)	(1.36)	(3.29)	(5.31)	(1.53)
Married	21.06***	30.19***	8.23***	21.39***	41.11***	9.67***
	(5.30)	(8.41)	(2.57)	(5.54)	(8.95)	(2.57)
Healthy	6.66***	11.27***	4.47***	9.49***	19.07***	6.22***
	(1.86)	(2.95)	(.90)	(2.27)	(3.66)	(1.05)
Family size	.29	−.90	.11	−.60	−2.40*	−.45
	(.87)	(1.39)	(.42)	(.88)	(1.44)	(.41)
Number of available	7.75***	8.83***	3.07***	7.02***	6.90***	2.67***
adults	(1.43)	(2.29)	(.69)	(1.51)	(2.48)	(.70)
Education	.52	1.49***	.31**	.50	1.97***	.32**
	(.33)	(.52)	(.16)	(.38)	(.62)	(.18)
Welfare	−23.06***	−35.32***	−10.34***	−23.48***	−38.17***	−10.48***
	(2.88)	(4.58)	(1.40)	(3.40)	(5.51)	(1.58)
Experimental	−2.20	8.62	−.96	−1.91	6.28	−1.22
status	(2.98)	(4.73)	(1.44)	(3.48)	(5.61)	(1.61)
Spline 2	−16.36	−42.68***	−6.32	−18.21	−64.34***	−9.65
	(12.87)	(20.40)	(6.24)	(15.02)	(24.24)	(6.97)
Spline 3	−24.79	28.87	−3.02	9.51	54.38**	11.05
	(16.97)	(26.93)	(8.23)	(19.78)	(31.94)	(9.18)
Spline 4	25.00	−37.71	−.45	−.84	−25.19	−4.03
	(26.08)	(41.36)	(12.64)	(30.45)	(49.14)	(14.13)
Spline 5	31.08	56.39	16.68	26.87	105.42**	23.54**
	(24.63)	(39.07)	(11.94)	(28.77)	(46.44)	(13.35)
Spline 6	13.56	44.10	4.77	5.89	55.49	2.67
	(21.09)	(33.45)	(10.23)	(24.60)	(39.71)	(11.41)
Negative	2.49	1.39	.42	−2.26	−5.85	−1.11
personality traits	(3.42)	(5.43)	(1.66)	(3.99)	(6.44)	(1.85)
Negative work	1.76	−1.83	.53	−1.31	−2.01	−.39
orientations	(3.49)	(5.54)	(1.69)	(4.06)	(6.56)	(1.88)

(continued)

339

Table 10.3 (*continued*)

	Second Year			Third Year		
	Percentage Employed	Average Earnings	Average Hours	Percentage Employed	Average Earnings	Average Hours
Negative personality traits by experimental status	−6.63 (4.62)	−9.09 (7.33)	−2.19 (2.24)	−1.34 (5.39)	−5.77 (8.71)	−.54 (2.50)
Negative work orientations by experimental status	−3.43 (4.66)	−3.06 (7.38)	−2.00 (2.26)	−1.18 (5.44)	−3.80 (8.78)	−1.22 (2.52)
R^2	.328	.378	.320	.280	.337	.287

NOTE: Coefficients are raw regression coefficients. Numbers in parentheses are standard errors.
** One-tailed test significant at the 5 percent level.
*** One-tailed test significant at the 1 percent level.

mographic variables, the social psychological variables have no significant and consistent main effect on work behavior, the one exception being the respondent's perception of his family's financial needs. Second, the attitudinal variables in interaction with experimental status also show no significant effect on work activity, except for present time orientation. In fact, of sixty-six possible interaction terms, only four were significantly different from zero. Similarly, when only the most "pathological" are considered—those scoring most negatively on several of the personality characteristics and work orientations—there is still no statistically significant disincentive effect.[17]

Various methodological issues have been raised which may invalidate the results of the experiment, including, for instance, problems arising from the short duration and narrow scope of the study and attrition losses, which may explain the lack of findings for the present analysis. Such concerns are addressed elsewhere in these volumes and need not be detailed here.

The absence of significant results may also be due to methodologically weak social psychological measures, as evidenced by the relatively low reliabilities of the scales. Three points suggest, however, that unreliability may not be such a severe problem. First, the factor analysis did indicate that the original items shared about 52 percent of the total variance among them, more than enough covariation to produce significant results if the independent and dependent variables were in fact empirically correlated. Moreover, the factors were relatively unambiguous in interpretation. Finally, other analyses show that all the scales, including the summary measures, are reasonably correlated with certain background characteristics of the respondents, while they are generally uncorrelated with the work behavior measures (Wright, 1973b).

Another reason for the lack of findings may be the conceptual inaccuracies in predicting the effects of social psychological characteristics on work. In response to pressing policy concerns, only recently has the problem of work incentives been addressed in the sociological literature. No conceptual approach allowed empirically based predictions about the effects of attitudinal variables on labor supply in an income-maintenance setting. Consequently, plausible yet contradictory hypotheses might have been entertained about the relationships between the variables. In an attempt to provide a more unified focus for this research the culture of poverty theory was examined as a source of hypotheses, its use here also

---

[17] Perhaps more stringent definitions of the "hard-core pathological" ought to be used, but data from the experimental sample do not allow it, since that would include even smaller proportions than those used here (see notes 14 and 15 above). An important finding by itself is that so few persons can even be assigned that label.

being due in large part to its prominent role as rationale for policy efforts.[18]

A final possibility is that the underlying theoretical perspective of this research is, in fact, inaccurate. A growing body of findings has questioned the theory's empirical and conceptual adequacy. The theory is one of a class which rests on the now tenuous assumption that attitudes determine behavior. Most recent research has indicated that the relationship between attitudes and behavior is not direct, frequently nonexistent, and always much less obvious than simple attitudinal models of behavior predict. It seems probable that this is the case here. The labor force participation of the poor has been shown to be determined by factors over which they generally have had little or no control: occupational and racial discrimination, inadequate training, poor health, restrictive and regressive welfare programs which penalize recipients for work, and so on. In the context of such external inhibitions, the particular attitudinal traits of the poor seem largely inconsequential, as indeed this chapter has generally shown.

In short, then, in spite of the pessimistic predictions derived from poverty subculture theories, there is no evidence that the work behavior of the poor would be adversely affected by a negative income tax program, nor would adverse social psychological characteristics pose an encumbrance.

APPENDIX A: THE ITEMS MAKING UP THE EIGHT DIMENSIONS EXPECTED TO INFLUENCE WORK BEHAVIOR

WORK INVOLVEMENT

The following items showed loadings of .50, or higher, on the first factor: (1) The most important things that happen to me involve my work. (2) The major satisfaction in my life comes from my job. (3) I think about my job all the time. (4) I am very much involved personally in my work.

---

[18] Thus, the results are "policy relevant" in that they speak to the social theory which is so often cited as "proof" why a negative income tax program would be unsuccessful as a national social welfare program. To be sure, one would not be able, on the basis of our results, to vary such programs according to the psychological and cultural characteristics of the poor; nor could these variables be "manipulated" in order to secure a more positive response to the negative income tax program. In this "social engineering" sense, then, they are basically irrelevant. But since adoption of a negative income tax program will in the end be decided by political (rather than economic or sociological) factors, the results are directly relevant to the political debate surrounding the efficacy of such a program.

(5) I'm really a perfectionist about my work. Response categories were the usual five Likert-type ranging from strongly agree to strongly disagree.

ANOMY

The next set of items loaded highest on factor two: (1) I often feel that many of the things our parents stood for are just going to ruin before our very eyes. (2) What is lacking in the world today is the old kind of friendship that lasted for a lifetime. (3) People were better off in the old days when everyone knew just how he was expected to act. (4) The trouble with the world today is that most people really don't believe in anything. (5) Everything changes so quickly these days that I often have trouble deciding what is right and what is wrong. They are all from the McClosky–Schaar (1965) anomy scale.

OCCUPATIONAL FLEXIBILITY

Four items had high loadings on the third factor:

1. Let's imagine that you heard about a job in (*city in which respondent lives*) that paid quite a bit more than you are now getting. To get it you would have to enroll in a training program that lasts for six months and pays a lower salary than you are presently getting. Would you take such a job?
2. Let's imagine that you heard about a job you could get in another city. The pay was good and it offered job security with little chance of being laid off. Would you seriously consider leaving (*city in which respondent lives*) and moving to the other city to take the job?
3. Let's imagine that you heard about another job that was part time and would still let you hold your present job. Would you be interested in "moonlighting" and take this second job?
4. Thinking ahead to the future, do you expect to have a better job, a worse job, or a job about the same as the one you have now?

The first three were coded as follows: Yes, don't know, no. The last was coded as follows: Better job, don't know, same ($N = 216$) or worse job ($N = 4$).

SELF-ESTEEM

Three items from the Rosenberg self-esteem scale produced loadings of .70 or higher on factor four: (1) I am able to do things as well as most other people. (2) I feel that I am a person of worth—at least equal to others. (3) I feel that I have a number of good qualities. Coded into four Likert-type ranging from agree strongly to disagree strongly. Two additional items from the Rosenberg scale, both negatively worded, did not cluster in the same factor. The hypothesis here is that those with low self-esteem will reduce their labor force participation if incomes are maintained.

PERSONAL EFFICACY

Three items loaded highest on the fifth factor: (1) Planning only makes a person unhappy since your plans hardly ever work out anyhow. (2) Nowadays, with world conditions the way they are, the wise person lives for today and lets tomorrow take care of itself. (3) There is no sense taking a chance failing at something new when I'm doing all right as I am. Response categories were the usual five Likert-type ranging from strongly agree to strongly disagree.

JOB SATISFACTION

Two items with loadings of .70 or higher on factor six measured job satisfaction: (1) Thinking about your job, how satisfied are you with it in general? (2) How would you compare your present (last) job to all other jobs you have had? Codes for the first were the usual five Likert-type ranging from very satisfied to very dissatisfied, and for the second, best, about the same, not as good.

TIME ORIENTATION

The three items with high loadings on the seventh factor were: (1) The present is more important to me than the future. (2) When I feel like doing something, I just go ahead and do it. (3) I usually wait until the last minute to get things done. Responses were the usual five Likert-type ranging from very accurate to very inaccurate.

PERCEPTION OF FINANCIAL NEED

Finally, the last factor contained only one item with a high loading: What is the smallest amount of money that your family would need each year to live comfortably? This item was coded in dollars, adjusted for family size. It was introduced into the factor analysis because it is the only one available which even resembles the concept of aspirations.

ACKNOWLEDGMENTS

I am grateful for the assistance of Dennis Bindley, David Elesh, and James Wright throughout this research. Harold Watts and Glen Cain offered helpful comments on an earlier draft.

REFERENCES

Allen, V. L. 1970. *Psychological factors in poverty.* Institute for Research on Poverty Monograph Series. Chicago: Markham.
Cain, G., and Watts, H., eds. 1973. *Income maintenance and labor supply. Econometric studies.* Institute for Research on Poverty Monograph Series. New York: Academic Press.
Conlisk, J., and Watts, H. 1969. A model for optimizing experimental designs for estimating response surfaces, pp. 150–156. Social Statistics Section of the American Statistical Association.
Crowne, D., and Marlowe, D. 1964. *The approval motive.* New York: Wiley.
Edwards, A. E. 1957. *Techniques of attitude scale construction.* New York: Appleton.
Goodwin, L. 1972. *Do the poor want to work? A social-psychological study of work orientations.* Washington, D.C.: Brookings Institution.
Himes, J. S. 1972. Some work-related cultural deprivations of lower class negro youths. In *Poverty in America,* ed. L. A. Ferman, J. L. Kornbluh, and A. Haber, pp. 384–389. Ann Arbor: University of Michigan Press.
Irelan, L. M.; Moles, O. C.; and O'Shea, R. M. 1969. Ethnicity, poverty, and selected attitudes: A test of the "culture of poverty" hypothesis. *Social Forces* 47: 405–413.
Johnson, N. J., and Sanday, P. R. 1971. Subcultural variations in an urban poor population. *American Anthropologist* 73: 128–143.
Lewis, O. 1966a. The culture of poverty. *Scientific American* 215: 19–25.
Lewis, O. 1966b. *La vida: A Puerto Rican family in the culture of poverty—San Juan and New York.* New York: Random House.
McClosky, H., and Schaar, J. H. 1965. Psychological dimensions of anomy. *American Sociological Review* 30: 14–40.
Garfinkel, I. Forthcoming. The effects of welfare on the labor-supply response. In *The New Jersey income-maintenance experiment.* Vol. 3. *Expenditures, health, and social behavior; and the quality of the evidence,* ed. H. Watts and A. Rees. New York: Academic Press.
Middleton, R., and Allen, V. Forthcoming. Social psychological consequences of income maintenance. In *The New Jersey income-maintenance experiment.* Vol. 3. *Expenditures, health, and social behavior; and the quality of the evidence,* ed. H. Watts and A. Rees. New York: Academic Press.
Roach, J. L., and Gursslin, O. R. 1967. An evaluation of the concept "culture of poverty." *Social Forces* 45: 383–392.
Rosenberg, M. 1965. *Society and the adolescent self-image.* Princeton: Princeton University Press.
Rossi, P., and Blum, Z. 1968. Class, status, and poverty. In *On understanding poverty,* ed. D. P. Moynihan, pp. 36–63. New York: Basic Books.
Spilerman, S., and Elesh, D. 1971. Alternative conceptions of poverty and their implications for income maintenance. *Social Problems* 18: 358–373.

Strodbeck, F. L. 1958. Family interaction, values, and achievement. In *Talent and society: New perspectives in the identification of talent,* ed. D. C. McClelland, A. L. Baldwin, U. Bronfenbrenner, and F. L. Strodbeck, pp. 135—194. Princeton: Van Nostrand.

Valentine, C. A. 1968. *Culture and poverty: Critique and counterproposals.* Chicago: University of Chicago Press.

Wright, S. 1973a. Social psychological characteristics and labor-force response of male heads. In *Final report of the New Jersey graduated work incentive experiment,* ed. H. Watts and A. Rees, Part B, Chapter 9. Madison: Institute for Research on Poverty, University of Wisconsin.

Wright, S. 1973b. Social psychological characteristics and work behavior among the urban poor. Ph.D. dissertation, Purdue University.

11 Information levels and labor response

Jon Helge Knudsen
John Mamer
Robert A. Scott
Arnold R. Shore

When human beings are subjects in a scientific experiment, attention must sometimes be given to the question of their comprehension of the experimental stimulus. The possibility exists that subjects may only partially comprehend the stimulus or possibly even completely fail to understand it. The problem warrants attention for at least two reasons. Under certain circumstances, interpretation of results can depend upon knowing how subjects understood and responded to the intended stimulus. And our ability to generalize findings of the experiment to a larger setting will, in certain circumstances, also depend upon how subjects comprehended the experimental stimulus.

The problem of comprehension of the experimental stimulus is especially worrisome in this kind of experiment. The stimulus of negative income taxation is fairly complicated as experimental stimuli go—involving, among other things, understanding of guarantee level, tax rate, and breakeven point; the interrelationships among these parameters; and the relationship of the plan as a whole to income. The experiences of persons both in experimental field offices and in the payments division suggest that there was more than a little confusion about tax plans, and that some subjects experienced recurrent difficulties in understanding the most rudimentary aspects of them. These experiences would indicate to us that the problem of subjects' comprehension of the experimental stimulus warrants further investigation.

At the outset, it is important to clarify the sense in which data about experimental subjects' comprehension of the plans to which they were assigned is relevant to the larger problem of generalizability of findings to a national program. First, the mere fact that some subjects fail to comprehend the stimulus is not, in and of itself, necessarily relevant to the issue of generalizability. We say this because, in a national negative income tax program, as in any similar program, subjects need not understand the intricacies of the program in minute detail in order to participate. In fact, it is likely that many will not comprehend very much; and this is not serious as long as they can get more information when they need it for some specific purpose. For example, if a person (either an experimental subject or an ordinary citizen under a national scheme) contemplates the possibility of working either more or less, he may then inquire and learn about the effects such a choice will have on his negative tax payments. In a sense, learning about tax plans, whether in an experimental context or in an ongoing national program, will depend upon both enrollment procedures *and* experience with the receipt of payments over the course of time.

In the case of the experiment, there exists the possibility that some of the confusion and misunderstanding about tax plans evident during the study may have been due to inadequacies (relative to a national program) in the enrollment procedures used to explain the stimulus to the subjects. In other words, some subjects may not have connected the receipt of these tax monies to their level of income. To the extent that this is true, serious questions arise concerning the straightforward generalizability of experimental results for purposes of planning a national program. It is for this reason that it is extremely useful to have information about knowledge levels in interpreting the results of the experiment.

An empirical study of the comprehension question raises almost as many problems as it addresses. Foremost among the problems raised by this issue is first how to conceptualize subjects' understanding of their participation in the program, and second how to relate that understanding to the issues raised in the preceding paragraph. In principle, the recipient of negative income tax benefits can understand his position in a number of ways. He may realize only that he receives money at regular intervals from some specific source; or he can have some idea that he is on a negative income tax plan and that his earned income bears some relationship to the amounts he receives; or he can understand his payments as calculated according to an exact formula; or, finally, he can realize that he is participating in a program in which payments are made to certain categories of families in particular ways.

We would argue that it is not sufficient to say that a subject comprehends the experimental stimulus if he recognizes only that money is given to him on a regular basis, without understanding any other feature of the program. Indeed, we assert that, for the purposes of generalizing experimental results to the operation of a national program, the recipient of payments in the experiment would have to be able to articulate, in some form, the relationship between tax plan and income. Our position is based on the fact that negative income tax plans differ from the mere receipt of money, in that the former are regular *and* systematic over time, whereas the latter may not be. This point of view is used as a guideline for operationalizing the variable of knowledge level in this paper.

Another equally complicated problem involves the source of data available for studying the comprehension problem. For numerous reasons, we had to rely entirely on interview data collected in a special postexperimental interview. This method makes questioning knowledge about the relationship between tax plans and income somewhat unrealistic, because it necessitates asking about knowledge levels apart from actual decisions that may have confronted subjects and in a context removed from the day-to-day operation of the program. To accept our findings, it is necessary also to accept the assumptions (1) that subjects who answer "correctly" on interview items about the logic and operation of their particular negative income tax plans differ significantly in their comprehension of the operational program from those who cannot articulate this relationship in an interview situation, and (2) that this difference is not a matter of intelligence but of genuine differences in levels of information. Again, only if recipients understand that there is some relationship between tax plans and income, can they make informed decisions in terms of tax plans or realize that they should make inquiries about the effects of their decisions on tax payments.

Finally, because the program will be national and public, it is likely that recipients in a permanent program will face some of the same comprehension problems with respect to knowledge of tax-plan parameters as those faced by recipients of payments in this experiment, even though the sources of tax information may differ in significant ways.

It is thus important to estimate as accurately as possible what comprehension problems recipients in the experiment actually faced. Indeed, it seems plausible to argue that not only is work response and its relationship to information level an important policy concern, the information level itself is also an important policy variable. In the end, of course, we must be able to assert how, if at all, information levels affect our regression estimates of labor supply, because the reliability of these estimates is critical to the generalization of findings from an experimental context to a national program of negative income taxation. If there are no discrepancies between the assigned negative income tax plan and the perception of that plan, then no additional analytic problems are posed. If understanding sufficient to make informed choices on the basis of plan parameters takes place only after a period of time, then the time period used in analysis may be adjusted to take this datum into account. If there is misperception, then we must ask about the nature of misperception, because not all cases of misperception are equally important.

Random misperceptions of negative income tax plans will result in regression estimates of labor supply which have wider variances than in the case where perceived and assigned tax plan are the same; however, the estimates will be unbiased. When misperceptions are not random, the degree of seriousness depends upon the nature of the misperception. Misperceptions of assigned plan might be a function of variables which themselves affect labor supply. Since these variables will affect recipients in a national program in much the same way, these misperceptions do not give misleading estimates. On the other hand, if misperceptions are a function of an activity or procedure directly related to the program—for example, enrollment and information practices—then extrapolation of results to a national program might be more difficult.

Thus, there are two parts to the information problem. The first concerns whether or not information levels affect labor-supply response. For this aspect of the problem, we can utilize standard labor-supply equations, insert information level variables, and note the effects. The second part of the problem concerns why the effects take place, if they do. Here answers may be less conclusive, for two reasons: (1) the relationship between information level and labor-supply variables may be difficult to determine in a final way since the number of potential variables is large; and (2) the number of cases for which the data are adequate for testing the relationship between perceived tax variables and other variables is rather small.

1. MODELS OF SUBJECTS' UNDERSTANDING

Following Nicholson (1975), our theoretical equation for labor supply is of the form $Y_i = \alpha + \beta X_i + \gamma E_i + U_i$, where Y_i represents labor supply, X_i represents factors related to labor supply, E_i represents the parameters of the individual family's assigned negative income tax plan, and U_i represents random error. Behaviorally speaking, we can rewrite the equation by substituting S for E, where S represents perception of the experimental stimulus. Thus, $Y_i = \alpha + \beta X_i + \gamma S_i + U_i$. If $S_i = E_i$, there is no problem. If not, we find that $Y_i = \alpha + \beta X_i + \gamma E_i + U_i$, where U_i is composed of the discrepancy between S_i and E_i as well as random error.

Various models of labor supply which include terms for information levels can be specified (Nicholson, 1975:7 ff). However, as we shall see, there is the practical problem of trying to measure information level either numerically (in terms of an index) or as a series of dummy variables. We shall employ both forms. For the case of a numeric measurement of information levels, the theoretically appropriate model is of the form

$$Y = a + f(x_1, x_2, \ldots, x_n) + b(G^* - G) + c(T^* - T) + G + T + U,$$

where G^* represents perceived guarantee level, G represents assigned guarantee level, T^* is perceived tax rate, and T is assigned tax rate. As we shall note below, this model will be amended to take account of certain difficulties encountered in measuring tax-rate information level.

For indicators consisting of dummy variables which represent degrees of information on tax rate and guarantee level as measured by responses to interview questions, the model we shall be using is the following:

$$Y_i = \alpha + \beta x_i + \gamma(E_{tr} \cdot S_{tr}) + \delta(E_{gl} \cdot S_{gl}) + U_i,$$

where dummy variables for tax rate and guarantee level are interacted with dummy variables for information level on tax rate and guarantee level, respectively. As a result of this formulation, the slope of the line fitted is the same for all levels of tax rate and guarantee level, but the constants (or y intercepts) vary from case to case. The important point is that the coefficients for variables usually included in the labor-supply equation can be compared to coefficients for these same variables when an information level indicator is included in the equation. The restriction on the slope of the line for all levels of the tax parameters does not affect the variability of signs and coefficients for variables in the original labor-supply equation.

In the presentation of findings, we shall assume that for practical purposes a simple model of labor supply suffices. We shall also assume that information levels can alter coefficients of variables in ways which are interpretable and understandable. Data necessary for the testing of the model are dummy variable indicators of information levels and numeric measurements. No attempt has been made to construct an overall index of information level. Rather, dummy variable indicators were constructed separately for tax rate and guarantee level, and numeric measurements of tax rate and guarantee level were used separately as well.

In addition, where numeric measurements of perceived tax rate and perceived guarantee level are available, these can be regressed on E_i and other factors to discover, in a regression format, whether $S_i = E_i$ or whether there is over- or underestimation of E in the aggregate. The model to be used assumes, as before, that information level can be ascertained as a number, at least for some of the families. The model also assumes that the variables most likely to affect information levels can be specified in advance. Data necessary for testing the model are arithmetic conversions of answers to interview questions on guarantee level and tax rate.

2. MEASUREMENT OF INFORMATION LEVELS

Data on information levels were collected as part of the thirteenth quarterly interview—which included questions on work supply, knowledge of operational rules of the experimental negative income tax program, and reactions both to the end of the experiment and to the quarterly interviews administered during the experiment. The list of contents of this quarterly reveals that it was an interview which dealt with special topics as well as with the measurement of labor supply after the conclusion of the experiment.

The timing of the interview—three months after the conclusion of the experiment—raises some problems. First, this interview yields the only measure of information level which was based on closed-end interview questions. There is no way to approach the problem of changes over time in level of information except, perhaps, to run the labor-supply equations for each quarter and assume that, all other things being equal, variations are attributable to changes in levels of information. We have not considered this a satisfactory way to proceed; therefore, no attempt has been made to measure the effect of (varying) information levels over time.

Second, because the interview was administered after the conclusion of the experiment, one has to question the accuracy of its data: Do measures taken after the conclusion of the experiment accurately reflect information levels operative during the experiment? A final, definitive answer is difficult to achieve, but it can be argued that learning was most likely to take place by the start of the second year and that a three-month lapse between the end of the experiment and the administration of the interview is not a sufficiently long time for experimental families to have forgotten what they knew about their negative income tax plans. The practical concern for reactive effects which could have resulted from repeated measurements of information level, coupled with our use of second-year data for labor response,[1] helps to ease the problems of interview timing, if it does not alleviate them altogether.

Nicholson has noted that asking families directly about information level takes the form of questions which require abstract and hypothetical thought (1975:29 ff). To rephrase Nicholson's point, the type of question—how abstract and how hypothetical—is a function to some extent of the level of knowledge which the question writer attributes to respondents. If respondents were assumed to be capable of perceiving the intricacies of carryover and averaging, then these aspects of accounting would have to be included as part of the question. On the other hand, if respondents are assumed, by and large, not to know very much about the accounting rules, then very simple questions are formulated—with the result that knowledge of some of the intricacies mentioned could result in a *wrong* answer.

Questions formulated for the New Jersey experiment assumed low to moderate levels of information and used simplified questions. The data on guarantee level were taken from a question series which first asked about the largest check the household ever received from the experiment. This question was designed to make the process less abstract, because the following question, which asked about the situation of the family's receiving no income for a year except from the experiment, related the amount to the previous question; the family was asked whether it received more or less than, or the same as, the amount mentioned in the previous question. The question for tax rate was more abstract than the question about guarantee level. It asked about the reduction in the amount of the payment per dollar of marginal income.[2] It did not deal with breakeven points or with the complexities of the accounting system.

It should therefore be noted that the questions asked about information level can be assumed to give a high number of "correct" responses, given the inherent complexity of negative income tax concepts. At the low end

---

[1] This is discussed in more detail in Section 4 of this chapter.

[2] In Trenton and Paterson–Passaic the question read:

If you had had a steady income for three or four months and then your income went up by $100.00 per month, would your payments from the Council have gone up, gone down, stayed the same, stopped coming, or what would have happened to them?

1. Would have gone up   By about how much per month? $_____ per month
2. Would have gone down
3. Would have stayed the same
4. Would have stopped coming
5. Don't know
6. Other (specify): _____
   Interviewer: Check box at right if respondent mentioned carry-over ☐.

of the indicators developed, answers represent practically no information; at the higher end, they represent low to moderate information levels.

3. NUMERIC MEASUREMENT OF TAX RATE AND GUARANTEE LEVEL

A number of difficulties were encountered in establishing numeric measures of perceived guarantee level and perceived tax rate. First, a large number of respondents answered "don't know" or, if they did answer the first part of the question, which dealt with the direction of payments (for guarantee level—whether larger or smaller than largest single check ever received; for tax rate—whether payments would go up or down), many did not venture an amount. All told, 318 respondents out of a possible 725 answered with a specific amount to questions on guarantee level; for numeric answers to the tax-rate question, the comparable numbers are 57 of 725.[3]

Numeric answers were converted to a measure which could be compared to assigned guarantee level and tax rate. For guarantee level this meant arithmetic conversion of answers to a percentage of the poverty level. Thus, perceived guarantee level

$$= \frac{\text{estimated negative tax payments in absence of income (\$ per year)}}{\text{guarantee level adjusted to 100 percent of poverty (\$ per year) plus filing fees}} \times 100.$$

For example, suppose a family of three with a 75 percent guarantee level answered that in the absence of income they would expect to receive biweekly checks of $70.00. The computer program calculated the perceived guarantee level as follows:

$$\text{perceived guarantee level} = \frac{70 \times 26}{(2103/.75) + 240} \times 100 = 60,$$

where $2103 is the family's guarantee for a year; 26 is the number of biweekly checks a family receives in a year's period of time; division by .75 is the conversion factor used to norm the guarantee level to 100 percent of the poverty level; and 240 represents the total filing fees received during a year. The addition of filing fee to the assigned guarantee level is

---

[3] The 725 represents the total number of families originally in the treatment group. In the regression equations which follow, the usable sample of 318 was further reduced because information on other variables was missing for some respondents. On average, the reduced sample for the information level–labor response equations consists of 275 subjects.

INFORMATION LEVELS AND LABOR RESPONSE

warranted by the fact that most families would probably not be able to distinguish filing fee from payments.

The computation of a tax rate figure is more involved and incurs a number of assumptions. The conceptual equation is:

(yearly guarantee level + amount of filing fee for a year) − (yearly earnings + $1200 increase in earnings stipulated in interview question) × X = yearly negative tax payments − respondent's estimate of reduction in earnings normed to a year,

where X represents the perceived tax rate and $1200 represents the increase in yearly income stipulated in the interview question. The equation represents the logic that the tax rate times earnings is subtracted from the guarantee level, and this amount represents the family's negative tax benefits for a year's period of time. Rearranging terms we have: perceived tax rate

$$= \frac{\text{(yearly guarantee + year's filing fee) + (estimated reduction in payments normed to a year)} - \text{yearly negative tax benefits}}{\text{yearly earnings} + \$1200 \text{ increase in yearly earnings stipulated by the interview question}}$$

For example, suppose a family with a tax rate of 30 percent had a guarantee level of $1950, earnings of $5421, and negative tax benefits of $770; and in response to the interview question they said that their biweekly check would be reduced by $20 if earnings were increased by $100 per month. In that case,

$$\text{perceived tax rate} = \frac{\$1950 + 240 + (\$20 \times 26) - 770}{\$5421 + \$1200} = 29\%.$$

An assumption in the above computation is that the family knows its assigned guarantee level or, alternatively, that a family can calculate reduction in payments without precise knowledge of guarantee level (though, of course, we must impute a value for purposes of calculation).

4. THE CHOICE OF EQUATIONS AND VARIABLES

Many fewer families answered the question about tax rate with statements that could be converted to numeric amounts than answered the guarantee level question. As can be seen in Table 11.1, the number of usable cases for tax rate is very much smaller than the number of cases usable for ascertaining knowledge of guarantee level. It is also clear from

Table 11.1 **Levels of Information: Guarantee and Tax Rate**

Guarantee percentage	Row N	Under	Within 10 Percent (±)	Over	Don't Know
50	(122)	25	11	7	79
75	(302)	78	20	34	170
100	(163)	54	12	13	84
125	(138)	55	11	8	64
Tax rate percentage					
30	(12)	0	4	7	1
50	(38)	13	16	8	1
70	(10)	2	3	4	1

Table 11.1 that, of those who did answer the guarantee level question, many underestimated it. Besides providing background description of the information level among participants, these numbers hold important implications for the kinds of equations we can utilize to study the effects of information level on labor supply.

Since the problem is to ascertain the effect, if any, of knowledge of tax rate and guarantee level on labor supply, the ideal or theoretically appropriate equation contains these terms for knowledge of guarantee level and tax rate, respectively: $G^* - G$, and $T^* - T$, where the asterisked letters represent perceived values. This formulation allows us to take account of discrepancy and direction. However, there are too few cases which can be formulated in this way for answers to tax-rate questions. To avoid a total loss of information about tax rate and its effect on labor supply, therefore, we employed a tax-rate measure which is not totally comparable to the $T^* - T$ formulation, but which may, nevertheless, be somewhat helpful, namely, knowledge of *direction* of tax rate effects. Thus, whereas we shall employ $G^* - G$ as the numeric formulation for guarantee level, in the absence of comparable formulation for the tax rate, we shall employ knowledge of the direction of tax rate effects.

The next concern is how to formulate the labor-supply equations because, while there is a general model to guide formulation, the actual number of possible equations is formidable. Our purpose is to present findings which relate to the general problem of the relationship between information levels and labor supply; and this guided our choice of variables as follows:

DEPENDENT VARIABLE

It was decided that two basic formulations of the dependent variable should be included, namely, the percentage difference in earnings and in hours between preenrollment and eighth quarterly. The earnings and hours differences measured as a percentage of preenrollment values are measures of labor supply that account well for differences which may be attributable to experimental effects. The choice of the preenrollment–eighth-quarterly comparison was made on the grounds that it represents a substantial passage of time while avoiding the difficulties in measurement related to phase-out. There are, however, a number of practical problems which stem from this formulation. First, because the percentage is derived by dividing a difference (eighth minus Pre) by an amount (Pre), the amount of preenrollment earnings cannot be allowed to be zero. Further, if the amount of preenrollment earnings is small, the percentage difference may be unrealistic. We have therefore chosen to eliminate those sample members whose preenrollment earnings amounted to less than \$25 per week, or whose hours worked were less than ten per week. Second, as a consequence of this operational measure of the percentage difference for hours and earnings, the female subsample was very severely restricted. Thus, for females we shall adopt the dependent variable of *level* of earnings and hours as of eighth quarterly, rather than the difference between eighth quarterly and preenrollment.

INFORMATION VARIABLES

The difference, $G^* - G$, will be included to represent numeric deviations from an assigned parameter; in addition, the formulation of over–correct–under will also be included, since it could be argued that direction might be important independent of margin of error. Knowledge of direction of tax rate will be included because this is the best available measure we have.

INDEPENDENT VARIABLES

The number of independent variables which could be included is rather large. We have therefore chosen to accept as given basic formulations derived by Nicholson (1975).

PARAMETERIZATION OF EXPERIMENTAL VARIABLES

Two parameterizations were chosen: $G - 75$ and $t - 50$, and dummy variables representing the various guarantee levels and tax rates. The first formulation represents an average effect around an arbitrary midpoint in the case of guarantee level and an obvious midpoint in the case of tax rate.

The second formulation represents effects for a given guarantee or tax rate.

The choices made regarding the formulation of variables and equations represent the boundaries for the following analysis. One can characterize these choices or boundaries as tending toward simplified versions of labor-supply equations, with the assumption implicit that if information levels do have an effect on labor supply, then these equations should be adequate to capture such an effect. It is entirely conceivable, however, that more elaborate formulations of labor supply might yield interesting qualifications to the findings reported here.

5. LABOR-SUPPLY EQUATIONS AND INFORMATION LEVEL

The subsample for analysis was chosen as follows. First, only experimental observations were included. Then, if information on variables presumed related to labor supply were missing, or if income information was inadequate, the observation was rejected. Finally, only those cases for which numerical measurements of perceived guarantee level were available were included in the final sample. Thus, the first cut was determined by experimental group, the second by labor-supply variables, and the third by an information level variable. It should be emphasized that this analysis is restricted to comparisons among families assigned to one of the experimental treatments. The response estimates provided here are, therefore, not conceptually the same as the total responses discussed in previous chapters, which are based on contrasts between control families and families assigned to experimental treatments. Estimates of the marginal effects of guarantee and tax levels—which are always based on between-treatment comparisons—are comparable to estimates in earlier chapters.

In all, approximately sixty labor-supply equations were fitted with various formulations of experimental parameters and information level variables for differences in hours and earnings for total family, husband, and wife. For the most part, information level was not related to labor response. However, in one or two instances, where formulations of the guarantee level information variables were interacted with the assigned experimental parameter, there did seem to be some effect, at least for differences in earnings equations. We shall be sparing in our presentation of equations and instead emphasize descriptively some of the implications of the few equations which indicated information level effects. For purposes of illustration, we have included one example of the basic labor-supply equations and a brief review of formulations which did not yield significant results.[4]

FAMILY EQUATIONS

The basic labor-supply equations for the total family are presented in Table 11.2. When the experimental parameters are added in the form of $G - 75$ and $t - 50$, these variables are not themselves significant and have little or no effect on other variables. However, when the variable $G^* - G$ is added to the $G - 75, t - 50$ information, there is an interesting effect in the hours equation: the coefficient for tax rate becomes significant.[5] This one major change must be qualified by the facts that (1) the coefficient itself is positive but rather small (.005), and (2) the coefficient for the variable $G^* - G$ is not significant, though it does approach statistical significance (1.611). In another hours equation, a similar result appears. Where $G^* - G$ is interacted with dummy variables for the various guarantee levels, the coefficient for the 70 percent tax rate is significant, and this time it is substantial; again, the $G^* - G$ variable singly and in interaction with guarantee dummies is not significant. Almost the same result is evident for percentage change in hours where the guarantee perception variable is formulated as over–correct–under: the coefficient for the 70 percent tax rate is significant, positive, and substantial; but the coefficients of the perception variables themselves are not.

Of course, one cannot interpret these few scattered cases of significant tax rate coefficients in a systematic way, especially since the sign of the effects is not in the expected direction. Similarly, it can be reported that in only one equation, an earnings equation where the guarantee perception variable was formulated as under–correct–over, was there an instance of a guarantee dummy variable coefficient becoming significant. Once again,

---

[4] In discussions which follow, we shall not cite the significance of variables included in equations for the purpose of controlling for regression toward the mean, namely, average hours and earnings in the total family and husband equations. The choice of an average in these two cases is based on the statistical criterion that these measures are not themselves correlated with the dependent variable. In the wife equations, hours and earnings at preenrollment were entered as independent variables to control for experimental–control differences for which we were unable to control with other variables. Thus, the coefficients on tax and guarantee parameters show the experimental response, abstracting from initial differences.

[5] It should be noted that where the significance of individual coefficients for dummy variables is discussed, significance must be related to the left-out category. Where the significance of tax rate and guarantee level dummy variable coefficients are discussed, this implicit comparison must be appreciated, since in all these equations the left-out category is not the control group but rather a certain guarantee or tax rate dummy variable.

Table 11.2 Basic Labor-Supply Equations for the Total Family

		Dependent Variable			
		Percentage Change in Hours (Eighth − Pre)/Pre		Percentage Change in Earnings (Eighth − Pre)/Pre	
Variable	Mean	Coefficient	t-Ratio	Coefficient	t-Ratio
Constant		−0.280	−1.351	.044	0.178
Trenton	.150	0.002	0.013	0.002	0.015
Paterson–Passaic	.242	−0.088	−0.725	−0.292	−1.923*
Jersey City	.317	−0.081	−0.637	−0.201	−1.279
White	.417	−0.188	−1.531	−0.169	−1.110
Black	.350	−0.027	−0.274	0.007	0.054
Age ≤ 35	.542	−0.102	−1.330	−0.108	−1.138
Age > 50	.079	.072	0.503	−0.016	−0.090
Education 0–4	.083	−0.224	−1.581	0.039	0.220
Education 5–8	.308	−0.106	−1.287	−0.072	−0.705
Education 12	.212	−0.132	−1.495	−0.242	−2.184
Education > 12	.004	−0.363	−0.703	−0.280	−0.438
Number of children	3.829	0.020	1.107	−0.025	−1.108
Number of adults	2.267	−0.121	−2.246**	−0.140	−2.129**
Average hours	39.24	0.016	6.407**	—	—
Average earnings	107.1	—	—	0.008	7.901
		$F = 4.246$**		$F = 5.256$**	

* Significant at the 10 percent level.
** Significant at the 5 percent level.

coefficients of the perception variables were not significant, and though the direction of guarantee effects was as expected, the lack of significance for most of the guarantee dummy variables meant that coefficients could well not be significantly different from zero.

In sum, the effects seen in the two basic equations are largely unchanged by the addition of other variables. Where changes are evident, the changes are linked to individual tax and guarantee levels, thus precluding any attempt to interpret these changes as systematic.

6. EQUATIONS FOR HUSBANDS

Beginning with the same basic equations used for the total family, we find somewhat different outcomes for husbands: in general, more variables seem to be significant. The addition of experimental parameters as $G − 75$ and $t − 50$ affects the hours equation but not the earnings equation: the coefficient of *guarantee* is positive, rather small, and significant; and the number of adults takes on significance. The addition of the variable of some knowledge of tax rate boosts these effects for percentage change in hours (not shown). However, it is the formulation of the guarantee perception variable as under–correct–over that seems to have systematic effects on percentage change in earnings (Table 11.3). Most of the interactions between perceived and assigned guarantee are significant, and the coefficients of guarantee are ordered as would be expected and are significant too.

To make the implications of this equation clear, it is useful to choose a hypothetical case and, with all other variables held constant except guarantee and information level, consider the impact of these two factors on labor supply (Table 11.4). For purposes of this illustration, we chose the hypothetical example of a white family with a male head who is less than thirty-five years of age, has completed the twelfth grade of school, and had exactly average earnings at preenrollment, plus a wife and one child.

The only consistent effects are found when holding information level constant. However, this is the case only for the category of "correct": the higher the guarantee level, the smaller are the increases in earnings. Holding guarantee level constant, effects are not ordered by our expectations for any of the guarantee categories. That is, we do not find the largest percentage increase in the "under" category, followed by "correct" and "over."

In sum, for a number of equations for husbands we found "spot" significance. Only for percentage change in earnings where the perception variables were formulated as under–correct–over and interacted with assigned guarantee did outcomes seem systematically related to guarantee information level. However, upon further inspection of the implications of the equation, it was found that outcomes were ordered as expected only for the "correct" category. (It should be noted that entering knowledge of direction of tax rate did not alter the results for this equation.)

7. EQUATIONS FOR WIVES

As mentioned earlier, it was not possible to formulate percentage difference equations for hours and earnings for wives, given the practical difficulties which stem from defining the dependent variable as a percentage difference. By restricting the sample to those who earned more than $25 per week at preenrollment or who worked more than ten hours, only forty-eight cases remained. Even if we had excluded only those wives who had zero earnings, the number in the sample would have been re-

Table 11.3 Husband Labor-Supply Equation, Interaction of Under–Correct–Over Information Dummy Variables with Guarantee Level Dummy Variables

Variable	Mean	Dependent Variable: Percentage Change in Earnings (Eighth − Pre)/Pre	
		Coefficient	t-Ratio
Constant		0.489	0.975
Trenton	0.141	−0.177	−1.084
Paterson–Passaic	0.247	−0.458	−3.138**
Jersey City	0.322	−0.313	−2.060**
White	0.418	−0.156	−1.064
Black	0.339	−0.080	−0.664
Age ≤ 35	0.542	−0.025	−0.270
Age > 50	0.075	−0.107	−0.608
Education 0–4	0.084	0.234	1.342
Education 5–8	0.304	0.015	0.147
Education 12	0.216	−0.245	−2.221**
Education > 12	0.004	0.326	0.544
Number of children	3.881	−0.010	−0.448
Number of adults	2.264	−0.073	−1.086
Average earnings	100.0	0.009	7.481**
Guarantee 75	0.370	−0.542	−1.000
Guarantee 100	0.264	−0.803	−1.709*
Guarantee 125	0.251	−0.956	−1.992**
Tax 50	0.555	−0.120	−0.978
Tax 70	0.238	−0.080	−0.524
Under	0.731	−0.571	−1.297
Over	0.181	−0.719	−1.397
$G75$ underestimated	0.238	0.474	0.836
$G75$ overestimated	0.119	0.815	1.303
$G100$ underestimated	0.198	0.932	1.873*
$G100$ overestimated	0.031	1.016	1.680*
$G125$ underestimated	0.207	0.967	1.916*
$G125$ overestimated	0.013	1.337	1.981**
		$F = 3.518**$	

* Significant at the 10 percent level.
** Significant at the 5 percent level.

duced almost to the same extent. Therefore, we chose to formulate the equations for wives as equations which predict level of earnings and hours at the eighth quarterly. Without repeating all the formulations employed, since they are the same as those used for total family and for husbands, we find that only for an hours equation where the guarantee information

Table 11.4 Predicted Percentage Differences in Earnings, (Eighth − Pre)/Pre, for a Hypothetical Husband

Perception of Assigned Guarantee	Plan			
	125–50	100–50	75–50	50–50
Under	0.520	0.638	0.441	0.509
Correct	0.124	0.277	0.538	1.080
Over	0.745	0.574	−0.446	0.361

variable is formulated as under–correct–over are individual tax and guarantee coefficients significant. As before, these outcomes cannot be interpreted systematically; therefore, for all intents and purposes we can say that information does not significantly affect labor response of female spouses.

8. REGRESSION OF PERCEIVED PARAMETERS ON ASSIGNED PARAMETERS AND OTHER VARIABLES

As noted earlier, even if perceived experimental parameters are related to labor-supply outcomes, these relationships do not automatically lead to difficulties in interpreting the experimental results. The nature of the relationship is also important. It is therefore appropriate to regress the perceived or information variable on assigned tax parameters and other variables to determine the nature of the perception. We can assume that a relationship between a perceived parameter and variables such as education, race, and an assigned tax parameter would not be indicative of a bias, since these variables are likely to affect labor supply in an experiment in much the same way as in a national program. The variable of city is likely to affect labor supply in a national program as well, but this variable can be taken as a proxy for enrollment practices since experience gained with time probably was reflected in somewhat different enrollment practices, especially in Scranton and Jersey City, the last cities to be enrolled.

There are two choices for the formulation of the dependent variable. The first is simply to define the dependent variable as the value of the perceived parameter; the second is to define it as the difference between the perceived and assigned values. However, both approaches are essentially identical. For our purposes we have chosen to present the first formulation.

In addition to city, race, education, and assigned tax parameters, we included an "experimental variable." The idea behind this last, constructed variable was the notion that experience, rather than enrollment practices alone, might determine a family's perception of tax parameters. For guarantee level, the constructed variable reflected a family's experience with low income—since we hypothesized that the lower the family's income (here we have used the income value during the last year of the experiment because our information-level data come from a postexperiment interview), the greater the opportunity to perceive and therefore learn about their assigned guarantee level. To construct a dummy variable, low income was related to a family's potential benefits as determined by assigned guarantee level, and families were assigned to medium high, medium low, and very low income groups.

Table 11.5 presents the equation in which perceived guarantee level is the left-hand or dependent variable. From the equation where perceived guarantee was entered as such, it can be seen that assigned guarantee level is significant. It is also apparent that assigned guarantee level is underperceived; all other variables constant, families perceive about 54 percent of this assigned guarantee parameter. Equally apparent is the importance of the constructed low-income variable: the lower the income, the higher the perceived value of the guarantee parameter.

For the equation with G^* as the dependent variable, we defined a hypothetical case similar to the one defined for the male's earnings equations.

Table 11.5 **Perceived Guarantee Level as the Dependent Variable**

Variable	Mean	Dependent Variable, G^*	
		Coefficient	t-Ratio
Constant		18.566	1.437
Trenton	0.136	−2.292	−0.231
Paterson–Passaic	0.307	1.215	0.139
Jersey City	0.292	−13.334	−1.462
Assigned guarantee	91.10	0.546	5.411**
White	0.364	−8.745	−1.135
Spanish-speaking	0.231	−5.583	−0.873
Education ≤ 4	0.087	6.434	0.703
Education 5–8	0.277	5.947	1.014
Education 12	0.208	2.214	0.346
Education > 12	0.015	−19.236	−0.999
Medium low income	0.280	13.357	2.388**
Very low income	0.235	21.719	3.575**

$F = 5.860^{**}$

** Significant at the 5 percent level.

In this case, we chose a white family living in Trenton whose head has a twelfth-grade education. We varied guarantee level and the experimental variable. From Table 11.6 it is apparent that in most cells guarantee level is underestimated, with the exception of two cells with a 50 percent guarantee level. In the main, however, experience with low or very low income does affect perception in sizable amounts.

To take account of the importance of groups of variables, one group at a time was dropped from the equations presented in Table 11.5, and changes in the F-ratio were inspected. This technique confirmed what could be derived intuitively from the original equations, namely, that city, race, and education did not contribute significantly to explanatory power, but that assigned guarantee level and experience with low income did.

Equations were run where $T^* - T$ and T^* were dependent variables. Inspection of the correlation coefficients for T^* and T revealed virtually no relationship; however, the small number of cases precludes making *any* tax-rate inferences, including whether or not a correlation exists between perceived and assigned tax rates. We shall have to await evidence from other income-maintenance experiments.

9. THE NATURE OF THE REDUCED SAMPLE

The decision to include observations in this analysis was based first on whether or not numerical answers had been supplied to questions on guarantee and tax rate. Further reductions in the sample were made based on the completeness of income and other information, and on the basis of level of hours and earnings. Since the use of a subsample could affect outcomes, it is proper to ask about the nature of the subsample. This we have done in a number of ways for the subsample of male heads, since it was for this group that some systematic differences by information level about the guarantee were found.

First, we regressed the constructed variable "included–excluded" on variables utilized in the equations presented above (Table 11.7). On the

Table 11.6 **Predicted Guarantee Level for a Hypothetical Family**

Income Level	Guarantee Level			
	125	100	75	50
Medium high	78	64	51	37
Medium low	91	78	64	50
Very low	100	86	72	59

Table 11.7 Probability of Being Excluded from the Sample

Variable	Mean	Dependent Variable: Included–Excluded	
		Coefficient	t-Ratio
Constant		0.337	2.089**
Trenton	0.107	−0.220	−2.194**
Paterson–Passaic	0.261	−0.059	−0.703
Jersey City	0.325	0.036	0.434
White	0.428	0.107	1.243
Black	0.362	0.099	1.441
Age ≤ 35	0.510	0.059	1.058
Age > 50	0.084	−0.045	−0.479
Education 0–4	0.090	0.134	1.497
Education 5–8	0.336	0.037	0.677
Education 12	0.199	−0.006	−0.099
Education > 12	0.011	0.140	0.619
Number of children	3.839	0.012	0.876
Number of adults	2.330	0.064	1.881*
Earnings at preenrollment	82.69	−0.001	−0.122
Guarantee 75	0.411	−0.081	−1.104
Guarantee 100	0.218	−0.195	−2.221**
Guarantee 125	0.233	−0.238	−2.783**
Tax 50	0.559	0.069	1.021
Tax 70	0.235	0.114	1.453
Number of children ≤ 6	0.769	−0.164	−2.480**
		$F = 1.682$**	

* Significant at the 10 percent level.
** Significant at the 5 percent level.

basis of this equation, we have constructed the probability of exclusion by plan for the hypothetical case used previously.[6] Then, assuming that the effects of tax rate and guarantee level were additive, we arrived at the probability of exclusion for various plans (Table 11.8). This table presents the implications of the regression equation. In the main, some of the

Table 11.8 Probability of Exclusion for a Hypothetical Case, by Plan

Tax Rate	Guarantee Level			
	50	75	100	125
30	.475	.393	—	—
50	.406	.462	.349	.306
70	—	.507	.394	—

[6] The child in the example was assumed to be older than six years of age.

INFORMATION LEVELS AND LABOR RESPONSE

higher plans (under the assumption of additivity of probabilities) are slightly underrepresented, whereas most of the lower plans are fairly evenly represented.

To show the inclusion or exclusion of observations by variables which could presumably affect perception of tax parameters, we have broken out the experimental sample by selected variables (Table 11.9). The categories which are most unrepresentative are those from the Trenton site and those who are Spanish-speaking. Average weekly earnings and average weekly hours for the two subsamples are rather similar.

10. CONCLUSION

Information level by and large was not found to be associated with labor response. However, those husbands whose perception of their guarantee level was "correct" were found to work less, the higher their guar-

Table 11.9 Included and Excluded Members of the Sample, by Selected Variables

	Included (N = 263)		Excluded (N = 204)	
	Percentage	N	Percentage	N
City				
Trenton	72	(36)	28	(14)
Paterson–Passaic	59	(72)	41	(50)
Jersey City	51	(78)	49	(74)
Scranton	54	(77)	46	(66)
Ethnicity				
White	54	(108)	46	(92)
Black	55	(93)	45	(76)
Spanish-speaking	23	(62)	77	(36)
Age				
≤35	58	(139)	42	(99)
35–50	55	(104)	45	(86)
>50	51	(20)	49	(19)
Education				
0–4	52	(22)	48	(20)
5–8	55	(86)	45	(71)
9–11	57	(108)	43	(80)
12	58	(54)	42	(39)
>12	40	(20)	60	(30)
Average weekly earnings at preenrollment (dollars)	83.33		81.85	
Average weekly hours worked at preenrollment (hours)	35.08		33.76	

NOTE: "Included–excluded" refers to the sample of experimentals with valid income and demographic data.

antee level. It was also found that those who had experienced low income—and hence were receiving higher payments than others on the same plan—had perceptions closer to the actual value of their assigned guarantee than those who had higher incomes.

The interpretation of these findings is not straightforward because it is difficult to know which came first, labor-supply response or information. Families could have made labor-supply response decisions with respect to their tax plans either because (1) they possessed information and decided, on the basis of that information, what they wanted to do, or (2) faced with a change in labor force participation externally inspired, they learned more about their tax plans. No doubt both kinds of situation existed in the experiment, just as they would no doubt exist in a national negative income tax program. However, the problem is how to interpret the results in light of both these possibilities.

An initial reaction is to say that the results for husbands seem to indicate that those who possess correct information will make choices as would be expected from economic theory—the higher the guarantee, the lower the incentive. Yet the regression of perceived guarantee on variables related to labor response, including experience with low income, is consistent with the interpretation that experience contributes heavily to one's perception of guarantee level. Probably both explanations apply.

In evaluating the implications of these findings, we must be aware that the information level of recipients can be controlled, to some degree, through administrative practices. Variability of income, and thus the opportunity to learn automatically about one's tax and guarantee rate by seeing the payments received fluctuate, is not administratively controllable. Thus, the importance of one factor vis-à-vis the other may ultimately depend on the uses made of the experimental data.

ACKNOWLEDGMENTS

We wish to thank Walter Nicholson for his advice and for providing us with his forthcoming paper on information levels issues. Albert Rees and Glen Cain provided helpful comments on the first draft of this paper.

REFERENCES

Nicholson, W. 1975. Participants' understanding of social science experiments: Issues in analysis and design. Unpublished paper. Princeton, N.J.: Mathematica Policy Research.

12 Spline functions and their applications in regression analysis

Dale J. Poirier

A *polynomial spline of degree n* is a piecewise polynomial function made up of polynomials of degree at most n such that the spline and its derivatives, up to and including the $(n-1)$th, are continuous. Throughout the analysis of the experiment, spline functions were used for two basic purposes.

First, interpreting their piecewise nature as reflecting the occurrence of "structural change" which manifests itself through jump discontinuities in the nth derivative, splines were used to test for changes in behavioral responses for adjoining groups in, say, the tax rate and guarantee dimensions or in the age and education dimensions.[1] With regard to the tax-rate and guarantee dimensions, it was noted early in the planning stages that the various experimental plans should not be treated as totally distinct, independent of each other, but that their similarities (common tax or guarantee rates) should be exploited. A continuous, but piecewise, function achieves precisely these goals.[2] Second, based on their great flexibility, splines were used as general functional forms to represent time dimensions.

[1] In all the applications discussed here, the points of potential structural change are assumed known.

[2] For a discussion of spline representations of the tax- and guarantee-rate dimensions, as well as other parameterizations of the treatment, see Poirier (1974).

The purpose of this chapter is to provide both readers and prospective researchers with an introduction to spline functions and to show how they were used in the analysis of the experiment.[3]

1. LINEAR SPLINES

A *linear spline* is a continuous piecewise linear function. An example of a linear spline $S(x)$ with three segments is given in Figure 12.1. The abscissa values $\bar{x}_1$ and $\bar{x}_2 (\bar{x}_1 < \bar{x}_2)$ are called *knots*.

In general, if $S(x)$ is a linear spline in x with knots $\bar{x}_1 < \bar{x}_2 < \cdots < \bar{x}_{k-1}$, then $S(x)$ can be written as

$$S(x) = \beta_0 + \beta_1 x_1 + \beta_2 x_2 + \cdots + \beta_k x_k, \tag{1}$$

where

$x_1 = x$
$x_2 = x - \bar{x}_1$ if $x > \bar{x}_1$, 0 if $x \leq \bar{x}_1$
.
.
.
$x_k = x - \bar{x}_{k-1}$ if $x > \bar{x}_{k-1}$, 0 if $x \leq \bar{x}_{k-1}$.

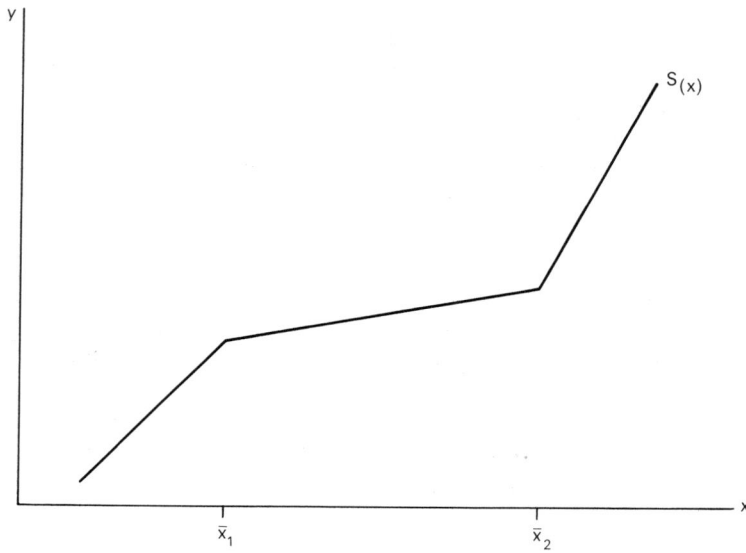

Figure 12.1 Linear spline with three segments.

---

[3] No attempt at exhaustiveness will be made. For more detailed discussions see Poirier (1973, 1976).

The coefficient β_1 represents the slope of the spline over the first interval, and each of the remaining coefficients $\beta_j (j = 2, 3, \ldots, k)$ represents the *change* in the slope from interval $(j - 1)$ to interval j, respectively. Hence, the first derivative of a linear spline is a step function with jump discontinuities equal to $\beta_j (j = 2, 3, \ldots, k)$ at the knots. The actual slope over the jth segment is $(\beta_1 + \beta_2 + \cdots + \beta_j)$.

As the deterministic part of a conventional regression model—that is, letting $S(x) = E(y)$—equation (1) is attractive because it is linear in the unknown regression parameters $\beta_0, \beta_1, \ldots, \beta_k$; there are no constraints on these parameters; the transformed variables $x_1, x_2, \ldots, x_k$ can be easily constructed using only transformation card operations permitted in standard regression packages; and, finally, under the classical disturbance term assumptions, the t-ratio corresponding to $\beta_j (j = 2, 3, \ldots, k)$ indicates the statistical significance of the change in slope over intervals $(j - 1)$ and j. Since $\beta_j = 0$ implies the same slope over intervals $(j - 1)$ and j, if β_j is significantly nonzero, then this is consistent with the idea of some sort of "structural change" occurring at $\bar{x}_{j-1}$.

It is interesting to note the relationship of the linear spline to two rather common regression functions. Since a linear polynomial is a linear spline in which $\beta_2 = \beta_3 = \cdots = \beta_k = 0$, the standard "linear in x" model is a special case. The familiar discontinuous piecewise linear model often used in regression analysis is a limiting case of a linear spline in which one of the knots approaches an adjacent knot. This is illustrated in Figure 12.2 for the case in which $\bar{x}_1$ approaches $\bar{x}_2$ and the second interval approaches zero.

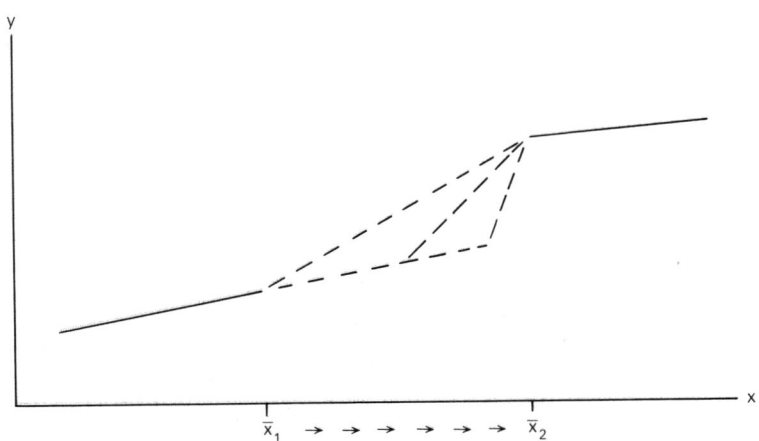

Figure 12.2 Limiting case in which one knot approaches another knot.

2. CUBIC SPLINES

In practice, a third-degree polynomial spline (that is, a *cubic spline*) is usually flexible enough to work satisfactorily whenever a higher degree spline than a linear spline is desired. However, the transformed variables needed to represent the cubic spline are not as easily constructed as in the case of a linear spline.[4] This section presents (without proof) the necessary ingredients for constructing these transformed variables.

To begin, let the set $\Delta = \{\bar{x}_0 < \bar{x}_1 < \cdots < \bar{x}_k\}$ of abscissa values be referred to as a *mesh* of $[\bar{x}_0, \bar{x}_k]$ and the $k + 1 \geq 3$ individual points $\bar{x}_j$ $(j = 0, 1, \ldots, k)$ as *knots*. Let $Y = \{y_0, y_1, \ldots, y_k\}$ be an associated set of ordinates. Then a *cubic spline on Δ interpolating to Y*, denoted $S_\Delta(x)$, is a function satisfying the following three conditions: (i) $S_\Delta(x) \in C^2[\bar{x}_0, \bar{x}_k]$; (ii) $S_\Delta(x)$ coincides with a polynomial of degree at most three on the intervals $[\bar{x}_{j-1}, \bar{x}_j]$ $(j = 1, 2, \ldots, k)$, and (iii) $S_\Delta(\bar{x}_j) = y_j$ $(j = 1, 2, \ldots, k)$. For the purposes of the applications discussed here, all cubic splines will also satisfy: (iv) $S_\Delta''(\bar{x}_0) = S_\Delta''(\bar{x}_k) = 0$. Cubic splines that satisfy "end condition" (iv) are known as *natural cubic splines*.

While many different parameterizations of the cubic spline are possible, in general the most convenient form is to express $S_\Delta(x)$ as a linear function of $\mathbf{y} = [y_0, y_1, \ldots, y_k]'$, the ordinate vector of values of $S_\Delta(x)$ at the knots. Thus, the purpose of this section is for any value x to obtain a vector of transformed variables $\mathbf{w} = [w_0, w_1, \ldots, w_k]$ such that

$$S_\Delta(x) = \mathbf{w}\mathbf{y}. \tag{2}$$

To obtain such a vector $\mathbf{w}$, let $h_j = \bar{x}_j - \bar{x}_{j-1}$ $(j = 1, 2, \ldots, k)$ be the interval lengths and let $\lambda_j = h_{j+1}/(h_j + h_{j+1})$. Also define the $(k + 1) \times (k + 1)$ matrices

$$\Lambda = \begin{bmatrix} 2 & 0 & 0 & \cdots & 0 & 0 & 0 \\ 1 - \lambda_1 & 2 & \lambda_1 & \cdots & 0 & 0 & 0 \\ 0 & 1 - \lambda_2 & 2 & \cdots & 0 & 0 & 0 \\ \vdots & \vdots & \vdots & & \vdots & \vdots & \vdots \\ 0 & 0 & 0 & \cdots & 2 & \lambda_{k-2} & 0 \\ 0 & 0 & 0 & \cdots & 1 - \lambda_{k-1} & 2 & \lambda_{k-1} \\ 0 & 0 & 0 & \cdots & 0 & 0 & 2 \end{bmatrix},$$

---

[4] While it is possible to parameterize a cubic spline in a fashion similar to that introduced for a linear spline (i.e., in terms of polynomial coefficients and jump discontinuities in the nth derivative), the resulting transformed variables produce severe ill-conditioning of the regressor matrix.

$$\Theta = \begin{bmatrix} 0 & 0 & 0 & \cdots & 0 & 0 & 0 \\ \dfrac{6}{h_1(h_1+h_2)} & \dfrac{-6}{h_1 h_2} & \dfrac{6}{h_2(h_1+h_2)} & \cdots & 0 & 0 & 0 \\ 0 & \dfrac{6}{h_2(h_2+h_3)} & \dfrac{-6}{h_2 h_3} & \cdots & 0 & 0 & 0 \\ \vdots & \vdots & \vdots & & \vdots & \vdots & \vdots \\ 0 & 0 & 0 & \cdots & \dfrac{-6}{h_{k-2}h_{k-1}} & \dfrac{6}{h_{k-1}(h_{k-2}+h_{k-1})} & 0 \\ 0 & 0 & 0 & \cdots & \dfrac{6}{h_{k-1}(h_{k-1}+h_k)} & \dfrac{-6}{h_{k-1}h_k} & \dfrac{6}{h_k(h_{k-1}+h_k)} \\ 0 & 0 & 0 & \cdots & 0 & 0 & 0 \end{bmatrix}$$

For $\bar{x}_{j-1} \leq x \leq \bar{x}_j$, define the row vectors $\mathbf{p} = [p_0, p_1, \ldots, p_k]$ and $\mathbf{q} = [q_0, q_1, \ldots, q_k]$ such that[5]

$$p_i = \begin{cases} [(\bar{x}_j - x)/6h_j][(\bar{x}_j - x)^2 - h_j^2], & \text{if } i = j-1 \\ [(x - \bar{x}_{j-1})/6h_j][(x - \bar{x}_{j-1})^2 - h_j^2], & \text{if } i = j \\ 0, & \text{otherwise} \end{cases}, \text{ and}$$

$$q_i = \begin{cases} [(\bar{x}_j - x)/h_j], & \text{if } i = j-1 \\ [(x - \bar{x}_{j-1})/h_j], & \text{if } i = j \\ 0, & \text{otherwise} \end{cases}.$$

Then $S_\Delta(x)$ is given by (2), where

$$w = \mathbf{p}\Lambda^{-1}\theta + \mathbf{q}. \tag{3}$$

Having obtained an expression for $S_\Delta(x)$ as a linear function of y, it becomes quite easy to use the natural cubic spline in regression analysis. All that needs to be done is to perform transformation (3) on each observation of the independent variable x, and then estimate the unknown regression coefficient vector y in the standard way. However, care must be exercised when there are other explanatory variables in the model, since implicit in estimating the vector y of ordinates is an intercept term for x.[6] In other words, either there can be no constant term or an exhaustive classification of dummy variables elsewhere in the regression equation; or one of the transformed variables, say w_0, must be omitted. This latter case implies that the ordinate value y_0 at the knot $\bar{x}_0$ must be zero.

To help serve as an example of how a natural cubic spline can be used, consider the natural cubic experimental time spline used in Chapter 14.

---

[5] For $x < \bar{x}_0$ or $x > \bar{x}_k$, $S_\Delta(x)$ is determined by using the polynomial segment for the first or last interval, respectively.

[6] A similar situation holds in the case of a linear spline for β_0 in (1).

Table 12.1 Transformed Variables for a Natural Cubic Spline over $\Delta = \{0, 2, 6, 12\}$

x	w_0	w_1	w_2	w_3
0	1.000	0.0000	0.0000	0.0000
1	0.4330	0.6071	−.04464	0.004464
2	0.0000	1.000	0.0000	0.0000
3	−.2009	1.025	0.1942	−.01786
4	−.2142	0.7679	0.4821	−.03571
5	−.1205	0.3772	0.7790	−.03571
6	0.0000	0.0000	1.000	0.0000
7	0.08185	−.2455	1.079	0.08482
8	0.1190	−.3571	1.024	0.2143
9	0.1205	−.3616	0.8616	0.3795
10	0.09524	−.2857	0.6190	0.5714
11	0.05208	−.1563	0.3229	0.7813
12	0.0000	0.0000	0.0000	1.000

Here the mesh in quarter time is $\Delta = \{0, 2, 6, 12\}$, the interval lengths are $h_1 = 2$, $h_2 = 4$, and $h_3 = 6$, respectively, and $\lambda_1 = 2/3$, $\lambda_2 = 3/5$. Performing transformation (3) on all possible experimental time (measured in quarters) observations, namely $x = 0, 1, \ldots, 12$, yields the transformed variables given in Table 12.1. Omitting w_0 from the regression equation, as is done in Chapter 14, implies a value zero for the ordinate y_0 of $S_\Delta(x)$ at preenrollment ($\bar{x}_0 = 0$).

3. PERIODIC CUBIC SPLINES

A cubic spline $S_\Delta(x)$ defined by conditions (i) through (iii) in Section 2 is said to be *periodic* with period $(\bar{x}_k - \bar{x}_0)$ if and only if

$$S_\Delta^{(m)}(\bar{x}_0) = S_\Delta^{(m)}(\bar{x}_k) \quad (m = 0, 1, 2). \tag{4}$$

Otherwise, $S_\Delta(x)$ is said to be *nonperiodic*.

Condition (4) serves as a sort of "end condition" for the periodic cubic spline analogous to condition (iv) in Section 2. Condition (4) merely says that in functional value and first two derivatives, $S_\Delta(x)$ is well behaved in the sense that a smooth hookup can be made if the curve is translated along the x-axis by $(\bar{x}_k - \bar{x}_0)$. Given the mesh Δ and the ordinate vector y, condition (4) uniquely defines a periodic cubic spline.

To obtain a mathematical formulation for the periodic cubic spline analogous to equation (2) of Section 2, the following procedure is used. Analogous to the matrices Λ and θ of Section 2, define the $k \times k$ matrices

SPLINE FUNCTIONS IN REGRESSION ANALYSIS

$$\tilde{\Lambda} = \begin{bmatrix} 2 & \lambda_1 & 0 & \cdots & 0 & 0 & 1-\lambda_1 \\ 1-\lambda_2 & 2 & \lambda_2 & \cdots & 0 & 0 & 0 \\ 0 & 1-\lambda_1 & 2 & \cdots & 0 & 0 & 0 \\ \cdot & \cdot & \cdot & & \cdot & \cdot & \cdot \\ \cdot & \cdot & \cdot & & \cdot & \cdot & \cdot \\ 0 & 0 & 0 & \cdots & 2 & \lambda_{k-2} & 0 \\ 0 & 0 & 0 & \cdots & 1-\lambda_{k-1} & 2 & \lambda_{k-1} \\ \lambda_k & 0 & 0 & \cdots & 0 & 1-\lambda_k & 2 \end{bmatrix},$$

$$\tilde{\Theta} = \begin{bmatrix} \frac{-6}{h_1 h_2} & \frac{6}{h_2(h_1+h_2)} & 0 & \cdots & 0 & 0 & \frac{6}{h_1(h_1+h_2)} \\ \frac{6}{h_2(h_2+h_3)} & \frac{-6}{h_2 h_3} & \frac{6}{h_3(h_2+h_3)} & \cdots & 0 & 0 & 0 \\ 0 & \frac{6}{h_3(h_3+h_4)} & \frac{-6}{h_3 h_4} & \cdots & 0 & 0 & 0 \\ \cdot & \cdot & \cdot & & \cdot & \cdot & \cdot \\ \cdot & \cdot & \cdot & & \cdot & \cdot & \cdot \\ 0 & 0 & 0 & \cdots & \frac{-6}{h_{k-2}h_{k-1}} & \frac{6}{h_{k-1}(h_{k-2}+h_{k-1})} & 0 \\ 0 & 0 & 0 & \cdots & \frac{6}{h_{k-1}(h_{k-1}+h_k)} & \frac{-6}{h_{k-1}h_k} & \frac{6}{h_k(h_{k-1}+h_k)} \\ \frac{6}{h_1(h_k+h_1)} & 0 & 0 & \cdots & 0 & \frac{6}{h_k(h_k+h_1)} & \frac{-6}{h_k h_1} \end{bmatrix},$$

and the vectors

$\tilde{\mathbf{w}} = [\tilde{w}_1, \tilde{w}_2, \ldots, \tilde{w}_k]$,
$\tilde{\mathbf{y}} = [\tilde{y}_1, \tilde{y}_2, \ldots, \tilde{y}_k]'$.

For $\bar{x}_{j-1} \le x \le \bar{x}_j$ ($j = 2, 3, \ldots, k$), define the row vectors $\tilde{\mathbf{p}} = [\tilde{p}_1, \tilde{p}_2, \ldots, \tilde{p}_k]$ and $\tilde{\mathbf{q}} = [\tilde{q}_1, \tilde{q}_2, \ldots, \tilde{q}_k]$ such that

$$\tilde{p}_{im} = \begin{cases} [(\bar{x}_j - x)/6h_j][(\bar{x}_j - x)^2 - h_j^2], & \text{for } m = j-1 \\ [(x - \bar{x}_{j-1})/6h_j][(x - \bar{x}_{j-1})^2 - h_j^2], & \text{for } m = j \\ 0, & \text{otherwise} \end{cases},$$

$$\tilde{q}_{im} = \begin{cases} (\bar{x}_j - x)/h_j, & \text{for } m = j-1 \\ (x - \bar{x}_{j-1})/h_j, & \text{for } m = j \\ 0, & \text{otherwise} \end{cases}.$$

For $j = 1$ define

$$\tilde{p}_{im} = \begin{cases} [(\bar{x}_1 - x)/6h_1][(\bar{x}_1 - x)^2 - h_1^2], & \text{for } m = k \\ [(x - \bar{x}_0)/6h_1](x - \bar{x}_0)^2 - h_1^2], & \text{for } m = 1 \\ 0, & \text{otherwise} \end{cases},$$

$$\tilde{q}_{im} = \begin{cases} (\bar{x}_1 - x)/h_1, & \text{for } m = k \\ (x - \bar{x}_0)/h_1, & \text{for } m = 1 \\ 0, & \text{otherwise} \end{cases}.$$

Then,

$$S_\Delta(x) = \tilde{w}\tilde{y}, \qquad (5)$$

where

$$\tilde{w} = \tilde{p}\tilde{\Lambda}^{-1}\tilde{\theta} + \tilde{q}. \qquad (6)$$

Again, to help serve as an example of how a periodic cubic spline can be used, consider the calendar periodic cubic time spline used in Chapter 3. Here the mesh in quarter time is $\Delta = \{0, 3, 6, 9, 12\}$, the interval lengths are $h_1 = h_2 = h_3 = h_4 = 3$, and $\lambda_1 = \lambda_2 = \lambda_3 = \lambda_4 = \frac{1}{2}$. Performing transformation (6) on all possible seasonal calendar time observations (measured in months) yields the transformed variables given in Table 12.2. Since $S_\Delta(x)$ defined by (6) contains an implicit intercept, the use of $S_\Delta(x)$ in an equation already containing an intercept would result in exact collinearity. Thus, one of the elements of $\tilde{w}$ must be dropped. In Chapter 3, $\tilde{w}_4$ was dropped, which implies that the parameters to be estimated are $\tilde{y}_1, \tilde{y}_2,$ and $\tilde{y}_3$, namely, the seasonal deviations from, say, the overall time trend.

4. BILINEAR SPLINES

One of the simplest ways of representing the relationship of the dependent variable y and two explanatory variables u and v is the bilinear form

$$y = a + bu + cv + duv \qquad (7)$$

which allows for both "main effects," as manifested through the terms bu and cv, and an "interaction effect," namely, duv. While it may be reasonable to expect equation (7) to be a valid representation over particular regions of u-v space, often it is not reasonable to expect this to be true over the entire u-v space. In such cases it may be appropriate to envision y as a "piecewise function" of u and v, where the "pieces" are functions of the form (7), but may have different coefficients. When it is possible to define the partitioning of u-v space in terms of well-defined rectangles, and the overall surface is also continuous (i.e., the pieces are joined together), then the resulting surface is a *bilinear spline*.[7]

---

[7] A bilinear spline can also be thought of as arising from the interaction of two linear splines.

Table 12.2 Transformed Variables for a Periodic Cubic Spline over $\Delta = \{0, 3, 6, 9, 12\}$

x	$\tilde{w}_1$	$\tilde{w}_2$	$\tilde{w}_3$	$\tilde{w}_4$
0	0.0000	0.0000	0.0000	1.000
1	0.3704	−.05556	−.1111	0.7963
2	0.7963	−.1111	0.05556	0.3704
3	1.000	0.0000	0.0000	0.0000
4	0.7963	0.3704	−0.5556	−.1111
5	0.3704	0.7963	−.1111	−.05556
6	0.0000	1.000	0.0000	0.0000
7	−.1111	0.7963	0.3704	−.05556
8	−.05556	0.3704	0.7963	−.1111
9	0.0000	0.0000	1.000	0.0000
10	−.05556	−.1111	0.7963	0.3704
11	−.1111	−.05556	0.3704	0.7963
12	0.0000	0.0000	0.0000	1.000

This section provides a mathematical formulation of a bilinear spline and a means for testing, in a regression context, whether the estimated pieces are significantly different.

Consider the two meshes $\Delta_u = \{\bar{u}_1 < \bar{u}_2 < \cdots < \bar{u}_{I-1}\}$ and $\Delta_v = \{\bar{v}_1 < \bar{v}_2 < \cdots < \bar{v}_{J-1}\}$. These meshes define a rectangular grid in $\bar{u}$-$\bar{v}$ space consisting of IJ rectangles as illustrated in Figure 12.3. For any point (u,v) define the transformed variables

$u_1 = u,$
$u_i = \max(u - \bar{u}_{i-1}, 0) \ (i = 2, 3, \ldots, I),$
$v_1 = v,$
$v_j = \max(v - \bar{v}_{j-1}, 0) \ (j = 2, 3, \ldots, J),$
$w_{ij} = u_i v_j (i = 1, 2, \ldots, I) (j = 1, 2, \ldots, J),$

and the corresponding row vectors

$\mathbf{u} = [u_1, u_2, \ldots, u_I],$
$\mathbf{v} = [v_1, v_2, \ldots, v_J],$
$w_i = [w_{i1}, w_{i2}, \ldots, w_{iJ}] \ (i = 1, 2, \ldots, I),$
$\mathbf{w} = [w_1', w_2', \ldots, w'_I].$

Then, given the coefficient vectors

$\boldsymbol{\alpha} = [\alpha_1, \alpha_2, \ldots, \alpha_I],$
$\boldsymbol{\delta} = [\delta_1, \delta_2, \ldots, \delta_J]',$
$\gamma_i = [\gamma_{i1}, \gamma_{i2}, \ldots, \gamma_{iJ}] \ (i = 1, 2, \ldots, I),$
$\boldsymbol{\gamma} = [\gamma_1', \gamma_2', \ldots, \gamma_I]',$

and the intercept β_0, y is defined to be a bilinear spline over Δ_u and Δ_v if

$$y = \beta_0 + \mathbf{u}\boldsymbol{\alpha} + \mathbf{v}\boldsymbol{\delta} + \mathbf{w}\boldsymbol{\gamma}. \tag{8}$$

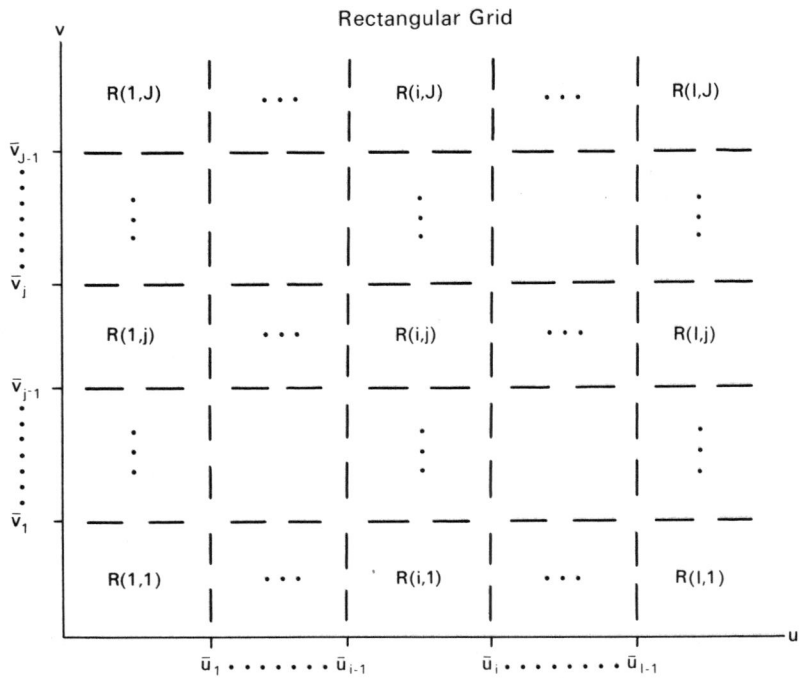

Figure 12.3 Rectangular grid.

If the bilinear spline is being used together with other independent variables in a regression equation, then β_0 must be dropped from (8) if a constant term or exhaustive dummy variable classification is included elsewhere in the equation.

While representation (8) is handy for regression purposes, since it expresses y as a linear combination of the $(1 + I + J + IJ)$ unknown parameters β_0, α, δ, and γ, it disguises the inherent piecewise nature of the bilinear spline. This can be corrected by defining the $4IJ$ coefficients a_{ij}, b_{ij}, c_{ij}, d_{ij} ($i = 1, 2, \ldots, I$) ($j = 1, 2, \ldots, J$) such that for $(u, v) \epsilon R\ (ij)$,

$$y = a_{ij} + b_{ij}(u - \bar{u}_{i-1}) + c_{ij}(v - \bar{v}_{j-1}) + d_{ij}(u - \bar{u}_{i-1})(v - \bar{v}_{j-1}), \quad (9)$$

where $\bar{u}_0 < \bar{u}_1$ and $\bar{v}_0 < \bar{v}_1$ are chosen arbitrarily. The intuitive appeal of representation (9) is that it expresses y as a simple bilinear surface over $R(i,j)$ with the origin translated to $(\bar{u}_{i-1}, \bar{v}_{j-1})$.[8] In this context, a_{ij} is the

---

[8] For $i = j = 1$ the origin is translated to $(\bar{u}_0, \bar{v}_0)$. For cases in which the natural origin is of little interest (e.g., age = 0 and education = 0, judicious selection of $\bar{u}_0$ and $\bar{v}_0$ can give coefficients for the first row and first column of rectangles which have easier interpretations.

SPLINE FUNCTIONS IN REGRESSION ANALYSIS   379

value of y when $u = \bar{u}_{i-1}$ and $v = \bar{v}_{j-1}$, b_{ij} is the partial of y with respect to u along $\bar{v}_{j-1}$, c_{ij} is the partial of y with respect to v along $\bar{u}_{i-1}$, and d_{ij} is the interaction coefficient between u and v.

To obtain a simple means for determining the above four IJ coefficients, define the $(I + 1) \times (J + 1)$ coefficient matrix:

$$\Pi = \begin{bmatrix} \beta_0 & \delta_1 & \cdots & \delta_J \\ \hline \alpha_1 & \gamma_{11} & \cdots & \gamma_{1J} \\ \cdot & \cdot & & \cdot \\ \cdot & \cdot & & \cdot \\ \cdot & \cdot & & \cdot \\ \alpha_I & \gamma_{I1} & \cdots & \gamma_{IJ} \end{bmatrix},$$

the $2I \times (I + 1)$ matrix

$$U = \begin{bmatrix} 1 & \bar{u}_0 & 0 & 0 & \cdots & 0 & 0 \\ 1 & \bar{u}_1 & 0 & 0 & \cdots & 0 & 0 \\ 1 & \bar{u}_2 & \bar{u}_2 - \bar{u}_1 & 0 & \cdots & 0 & 0 \\ \cdot & \cdot & \cdot & \cdot & & \cdot & \cdot \\ \cdot & \cdot & \cdot & \cdot & & \cdot & \cdot \\ \cdot & \cdot & \cdot & \cdot & & \cdot & \cdot \\ 1 & \bar{u}_{I-1} & \bar{u}_{I-1} - \bar{u}_1 & \bar{u}_{I-1} - \bar{u}_2 & \cdots & \bar{u}_{I-1} - \bar{u}_{I-2} & 0 \\ 0 & 1 & 0 & 0 & \cdots & 0 & 0 \\ 0 & 1 & 1 & 0 & \cdots & 0 & 0 \\ 0 & 1 & 1 & 1 & \cdots & 0 & 0 \\ \cdot & \cdot & \cdot & \cdot & & \cdot & \cdot \\ \cdot & \cdot & \cdot & \cdot & & \cdot & \cdot \\ \cdot & \cdot & \cdot & \cdot & & \cdot & \cdot \\ 0 & 1 & 1 & 1 & \cdots & 1 & 1 \end{bmatrix},$$

and the $(J + 1) \times 2J$ matrix

$$V = \begin{bmatrix} 1 & 1 & 1 & \cdots & 1 & 0 & 0 & 0 & \cdots & 0 \\ \bar{v}_0 & \bar{v}_1 & \bar{v}_2 & \cdots & \bar{v}_{J-1} & 1 & 1 & 1 & \cdots & 1 \\ 0 & 0 & \bar{v}_2 - \bar{v}_1 & \cdots & \bar{v}_{J-1} - \bar{v}_1 & 0 & 1 & 1 & \cdots & 1 \\ 0 & 0 & 0 & \cdots & \bar{v}_{J-1} - \bar{v}_2 & 0 & 0 & 1 & \cdots & 1 \\ \cdot & \cdot & \cdot & & \cdot & \cdot & \cdot & \cdot & & \cdot \\ \cdot & \cdot & \cdot & & \cdot & \cdot & \cdot & \cdot & & \cdot \\ \cdot & \cdot & \cdot & & \cdot & \cdot & \cdot & \cdot & & \cdot \\ 0 & 0 & 0 & \cdots & \bar{v}_{J-1} - \bar{v}_{J-2} & 0 & 0 & 0 & \cdots & 1 \\ 0 & 0 & 0 & \cdots & 0 & 0 & 0 & 0 & \cdots & 1 \end{bmatrix}.$$

Then it can be shown that

$$\mathbf{U}\Pi\mathbf{V} = \left[\begin{array}{c|c} A & C \\ \hline B & D \end{array}\right],$$

where

$$\mathbf{A} = \begin{bmatrix} a_{11} & \cdots & a_{1J} \\ \cdot & & \cdot \\ \cdot & & \cdot \\ \cdot & & \cdot \\ a_{I1} & \cdots & a_{IJ} \end{bmatrix}, \quad \mathbf{C} = \begin{bmatrix} c_{11} & \cdots & c_{1J} \\ \cdot & & \cdot \\ \cdot & & \cdot \\ \cdot & & \cdot \\ c_{I1} & \cdots & c_{IJ} \end{bmatrix},$$

$$\mathbf{B} = \begin{bmatrix} b_{11} & \cdots & b_{1J} \\ \cdot & & \cdot \\ \cdot & & \cdot \\ \cdot & & \cdot \\ b_{I1} & \cdots & b_{IJ} \end{bmatrix}, \quad \mathbf{D} = \begin{bmatrix} d_{11} & \cdots & d_{1J} \\ \cdot & & \cdot \\ \cdot & & \cdot \\ \cdot & & \cdot \\ d_{I1} & \cdots & d_{IJ} \end{bmatrix}.$$

If the piecewise nature of the bilinear spline is thought to reflect some sort of "structural change," then it is necessary to develop a testing procedure for determining when the estimated surfaces over two adjacent rectangles are "significantly different."

To do this, consider the case of comparing the surfaces over $R(i,j)$ and $R(i + 1, j)$. If there is no structural change along $\bar{u}_i$, then at any point (u, v) in the interior of $R(i + 1, j)$, the surface could be evaluated by merely extending the surface which lies over $R(i, j)$. However, if the surface over $R(i + 1, j)$ is used instead, it can be seen from (8) that the presence of the transformed variable u_{i+1} implies that these two estimates will differ by

$$\alpha_{i+1}(u - \bar{u}_i) + \sum_{m=1}^{j} \gamma_{i+1,m}(u - \bar{u}_i)(v - \bar{v}_{m-1}), \tag{10}$$

where $\bar{v}_0 = 0$. Thus no structural change occurs between $R(i,j)$ and $R(i + 1, j)$ iff expression (10) equals zero.

If (10) equals zero, then since $u > \bar{u}_i$, (10) may be divided by $u - \bar{u}_i$ and rearranged to give

$$\alpha_{i+1} - \sum_{m=1}^{j} \gamma_{i+1,m}\bar{v}_{m-1} + v\sum_{m=1}^{j} \gamma_{i+1,m} = 0. \tag{11}$$

Since (11) must hold identically in $\tilde{v}$, (11) holds if

$$\alpha_{i+1} - \sum_{m=1}^{j} \gamma_{i+1,m} \bar{v}_{m-1} = 0, \qquad (12)$$

and

$$\sum_{m=1}^{j} \gamma_{i+1,m} = 0. \qquad (13)$$

Hence in a regression context, the null hypothesis that the surfaces over $R(i,j)$ and $R(i+1,j)$ are the same can be rejected iff the estimated regression coefficients fail to satisfy the null hypothesis given by restrictions (12) and (13).

Similarly, the restrictions analogous to (12) and (13), which hold if the surfaces over $R(i,j)$ and $R(i,j+1)$ are the same, can be easily shown to be

$$\delta_{j+1} - \sum_{m=1}^{i} \gamma_{m,j+1} \bar{u}_{m-1} = 0, \qquad (14)$$

and

$$\sum_{m-1}^{i} \gamma_{m,j+1} = 0. \qquad (15)$$

REFERENCES

Poirier, D. J. 1973. Piecewise regression using cubic splines. *Journal of the American Statistical Association* 68: 515–524.

———. 1974. Parameterizations of the "treatment" in negative income tax experiments. University of Wisconsin Institute for Research on Poverty Discussion Paper 215-74, Madison.

———. 1976. *The econometrics of structural change with special emphasis on spline functions.* Amsterdam: North-Holland Publishing.

13 The application of an error components model to experimental panel data

Robert Avery
Harold W. Watts

Most of the variables in the New Jersey experiment were measured at several points in time over the three-year experimental period. Thus analysts have had to cope with two sources of variation or difference: cross-sectional differences across a sample of individuals and variation for a given individual over time. Several methods have been employed to handle the panel data, ranging from analysis of each time period separately to averaging variables across time periods. An alternative method, used widely in this volume, pools the intertemporal and cross-sectional variation in a single analysis. The advantages include additional degrees of freedom and the ability to examine the experimental response as an explicit function of time.[1]

A potential problem of such pooling, however, is that it may lead to a violation of the assumption of independence of stochastic error terms which underlies ordinary least squares regression. For example, variables such as motivation and intelligence cannot be entered explicitly into a labor-supply model, and are assumed to be part of the error term. We might expect, however, that a poorly motivated individual will have a consistently lower work effort than predicted, leading to a correlation of

---

[1] See Chapters 2 and 12 for a discussion of the treatment of time.

residuals over time. Similarly, neglected macroconditions, such as changes in the unemployment rates, may lead to a correlation of the errors of all individuals in a given time period. While still yielding unbiased coefficients, the violation of the independence assumption produces inefficient estimates and an overstatement of the precision of those estimates which may be major.

There are several methods available for dealing with nonindependence of residuals, the choice depending to a large extent upon the source of the nonindependence and the objectives of the analysis. Perhaps the most common method is to use dummy variables. The most extreme treatment, labeled a covariance model, is a separate fixed effect (dummy) for each time period and each individual. The use of a covariance model, however, complicates the examination of intercept shifts between large groups of individuals, a factor which may be of great interest in measuring experimental–control differentials.[2] An alternative approach is to assume the unique time or individual effects are random and to use generalized least squares (GLS) to take explicit account of the correlation among composite errors. A common specification used primarily for purely temporal models, which may also be applicable to panel data, is an autoregressive error structure. An autoregressive scheme is particularly attractive when the residuals are cumulative or when neighboring time periods are more highly correlated than errors of widely separated time periods.[3] For example, if health were not directly included in a model, we might expect health effects to produce an autoregressive error.

A more prevalent view of the residual terms in many of the experimental models is to view them as primarily constituted of such factors as ability, motivation, and special skills, which are constant over time (or at least over a period as short as three years). This, coupled with the potential complications of the covariance model, has led to the use of a third method of dealing with residual correlation, an error components model.

1. THREE-COMPONENT ERROR COMPONENTS MODEL

Assume a sample of N individuals observed over T time periods. Furthermore, let there be a linear relationship between a dependent variable,

---

[2] If separate dummies are used for each individual, the use of any additional dummy variables, such as an experimental–control dummy, will produce multicollinearity. However, restrictions can be applied which allow the calculation of intercept shifts between groups of individuals. This may be a complicated or costly process.

[3] The autoregressive model for panel data differs slightly from normal time series autocorrelations. There is no reason to believe that the errors of one individual are correlated with those of another. Thus the model can be thought of as a series of autocorrelated errors correlated over time for each individual, but independent of the errors of other individuals.

APPLICATION OF AN ERROR COMPONENTS MODEL

y, and a set of K independent variables, $x^{(K)}$, of the following form:

$$y_{nt} = x_{nt}^{(1)}\beta^{(1)} + \cdots + x_{nt}^{(K)}\beta^{(K)} + u_{nt}, \quad n = 1, \ldots, N \quad (1)$$
$$t = 1, \ldots, T$$

where u_{nt} is a stochastic random error term with zero mean and variance σ^2. The standard assumption made in error components models[4] is that u_{nt} can be decomposed into three components,

$$u_{nt} = \mu_n + \nu_t + \epsilon_{nt}, \quad (2)$$

where μ_n, ν_t, and ϵ_{nt} are each random, have zero mean, are independent of one another, and

$$\begin{aligned}
E(\mu_n\mu_{n'}) &= \sigma_\mu^2 & n &= n' \\
&= 0 & n &\neq n' \\
E(\nu_t\nu_{t'}) &= \sigma_\nu^2 & t &= t' \\
&= 0 & t &\neq t' \\
E(\epsilon_{nt}\epsilon_{n't'}) &= \sigma_\epsilon^2 & n &= n' \text{ and } t = t' \\
&= 0 & n &\neq n' \text{ or } t \neq t'
\end{aligned} \quad (3)$$

yielding,

$$\sigma^2 = \sigma_\mu^2 + \sigma_\nu^2 + \sigma_\epsilon^2. \quad (4)$$

The error structure defined in (2), (3), and (4) can be conveniently summarized by σ^2 and the following two ratios:

$$\rho = \sigma_\mu^2/\sigma^2 \quad (5)$$
$$\omega = \sigma_\nu^2/\sigma^2.$$

If observations are ordered first by individuals and then by time period, the model can be rewritten in more convenient matrix notation. Defining the following matrices,

$$Y = \begin{bmatrix} y_{11} \\ \vdots \\ y_{1T} \\ y_{21} \\ \vdots \\ y_{2T} \\ \vdots \\ y_{N1} \\ \vdots \\ y_{NT} \end{bmatrix}; \quad X = \begin{bmatrix} x_{11}^{(1)} & \cdots & x_{11}^{(K)} \\ \vdots & & \vdots \\ x_{1T}^{(1)} & \cdots & x_{1T}^{(K)} \\ x_{21}^{(1)} & \cdots & x_{21}^{(K)} \\ \vdots & & \vdots \\ x_{2T}^{(1)} & \cdots & x_{2T}^{(K)} \\ \vdots & & \vdots \\ x_{N1}^{(1)} & \cdots & x_{N1}^{(K)} \\ \vdots & & \vdots \\ x_{NT}^{(1)} & \cdots & x_{NT}^{(K)} \end{bmatrix}; \quad U = \begin{bmatrix} u_{11} \\ \vdots \\ u_{1T} \\ u_{21} \\ \vdots \\ u_{2T} \\ \vdots \\ u_{N1} \\ \vdots \\ u_{NT} \end{bmatrix}; \quad B = \begin{bmatrix} \beta^{(1)} \\ \beta^{(2)} \\ \vdots \\ \beta^{(K)} \end{bmatrix} \quad (6)$$
$(NT \times 1) \qquad (NT \times K) \qquad (NT \times 1) \qquad (K \times 1)$

---

[4] The error components model can be properly used only if lagged independent variables do not appear on the right hand side. Similar to autoregression, this leads to a violation of the assumption of independence between independent variables and error term. See Maddala (1971).

the model stated in equation (1) can be expressed as

$$Y = X\beta + U. \tag{7}$$

From previously stated assumptions about the error terms, the variance–covariance matrix of the residuals can now be written as the $NT \times NT$ matrix:

$$E(UU') = \sigma^2\Sigma = \sigma^2\{(1 - \rho - \omega)I_{NT} + \rho(I_N \otimes \iota_T\iota_T') + \omega(\iota_N\iota_N' \otimes I_T)\}, \tag{8}$$

where I_i is an $i \times i$ identity matrix, ι_i is an $i \times 1$ vector consisting entirely of ones, and $\otimes$ is the notation of Kronecker product. Putting the model in the form of equations (7) and (8), the Aitken theorem can be used to obtain efficient estimates of β and its estimated variance–covariance matrix. The estimate of β is simply:

$$\hat{\beta} = (X'\Sigma^{-1}X)^{-1}(X'\Sigma^{-1}Y). \tag{9}$$

The problem of obtaining Σ^{-1}, hence $X'\Sigma^{-1}X$ and $X'\Sigma^{-1}Y$, represented a potential stumbling block; however, it has been reduced to a relatively simple procedure developed first by Wallace and Hussain (1969) and later by Nerlove (1971). For the sake of simplicity we shall present only the form of the product $X'\Sigma^{-1}X$. (The product $X'\Sigma^{-1}Y$ can be expressed analogously, the complete derivation appearing in Nerlove [1971].)

$$\begin{aligned}X'\Sigma^{-1}X =\ & \frac{1}{1 - \rho - \omega + \omega N + \rho T} \cdot NT\bar{\bar{X}}\bar{\bar{X}}' \\ & + \frac{1}{1 - \rho - \omega + \omega N} \cdot \left[N \sum_{t=1}^{T} \bar{X}_t\bar{X}_t' - NT\bar{\bar{X}}\bar{\bar{X}}'\right] \\ & + \frac{1}{1 - \rho - \omega + \rho T} \cdot \left[T \sum_{n=1}^{N} \bar{X}_n\bar{X}_n' - NT\bar{\bar{X}}\bar{\bar{X}}'\right] \\ & + \frac{1}{1 - \rho - \omega}\left[X'X - T\sum_{n=1}^{N}\bar{X}_n\bar{X}_n' - N\sum_{t=1}^{T}\bar{X}_t\bar{X}_t' + NT\bar{\bar{X}}\bar{\bar{X}}'\right]\end{aligned} \tag{10}$$

where $\bar{X}_t$ and $\bar{X}_n$ are the vectors of variable means for time period t and individual n respectively and $\bar{\bar{X}}$ is the vector of grand means.[5] Generalized least squares coefficients follow directly from (9).

[5] The terms $\bar{\bar{X}}\bar{\bar{X}}'$, $N \cdot \sum_{t=1}^{T} \bar{X}_t\bar{X}_t'$, and $T \cdot \sum_{n=1}^{N} \bar{X}_n\bar{X}_n'$ can be calculated in advance and stored as matrices. Note that the last two terms are the familiar between-time and between-unit moment matrices respectively.

2. PARAMETER ESTIMATES

In general, the population parameters σ^2, ρ, and ω are not known. However, consistent estimates can be derived from the least squares residuals by a decomposition of the total sum of squares ($TRSS$). Using familiar two-way analysis of variance (Haggard, 1958), we can decompose $TRSS$ into three components as follows:

$$BNRSS = T \cdot \sum_{n=1}^{N} (\bar{\mathbf{Y}}_n'\bar{\mathbf{Y}}_n - \bar{\mathbf{Y}}_n'\bar{\mathbf{X}}_n\mathbf{b} - \mathbf{b}'\bar{\mathbf{X}}_n'\bar{\mathbf{Y}}_n + \mathbf{b}'\bar{\mathbf{X}}_n'\bar{\mathbf{X}}_n\mathbf{b})$$

(between individuals)

$$BTRSS = N \cdot \sum_{t=1}^{T} (\bar{\mathbf{Y}}_t'\bar{\mathbf{Y}}_t - \bar{\mathbf{Y}}_t'\bar{\mathbf{X}}_t\mathbf{b} - \mathbf{b}'\bar{\mathbf{X}}_t'\bar{\mathbf{Y}}_t + \mathbf{b}'\bar{\mathbf{X}}_t'\bar{\mathbf{X}}_t\mathbf{b}) \quad (11)$$

(between time)

$WRSS = TRSS - BNRSS - BTRSS$

(within residual sums of squares)

where $\bar{\mathbf{Y}}_n$ and $\bar{\mathbf{Y}}_t$ are defined analogously to $\bar{\mathbf{X}}_n$ and $\bar{\mathbf{X}}_t$, and $\mathbf{b}$ is the ordinary least squares estimate of β.

The parameters may then be consistently estimated by:

$$\hat{\rho} = \frac{(BNRSS)/(NT - T) - (WRSS)/T(NT - K - N - T + 2)}{(BNRSS)/(NT - T) + BTRSS/(NT - N) + [(WRSS)(1 - 1/T - 1/N)]/(NT - K - N - T + 2)}$$

$$\hat{\omega} = \frac{(BTRSS)/(NT - N) - (WRSS)/T(NT - K - N - T + 2)}{(BNRSS)/(NT - T) + (BTRSS)/(NT - T) + [(WRSS)(1 - 1/T - 1/N)]/(NT - K - N - T + 2)}. \quad (12)$$

3. TWO-COMPONENT MODEL

The above model was developed under the assumption that there are three error components, μ_n, ν_t, and ϵ_{nt}. With the experimental data, however, there are several reasons for adopting an alternative treatment of variation along the time dimension. First of all, because of lagged and/or anticipatory adjustment, a time effect in the response to the experimental treatment is possible. Second, the sequential site enrollment process and the measurement design produce data arrays that are synchronous in experimental time but not in calendar time (except within each site). Third, there are ample degrees of freedom for estimating "fixed effect" time patterns (explicit specifications with dummy variables, trends, splines, etc.). Finally, the explicit treatment of time in the regression model permits the use of a simpler two-component model for the distribution, i.e.,

$$u_{nt} = \mu_n + \epsilon_{nt}, \tag{13}$$

where μ_n and ϵ_{nt} are defined as in (2) and (3). That is, we assume $\nu_t = 0$ for all t, therefore $\omega = 0$, $\sigma^2 = \sigma_\mu^2 + \sigma_\epsilon^2$, with ρ still defined as σ_μ^2/σ^2.

The variance–covariance matrix of the residuals can be written as the $NT \times NT$ matrix:

$$E(\mathbf{U}\mathbf{U}') = \sigma^2 \mathbf{\Sigma} = \sigma^2\{(1 - \rho)\mathbf{I}_{nt} + \rho(\mathbf{I}_n \otimes \iota_T \iota_T')\}. \tag{14}$$

Note that the $\mathbf{\Sigma}$ matrix is block diagonal where each $T \times T$ block is

$$\begin{bmatrix} 1 & \rho & \rho & \cdots & \rho \\ \rho & 1 & \rho & \cdots & \rho \\ \rho & \rho & 1 & \cdots & \rho \\ \cdot & \cdot & \cdot & & \cdot \\ \rho & \rho & \rho & \cdots & 1 \end{bmatrix}. \tag{15}$$

The similarities between the two-component and autocorrelation model are quite apparent when viewed in this fashion. The residual covariance matrix of an autocorrelation model for panel data is also block diagonal with blocks of $T \times T$. The off-diagonal covariances, however, are declining, that is

$$\begin{bmatrix} 1 & \rho & \rho^2 & \cdot & \cdot & \rho^{T-1} \\ \rho & 1 & \rho & \cdot & \cdot & \rho^{T-2} \\ \rho^2 & \rho & 1 & \cdot & \cdot & \cdot \\ \cdot & & & \cdot & & \cdot \\ & & & \cdot & 1 & \rho \\ \rho^{T-1} & \rho^{T-2} & \cdot & \cdot & \rho & 1 \end{bmatrix}. \tag{16}$$

The generalized least squares coefficients and parameter estimates are derived in the same manner as the three-component model. Computations, however, are significantly easier. The term $\mathbf{X}'\mathbf{\Sigma}^{-1}\mathbf{X}$ (and analogously $\mathbf{X}'\mathbf{\Sigma}^{-1}\mathbf{Y}$) defined in (10) reduces to:

$$\mathbf{X}'\mathbf{\Sigma}^{-1}\mathbf{X} = \frac{1}{1 - \rho + \rho T} \cdot T \sum_{n=1}^{N} \bar{\mathbf{X}}_n \bar{\mathbf{X}}_n' \tag{17}$$

$$+ \frac{1}{1 - \rho}\left[\mathbf{X}'\mathbf{X} - T \cdot \sum_{n=1}^{N} \bar{\mathbf{X}}_n \bar{\mathbf{X}}_n'\right].$$

Similarly, ρ can be consistently eliminated by

$$\hat{\rho} = \frac{(BNRSS)/(NT - T) - (WRSS)/T(NT - K - N + 1)}{(BNSS)/(NT - T) + (WRSS)(1 - 1/T)/(NT - K - N + 1)} \quad (18)$$

where $BNRSS$ and $TRSS$ are defined in (11) and $WRSS = TRSS - BNRSS$.

4. TWO-COMPONENT MODEL WITH MISSING DATA

The two- and three-component models derived in the previous sections are based on the assumption of a full panel data set, that is, all individuals are present for all quarters. However, because of missing interviews, refusals, and so on, individuals in the experiment's data base may be missing observations at one or several points in time. Observations may also be excluded because of specifications of the model. For example, unemployed persons do not have a wage rate, thus should be excluded from a wage model. An error components specification can still be applied; however, the computational algorithms change slightly.

Assume a sample of N individuals, where each individual is observed for T_n time periods where $T_n \le T$. The total number of observations is

$$M = \sum_{n=1}^{N} T_n.$$

Assume, as before, a two-component model with error specification as in (13), (2), and (3).[6] Because of the uneven structure of the data, the variance–covariance matrix of the residuals cannot be expressed in compact form as in (14). The Σ matrix is again block diagonal; however, the blocks are of varying size. That is, the block corresponding to the nth individual will be of order $T_n \times T_n$. Each block, however, will have the same internal form as (15).

The derivation of generalized least squares and parameter estimates is quite similar to the full two-component model. The product $\mathbf{X}'\mathbf{\Sigma}^{-1}\mathbf{X}$ (and again analogously $\mathbf{X}'\mathbf{\Sigma}^{-1}\mathbf{Y}$) reduces to:

$$\mathbf{X}'\mathbf{\Sigma}^{-1}\mathbf{X} = \frac{1}{1-\rho}\mathbf{X}'\mathbf{X} + \sum_{n=1}^{N}\left(\left[\frac{1}{1+\rho+\rho T_n} - \frac{1}{1-\rho}\right]T_n\bar{\mathbf{X}}_n\bar{\mathbf{X}}_n'\right). \quad (19)$$

If $T_n = T$ for all n (full two-component model), equation (19) reduces to

---

[6] The missing observation problem could also be applied to a three-component model. However, an algorithm has not been developed for easily computing $\mathbf{\Sigma}^{-1}$ which may make the specification impractical.

(17). If observations are not missing, $\Sigma_{n=1}^{N}\bar{X}_n\bar{X}_n'$ is invariant to changes in the parameter ρ, therefore it can be pre-summed and stored as a matrix. If data are missing, however, the parameter estimate of ρ enters into the sum. Thus individual mean vectors must be stored and summed for each equation. And ρ can be estimated similarly to equation (18) with the average number of time periods per individual,

$$\bar{T} = \frac{1}{N-1}\left(M - \sum_{n=1}^{N} T_n^2/M\right),$$

substituted for T (again note $\bar{T}$ reduces to T in the full data model). Thus,

$$\hat{\rho} = \frac{(BNRSS)/(M - \bar{T}) - (WRSS)/\bar{T}(N - K - N + 1)}{(BNRSS)/(M - \bar{T}) + (WRSS)(1 - 1/\bar{T})/(M - K - N + 1)}. \quad (20)$$

5. SUMMARY

In practice, only the two-component model, with or without missing observations, was actually employed in the experimental analysis. Preliminary testing on sample equations indicated that the presence of fixed effect time variables all but eliminated the time component. The most apparent effect of using error components versus least squares was generally to change the significance of estimated coefficients, not their magnitude. However, to the extent that inferences are drawn not only from the magnitude of predicted experimental response but from their precision, correct specification of the error structure is important for accurate and believable results. It was found that coefficients of variables which are constant over time (race, experimental status, etc.) tended to show the largest changes in their significance levels in the two-component case.

A word of caution should be exercised for potential users. As mentioned in footnote 4, lagged dependent variables cannot properly be used with error components. This may present a conflict with the use of preenrollment values of the dependent variable as a regressor. It is also suggested that users consider carefully the nature of their error term. If the residuals do not fit the error components assumption of constant effect, alternative specifications such as a covariance model or autoregressive scheme should be considered.

A computer program was developed during the analysis of this experiment to handle many types of statistical analysis using large panel data sets. Among its capabilities are two- or three-component models with or without missing observations, autoregressive and covariance models, heteroskedastic models, two- and three-stage least squares, and Zellner seemingly unrelated least squares with or without error components. The program, entitled AVETRAN, is available in IBM or UNIVAC versions with accompanying manual and sample run. It can be obtained in machine processable form on a nonprofit basis from the University of Wisconsin Data and Program Library Service. Inquiries should refer to the program by name and be addressed to:

> Data and Program Library Service
> 4451 Social Science Building
> University of Wisconsin
> Madison, Wisconsin 53706

REFERENCES

Haggard, E. A. 1958. *Intraclass correlation and the analysis of variance.* New York: Dryden Press.

Maddala, G. S. 1971. The use of variance components models in pooling cross-section and time series data. *Econometrica* 39: 341–358.

Nerlove, M. 1971. A note on error components models. *Econometrica* 39: 383–396.

Wallace, T. D., and Hussain, A. 1969. The use of error components models in combining cross-section with time-series data. *Econometrica* 37: 55–72.

14 The estimation of normal wage rates and normal income

Harold W. Watts
Dale Poirier

Normal wage rates, $\hat{W}$, and normal income $\hat{Y}$ variables have been used in many parts of the labor-supply analyses in preceding chapters. Chapter 2 provided an explanation of the basic approach and strategy. This chapter provides an expanded discussion of the rationale for constructing these variables and then provides the technical specifications, details of their estimation, and a summary of the estimates. Before proceeding with the more specific explanation of the measures developed in this experiment, it will be useful to discuss the need for such estimates and some possible alternatives.

It must be emphasized that the primary objective of any analysis of experimental data is to control the sources of extraneous variation in the variable(s) of interest so that the variation produced by the experimental stimulus can be isolated. Here variables describing aspects of labor supply are of primary concern, and the stimuli are provided by changes in net wage rates and augmentation of income in the form of a negative income tax.

Since the gross wage rates and family income, and both cross-sectional and temporal variations in them, are not directly under the control of the experimenter, it is important to be able to control for these sources of labor-supply variation. In a true laboratory situation, it might be possible to secure direct control and constancy of some sources of variation, but in a field experiment such control is limited.

Simple randomization provides one means of control which is weak but dependable. It is weak because the variation coming from all the extraneous sources is left in the unexplained error; hence the precision of estimation for a simple difference in means to be attributed to the treatment is reduced. It is dependable, however, because with large enough samples, a random assignment to two groups will ensure that equivalent extraneous variation is added to both. More important, it is not even necessary to be able to name, much less measure, these extraneous influences.

The dependability of randomization is enough to ensure its continued role in field experimentation, but its weakness leads to attempts to reduce the residual variation by identifying, measuring, and estimating the effects of as many sources of variation as possible.

In addition, when one goes beyond the estimation of simple, mean differences between treated and untreated groups and seeks to estimate a more complex structure of response, it is possible that some of those variables which produce variation in, say, labor supply will also interact with the treatment variables in the response function. This possibility may even lead, as it did in this experiment, to the use of income for stratification in the design and sample assignment process. For this reason, and for reasons of general "noise reduction," it is therefore important to have some means of control for wage rates and family income in an experiment estimating labor-supply response, even though variation in those variables is *not* the primary source of variation producing the response.

At least three possible approaches may be suggested for this purpose. The first is to use baseline or preenrollment values of wages and income. In this experiment, we had only a single observation made in the preenrollment interview, but in principle a more extended period of observation could have been used to form a more precise estimate of preexperimental status. This approach has the drawback that it is not sensitive to changes in family composition or external changes in the labor market concurrent with the experimental stimulus. Its strength lies in that it is patently free of experimental influence, being measured prior to determination of experimental–control status.

Another approach is to use the control sample for estimation of permanent income or wage models, and to use these models to attribute "permanent" wages and income to the treated sample as well. This approach also keeps the estimated "permanent" components free of possible responses, but it cannot take advantage of the multiple observations available that could indicate persistent deviations from such average functions caused by unmeasured factors. Second, because the fitted model will not have the same orthogonality properties in the sample for control and experimental groups, it is possible for subsequent estimates of response interactions to be biased.

Finally, there is the approach explained in detail below and described generally in Chapter 2. The main weakness of this approach is that it is dependent on the adequacy of specification and precision in measurement of the experimental component that is removed to form the "ex ante" estimate. Any bias introduced from the specification or error from the estimation will be transmitted back into the normal wage and income series. On the other hand, this more elaborate approach does allow the introduction of persistent inter-unit differences that can be estimated from a panel and can, at the same time, make use of whatever baseline information is available.

None of the approaches shows a clear-cut superiority, and their different strengths and weaknesses suggest that it would be prudent to use all of them. Indeed they are all used at various points in the analysis, and the most robust findings seem to be consistent, although not equally precise, regardless of which method is used. But because the third approach is most elaborate and novel, the balance of this chapter will be devoted to its specification and estimation.

1. SPECIFICATION OF MODELS

As outlined in Chapter 2, the basic formulation of the observed wage rates or family income specifies a four-component multiplicative model written in log form as

$$\ln W_{it} = \ln W_{it}^* + \ln \tilde{W}_{it} + \ln u_i + \gamma_{it}. \tag{1}$$

Again we will explain the model only in terms of wage rates, where the specification applies to both. The last two terms form a two-component error term:

$$\epsilon_{it} = \ln \mu_i + \gamma_{it},$$

where ϵ_{it} is assumed to have a zero mean and to be uncorrelated with all variables entering the specification of $\ln W^*$ or $\ln \tilde{W}$. Both components of ϵ are assumed to be mean-independent of the regressor variables and mean-independent of each other. Consequently the variance of ϵ, σ_ϵ^2, is the sum of the two component variances, $\sigma_{\ln\mu}^2$ and σ_γ^2, and the usual independence and homoskedasticity specifications are imposed. An estimation procedure consistent with this specification is presented and discussed in Chapter 13.

The possibility of specifying a third component of ϵ_{it}, say $\ln \lambda_t$, which varies over time but is constant for all individuals at a point in time, was considered and rejected. Time is introduced explicitly in the specification of $\ln W^*$ and $\ln \tilde{W}$ and preliminary testing indicated that there was no substantial or significant time-varying component remaining in ϵ when this is done.

Now consider the specification of the "normal" or "control" part of the model, $\ln W^*$ or $(\ln Y^*)$. The basic variables used are as follows:

Z_1 = current age in years of a person
Z_2 = the educational level in years of a person
Z_3 = the person's industrial category (6 classes)
Z_4 = the person's occupational category (6 classes)
Z_5 = the experimental site (4 sites)
Z_6 = the current calendar time in months (Aug 1968 = 0)
Z_7 = the number of the month within each year (Jan = 1)
Z_8 = family composition
Z_9 = employment status of spouse
Z^{10} = health of male head at quarters 2 and 6.

In the family income regression, Z_1 and Z_2 will be further subscripted by m and f to denote the male head and female spouse respectively.

The specification of the control models can be organized by a further subdivision of additive parts. Let

$$\log_{10} W^* = f_1(Z_1, Z_2) + f_2(Z_3, Z_4) + f_3(Z_5) + f_4(Z_6) \\ + f_5(Z_9), \quad (2)$$

$$\ln Y^* = f_{1m}(Z_{1m}, Z_{2m}) + f_{1f}(Z_{1f}, Z_{2f}) + f_3(Z_5) \\ + f_4(Z_6) + f_6(Z_7) + f_8(Z_8) + f_9(Z_{10})[1]. \quad (3)$$

The subfunctions, f_1, f_{1m}, and f_{1f}, are formed as bilinear splines in age and education. In particular: $f_1(Z_1, Z_2)$ is a simple linear function of eight variables where

$X_1 = Z_1$ $\qquad\qquad X_5 = \text{Max}(Z_2 - 8, 0)$
$X_2 = \text{Max}(Z_1 - 25, 0)$ $\qquad X_6 = X_1 * X_4$
$X_3 = \text{Max}(Z_1 - 45, 0)$ $\qquad X_7 = X_3 * Z_4$
$X_4 = Z_2$ $\qquad\qquad X_8 = X_3 * Z_5.$

---

[1] For no significant reason, the wage function used common logarithms and the income function used natural logarithms.

This formulation produces a set of piecewise linear age profiles, one for each level of education, but varying continuously to produce a continuous surface. The "knots," or points where the linear segments join, are at ages twenty-five and forty-five, and at eight years of education in that dimension. The same subfunction applied to the husbands' ages and education was used in the normal income function, and a shortened form (omitting X_6, X_7, and X_8) was applied to the wives' characteristics in the normal income function. For the female normal wage model, where all groups were combined, twelve additional terms were added to this subfunction to allow for distinct age–education patterns for each ethnic group. They consisted of a simple binary variable for blacks and Spanish-speaking respectively and the product of each of these with X_1, X_2, X_3, X_4, and X_5 making a total of 12.

Industry and occupation variables are combined in $f_2(Z_3, Z_4)$, which is a simple sum of 11 terms. Five are simple binary (dummy) variables representing the contrasts of five industry categories with the heterogeneous excluded category. Five more are binary variables representing occupational categories, and a final one allows for an interaction or free parameter for operatives in durable manufacturing. Table 14.1 gives the specification for the ten basic binary variables. This subfunction was used for the normal wage estimates for males in each ethnic group but, because of nonsignificance, a shortened form was used for the (combined) female wage models; specifically, a combined manufacturing binary ($X_9 + X_{10}$) and one binary for household and service workers (X_{17}) were introduced. This subfunction was not used in the normal income model.

Allowance for intersite differences in normal wage rates and normal income is provided by $f_3(Z_5)$. Again this subfunction is a simple sum of three binary terms ($X_{20} - X_{22}$) representing the contrasts of Paterson–Passaic, Jersey City, and Scranton, with Trenton as the base. For

Table 14.1 **Binary Variable Specification for $f_2(Z_3, Z_4)$**

Industry (Z_3)	Occupation (Z_4)
X_9: durable manufacturing	X_{14}: clerical and sales
X_{10}: nondurable manufacturing	X_{15}: craftsmen, foremen
X_{11}: transportation, communication, utilities	X_{16}: operatives
X_{12}: wholesale and retail trade	X_{17}: private households and service workers
X_{13}: services	X_{18}: laborers
(basis) All other industries	(basis) All other occupations

Interaction: $X_{19} = X_9 * X_{16}$: operatives in durable manufacturing.

estimates limited to black or Spanish-speaking, the term for Scranton was omitted because these groups were virtually unrepresented in Scranton.

Time is introduced into the normal wage model by $f_4(Z_6)$ which is specified as a cubic spline with knots 0, 16, 32, 48 months (covering the period of activity at all four sites). It is further required that $f_4(0) = 0$ so that the anti-log (times 100) of f_4 directly produces an index number for wage rates or family incomes. This spline formulation requires the introduction of three variables (X_{23} through X_{25}), each of which is a complex transformation of Z_6. The details of this transformation are provided in Chapter 12.

The employment status of an individual's spouse is introduced only in the normal wage function by $f_5(Z_9)$. This is a single binary (X_{26}) set equal to one for individuals who have spouses who are employed during the week preceding the interview.

The discussion so far covers all the subfunctions incorporated into the normal wage models, some of which are also part of the normal income functions. The last three subfunctions were used only in the normal income model. A seasonal pattern was observed in the family income data (but not in wage rates), and a periodic cubic spline (see Chapter 12), $f_6(Z_7)$, was added to allow for this source of fluctuation. This subfunction involves three variables (X_{27} through X_{29}) which are transforms of the month index, Z_7.

Family composition was introduced by a series of four variables, each representing the number of family members in an age class as follows:

X_{30} = number of adults over 21 not counting primary husband or wife
X_{31} = number of adults 16–21 years of age
X_{32} = number of children 6–15 years of age
X_{33} = number of children 0–5 years of age.

The subfunction, $f_8(Z_8)$, is a simple linear form in these variables.

The final variable introduced was the health status of the husband, in $f_9(Z_{10})$. Only one variable is involved, and it is not allowed to vary from quarter to quarter. This variable was defined as follows:

$X_{33} \begin{cases} = 0 \text{ if no chronic illness or disability at quarters 2 and 6} \\ = 1/2 \text{ if chronic illness reported } one \text{ of these quarters} \\ = 1 \text{ if chronic illness reported both of these quarters} \end{cases}$

This completes the discussion of the control submodels. No extensive justification is required for the basic selection of variables; all are quite conventional components of "permanent" wage or income models as adapted to quarterly panel data. Several other variables suggested by previous studies were tested in the development of these models but were rejected as providing little additional explanation and showing implausible coefficients. The only novelty here lies in the functional forms involving spline transformation. While new to econometric analysis, they have a longer history in mathematics for providing economical (in terms of parameters) but flexible continuous approximations that are linear-in-parameters. These properties make them very useful in formulating econometric models.

The experimental component models will be specified next. The $\ln \tilde{W}$ component is much simpler than that for $\ln \tilde{Y}$. We will, therefore, discuss it first, and then explain the added features of $\ln \tilde{Y}$. Four variables are involved in $\tilde{W}$:

Z_{11} = a binary variable equal to one for all families assigned to an experimental treatment ($=$ zero for controls)
Z_{12} = tax rate assigned to an experimental family ($=$ zero for controls)
Z_{13} = guarantee rate assigned to an experimental family ($=$ zero for controls)
Z_{14} = time since enrollment in quarters of experimental time (preenrollment $= 0$).

We may now specify the experimental component as

$$\ln \tilde{W} = f_{10}(Z_{11}, Z_{14}) + f_{12}(Z_{11}, Z_{12}, Z_{13}) \tag{4}$$

The first subfunction is the product of Z_1 and a cubic spline function of experimental time with knots at preenrollment, and quarters 2, 6, and 12. Imposing the restriction $f_{10}(1, 0) = 0$ produces three variables ($X_{34} - X_{36}$) which are identically equal to zero when $Z_{11} = 0$ and are otherwise equal to the required spline transformations of Z_{12}. This subfunction provides an estimate of a time profile of experimental response which is smooth (continuous first and second derivatives) and has its greatest flexibility during the first half of the experiment by the choice of knot location.

The second subfunction, as described in Chapter 2, is a bilinear spline. This function provides nonlinear additive effects for both tax rates and guarantee which are centered at $t = .5$, $G = .75$; that is, $f_{12}(1, .5, .75) = 0$. We may now interpret the spline function, f_{11}, as yielding the estimated response for experimentals with $t = .5, G = .75$ and the function f_{12} as yielding constant (multiplicative) adjustments to that spline for other combinations of tax and guarantee. We also know that $f_{12}(0, 0, 0) = 0$. That is, all five transformed spline variables (X_{37} through X_{41}) are equal to zero for control families. The entire $\ln \tilde{W}$ function is thus definitionally zero for control families.

For the female wage model, where the three ethnic groups are combined for estimation, two added cubic spline functions were used. They were formed as the product of f_{11} and two binary variables for black and Spanish-speaking individuals. This specification allowed each ethnic group to have its own time pattern of experimental response.

The experimental component of income ln $\tilde{Y}$ is substantially more complex, involving thirty parameters in total. As mentioned before, this component involves normal income, Y^*, as an interacting variable. Thus, in addition to Z_{11} through Z_{14} (defined above), we must introduce a new variable:

$Z_{15} = \hat{Y}^*/PL(n)$ where $\hat{Y}^*$ is the most recent iteratively estimated value for $\hat{Y}^*$ and $PL(n)$ is the appropriate "poverty line" used to define guarantee variations, $PL(n)$ is adjusted annually to reflect changes in the consumer price index.

This "welfare ratio" variable is interacted with cubic splines in experimental time and linear tax and guarantee variables to provide a response subfunction that is linear in the welfare ratio for fixed Z_{12}, Z_{13}, Z_{14}; varies continuously with experimental time; and varies linearly with tax and guarantee values. This subfunction, call it $f_{13}(Z_{11}, Z_{12}, Z_{13}, Z_{14}, Z_{15})$, consists of six natural cubic splines with knots at 0, 4, 8, and 12, each interacted with a different combination of experimental variables. These splines are not required to equal zero at preenrollment ($Z_{14} = 0$). The six combinations are Z_{11}, $Z_{11} * Z_{15}$, $Z_{11} * (Z_{12} - .5)$, $Z_{11} * Z_{15} * (Z_{12} - .5)$, $Z_{11} * (Z_{15} .75)$, $Z_{11} * Z_{15} * (Z_{13} - .75)$.

Another interpretation of f_{13} is that it provides a planar response surface over the tax and guarantee space for any fixed values of Z_{14} (experimental time) and Z_{15} (welfare ratio of Y^* or normalized "permanent income"). The subfunction, $f_{14}(Z_{12}, Z_{13})$, was then introduced. It contains five binary terms to allow time-constant deviations from the plane given by f_{13} for five of the eight distinct tax–guarantee combinations, thus relaxing the restrictions of a planar response. One final term was added to complete the specification of ln $\tilde{Y}$. The possibility that health status of the head might affect income differently for experimental families was allowed for by introducing the product $Z_{11} * X_{33}$.

This completes the specification of the model used for estimation of normal income. To summarize, the "permanent" components explain income or wage rates in terms of quite conventional variables, with only some novel adaptations in form to take time into account. The experimental response components, $\tilde{W}$ and $\tilde{Y}$, were specified to capture as much as possible of the variation which is correlated with the experimental treatment. The objective was to remove the experimental component of observed wages or income so as to get appropriate ex ante measures for controlling experimental–control contrasts. To this end quite generous or even prodigal use of parameters was justified.[2] To repeat, for present purposes the experimental component was simply intended to cast a wide net so that all variation which could conceivably be systematically related to the experimental treatments could then be removed.

2. ESTIMATES OF THE SYSTEMATIC COMPONENTS OF WAGE RATES AND FAMILY INCOME

The models specified above were estimated using generalized least squares techniques appropriate for a two-component model of error. In the case of the wage functions this was straightforward, but for the family income model an iterative technique was necessary to incorporate Y^* into the experimental component as described above.

The nature of the estimated relationships will be displayed here in graphic form, because a substantial amount of manipulation (and mental gymnastics) is required to interpret the raw coefficients of the transformed variables used in the models.[3] The magnitudes and plausibility of the estimates can be most easily appreciated and evaluated from summaries in graphic form.

Figure 14.1 displays the pattern of wage rates generated by the age–education function for males. They are shown in the form of age profiles for two different education levels and for each of the three ethnic groups. The level of the various curves is determined by the choices of site, time, industry, occupation, and work status of wife, as detailed in the figure heading. Because the graph is presented in logarithmic scale, one may visualize each curve being shifted up or down by a constant amount if a different site or time were to be displayed. Since separate sets of coefficients were estimated for each ethnic group of males, the three pairs of curves would in general shift relative to each other if alternative base situations were chosen. A comparable display of profiles for females is shown in Figure 14.2, and selected family income profiles are shown in Figures 14.3 and 14.4.

Obviously, these estimates were obtained from a sample which is truncated in terms of family income (only those with incomes below 150 percent of the poverty line). Hence one should not expect the age–education relationships to be similar to those estimated from untruncated samples. For purposes of controlling comparisons among control and experimental

---

[2] Chapter 6 is concerned with the estimation and interpretation of more parsimonious and theoretically interesting models of family income response to the experiment.

[3] The numerical coefficients are available in Watts and Rees (1973: Part B, Chapter 1).

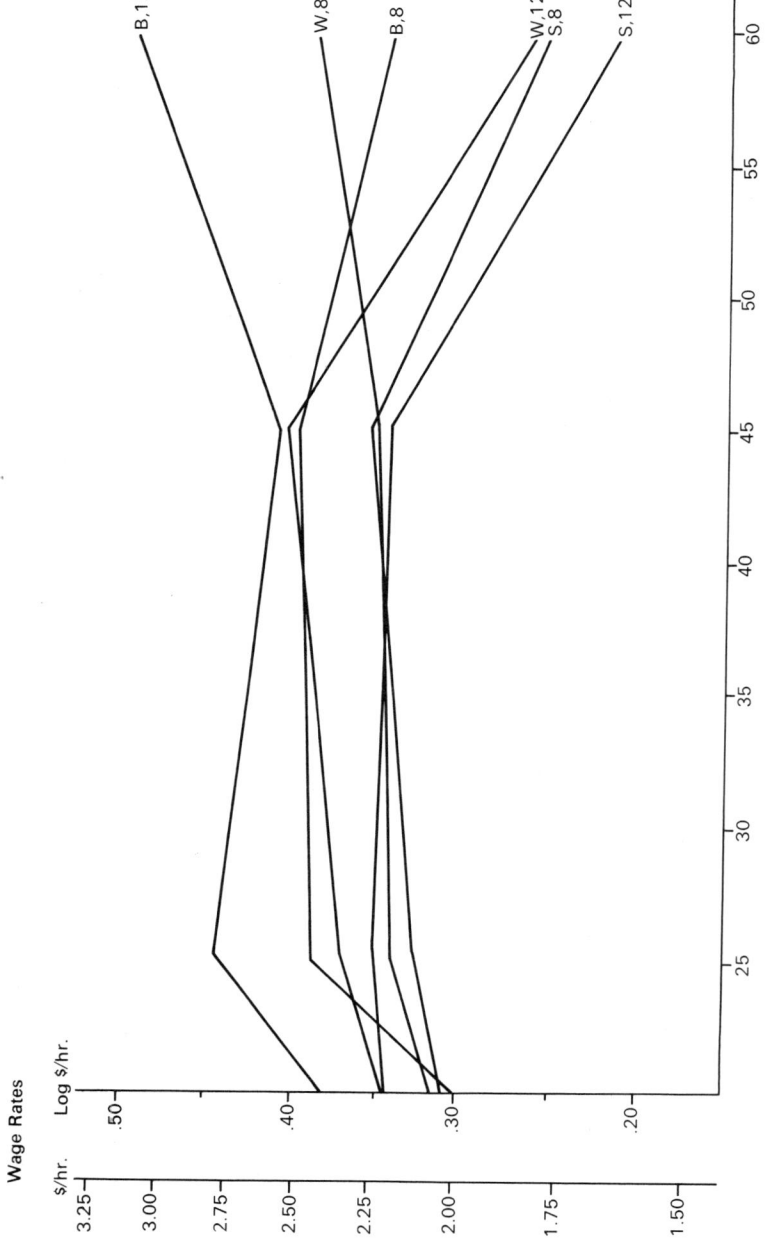

Figure 14.1 Male age profiles for full-time wage rates in Trenton, at preenrollment, for an operative in durable manufacturing whose wife is not employed.

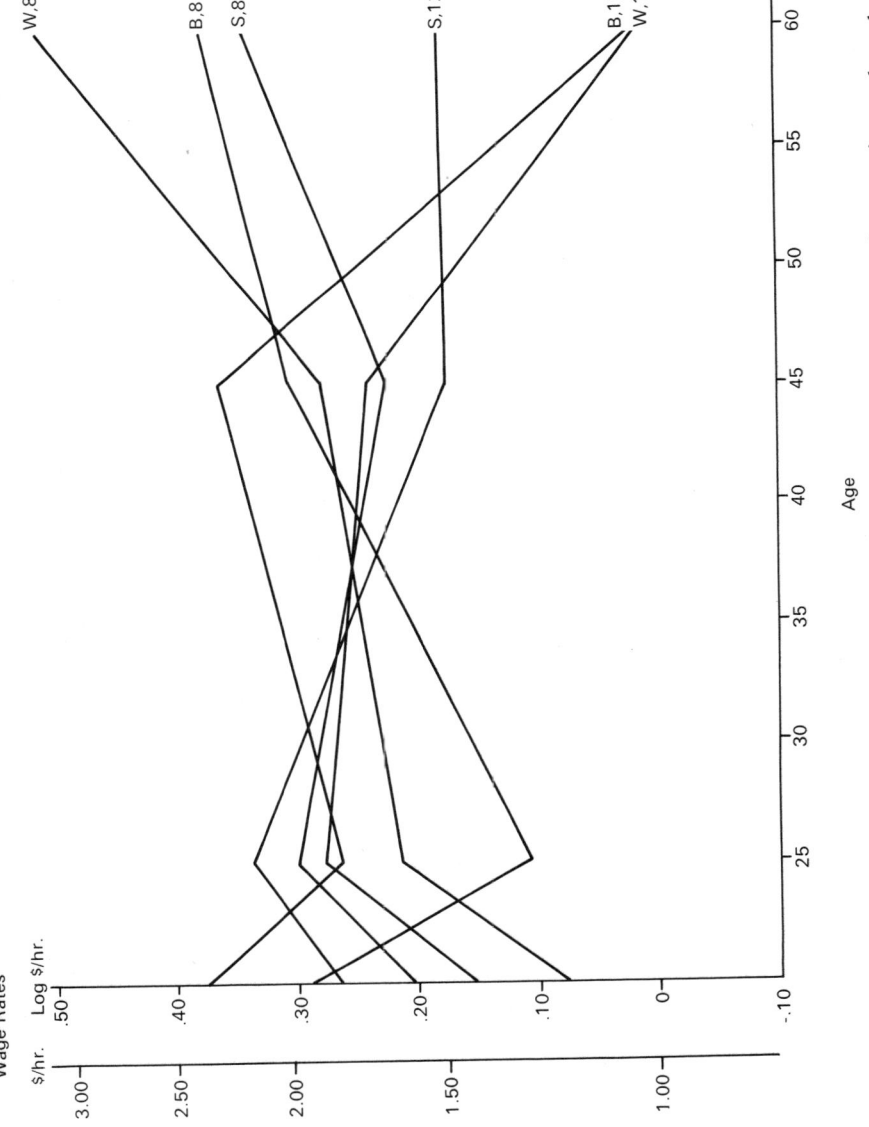

Figure 14.2 Female age profiles for full-time wage rates in Trenton, at preenrollment, for a service worker whose husband is employed.

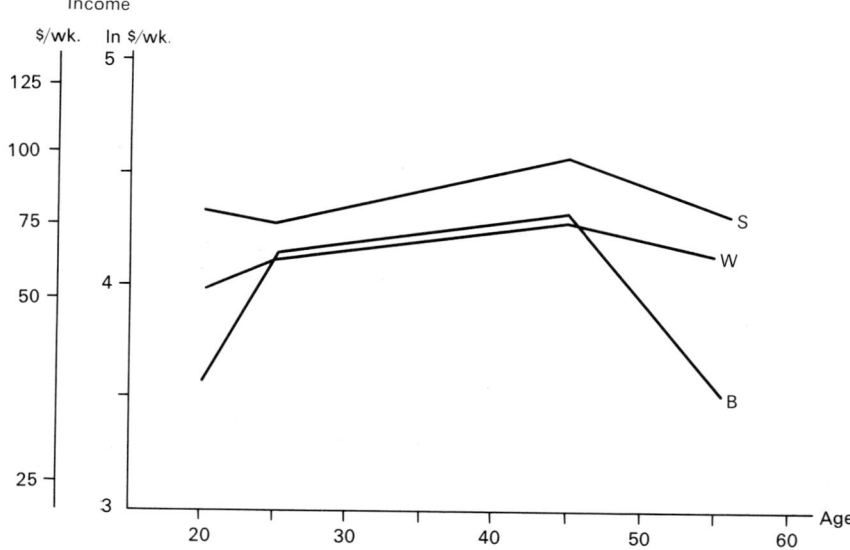

Figure 14.3 Family age–income profiles for like-aged couple, both with eight years of education, living in Trenton at preenrollment, husband healthy.

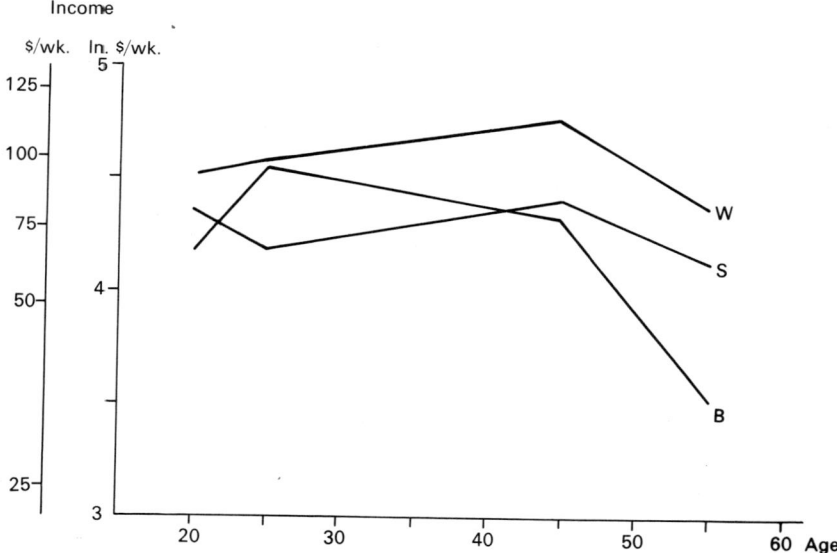

Figure 14.4 Family age–income profiles for like-aged couple, both with twelve years of education, living in Trenton at preenrollment, husband healthy.

groups in this truncated sample, these relations are appropriate. They should not be interpreted, however, as reasonable estimations for the entire population.[4]

The age–education subfunctions are all statistically significant at least at the 5 percent level. This does not mean that every parameter estimate is significant for each ethnic group, however. Nevertheless, since the mean objective was to provide equivalent ceteris paribus comparisons, no attempt was made to leave nonsignificant parameters out of the model so long as they were well precedented or grounded in theory and were sometimes significant.

The estimated effects of industry, occupation, site, and employment status of wife for the wage function will not be shown here—again, their values cannot be compared with full population estimates or intuition. Similarly site, family composition, and health status estimates will not be presented in detail for the income model. The subfunctions involving these variables were capable of shifting wages or income by from 15 to 20 percent, with the exception of the health status of the family head. A chronic disease or disability at both observed quarters tended to reduce income by from 40 to 60 percent.

The movement of wage rates and income through time are displayed in Figures 14.5 through 14.7. Vertical scales are provided both for the log scale of the appropriate subfunction and for the anti-log, which can be regarded as an index which multiplicatively shifts the entire wage (or income) structure through time. These curves should be regarded as describing the trends for control families or, hypothetically, for experimental families ex ante the experiment. It is noteworthy that wage rates for low-income males rose during the entire period, but at a distinctly lower rate for blacks. For females, an initial fall was estimated, at which point increases were observed at rates comparable to those for white males.

The plotted curves for family income include the seasonal component. The seasonal component appears to cause swings as large as ± 5 percent during a year. The white sample shows here a generally increasing trend which accelerates during the latter part of the period. The blacks show a decline after an initial increase, and the Spanish-speaking improve during the early period and then level off.

With regard to the experimental component for wage rates, Figures 14.8 and 14.9 show the pattern of wage-rate adjustments for the various

---

[4] Initially the strategy was to use extraneous estimates of age, income, occupation, and industry effects, but these were found almost useless for predicting wages or incomes in this low-income sample.

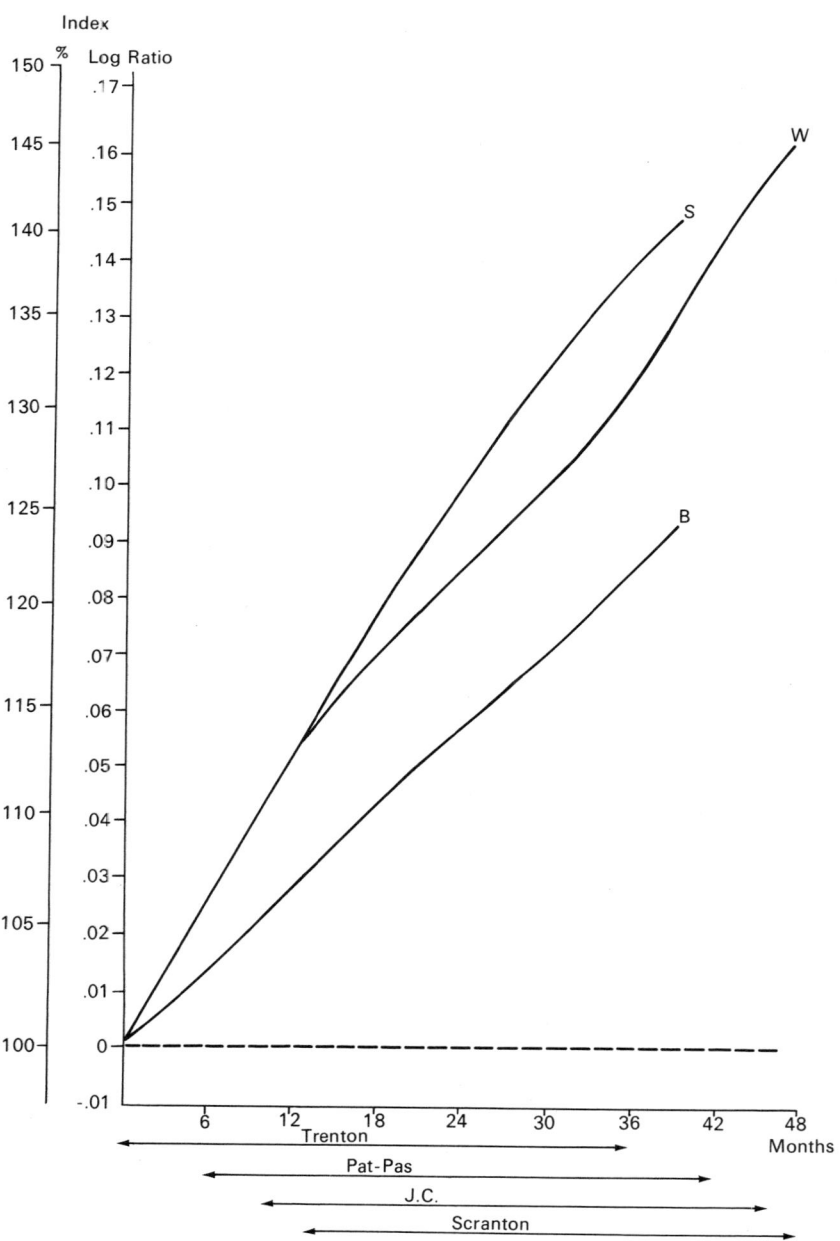

Figure 14.5 Wage-rate index for male sample during experimental period, estimated natural cubic calendar time splines.

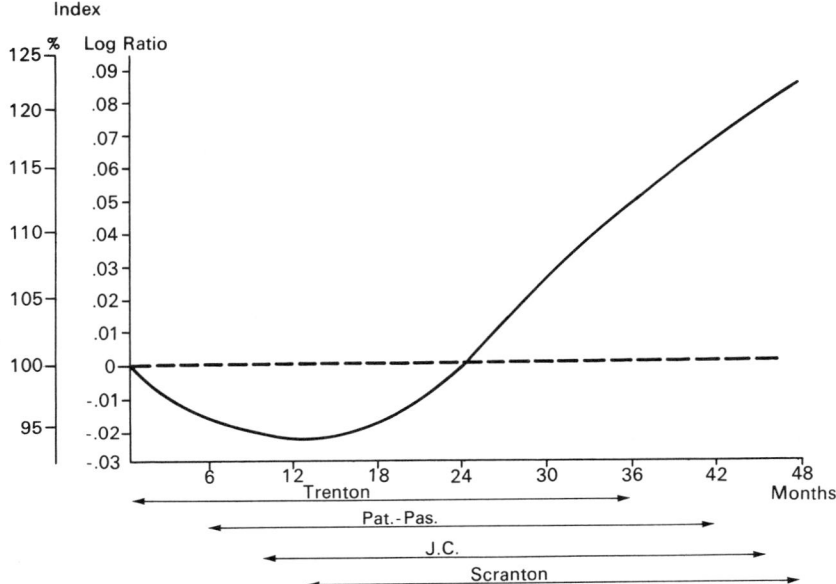

Figure 14.6 Wage-rate index for female sample during experimental period, estimated natural cubic calendar time spline.

experimental combinations of tax (t) and guarantee (G) rates. Note that $t = .5, G = .75$, is constrained to equal zero (or 100 percent). These patterns were not statistically significant, but were retained in the model to assure that all variation associated with the treatment would be removed. Figures 14.10 and 14.11 present the cubic spline function in experimental time which measures the central experimental differential. For males, the spline is strongly significant only for blacks, who show an 8.8 percent differential by the end of the experiment. The white differential is significant at the 5 percent level during the early and middle period, but it deteriorates towards the end. The Spanish-speaking differential is never significant. For females, in contrast, the Spanish-speaking show the only significant departure from controls, but that difference vanishes by the experiment's end. A number of interesting questions are raised by these differentials, and they are discussed at greater length elsewhere.[5] We simply note here that the differential rose sharply at the start of the experiment for all except the white females. At the end of the experiment, the differential was very small or vanishing except for black males. (These pat-

---

[5] The wage differentials are analyzed from a substantive point of view by Watts and Mamer (forthcoming).

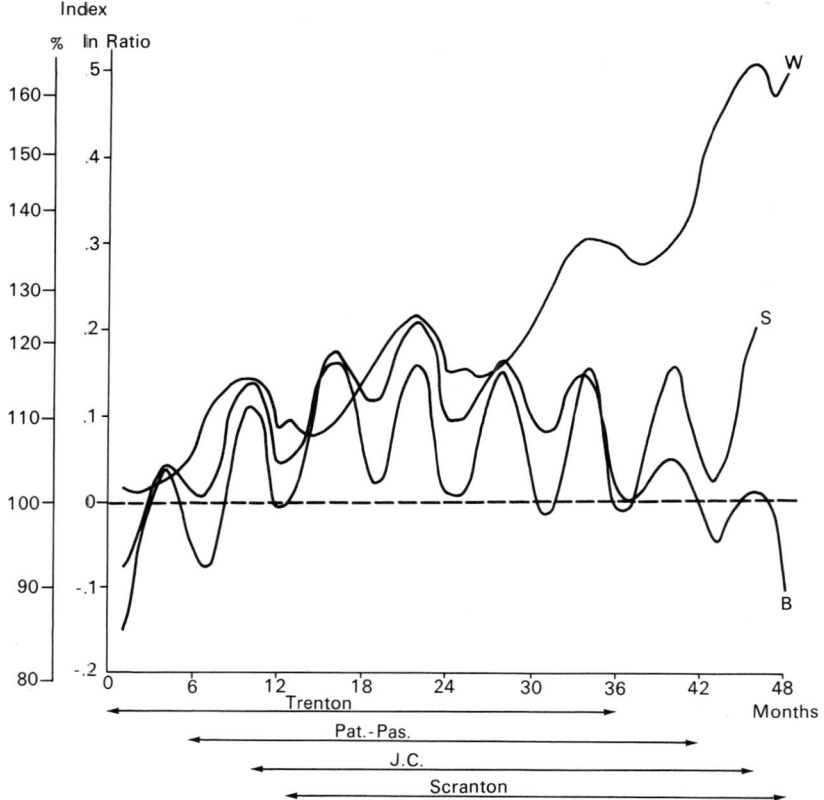

Figure 14.7 Index of total family income during experimental period for control families, including seasonal pattern.

terns are consistent with the differential being the result of measurement error and hence spurious.)

From the very much more complex experimental component used in the family income model, a selection of estimated response splines is shown. All are for families at the poverty threshold in terms of estimated Y^* (the systematic part of normal income) and have 50 percent tax rates. The guarantee level varies, among the three figures, from 75 percent to 125 percent. If income were in fact equal to the poverty level, payments would be made in the amounts of 25 percent of income to those on the $G = 0.75$ plan, up to 75 percent of income for those on the $G = 1.25$ plan. That the specification of $\tilde{Y}$ afforded a great deal of flexibility in capturing experimental effects is evident in these graphs. But, because of this, it would be hazardous to attempt much interpretation of these or a more complete set of estimated responses. Taken as a whole, the $\tilde{Y}$ function

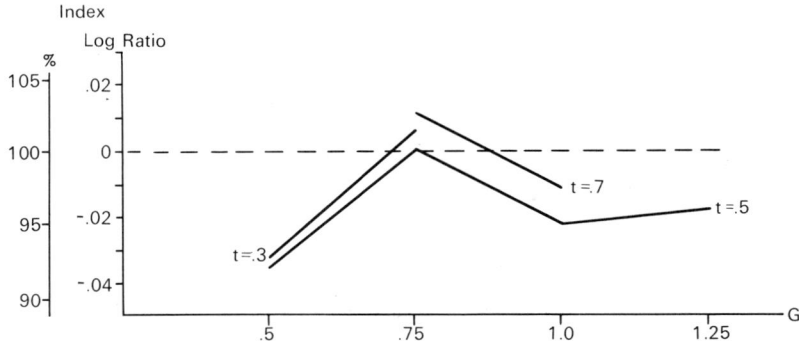
Tax-Guarantee Spline for White Male Wage Rates

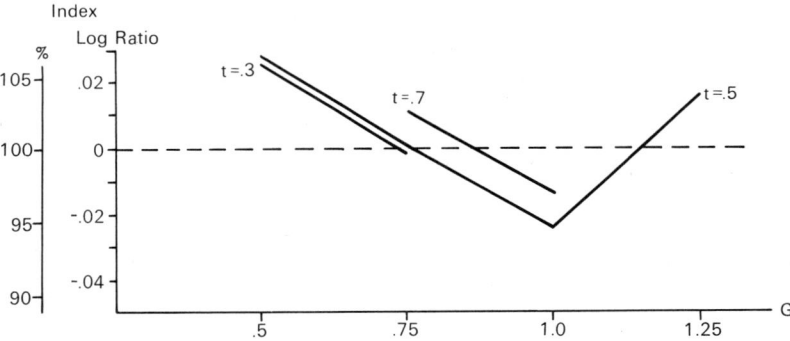
Tax-Guarantee Spline for Black Male Wage Rates

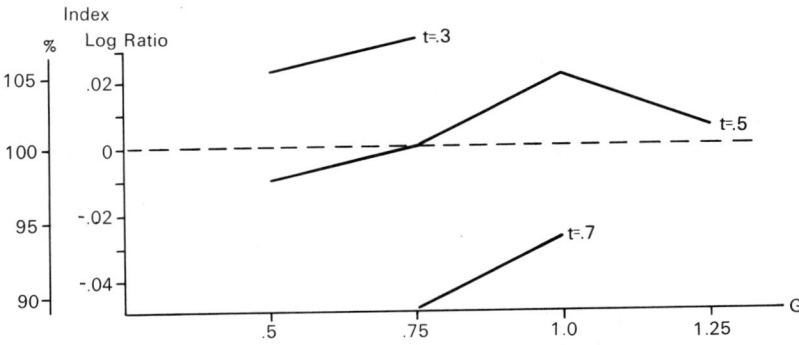
Tax-Guarantee Spline for Spanish-Speaking Male Wage Rates

Figure 14.8 Structure of experimental component by plan, tax–guarantee splines for male wage rates, by ethnic group.

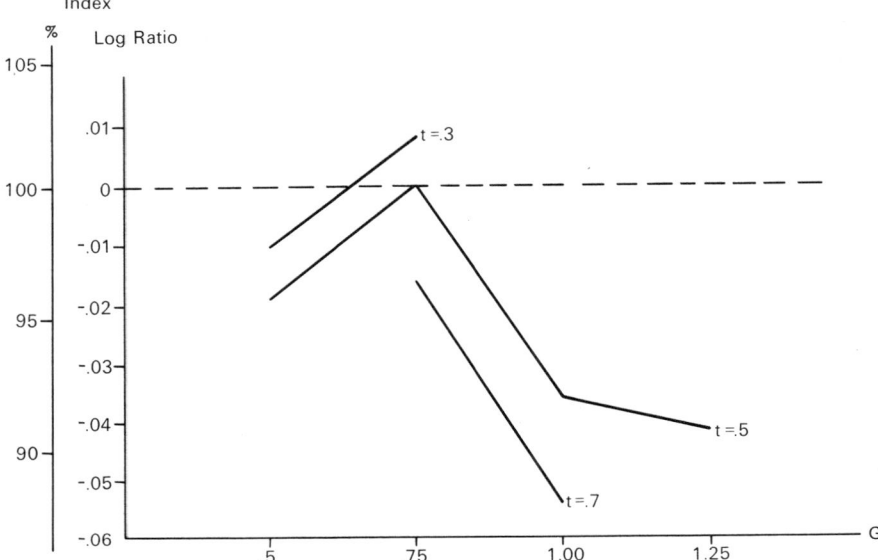

Figure 14.9 Structure of experimental component by plan, tax–guarantee spline for female wage rates.

was statistically significant. The analysis of family income presented in Chapter 6 is aimed at substantive interpretation of the response. (Note also that these responses will be affected by the same reporting error noted elsewhere, so that a part of what appears here may be spurious in any case.)

3. CALCULATION OF INDIVIDUAL DEVIATIONS

Given the estimates of the control and experimental components of the wage and income models, the next step was to obtain estimates of the average individual deviations from the respective models. In the case of family income, this was quite straightforward since the panel was essentially complete (the few missing observations have been imputed values equal to the preceding observation for the same family). Hence the estimated income function was simply evaluated for each family and quarter and the residual calculated:

$$e_{it} = \ln Y_{it} - \ln \hat{Y}_{it}^* - \ln \tilde{Y}_{it}. \tag{5}$$

These were then averaged over all thirteen quarters for each family, and that average was used as the estimate of $\ln \mu_i$ from equation (1). In the

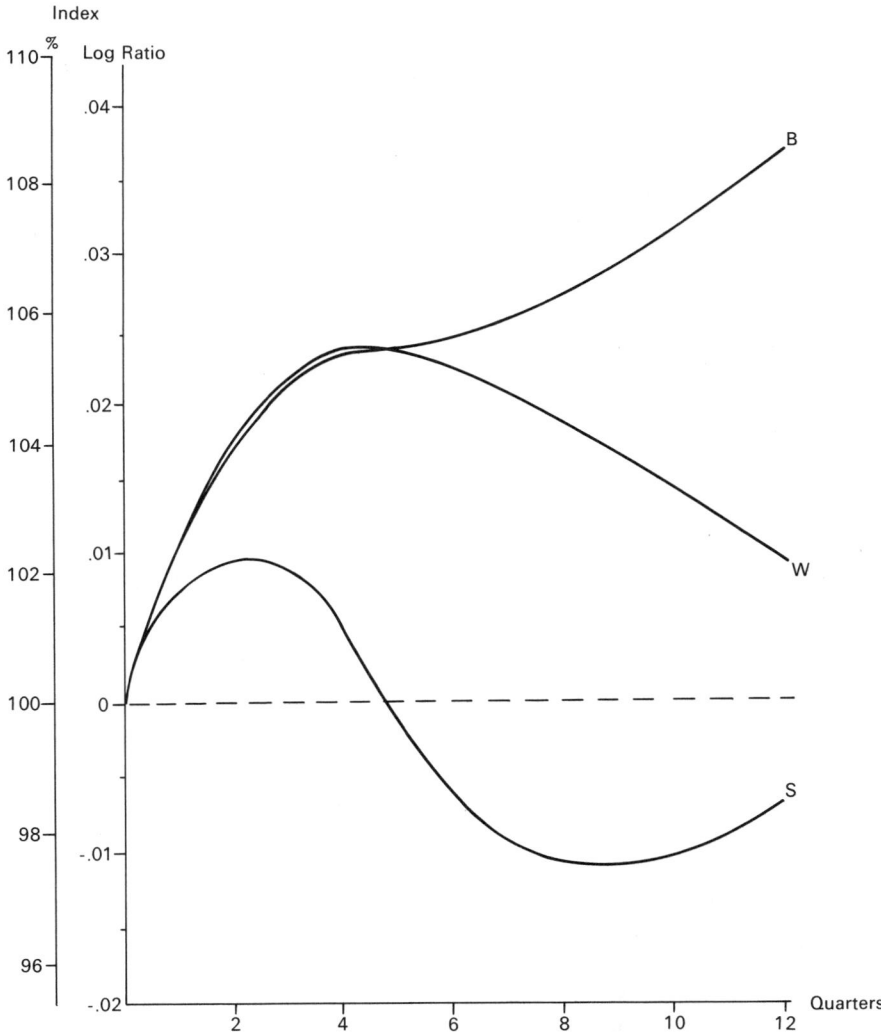

Figure 14.10 Relative experimental–control differential for male wage rates.

process of averaging, the standard deviation of the residuals was also calculated for each family. This variable has not so far been used. The estimates having been obtained, $\ln \hat{\mu}_i$ was then added to the control estimate for each quarter and exponentiated to produce normal income, $\hat{Y}_{it}$. In symbols we have

$$\hat{Y}_{it} = \exp(\ln \hat{Y}_{it}^* + \ln \hat{\mu}_i). \qquad (6)$$

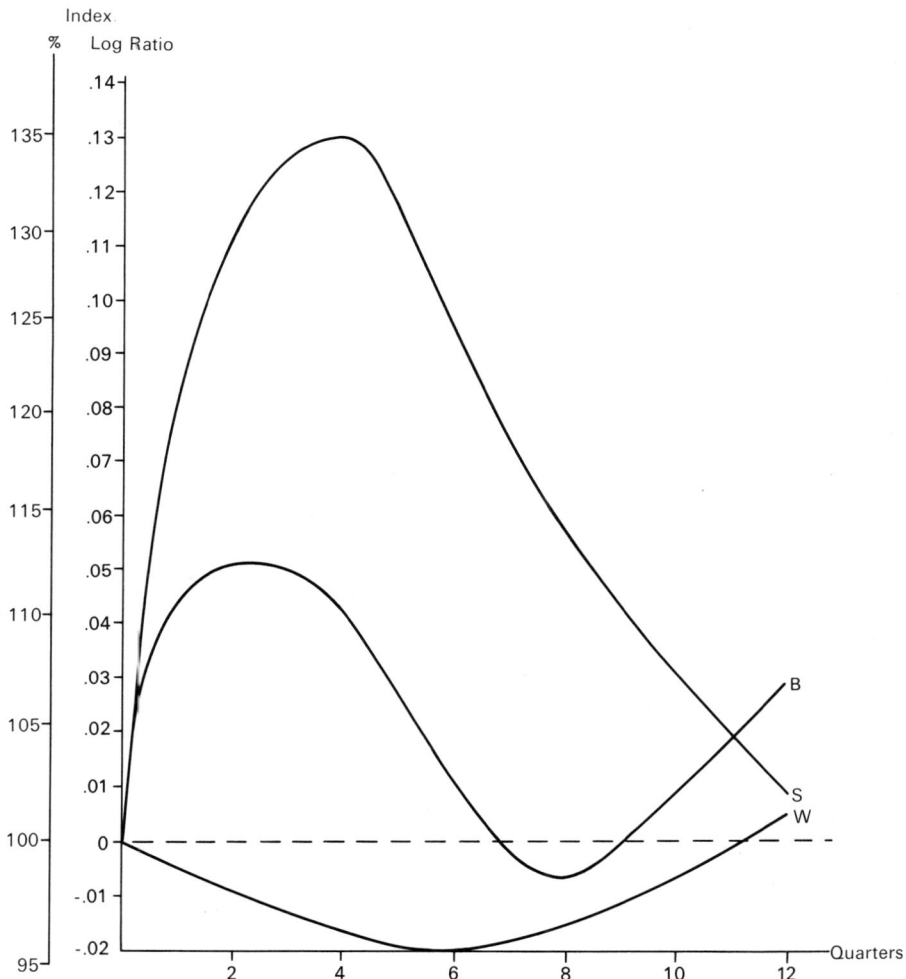

Figure 14.11 Relative experimental–control differential for female wage rates.

For the wage model, essentially the same steps were carried out, except that certain individuals did not have observed wages for some or all quarters. It will be recalled that only full-time wage rates were used for estimating the wage model. Residuals analogous to those defined above in equation (5) were calculated for all observations, which permitted the calculation of a wage rate for all quarterly observations with positive hours and earnings.

This produced a number of observed deviations, e_{it}, for each adult individual, which varied over the sample. For those who had no work record during the experiment, $\ln \hat{\mu}_i$ was set equal to zero—that is, the normal wage was simply W_{it}^* for them. For those with anywhere from one to thirteen usable deviations, the arithmetic average was calculated for the available quarters (the standard deviation was also estimated for anyone having at least two observations). The $\hat{W}_{it}$ estimates were then formed in precisely the same way as normal income shown in equation (6).

In the case of the normal income estimates, adding back the individual components, $\ln \hat{\mu}_i$, restored around 30 percent of the variation in the estimated deviations to the normal income variable—a little more for whites and a little less for Spanish-speaking. The experimental variation which was removed accounted for about 25 percent of the systematic variation in observed incomes of whites and blacks—but more like 44 percent for the Spanish-speaking. Because the sample used for estimating the wage model was only a part of the entire sample of adults, we cannot use the variance component share to say how much variation has been added to $\hat{\mu}$ by our method. For the part of the sample that was used for estimation of W^* and $\tilde{W}$, however, around half of the variance of e is accounted for by individual deviations for women and black and Spanish-speaking men. For white males, fully two-thirds appears to be persistent through time.

The means and standard deviations of the normal wage and income variables are displayed in Table 14.2, along with the estimated components from which they were formed. It should be noted that the use of a semi-logarithmic model for estimating the various components biases

Table 14.2 Sample Statistics for Normal Wage and Income Variables and Their Components, Husband–Wife Continuous Sample

	White (N = 310)		Black (N = 234)		Spanish-speaking (N = 149)	
	Mean	s.d.	Mean	s.d.	Mean	s.d.
Male heads						
$\hat{W}$	2.82	0.85	2.87	0.61	2.71	0.53
$\hat{W}*$	1.87	0.27	4.07	0.71	3.29	0.56
$\hat{\mu}$	1.521	0.441	0.719	0.158	0.839	0.175
Female spouses						
$\hat{W}$	3.43	1.31	3.24	1.53	2.79	1.12
$\hat{W}*$	4.27	1.19	4.17	1.60	3.06	1.12
$\hat{\mu}$	0.836	0.274	0.816	0.274	0.928	0.171
Families						
$\hat{Y}$	113.19	55.24	98.41	49.53	95.17	41.18
$\hat{Y}*$	102.77	33.91	89.69	31.01	88.55	26.23
$\hat{\tilde{Y}}$	0.977	0.132	1.079	0.130	1.033	0.210
$\hat{\mu}$	1.117	0.493	1.117	0.487	1.089	0.437

these mean values below the arithmetic means of observed wage rates. That is, the multiplicative model is analogous to geometric averaging, and such averages are always lower than arithmetic ones. The difference is more substantial for income, because the residual variation, σ_v^2, is quite large.

REFERENCES

Watts, H. W., and Mamer, J. Forthcoming. The problem of a spurious wage-rate response. In *The New Jersey income-maintenance experiment.* Vol. 3. *Expenditures, health, and social behavior; and the quality of the evidence,* ed. H. W. Watts and A. Rees. New York: Academic Press.

Watts, H. W., and Rees, A. 1973. Final Report of the Graduated Work Incentive Experiment. Madison: Institute for Research on Poverty, University of Wisconsin.

Subject index

A

Aid to Families with Dependent Children and Unemployed Parents, 11, 58
Annual Income Supplement, 46
Anomy, work behavior and, 325, 343
AVETRAN program, 390–391

B

Benefit levels, health factor in, 307–309
  see also Cash payments; Plan generosity
Benefit schedule, asymmetrical nature of, 86
Bilinear splines, 376–381
Black families
  labor-supply differentials in, 198
  labor-supply response of, 190–191
  plan generosity and, 214
  proxy income control variable for, 206
Black husbands
  job changes by, 259
  job status decline for, 275
  labor-supply response of, 112–113
Black wives
  disincentives for, 158
  treatment effects in, 155
  treatment interaction coefficient for, 143
Black workers
  job changes by, 271–274
  job characteristics among, 228
  job status equations for, 271–272

C

Cash payments
  average amount of, 20–21
  as basis of experiment, 17
  number of families receiving, 18

Census, U.S., 14
College attendance, probability of, 172
Compulsory education law, 164 n.
Consumer Price Index, 19
Control variables, 16–17
CPI, *see* Consumer price index
Cubic spline, 372–374
  periodic, 374–376
Cycle of poverty, breaking of, 171

D

Dependent variables, 15–16
Disabled workers, in labor force, 291
Disincentive effect, 119–120
  measures of, 121
Duncan scale, in job selection or change, 259, 265, 271, 276

E

Earning capacity, labor-supply response and, 85–110
Earning rate, health and, 290
Earnings
  in job selection, 255–279
  treatment effects on, 151–154
Earnings variable, 44
  see also Weekly income
Education
  differentials in years of schooling and, 174
  income-maintenance program and, 167–168
  lifetime earnings and, 170
Educational attainment, market wages and, 170
Educational response, negative income tax and, 175–176

415

Education programs, compensatory education in, 170
  see also Compulsory education law
Employment, versus participation, 93
Employment status, as variable, 43
  see also Job (*adj.*)
Equations and variables, choice of in information level studies, 355–358
Error components model
  application of to experimental panel data, 383–391
  parameter estimates in, 387
  three-component, 384–386
  two-component, 387–389
  two-component with missing data, 389–390
Experimental combinations, statistics associated with entering of, 74
Experimental panel data, error components model in, 383–391
Experimental treatment
  cash payments as basis of, 17
  effects of, *see* Treatment effects

F

Family, young adult responses in, 163–184
  see also Black families; Spanish-speaking families
Family age–income profiles, for like-aged couples, 404
Family health, budget and, 291
  see also Health
Family income, estimates of, 401–410
  see also Income; Wage rates,; Weekly wage
Family income model, response splines in, 408–409
Family labor supply, 28–30
Family labor-supply equations, 359–360
Family labor-supply response, 185–219
  basic experimental response in, 187–197
  control-based estimates of normal earnings and hours in, 216–217
  control-based proxy income variable in, 211
  and control variables for normal earnings when interacted with experimental effects, 202–212
  and differential response among individuals, 212–215
  and interaction biases with control-based instruments, 207–209
  labor-supply differentials in, 195–200
  mean earnings and labor supply for husband and wife in, 188–189
  normal income equations in, 203
  plan generosity and, 214
  preenrollment earnings measure in, 203
  quantifying bias in, 209–212
  total family earnings and, 218–219
  total family hours in, 194–195, 218–219
  Watts income proxies in, 204–205, 210
Family members, individual labor-supply responses of, 186
  see also Husbands; Wives; Young adults
Family size, by ethnic group and site, 38
Female age profiles, age rates and, 403
  see also Wives; Women
Financial need, work behavior and, 326, 344
Four-component multiplicative model, for wage rates, 395–396

G

Gross wage rates, labor-supply variation in, 393–394

H

Health
  age factor in, 300
  benefit levels and, 307–309
  control variables in, 299–301
  data on, 294–295
  earning rate and, 290
  family budget and, 291
  and hours worked per week, 308
  and husband's labor supply, 303–309
  labor supply and returns to labor in relation to, 297–298
  in labor-supply model, 290
  in labor-supply response, 287, 289–318
  methodological issues in, 294–303
  operational definition of, 296–297
  operational definitions of variables in, 312–314
  and parameterization of experimental plans, 298–299
  and response during various time periods, 306

SUBJECT INDEX

supplementary detailed tabulations in, 315–318
tabular presentation format for, 301–303
wives' labor supply and, 309–311
work effort and, 292
Health variables
 construction of, 295–296
 in wives' labor-supply response model, 132–133
High school completion, probability of, 173
Hours of work, negative income effect and, 12–15
Hours worked per week
 ethnicity and, 108
 as variable, 43–44
 for white husbands, 106–107
Husbands
 see also Male family heads
 basic experimental differentials for, 61
 black, *see* Black husbands
 employment and unemployment responses in, 58–60, 93–99
 hours worked per week conditional on employment, 106–108
 hours worked per week, whites versus blacks, 100–101
 "normal" wage or income for, 86
 Spanish-speaking, *see* Spanish-speaking husbands
 summary of findings for, 58–64
 work behavior of, 22
Husbands' employment, by ethnic group, 58–60, 94, 99
Husbands' equations, in information level studies, 360–361
Husbands' hours worked per week
 by ethnicity, 110
 theta factor for, 111
Husbands' labor-force response, social psychological characteristics and, 321–344
Husbands' labor-supply response, 57–113
 earning capacity and, 85–110
 ethnicity and, 90
 example of, 111–112
 at extremely low earning power, 112
 health factor in, 303–309, 315–317
 hours worked per week, black versus white, 100–101
 hours worked versus employment factors in, 99–110
 interpretations of, 110–113
 labor force participation and, 90–93
 regression estimates for, 89
 by time and ethnic group, 77–85
 welfare ratio and, 83
Husbands' labor-supply response coefficients, 68–69
Husband–wife samples
 mean earnings and labor supply of, 188–189
 size of, 35
 see also Wives

I

"Immune" variable, theta, 86–87, 112
Income
 normal, 393–411
 weekly, *see* Weekly income
Income-guarantee plans, *see* Income maintenance plans
Income-maintenance experiment, *see* New Jersey income maintenance experiment
Income-maintenance plans
 disincentive effect of, 119–120
 education effects on, 167–168
 family response differences in, 197–202
Income variables, *see* Wage and income variables
Information level
 choice of equations and variables in, 355–358
 family equations and, 359–360
 husband's equations in, 360–361
 labor-supply equations and, 358–360
 in labor-supply response, 288, 347–368
 measurement of, 352–354
 received and assigned parameters and other variables in, 363–365
 reduced sample in, 365–367
 subjects' understanding of, 350–352
 wives' equations in, 361–363

J

Job change
 ethnic factors in, 256–258, 271–272
 experimental variables in, 268–270

Job characteristic
  average earnings and, 260–266
  ethnic factors and, 228–230, 262–266
  job changes and, 256–258
  tax rate and, 276–277
Job content, satisfaction with, 228
  see also Job satisfaction
Job departure decision, negative income tax and, 234–235
Job satisfaction
  job content and, 228
  job selection and, 279–281
  negative income tax and, 247–248
  work behavior and, 326, 344
Job search, unemployment insurance and, 9–10
Job selection
  earnings and status in, 255–279
  impact of experiment on, 253–283
  plan generosity and, 281
Job turnover, negative income tax and, 221–250

L

Labor-force activity, social-psychological and experimental effects on, 330–333
  see also Labor force participation; Labor-supply response
Labor force participation
  as factor in husbands' labor-supply response, 90–93
  null hypothesis for, 24
  transfer payments and, 12
  as variable, 42–43
Labor-force variables, 41–44
Labor-leisure choices, weekly income and, 6
Labor market, withdrawal from, 113
Labor response, *see* Labor-supply response
Labor-supply disincentives, welfare reform and, 169–171
Labor-supply equations, information level and, 358–360
Labor-supply experiment
  see also New Jersey Income Maintenance Experiment
  dynamic considerations in, 8–11
  expected findings in, 5–15
  limited duration of, 10
  results of, 5–32
  static theory in, 6–8

Labor-supply function, inelasticity of for poor families, 162
Labor-supply model
  in analysis of husband's labor-supply response, 64–76
  basic findings of, 66–74
  elaborated, 63
  health factor in, 290
  one-parameter, 62–63
  pattern of adjustment in, 75–76
  qualifications to, 166
  simplified, 62
  theoretical background of, 64–66
  variable Q in, 73–75
Labor-supply response
  anomy and, 325, 343
  earning capacity and, 85–110
  at extremely low earning power, 112
  factors affecting, 287$ff.$
  financial need and, 326, 344
  of husbands, *see* Husbands' labor-supply response
  information levels and, 347–368
  job satisfaction and, 326, 344
  occupational flexibility and, 343
  pattern of, 22–30
  personal inefficacy and, 326, 344
  response differences among experimental plans in, 197–202
  self-esteem and, 325–326, 343–344
  by time and ethnic group, 77–85
  time orientation and, 326–327, 344
  work involvement and, 326, 342–343
Labor-supply variables, variation in, 86–88
Linear spline, 370–371

M

Male age profiles, wage rates and, 402
Male family heads
  see also Husbands
  characteristics of at preenrollment, 226
  number of employed, 39
  weekly hours worked by, 39
Male unemployment rate, 22–23
Market work, reduction of by wives, 117
Married women, *see* Wives
Multiple regression technique, 23–24

N

National Center for Health Statistics, 295

SUBJECT INDEX

National Health Surveys, 289
National Longitudinal Survey of Work
    Experience, 224
    see also Parnes samples
Negative income tax
    additive effects in, 231–233, 240–243
    adult family members and, 165
    declining real output and, 183
    educational response to, 175
    experimental effect in, 225–227
    health factor in, 293
    interaction effects of, 233–239, 241–247
    job characteristics and, 224–225,
        228–230
    job departures and, 234–238
    job effort and, 10
    job satisfaction measures and, 247–248
    job turnover and, 230–239
    misinterpretations of, 349–350
    numeric measurement of, 354
    occupational characteristics of at
        preenrollment, 227–230
    plan generosity and, 233
    "pleasant" jobs and, 9
    response to, 6
    unemployment duration and, 239–247
    work–leisure–education model and, 167
New Jersey compulsory education law,
    164 n.
New Jersey Income Maintenance
    Experiment
    cash payments in, 19–21
    control variables in, 16
    data analysis in, 15–21
    data cleaning in, 44–45
    dependent variables in, 15–16
    duration of, 10
    expectations in, 14–15
    experimental time in, 21
    findings in, 22–30
    job selection and, 252–283
    labor-force variables in, 41–44
    male unemployment rate in, 22
    negative effect of, 158–160
    sample size in, 33–40
    short-run effect of, on wives' work,
        120–121
    treatment variables in, 17–21
    welfare and, 11
    wives in, 26–28

Nonearned income
    by income category, 40–41
    measurement of, 45–47
Nonexperimental literature, 11–12
Nonlabor income, 13–14
Nonperiodic cubic spline, 374
Normal income, individual deviations from,
    410–411
Normal wage rates
    estimation of, 393–411
    individual deviations from, 410–414
    specification of models in, 395–401

O

Occupational flexibility, work behavior and,
    326, 343

P

Parnes file, 266 n.
Parnes samples, negative income tax and,
    224–225, 227, 230, 247, 249
Payments, cash, *see* Cash payments
Personal inefficacy, work behavior and, 326,
    344
Plan generosity
    black families and, 214
    job selection and, 281
    negative income tax and, 233
    Spanish-speaking families and, 215
Polynomial spline, defined, 369
Poor, disengagement of from society, 322
Positive income tax, 221
Poverty culture, 322–323, 334
Poverty integration, social-psychological
    effects on, 336–340
Poverty cycle, breaking of, 171
Preenrollment
    family income classification at, 84
    welfare ratio at, 83
Probit probability model, young adults and,
    168–169
Proxy income control variable, in family
    labor-supply response, 204–205
Public assistance, as alternative to work,
    119–120

Q

Q variable, 73–75

R

Reemployment, negative income tax and, 223
Regression analysis, spline functions in, 369–381
Response function, new specification for, 86–90

S

Sample, dimensions of, 33–40
Sample families, distribution of by plan and ethnicity, 78–82
Screening hypothesis, educational attainment and, 170
Self-esteem, work behavior and, 325–326, 343–344
Social psychological characteristics
  dependent and independent variables in, 327–328
  experimental parameters in, 329
  husbands' response in, 321–344
  in labor-supply response, 288
  poverty culture and, 334
  results of study in, 329–335
  variables in, 324–326
Society, disengagement of poor from, 322–323
Spanish-speaking families
  labor-supply differentials for, 198
  labor-supply response of, 29–30
  plan generosity factor and, 215
  proxy income control variable for, 207
Spanish-speaking husbands
  see also Husbands
  employment response for, 95
  hours worked per week by, 101–102
  job change and, 259
  job characteristics of, 228
  labor force participation for, 24–25, 58, 92
  mean theta variable for, 104
  unemployment percentiles for, 95–98
Spanish-speaking wives
  disincentives for, 158
  treatment interaction coefficients for, 143
Spline
  bilinear, 376–381
  cubic, 372–374
  defined, 369
  linear, 370–371
  polynomial, 369
Spline functions, in regression analysis, 369–381
Survey of Economic Opportunity, 14

T

Tax rate, numeric measurement of, 354–355
  see also Negative income tax
Theta variable
  defined, 86
  mean and standard deviations of, 87
  and reduction in labor supply, 112
Time orientation, work behavior and, 326, 344
Time variables, 50
Treatment effects
  earnings and, 151–154
  negative, 152
  other interactions and, 154
  preexperimental labor supply and, 153
  three-variable parametrization of, 142–144
  in wives' labor-supply response model, 134–154
Treatment variables, 17–21, 47–50
  experimental status and, 148–150
  payment level and, 148–150
  wives' income and, 158
  in wives' labor-supply response model, 126–127
  for young adults, 169

U

Unemployment, of Spanish-speaking husbands, 95–96
  see also Employment; Work behavior
Unemployment duration, negative income tax and, 239–247

V

Variables, types of, 16–21, 41–44, 128–150; *see also* Time variables; Treatment variables; Wage and income variables

SUBJECT INDEX

W

Wage and income variables, 51–55
Wage change, endogenous, 9
Wage-rate index, for male and female samples, 406–407
Wage rates
 age–education subfunctions in, 405
 decomposition of, 53
 labor-supply variation in, 393–394
 male age profiles for, 402
 normal, 393–414
 systematic components of, 401–410
Watts income proxies, 204–206, 210
Weekly income
 by ethnic group and site, 36–37
 labor-leisure choices and, 6
 as variable, 44
Welfare, general effect of, 11
 see also Public assistance
Welfare ratio
 at preenrollment, 83
 as variable, 400
Welfare reform, labor-supply disincentives and, 169
White family head, labor supply response of, 111–113
 see also Husbands
Wisconsin, University of, 391
Wives
 compensated wage elasticities for, 119
 fluidity of in labor-force behavior, 119
 health as factor for, 292
 income-maintenance effects on work by, 117–120
 labor-supply and wage rates for, 118
 latitude of for varying amount of market work, 118
 reduction in market work by, 117
Wives' labor force participation, 26
Wives' labor-supply response, 27, 115–162
 additional results with various models of, 154–158
 alternative welfare plans and, 161–162
 health factor in, 300–301, 309–311, 318
 interpretation of findings in, 158–162
 labor-force attachment and, 156–157
 labor-force-participation rates and, 122
 labor-supply reduction in, 160–161
 mobility and, 160
 negative effects in, 158–160
 pooled data for, 156–157
 regression results for, 135–136
 regression results excluding welfare recipients in, 155–156
 statistical model of, 121–125
 summary of results in, 115–117
 treatment plans and, 137–142
 treatment variables versus income for, 158
Wives' labor-supply response models, 123
 see also Wives' labor-supply response
 age-of-wife variables in, 131
 application of, 126–154
 education variables in, 131–132
 ethnicity interactions in, 138–141
 experimental labor-supply variables in, 129–130
 family income and, 133
 health variables in, 132–133
 independent variables in, 128–129
 other variables in, 124–133
 and presence of children and other family members, 132
 regression coefficients in, 144–147
 regression results for independent variables in, 130
 site-ethnicity variables in, 131
 treatment effects in, 134–154
 treatment variables in, 126–127, 142–150
Wives' work behavior
 short-run effects of experiment on, 120–121
 special importance of, 117–121
Women, health of, 292
 see also Wives
Work, hours of, see Hours of work
Work activity, social-psychological and experimental effects on, 336–340
Work behavior
 eight dimensions influencing, 342–344
 job satisfaction and, 344
 occupational flexibility and, 343
 and perception of financial need, 344
 personal efficacy and, 344
 self-esteem and, 343–344
Work disincentive hypothesis, young adults and, 163
Work–leisure–education model, 167
 human capital theory and, 166

negative income tax and, 167
probability model and, 168–169

Y

Young adults
  activity rates in simultaneous models for, 181–183
  educational attainment of, 171–172
  educational and labor-supply responses of, 163–184
  educational response of, 169–178
  high school completion rate for, 164
  labor-force participation by, 180
  labor-supply disincentive and, 178
  labor-supply response of, 178–181
  methodological considerations in responses of, 165–167
  negative income tax and, 175
  treatment response in educational activity of, 176
  treatment response in labor-supply activity of, 179–180
  work disincentive hypothesis and, 163, 178